"'Information sharing and data mining are integral IT components of the White House's newly released national strategy for homeland security,' said Steve Cooper, chief information officer of the Homeland Security Office. 'What we're talking about is pattern recognition, or use of software intelligent agents to peruse data, [which is] driven by algorithms and rules that define themselves over time; such tools can marry statistically derived outcomes from known events to predictive models.'"

—Washington Technology

"The FBI has selected 'investigative data warehousing' as a key technology to use in the war against terrorism. The technique uses data mining and analytical software to comb vast amounts of digital information to discover patterns and relationships that indicate criminal activity."

—Federal Computer Week

"Data mining and information sharing techniques are principal components of the White House's recently released National Strategy for Homeland Security."

—Intelligent Enterprise

"Many of the nation's businesses have long trolled through commercial databases hoping to divine which consumers are most likely to buy a luxury car or life-insurance policy. Now, the FBI hopes to explore the same data to uncover potential terrorists before they strike."

—Chicago Tribune

"By Sept. 11, 2011, the FBI hopes to use artificial-intelligence software to predict acts of terrorism the way the telepathic 'precogs' in the movie *Minority Report* foresee murders before they take place. The goal is to skate where the puck's going to be, not where the puck was."

—Los Angeles Times

Investigative Data Mining for Security and Criminal Detection

Investigative Data Mining for Security and Criminal Detection

Jesús Mena

An imprint of Elsevier Science
www.bh.com

Amsterdam • Boston • London • New York • Oxford • Paris • San Diego
San Francisco • Singapore • Sydney • Tokyo

Butterworth Heinemann is an imprint of Elsevier Science.

Library of Congress Cataloging-in-Publication Data
A catalog record for this book is available from the Library of Congress.

ISBN: 0-7506-7613-2

British Library Cataloguing-in-Publication Data
A catalogue record for this book is available from the British Library.

The publisher offers special discounts on bulk orders of this book.
For information, please contact:

Manager of Special Sales
Elsevier Science
200 Wheeler Road
Burlington, MA 01803
Tel: 781-313-4700
Fax: 781-313-4882

For information on all Butterworth Heinemann publications available, contact our World Wide Web home page at: http://www.bh.com.

10 9 8 7 6 5 4 3 2 1

Printed in the United States of America

To Deirdre

Contents

Introduction

During congressional hearings regarding the intelligence failures of the 9/11 attacks, FBI director Robert S. Mueller indicated that the primary problem the top law enforcement agency in the world had was that it focused too much on dealing with crime after it had been committed and placed too little emphasis on preventing it. The director said the bureau has been too involved in investigating, and not involved enough in *analyzing* the information its investigators gathered—which is what this book is specifically about: the prevention of crime and terrorism before it takes place (precrime), using advanced data mining technologies, tools, and techniques.

The FBI director went on to tell Congress that the bureau would shift its focus from reacting to crime to preventing it, acknowledging that this could be done only with better technology, which, again, is what this book is about, specifically:

- *Data integration* for access to multiple and diverse sources of information
- *Link analysis* for visualizing criminal and terrorist associations and relations
- *Software agents* for monitoring, retrieving, analyzing, and acting on information
- *Text mining* for sorting through terabytes of documents, Web pages, and e-mails
- *Neural networks* for predicting the probability of crimes and new terrorist attacks
- *Machine-learning algorithms* for extracting profiles of perpetrators and graphical maps of crimes

This book strives to explain the technologies and their applications in plain English, staying clear of the math, and instead concentrating on how they work and how they can be used by law enforcement investigators, counter-intelligence and fraud specialists, information technology security personnel, military and civilian security analysts, and decision makers responsible for protecting property, people, systems, and nations—individuals who may have experience in criminology, criminal analysis, and other forensic and counter-intelligence techniques, but have little experience with data and behavioral analysis, modeling, and prediction. Whenever possible, case studies are provided to illustrate how data mining can be applied to precrime.

Ironically, a week after this manuscript was submitted to the publisher, this headline appeared in *Federal Computer Week*: "Investigative Data Mining Part of Broad Initiative to Fight Terrorism" (June 3, 2002). The story went on to announce:

> The FBI has selected 'investigative data warehousing' as a key technology to use in the war against terrorism. The technique uses data mining and analytical software to comb vast amounts of digital information to discover patterns and relationships that indicate criminal activity.

Investigative data mining in an increasingly digital and networked world will become crucial in the prevention of crime, not only for the bureau, but also for other investigators and analysts in private industry and government, where the focus will be on more and better analytical capabilities, combining the intelligence of humans and machines. The precision of this type of data analysis will ensure that the privacy and security of the innocent are protected from intrusive inquiries. This is the first book on this new type of forensic data analysis, covering its technologies, tools, techniques, modus operandi, and case studies—case studies that will continue to be developed by innovative investigators and analysts, from whom I would like to hear at:

mail@jesusmena.com

Data mining and information sharing techniques are principal components of the White House's national strategy for homeland security.

Precrime Data Mining

1.1   Behavioral Profiling

With every call you make on your cell phone and every swipe of your debit and credit cards, a digital signature of when, what, and where you call or buy is incrementally built every second of every day in the servers of your credit card provider and wireless carrier. Monitoring the digital signatures of your consumer DNA-like code are models created with data mining technologies, looking for deviations from the norm, which, once spotted, instantly issue silent alerts to monitor your card or phone for potential theft. This is nothing new; it has been taking place for years. What is different is that since 9/11, this use of data mining will take an even more active role in the areas of criminal detection, security, and behavioral profiling.

Behavioral profiling is not racial profiling, which is not only illegal, but a crude and ineffective process. Racial profiling simply does not work; race is just too broad a category to be useful; it is one-dimensional. What is important, however, is suspicious behavior and the related digital information found in diverse databases, which data mining can be used to analyze and quantify. Behavioral profiling is the capability to recognize patterns of criminal activity, to predict when and where crimes are likely to take place, and to identify their perpetrators. Precrime is not science fiction; it is the objective of data mining techniques based on artificial intelligence (AI) technologies.

The same data mining technologies that have been used by marketers to provide *personalization,* which is the exact placement of the right offer to the right person at the right time, can be used for providing the right inquiry to the right perpetrators at the right time, before they commit crimes. Investigative data mining is the visualization, organization, sorting, clustering, segmenting, and predicting of criminal behavior, using such data attributes as age, previous arrests, modus operandi, type of building, household income, time of day, geo code, countries visited, housing type, auto make, length of residency, type of license, utility usage, IP address, type of bank account, number of children, place of birth, average usage of ATM card, number of credit cards, etc.; the data points can run into the hundreds. Precrime is the interactive process of predicting criminal behavior by mining this vast array of data, using several AI technologies:

- *Link analysis* for creating graphical networks to view criminal associations and interactions

- *Intelligent agents* for retrieving, monitoring, organizing, and acting on case-related information

- *Text mining* for examining gigabytes of documents in search of concepts and key words

- *Neural networks* for recognizing the patterns of criminal behavior and anticipating criminal activity

- *Machine-learning algorithms* for extracting rules and graphical maps of criminal behavior and perpetrator profiles

1.2   Rivers of Scraps

"It's not going to be a cruise missile or a bomber that will be the determining factor," Defense Secretary Donald Rumsfeld said over and over in the days following September 11. "It's going to be a scrap of information." Make that multiple scraps, millions of them, flowing in a digital river of information at the speed of light from servers networked across the planet. Rumsfeld is right: the landscape of battle has changed forever and so have the weapons—if commercial airliners can become missiles. So also has how we use one of the most ethereal technologies of all human creativity and imagination: AI.

AI in the form of text-mining robots scanning and translating terabyte databases able to detect deception, 3-D link analysis networks correlating human associations and interpersonal interactions, biometric identification devices monitoring for suspected chemicals, powerful pattern recognition neural networks looking for the signature of fraud, silent intrusion detection systems monitoring keystrokes, autonomous intelligent agent software retrieving e-mails able to sense emotions, real-time machine-learning profiling systems sitting in chat rooms: all of these are bred from (and fostering) a new type of alien intelligence. These are the weapons and tools for criminal investigations of today and tomorrow, whether we like it or not.

Which of the 1.5 million people who cross U.S. borders each day is the courier for a smuggling operation? Which respected merchant on ebay.com is about to abandon successful auction bidders, skipping out with hundreds of thousands of dollars? What tiny shred of the world's $1.5 trillion in daily foreign exchange transactions is the payment from an al-Qaeda cell for a loose Russian nuke? How many failed passwords attempts to log into a network are a sign of an organized intrusion attack? Finding the needles in these types of moving haystacks and the answers to these kinds of questions is where data mining can be used to anticipate crimes and terrorist attacks.

1.3   Data Mining

Data mining is the fusion of statistical modeling, database storage, and AI technologies. Statisticians have been using computers for decades as a means to prove or disprove hypotheses on collected data. In fact, one of the largest software companies in the world "rents" its statistical programs to nearly every government agency and major corporation in the United States: SAS. Linear regressions and other types of modeling analyses are common and have been used in everything from the drug approval process by the Food and Drug Administration to the credit rating of individuals by financial service providers.

Another element in the development of data mining is the increasing capacity for data storage. In the 1970s, most data storage depended upon COBOL programs and storage systems not conducive to easy data extraction for inductive data analysis. Today, however, organizations can store and query terabytes of information in sophisticated data warehouse systems. In addition, the development of multidimensional data models, such as those used in a relational database, has allowed users to move from a transactional view of customers to a more dynamic and analytical way of marketing and retaining their most profitable clients.

However, the final element in data mining's evolution is with AI. During the 1980s machine-learning algorithms were designed to enable software to learn; genetic algorithms were designed to evolve and improve autonomously; and, of course, during that decade, neural networks came into acceptance as powerful programs for classification, prediction, and profiling. During the past decade, intelligent agents were developed that were able to incorporate autonomously all of these AI functions and use them to go out over networks and the Internet to scrounge the planet for information its masters programmed them to retrieve. When combined, these AI technologies enable the creation of applications designed to listen, learn, act, evolve, and identify anything from a potentially fraudulent credit card transaction to the detection of tanks from satellites, and, of course, now more then ever, to prevent potential criminal activity.

As a result of these developments, data mining flowered during the late 1990s, with many commercial, medical, marketing, and manufacturing applications. Retail companies eagerly applied complex analytical capabilities to their data to increase their customer base. The financial community found trends and patterns to predict fluctuations in stock prices and economic demand. Credit card companies used it to target their offerings, microsegmenting their customers and prospects, maneuvering the best possible interest rates to maximize their profits. Telecommunication carriers used the technology to develop "churn" models to predict which customers were about to jump ship and sign with one of their wireless competitors.

The ultimate goal of data mining is the prediction of human behavior, which is by far its most common business application; however, this can easily be modified to meet the objective of detecting and deterring criminals. These and many more applications have demonstrated that rather than requiring a human to attempt to deal with hundreds of descriptive attributes, data mining allows the automatic analysis of databases and the recognition of important trends and behavioral patterns.

Increasingly, crime and terror in our world will be digital in nature. In fact, one of the largest criminal monitoring and detection enterprises in the world is at this very moment using a neural network to look for fraud. The HNC Falcon system uses, in part, a neural network to look for patterns of potential fraud in about 80% of all credit card transactions every second of every day. Likewise, analysts and investigators will come to rely on machines and AI to detect and deter crime and terrorism in today's world. Breakthrough applications are already taking place in which neural networks are being used for forensic analysis of chemical compounds to detect arson and illegal drug manufacturing. Coupled with agent technology, sensors can be deployed to detect bioterrorism attacks. The Defense Advanced Research Projects Agency (DARPA) has already solicited a prototype for such a system.

1.4 Investigative Data Warehousing

Data warehousing is the practice of compiling transactional data with lifestyle demographics for constructing composites of customers and then decomposing them via segmentation reports and data mining techniques to extract profiles or "views" of who they are and what they value. Data warehouse techniques have been practiced for a decade in private industry. These same techniques so far have not been applied to criminal detection and security deterrence; however, they well could be.

Using the same approach, behavioral data from such diverse sources as the Internet (clickstream data captured by Internet mechanisms, such as cookies, invisible graphics, registration forms); demographics from data providers, such as ChoicePoint, CACI, Experian, Acxiom, DataQuick; and utility and telecom usage data, coupled with criminal data, could be used to construct composites representing views of perpetrators, enabling the analysis of similarities and traits, which through data mining could yield predictive models for investigators and analysts. As with private industry, better views of perpetrators could be developed, enabling the detection and prevention of criminal and terrorist activity.

1.5   Link Analysis

Effectively combining multiple sources of data can lead law enforcement investigators to discover patterns to help them be proactive in their investigations. Link analysis is a good start in mapping terrorist activity and criminal intelligence by visualizing associations between entities and events. Link analyses often involve seeing via a chart or a map the associations between suspects and locations, whether by physical contacts or communications in a network, through phone calls or financial transactions, or via the Internet and e-mail. Criminal investigators often use link analysis to begin to answer such questions as "who knew whom and when and where have they been in contact?"

Intelligence analysts and criminal investigators must often correlate enormous amounts of data about individuals in fraudulent, political, terrorist, narcotics, and other criminal organizations. A critical first step in the mining of this data is viewing it in terms of relationships between people and organizations under investigation. One of the first tasks in data mining and criminal detection involves the visualization of these associations, which commonly involves the use of link-analysis charts (Figure 1.1).

Link-analysis technology has been used in the past to identify and track money-laundering transactions by the U.S. Department of the Treasury, Financial Crimes Enforcement Network (FinCEN). Link analysis often explores associations among large numbers of objects of different types. For example, an antiterrorist application might examine relationships among suspects, including their home addresses, hotels they stayed in, wire transfers they received and sent, truck or flight schools attended, and the telephone numbers that they called during a specified period. The ability of link analysis to represent relationships and associations among objects of different types has proven crucial in helping human investigators comprehend complex webs of evidence and draw conclusions that are not apparent from any single piece of information.

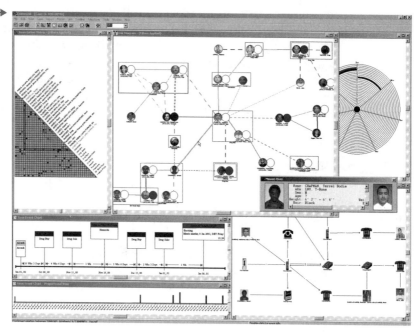

Figure 1.1
*A link analysis
can organize
views of
criminal
associations.*

1.6   Software Agents

Another AI technology that can be deployed to combat crime and terrorism is the use of intelligent agents for such tasks as information retrieval, monitoring, and reporting. An agent is a software program that performs user-delegated tasks autonomously; for example, an agent can be set up to retrieve information on individuals or companies via the Web or proprietary secured networks. An agent can be assigned tasks, such as compiling a dossier, interpreting its findings, and, following instruction, to act on those findings by issuing predetermined alerts. For example, agent technology is increasingly being used in the area of intrusion detection, for monitoring systems and networks and deterring hacker attacks. An agent is composed of three basic abilities:

1.   *Performing tasks*: They do information retrieval, filtering, monitoring, and reporting.

2.   *Knowledge*: They can use programmed rules, or they can learn new rules and evolve.

3.   *Communication skills*: They have the ability to report to humans and interact with other agents.

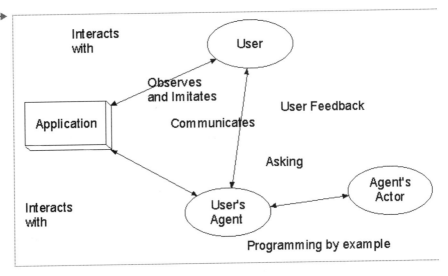

Figure 1.2
*Software
agents can
autonomously
monitor events.*

Over the past few years, agents have emerged as a new paradigm: they are in part distributed systems, autonomous programs, and artificial life. The concept of agents is an outgrowth of years of research in the fields of AI and robotics. They represent the concepts of reasoning, knowledge representation, and autonomous learning. Agents are automated programs and provide tools for integration across multiple applications and databases running across open and closed networks. They are a means of managing the retrieval, dissemination, and filtering of information, especially from the Internet.

Agents represent new type of computing systems and are one of the more recent developments in the field of AI. They can monitor an environment and issue alerts or go into action, all based on how they are programmed. For the investigative data miner, they can serve the function of software detectives, monitoring, shadowing, recognizing, and retrieving information on suspects for analysis and case development (Figure 1.2).

Intelligent agents can be used in conjunction with other data mining technologies, so that, for example, an agent could monitor and look for hidden relationships between different events and their associated actions and at a predefined time send data to an inference system, such as a neural network or machine-learning algorithm, for analysis and action. Some agents use sensors that can read identity badges and detect the arrival and departure of users to a network, based on the observed user actions and the duration and frequency of use of certain applications or files. A profile can be created by another component of agents called actors, which can also query a remote database to confirm access clearance. These agent sensors and actor mechanisms can be used over the Internet or other networks to monitor individuals and report on their activities to other data mining models which can issue alerts to security, law enforcement, and other regulatory personnel.

1.7 Text Mining

The explosion of the amount of data generated from government and corporate databases, e-mails, Internet survey forms, phone and cellular records, and other communications has led to the need for new pattern-recognition technologies, including the need to extract concepts and keywords from unstructured data via text mining tools using unique clustering techniques. Based on a field of AI known as natural language processing (NLP), text mining tools can capture critical features of a document's content based on the analysis of its linguistic characteristics. One of the obvious applications for text mining is monitoring multiple online and wireless communication channels for the use of selected keywords, such as *anthrax* or the names of individual or groups of suspects. Patterns in digital textual files provide clues to the identity and features of criminals, which investigators can uncover via the use of this evolving genre of special text mining tools.

Text mining has typically been used by corporations to organize and index internal documents, but the same technology can be used to organize criminal cases by police departments to institutionalize the knowledge of criminal activities by perpetrators and organized gangs and groups. This is already being done in the United Kingdom using text mining software from Autonomy. More importantly, criminal investigators and counter-intelligence analysts can sort, organize, and analyze gigabytes of text during the course of their investigations and inquiries using the same technology and tools. Most of today's crimes are electronic in nature, requiring the coordination and communication of perpetrators via networks and databases, which leave textual trails that investigators can track and analyze. There is an assortment of tools and techniques for discovering key information concepts from narrative text residing in multiple databases in many formats and multiple languages.

Text mining tools and applications focus on discovering relationships in unstructured text and can be applied to the problem of searching and locating keywords, such as names or terms used in e-mails, wireless phone calls, faxes, instant messages, chat rooms, and other methods of human communication. Unlike traditional data mining, which deals with databases that follow a rigid structure of tables containing records representing specific instances of entities based on relationships between values in set columns, text mining deals with unstructured data (Figure 1.3).

Text mining can be used to extract and index all the words in a database, or a network, as the example shown in Figure 1.3 demonstrates, to find key

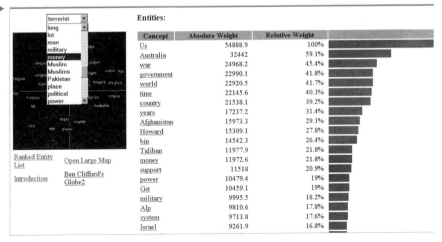

Figure 1.3 *Text mining can extract the core content from millions of records.*

intelligence, which can also be used for criminal and counter-intelligence purposes. Text software developed at the University of Texas exists that can detect when a person is lying three out of four times. The program looks at the words used and the structure of the message, which could be an e-mail.

1.8 Neural Networks

Probably one of the most powerful tools for investigative data miners, in terms of detecting, identifying, and classifying patterns of digital and physical evidence is the neural network, a technology that has been around for 20 years. Although neural networks were proposed in the late 1950s, it wasn't until the mid-1980s that software became sufficiently sophisticated and computers became powerful enough for actual applications to be developed. During the 1990s, the development of commercial neural network tools and applications by such firms are Nestor, NeuralWare, and HNC became reliable enough, enabling their widespread use in financial, marketing, retailing, medical, and manufacturing market sectors. Ironically, one of the first and most successful applications was in the area of the detection of credit card fraud.

Today, however, neural networks are being applied to an increasing number of real-world problems of considerable complexity. Neural networks are good pattern-recognition engines and robust classifiers with the ability to generalize in making decisions about imprecise and incomplete data. Unlike other traditional statistical methods, like regression, they are able to work with a relatively small training sample in constructing predictive models; this makes them ideal in criminal detection situations because, for example, only a tiny percentage of most transactions are fraudulent.

Figure 1.4
*A neural net
can be trained
to detect
criminal
behavior.*

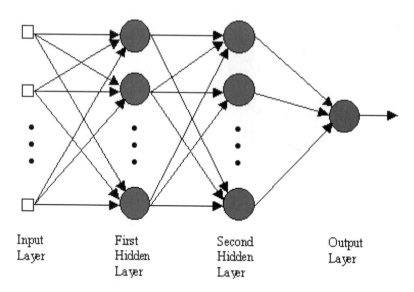

Input
Layer

First
Hidden
Layer

Second
Hidden
Layer

Output
Layer

A key concept about working with neural networks is that they must be trained, just as a child or a pet must, because this type of software is really about remembering observations. If provided an adequate sample of fraud or other criminal observations, it will eventually be able to spot new instances or situations of similar crimes. Training involves exposing a set of examples of the transaction patterns to a neural-network algorithm; often thousands of sessions are recycled until the neural network learns the pattern. As a neural network is trained, it gradually become skilled at recognizing the patterns of criminal behavior and features of perpetrators; this is actually done through an adjustment of mathematical formulas that are continuously changing, gradually converging into a formula of weights that can be used to detect new criminal behavior or other criminals (Figure 1.4).

Neural networks can be used to assist human investigators in sorting through massive amounts of data to identify other individuals with similar profiles or behavior. Neural networks have been used to detect and match the chromatographic signature of chemical components, such as kerosene in arson cases, by forensic investigators at the California Department of Justice.

One unique type of neural networks known as Kohonen nets or self-organizing maps (SOM), can be used to find clusters in databases for the autonomous discovery of similarities. SOMs have been used to cluster and match

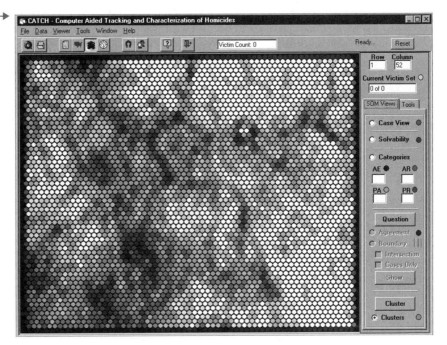

Figure 1.5
*CATCH:
Computer Aided
Tracking and
Characterization
of Homicides.*

unsolved crimes and criminals' modi operandi (MOs) or methods of operation. SOMs work through a process known as *unsupervised learning,* because
this type of neural network does not need to be trained. Instead it automatically searches and finds clusters hidden in the data. Police departments in the
United Kingdom and in the state of Washington are already doing this type of
clustering analysis. Investigators from the West Midlands Police in Birmingham used SOMs to model the behavior of sex offenders, while the Americans
used the clustering neural networks to map homicides in the CATCH project
(Figure 1.5).

1.9 Machine Learning

Probably the most important and pivotal technology for profiling terrorists
and criminals via data mining is through the use of machine-learning algorithms. Machine-learning algorithms are commonly used to segment a database—to automate the manual process of searching and discovering key
features and intervals. For example, they can be used to answer such questions
as when is fraud most likely to take place or what are the characteristics of a
drug smuggler. Machine-learning software can segment a database into statistically significant clusters based on a desired output, such as the identifiable
characteristics of suspected criminals or terrorists. Like neural networks, they
can be used to find the needles in the digital haystacks. However, unlike nets,

they can generate graphical decision trees or IF/THEN rules, which an analyst can understand and use to gain important insight into the attributes of crimes and criminals.

Machine-learning algorithms, such as CART, CHAID, and C5.0, operate somewhat differently, but the solution is basically the same: They segment and classify the data based on a desired output, such as identifying a potential perpetrator. They operate through a process similar to the game of 20 questions, interrogating a data set in order to discover what attributes are the most important for identifying a potential customer, perpetrator, or piece of fruit. Let's say we have a banana, an apple, and an orange. Which data attribute carries the most information in classifying that fruit? Is it weight, shape, or color? Weight is of little help since 7.8 ounces isn't going to discriminate very much. How about shape? Well, if it is round, we can rule out a banana. However, color is really the best attribute and carries the most information for identifying fruit. The same process takes place in the identification of perpetrators, except in this case an analysis might incorporate hundreds, if not thousands, of data attributes.

Their output can be either in the form of IF/THEN rules or a graphical decision tree with each branch representing a distinct cluster in a database. They can automate the process of stratification so that known clues can be used to "score" individuals as interactions occur in various databases over time and predictive rules can *"fire"* in real-time for detecting potential suspects. The rules or *"signatures"* could be hosted in centralized servers, so that as transactions occur in commercial and government databases, real-time alerts would be broadcast to law enforcement agencies and other point-of-contact users; a scenario might be played as follows:

1. An event is observed (INS processes a passport), and a score is generated:

    ```
    RULE 1:
    IF social security number issued <= 89-121 days ago,
    THEN target 16% probability,
    Recommended Action: OK, process through.
    ```

2. However, if the conditions are different, a low alert is calibrated:

    ```
    RULE 2:
    IF social security number issued <= 89-121 days ago,
    AND 2 overseas trips during last 3 months,
    THEN target 31% probability,
    Recommended Action: Ask for additional ID, report
    on findings to this system.
    ```

3.   Under different conditions, the alert is elevated:

> RULE 3:
> IF social security number issued <= 89-121 days ago,
> AND 2 overseas trips during last 3 months,
> AND license type = Truck,
> THEN target 63% probability,
> Recommended Action: Ask for additional information
> about destination, report on findings to this
> system.

4.   Finally, the conditions warrant an escalated alert and associated action:

> RULE 4:
> IF social security number issued <= 89-121 days ago,
> AND 2 overseas trips during last 3 months,
> AND license type = Truck,
> AND wire transfers <= 3-5,
> THEN target 71% probability,
> Recommended Action: Detain for further
> investigation, report on findings to this system.

Presently, all of this information exits: it is sitting idly in the government databases from the Social Security Administration and the Departments of State, Transportation, and the Treasury. Obviously the future of homeland security is going to require the application of data mining models in realtime, utilizing many different databases in support of multiple agencies and their personnel. Already the Visa Entry Reform Act of 2001 is addressing the modernization of the U.S. visa system in an effort to increase the ability to track foreign nationals. Amazingly, in the summer of 2000 ، full year before the attacks of September 11, Representative Curt Weldon from Pennsylvania, who chairs the House Military Research and Development Subcommittee, had proposed a government-wide *data mining agency* tasked with supporting the intelligence community in developing threat profiles of terrorists.

To quote Weldon, *"In the 21st century, you have to be able to do massive data mining, and nobody can do that today."* The data mining agency proposed in 2000 by Weldon was to be known as the National Operations and Analysis Hub (NOAH) and would support high-level government policy makers by integrating more than 28 intelligence community networks, as well as the databases from a vast array of federal agencies. However, simply aggregating the data is not enough; it must also be mined to extract digital signatures of suspected terrorists and criminals.

1.10 Precrime

The probability of a crime or an attack involves assessing *risk*, which is the objective of data mining. A determination involves the analysis of data pertaining to observed behavior and the modeling of it in order to determine the likelihood of its occurring again. Closely linked to risk are *threats* and *vulnerabilities*, weaknesses or flaws in a system, such as a hole in security or a back door placed in a server, which increases the likelihood of a hacker attack. As with the deductive method of profiling, almost as much time is spent in profiling each individual victim as in rendering characteristics about the offender responsible for the crime.

Assessing probability or predicting that a crime or an attack is going to take place involves either the interrogation of witnesses by investigators or field observation and inspection by security professionals of a property or the review of documents by intelligence analysts. In the case of computer systems, it may involve the testing of hardware and software or an evaluation of the design of firewalls against hacker and virus attacks. Data mining performs a similar type of risk assessment in computing the probability of crimes by analyzing hundreds of thousands of records and data points using pattern-recognition technologies.

Estimating the probability of crimes has traditionally involved the use of criminal statistics and documented historical data, such as crime reports or documented terrorist attack procedures. For a security professional, this may entail the documented statistics of car thefts for a building over a one-year period. For a criminal profiler, it is reconstructive techniques (e.g., wound-pattern analysis, bloodstain-pattern analysis, bullet-trajectory analysis), or the results of any other accepted form of forensic analysis that has a bearing on victim or offender behavior. The same holds true with data mining, in which predictive models or rules are generated based on the examination of criminal behavior and perpetrators.

In the aftermath of 9/11, the director of the FBI announced, "The Bureau needs to do a better job of analyzing data and expand the use of data mining, financial record analysis, and communications analysis to combat terrorism." The FBI hopes to use AI software to predict acts of terrorism the way the telepathic "precogs" in the movie *Minority Report* foresee murders. The goal is to "skate where the puck's going to be, not where the puck was." The technology plan reflects a belief that the chief weapon against crime and terrorism will not be bullets or bombs. It will be information.

1.11 **September 11, 2001**

Criminals leave digital clues, which represent patterns of behavior that data mining software and techniques can uncover. It is virtually impossible to exist in a modern society without leaving a trail of digital transactions in commercial and private databases and networks. Data mining has traditionally been used to predict consumer behavior, but the same tools and techniques can also be used to detect and validate the identity of criminals for security purposes. These data mining techniques will herald a new method of validating individuals for security applications over the Internet and proprietary networks and databases.

The need for a predictive enemy detection and comprehensive threat and risk assessment capability cannot be underestimated in matters of national security. In the words of the National Defense Panel, it is of pivotal importance to *"Improve predictive capabilities through latest technologies in data collection, storage, dissemination, and analysis."* Data is everywhere, and with it are the clues to anticipate, prevent, and solve crimes; enhance security; and discover, detect, and deter unlawful and dangerous entities. In the twenty-first century, investigators must begin to use advanced pattern-recognition technologies to protect society and civilization. Analysts need to use data mining techniques and tools to stem the flow of crime and terror and enhance security against individuals, property, companies, and civilized countries.

1.12 **Criminal Analysis and Data Mining**

Data mining is a process that uses various statistical and pattern-recognition techniques to discover patterns and relationships in data. It does not include business intelligence tools, such as query and reporting tools, on-line analytic processing (OLAP), or decision support systems. Those tools report on data and answer predefined questions, whereas data mining tools focus on finding previously unknown patterns and relationships among variables—in this case, for detecting and preventing criminal activity. While some will argue that forensics only applies to sciences used in court for convictions, the objective of recognizing threats and crime is also extremely important.

Unlike criminology, which re-enacts a crime in order to solve it, criminal analysis uses historical observations to come up with solutions. In criminal analysis, statistical examinations are performed on the frequency of specific crimes in order to evaluate the security of property and persons. Criminal analysis involves very careful evaluation of the location, time, and type of crime that has been committed at a building, neighborhood, beat, city, county, etc. Crime statistics, risks and probabilities are very much what criminal analysis is all about. Data mining, as with criminal analysis, has the same overall goal: the detection and prevention of crimes. The following scenario provides a good example of how criminal analysis works: A security professional in a large office building maintains information about all the criminal activity that has taken place on his property over three years, including the following incidents:

Auto Thefts	179
Office Thefts	142
Auto Break-in Thefts	211
Robberies	17
Burglaries of Offices	46
Aggravated Assaults	21
Rapes	2
Murders	0

One of the most important tasks of criminal analysis is to breakdown the pattern of crimes to evaluate when, where, and why they are occurring. In the case of this particular building, for example, the objective is to reduce crime by improving security. This type of analysis, however, is not as much offender-specific as target-specific; in other words, it begs the question *"why is the garage a target for such a high rate of thefts?"* By focusing on when, where, and why break-in auto thefts are taking place, preventive security measures can be taken to deter future criminal acts. Through research and the documentation of crimes and categorization by type of offenses, location, and time, gradual patterns and trends will emerge, which will lead to preventive solutions. This type of criminal analysis can be automated through the use of data mining for uncovering subtle patterns in large data sets.

Obviously, understanding the environment in which crime takes place is very important in criminal analysis. In this example, examining where crimes are taking place is critical; locations must be broken down by categories into main areas, such as the main entrance, side entrances, offices, common areas, walkways to the building from the garage, walkways from the streets, and the parking garage. In addition, the surrounding areas must be considered, such as adjoining buildings, strip malls, parks, residential neighborhood, etc.

In order to gauge the level of crime at this particular building, a comparison of crime data statistics can be considered by the analyst; for example, how does the rate of auto thefts for the property compare with the rate for the same crime at the local law enforcement agency levels, at the beat, district, precinct, city, county, metropolitan statistical area (MSA), state, and national levels. Using the FBI's Uniform Crime Report (UCR) codification system, rate comparisons can be made by following categories:

1. Murder
2. Rape
3. Robbery
4. Aggravated assault
5. Burglary
6. Theft
7. Motor vehicle theft
8. Arson
9. Other assaults
10. Forgery and counterfeiting
11. Fraud
12. Embezzlement
13. Stolen property (buying, receiving, possessing)
14. Vandalism
15. Weapons (carrying, possessing, etc.)
16. Prostitution and commercialized vice
17. Sex offenses
18. Drug abuse violations
19. Gambling
20. Offense against the family and children
21. Driving under the influence
22. Liquor laws
23. Drunkenness
24. Disorderly conduct
25. Vagrancy
26. All other offenses
27. Suspicion

28.   Curfew and loitering laws (persons under 18)

29.   Runaways (persons under 18)

To compute the comparison crime rates the following formulas can be used:

```
For violent crime rate (VCR) formula for building
property:

        VCR = (total violent crime/average
                daily traffic) x 1,000

For violent crime rate (VCR) formula for beat,
city, county, state, and nation:

        VCR = (total violent crime/population) x 1,000

For property crime rate (PCR) formula for building
property:

        PCR = (total property crime/number
                of targets) x 1,000
```

Because property crime is target-specific it must be computed differently as these crimes are not against individuals. It is worth noting that criminal analysis is very much interested in statistics, rates of occurrence, risk, probabilities, trend, and patterns, all of which can be improved through the use of data mining for detection and deterrence. A similar understanding of the environment and the targets of crime can be applied to other situations, so that rather than a building, we might perform a criminal analysis inventory of an e-commerce Web site for illegal hacking intrusions into a server.

The next phase of this type of criminal analysis is to use data mining, given the fact that a security expert or law enforcement investigator must deal with hundreds of thousands of transactions, e-mails, system calls, wire transfers, and the like for examining digital crimes. This calls for an automated methodology for behavioral profiling via pattern-recognition techniques. Data mining can provide a new dimension to criminal analysis, especially in digital crimes such as entity theft; credit card, insurance, Internet, and wireless fraud; and money laundering, where investigators and analysts must deal with large volumes of transactions in large databases. Data mining has traditionally been used to predict consumer preferences and to profile prospects for products and services; however, in the current environment, there is a compelling need to use this same technology to discover, detect, and deter criminal activity to improve the security of property, people, and countries.

1.13   Profiling via Pattern Recognition

Profiles constructed by criminologists, clinical psychologists, and other investigators are typically drawn from samples of behaviors, motives, and similar methods of operation. This type of profiling is *deductive* by nature and is based on work experiences and evidence an investigator assembles and examines to arrive at a conclusion. It is a top-down form of generalization, from samples to a profile of a potential suspect. Similar to the way an expert system works, the investigators follow a set of rules to arrive at an inference or conclusion about a particular case. For example, the case data collected by FBI profilers is passed down over time based on investigative experience by the agents and applied to new investigations. This type of profiling may be based on personal human experience and the insight and collective knowledge of seasoned investigators rather than empirical data.

The noted author, forensic scientist, and criminal profiler Brent Turvey offers this definition of the deductive method of criminal profiling: "A deductive criminal profile is a set of offender characteristics that are reasoned from the convergence of physical and behavioral-evidence patterns within a crime or a series of related crimes." Turvey goes on to state that the profile of offender characteristics must be supported by pertinent physical evidence suggestive of behavior, victimology, and crime-scene characteristics.

Turvey emphasizes, "A full forensic analysis must be performed on all available physical evidence before (a deductive) type of profiling can begin." Such is the case with data mining for behavioral profiling; the tools are different, but the methodology is the same. Criminals leave evidence, which may be digital by nature, but it represents patterns of crimes and intent. For example, investigative data miners can examine behavioral evidence found in a system's log files to study and analyze the victim's characteristics, which in this case may be a network, a server, or a Web site.

Profiling is an investigative technique and forensic science with many names and a history of being practiced on many levels for years. Dictionaries and encyclopedias tend to call it *offender profiling* or *criminal profiling*. The second most common name for it is *psychological criminal profiling*, or simply *psychological profiling*. The FBI approach produced the name *criminal personality profiling*. Criminologists tend to think of it as a type of applied criminology or clinical criminology. Some people prefer the name sociopsychological profiling, or think of it as a type of behavioral investigative analysis or criminal investigative analysis. The basic components of a criminal profile in some of the literature in this area include the following data features about the suspect:

1.   Probable AGE

2.   Probable SEX

3.   Probable RACE

4.   Probable RESIDENCE

5.   INTELLIGENCE *level* the suspect is operating at

6.   Probable OCCUPATION

7.   Probable MARITAL STATUS

8.   Probable LIVING ARRANGEMENTS

9.   The PSYCHOSEXUAL MATURITY

10. Probable TYPE AND CONDITION OF VEHICLE driven

11. Probable MOTIVATING FACTORS

12. Probable ARREST RECORD

13. PROVOCATION FACTORS that might drive the suspect out

14. INTERROGATION TECHNIQUES that would work best with the suspect

Out of the 14 data components, several can be obtained from demographic databases (1 through 4); intelligence level (5) may be estimated by level of education, also obtainable from demographic data providers; items 6 through 8, as well as item 10, are also available by third-party data providers. So of the 14 data items, commercial data providers can provide approximately 9 items. The arrest records can be obtained from government databases. In the end, 10 data components can be gleaned from commercial and government data sources. This is important because in commercial applications, data mining is often used to profile potential customers using lifestyle information, such as occupation or marital status, to segment product offerings and develop predictive models. Similar applications of data mining models can be made for criminal profiling analyses.

Data mining is also a deductive method of profiling; however, the conclusions or rules are generated from data rather than from a human expert's experience. It is an empirically based approach where conclusion are derived from data analysis using modeling software driven by neural networks or machine-learning algorithms. For example, the following rule may be developed to profile a dummy corporation set up as a front for money laundering:

```
IF    Standard Industry Code Number     = 7813
AND   Number of Physical Locations      < 2
AND   Number of employees               -50
AND   Uniform Commercial Code Number    = 0
THEN  Legal Entity                      32%
      Questionable Entity               78%
```

The conditional rules are derived not from an expert who has worked these types of investigations, but are instead driven by observation from samples of hundreds of thousands of cases. Using pattern-recognition technology, coupled with powerful computing power, enables the construction of this type of digital profile. Profiling via data mining looks for emerging patterns in large databases, which can lead to new insight for reducing the probability of crimes. Criminal profiling and victimology is the thorough study and analysis of victim characteristics. The characteristics of an individual offender's victims can lend themselves to inferences about the offender's motive, modus operandi, and signature behavior. Part of victimology is risk assessment, and so it is with data mining, which also seeks to identify the signature behavior of a perpetrator. To do so, it also relies on the need to examine the crime-scene characteristics and the victim to determine a quantifiable risk assessment.

In the end, the ideal profiling method is a hybrid of machine learning and human reasoning, domain experience, and expertise. Some of the most effective techniques for detecting fraud, for example, use the rules derived from trained specialists, coupled with data mining models constructed with pattern-recognition software, such as neural networks. There are some hardwire conditions, which may indicate foul play, such as using a social security number in an application for a credit card with no activity or record, or in Internet fraud, using an e-mail address that is exclusively Web based, such as Hotmail, coupled with a credit card number that doesn't match the billing Zip code. These are hard, fast red flags for detecting potential fraud in e-commerce; however, when coupled with data mining models, the chances of profiling fraudulent transactions will increase. It is in the marriage of humans and machines that the best chance of criminal detection lies.

In criminal profiling the term *signature* is used to describe behaviors committed by offenders that serve their psychological and emotional needs. A signature can assist investigators in distinguishing offender behaviors and modus operandi. In data mining, however, a signature is used to assign a probability to a crime or to profile a criminal. For example, the following is a signature developed from a data mining analysis using demographics, department of motor vehicle records, and insurance information in which a vehicle at a point-of-entry border crossing is being identified as having a HIGH probability of being used for smuggling:

```
Condition data fields:

    DRIVER HOUSEHOLD TYPE is Apt Or Co-op Owner
    INSURER STATUS is None
    VEHICLE YEAR is 1988
    TITLE OWNERSHIP is Owned
    VEHICLE PURCHASED is 1994-06-30
    VEHICLE MAKE is CHEVROLET
    DRIVER CITY is El Paso, TX
    DEMOGRAPHIC NEIGHBORHOD is High Rise Renters


Prediction # 1: ALERT is High
```

Criminal profiling, like data mining, is a matter of expertise. Just as the deductive method of criminal profiling is a skill, requiring some investigative heuristics, so is data mining. The data is the evidence, but some skill is required to extract a model or rules from the raw records. A methodology exists for data extraction, preparation, enhancement, and mining; however, it is a skill not a science. As with deductive profiling, no two criminals are exactly alike, and neither are the profiles or MOs constructed from data mining analyses. Every database is different, and so are the profiles extracted via data mining.

1.14 Calibrating Crime

The probability of a crime or an attack involves assessing *risk*, which is the objective of data mining. Making a determination involves the analysis of data pertaining to observed behavior and the modeling of it, in order to determine the likelihood of its occurring again. Closely linked to risk is the probability of *threats* and *vulnerability*, such as a weakness or flaw in a system, a hole in security or a back door placed in a server, which increase the likelihood of a hacker attack taking place. As with the deductive method of profiling, almost as much time is spent profiling each individual victim as rendering characteristics about the offender responsible for the crime.

An estimate of the probability of a crime or attack occurring is made using documented historical data, such as crime reports or documented terrorist attack procedures. For a security professional, this may entail the documented statistics on car thefts for a building over a one-year period. For a criminal profiler, it is the reconstructive techniques, such as wound-pattern analysis, bloodstain-pattern analysis, bullet-trajectory analysis, or the results of any other accepted form of forensic analysis that can be performed, that have a bearing on victim or offender behavior.

However, for a counter-intelligence analysts, predicting the risk of a terrorist attack is much more difficult because such events seldom occur or only occur rarely. Still, although a crime, such as embezzlement or a bomb attack rarely happens, there is a need to make some intelligent estimates of the probability it may happen and to perform a risk analysis. Obviously, threat occurrence rates and risk probabilities can be estimated from crime reports or other historical data. However, other seemingly unrelated data, using data mining techniques, may serve the same purpose; for example Department of Motor Vehicle information containing ownership and insurance information along with model, make, and year may serve as a viable input into a neural network for detecting vehicles smuggling narcotics or weapons by generating a probability score at a border point of entry.

This is where data mining techniques can be used to transform vast amounts of data generated from multiple sources in order for investigators and analysts to take preventive action to discover, detect, and deter crime and terror. Data mining tools can enable them to use quantifiable observations to construct predictive models in order to identify threats and assess the probability of crimes and attacks rapidly and to uncover perpetrators, as with criminal profiling, by analyzing forensic and behavioral evidence.

The new Patriot Act expands the ability to monitor multiple phone calls; it also facilitates the search of billing records with nationwide search warrants and the hunt into the flow of money. Under the new law, the police can conduct Internet wiretaps in some situations without court orders, and the powers of the federal courts are expanded. The new act also updates wiretapping laws to keep up with changing technologies, such as cell phones, voicemail, and e-mail. Coupled with data mining techniques, this expanded ability to access multiple and diverse databases will allow the expanded ability to predict crime.

Security and risk involving individuals, property, and nations involves probabilities that data mining models can be used to anticipate, predict, and in the end reduce. Decision makers need to be aware that every day more and more data is being aggregated, which can be mined for profiling criminals, as well as for uncovering patterns of behavior involving medical shams, insur-

Figure 1.6
*September 11,
Boston to New
York, 8:30AM.*

ance fraud, cyber crime, money laundering, bio-terrorism, entity theft, and other types of digital crimes, which data mining could be used to identify and prevent, such as the attacks of 9/11.

We always remember where we were, at the time that a tragic event took place. On 9/11, I was sitting in seat 6D on a Boston tarmac, taxiing for a take-off to New York City that never took place (Figure 1.6). Forensic data mining introduces a new methodology to criminal analysis and entity profiling that we must use to ensure such attacks do not occur again. As is the case throughout the book, case studies will be provided to illustrate how data mining technologies are being applied to solve crime and deter terror. What follows is the first.

1.15   Clustering Burglars: A Case Study

The following case study is presented in its original format. The author would like to thank Inspector Rick Adderley for contributing the paper, which demonstrates how the use of a Kohonen neural network, or self-organizing map (SOM), was used to link crimes to perpetrators. This type of neural network is used to discover clusters in data sets.

Data Mining at the West Midlands Police: A Study of Bogus Official Burglaries

Richard Adderley
West Midlands Police,
Bournville Lane Police Station
e-mail: r.adderley@west-midlands.police.uk

P. B. Musgrove
School of Computing and Information Technology,

University of Wolverhampton
e-mail: P.B.Musgrove@wlv.ac.uk

Abstract

Bogus official burglaries refer to crimes where a person(s) gains access to a premises by deception with the intention of stealing property. Experience has shown that such offenders tend to commit several similar crimes. The offender(s) may also be active across a wide geographical region covered by different police areas. That, together with the sheer volume of such crimes, makes it very difficult for the police to link crimes together in order to form composite descriptions of offender(s) and identify patterns in their activities.

This paper describes the results of applying a Kohonen self-organizing map (SOM) to a set of data derived from reported bogus official crimes with the objective of linking crimes committed by the same offender. The issues involved with how crime data is selected, cleaned, and coded are also discussed.

The results were independently validated and show that the SOM has found some links that warrant follow-up investigations. Some problems with data quality were experienced. Their effect on the map produced by the SOM algorithm is also discussed.

1.15.1 Introduction

Today computers are pervasive in all areas of business activity. This enables the recording of all business transactions, making it possible not only to deal with record keeping and control information for management, but also, via the analysis of those transactions, to improve business performance. This has led to the development of the area of computing known as data mining [1].

The police force, like any other business, now relies heavily on the use of computers. In the police force, business transactions consist of the reporting of crimes. A great deal of use is made of computers for providing management information via monitoring statistics that can be used for resource allocation. The information stored has also been used for tackling major serious crimes (usually crimes such as serial murder or rape), the primary techniques used being specialized database management systems and data visualization [2]. However, comparatively little use has been made of stored information for the detection of volume crimes, such as burglary. This is partly because major crimes can justify greater resources on the grounds of public safety but also because there are relatively few major crimes, making it easier to establish links between offenses. With volume crimes, the sheer number of offenses, the paucity of information, the limited resources available, and the high degree of similarity between crimes render major crime techniques ineffective.

There have been a number of academic projects that have attempted to apply AI techniques, primarily expert systems, to detecting volume crimes, such as burglary [3,4]. While usually proving effective as prototypes for the specific problem being addressed, they have not made the transfer into practical working systems. This is because they have been stand-alone systems that do not integrate easily into existing police systems, thereby leading to high running costs. They tended to use a particular expert's line of reasoning, with which the detective using the system might disagree. Also they lacked robustness and could not adapt to changing environments. All this has led to wariness within the police force regarding the efficacy of AI techniques for policing.

The objective of the current research project is therefore to evaluate the merit of data mining techniques for crime analysis. The commercial data mining package Clementine (SPSS) is being used in order to speed development and facilitate experimentation. Clementine also has the capability of interfacing with existing police computer systems. The requirement for purpose-written software outside the Clementine environment is being kept to a minimum.

In this paper we report the results from applying one specific data mining technique, the self-organizing map (SOM) [5] to descriptions of offenders for a particular type of crime, bogus official burglaries. The stages of data selection, coding, and cleaning are described together with the interpretation of the meaning of the resulting map. The merit of the map was independently validated by a Police Officer who was not part of the research team.

1.15.2   The Application Task

The specific application task reported here consists of a particular type of burglary. A *bogus officials* offense (sometimes known as a *distraction burglary*) refers to a burglary where the offender gains access to a premises by deception. The offender(s) may pose as a member(s) of the utilities, police, social services, salespersons, even children who are looking for pets or toys, to gain entry to the property. Typically, once inside, the victim is engaged in conversation while an accomplice searches for and steals property. In this type of burglary, the victim always meets the offender(s) and, therefore, should be able to provide a description.

A problem with this type of crime is that the sheer number of offenses committed over a wide geographical area makes it difficult to link crimes committed by the same offender(s). The objective in this study is to see whether a SOM can be used to link crimes based on offender descriptions. This will result in a map (more accurately a matrix) where each cell represents a cluster of offender descriptions. The ideal solution would be a SOM where each cell contains various descriptions of all the crimes involving a single offender. Neighboring cells in the map would contain descriptions of different offenders who bear a physical resemblance.

The ideal solution will always be unattainable due to the same offender being described differently by victims of different crimes. In addition, the high degree of similarity between some offenders (e.g., young, average build, average height) will inevitably mean the same cell will contain descriptions of different offenders. Just how far the map derived in practice differs from the ideal would help determine the efficacy of the technique. Unfortunately, few of the crimes have been successfully detected (i.e., solved) and, hence, there is no perfect solution to act as a comparison.

Consequently, a subjective assessment of the merit of the resulting map needs to be made. This subjective assessment can be supported/influenced by information from those crimes that have been detected.

1.15.3 Data Selection, Cleaning, and Coding

The victims of this type of crime tend to be elderly. Their age, together with the distressed state brought on by the crime, might be thought to lead to unreliable descriptions being provided. However, a recent study commissioned by the Metropolitan Police concluded, "There is no evidence that their attention, language, recognition, recency judgements or memory for the past is affected by age" [6]. The study included an experiment on older persons that indicated that the offender characteristics most likely to be accurately recalled are (in the order of most common to least frequently mentioned) gender, accent, race, age, general facial appearance, build, voice, shoes, eyes, clothes, and hair color and length.

When a bogus official crime is reported, a police officer attends the scene and takes a number of witness statements, and then completes a paper-based report called the *crime report,* which includes information abstracted from the witness statements. The crime reports are then summarized by civilian data entry clerks when they enter the details of the crime into the computerized database system. The crime record contains numerous fields. Fixed fields contain names, addresses, beat number, and other administrative data. In addition, there are two free-text fields: The first contains a description of the offender(s). The second describes how the crime was committed (the *modus operandi,* or MO).

While providing valuable information, the free-text nature of these fields makes automated analysis difficult. Consequently, it was necessary to write a simple parser program to pick out key words and phrases. This proved more difficult than expected due to the widely varying styles used by police officers and data entry clerks. Spelling mistakes were common, abbreviations were inconsistent, and word sequencing varied (for example, accent might be described as "Birmingham acent," "Birmingham accent," "Bham accent," "local accent," "accent: Birmingham," or even "not local accent"). As a consequence, the coding was part automatic and part manual.

Once key words had been abstracted from the description field, they showed some agreement with that found by Barber [6] with the exception of shoes and eyes, which were rarely mentioned. Because of the diversity of possible clothing and the likelihood of it changing between crimes, it was decided to omit this from the coded descriptions. This provided fields for age, gender, height, hair color, hair length, build, accent, and race. Fields not mentioned by Barber but included in this study are the person's height and the number of accomplices.

Care needs to be taken when encoding data from its symbolic form to the numeric form required by the SOM. Data could be a number on a continuous scale (such as age), binary (such as gender), nominal (such as hair color), and ordinal (such as hair length, which can be ordered as short, medium, or long). Nominal and ordinal variables can each be represented by a set of binary variables, although some information could be lost (i.e., order information) [7]. A further problem when dealing with continuous variables can arise due to certain variables swamping the effect of others due to their range being greater. It is common to standardize variables, but this can in itself cause problems, particularly for unsupervised techniques (such as SOM). This is due to the discriminating effect of the variable being lost. For example, in scaling age, which might range from 15 to 65, into a range of 0 to 1 would lead to a 20 year-old being scaled as 0.1 and a 30 year old 0.3. Thus, a difference of 10 years in age (a value of 0.2) would be 10 times less important compared to a difference in an attribute, such as build, which is coded as a strict 0 or 1 (NB: a difference in build would score two, one for each difference). For example, if offender A was described as being aged about 30 with medium build and offender B as being aged about 30 but with small build, there would be a difference of 2 between the descriptions. However, if offender A was described as having a medium build and being aged about 20 (scaled to

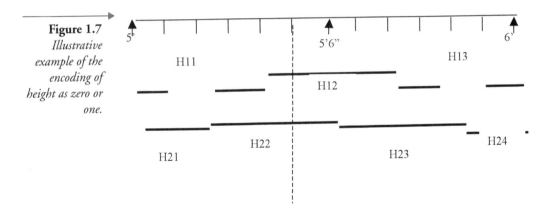

Figure 1.7
Illustrative example of the encoding of height as zero or one.

0.1) and offender B was described as having a medium build but being aged about 30 (scaled to 0.3) the difference would be 0.2. Due to these problems, it was decided to code the continuous age and height variables using a binary encoding, thereby placing them on a similar level of importance as the other binary variables.

The continuous age and height attributes were each expressed as ranges split into a number of intervals. If the height given in the description lay within a specified range, it was coded as a one and the other intervals as zero. In order to allow for slight discrepancies between descriptions of the same offender and to incorporate some aspect of ordering, two sets of overlapping intervals were used for each variable. This means that each height was encoded as a set of binary variables, two of which would be set to 1 for any given height and the remainder set to 0, and similarly for age.

To illustrate, consider an offender who is estimated as being about 5'5" (people still do not think in metric units). This would be encoded as a 1 for the interval 5'2" to 5'6" (e.g. H11=0 H12=1 and H13=0) and also a one for the interval 5'4" to 5'8" (i.e. H21=0 H22=1, H23=0 and H24=0) (Figure 1.7). This incorporates a degree of fuzziness in the description of age and height. However, it is at the cost of effectively giving age and height a double count when it comes to comparing similarities between descriptions.

A further problem encountered in producing comparable descriptions is that of missing attributes. Sometimes attributes such as build are not recorded. This means in our system of encoding that all build binary variables will be set to 0. This does not mean that the person does not have a build! The problem of missing values is notorious in statistical data analysis. There is no universal solution for dealing with this problem adequately. What is of interest is how robust the technique is, faced with the inevitable missing values.

Over the three-year period under consideration, there were 800 bogus official crimes involving 1,292 offenders in the police areas under consideration. Dealing with all 800 would generate a solution that was intractable regarding analysis and validation. Consequently, it was decided to deal with a subset of the crimes. Those crimes involving female offenders were selected as they represented a reasonable time cross-section and consisted of just 105 offender descriptions associated with 89 crimes. The SOM algorithm was provided with records consisting of offender descriptions. There could be more than one description associated with a particular crime (i.e., in crimes where more than one female is involved). Each of these descriptions was represented by up to eight attributes: race, age, height, number of accomplices, build, hair color, hair length, and accent. When translated into a binary encoding, this resulted in 46 binary variables out of which at most 10 would be given a value of 1 (each height and age being represented by two binary variables). In practice, due to incomplete descriptions, the number of binary variables per description taking a value of 1 varied between 3 and 9 with an average of 7.5.

1.15.4 Application Construction

The SOM [5] is an unsupervised neural network training method. It takes data consisting of a number of unordered records (in this task the 105 offender descriptions), each of which is measured by a variety of attribute values (in this task 46 binary variables). It iteratively organizes the input records by grouping them into clusters. The clusters are themselves ordered into a two-dimensional spatial configuration where the members of one cluster bear a resemblance to neighboring clusters, but not as strong a resemblance as they do to members of their own. The SOM can be viewed as a dimension-reduction visualization technique, in this case reducing from 46-dimensional space to two dimensions. The resulting two-dimensional configuration is a topological, rather than spatial map, (i.e., it is like a London underground map, rather than a road map). The implementation of the SOM algorithm used was that provided by the Clementine data mining package.

A design consideration when constructing a SOM is to decide on the dimensions of the resulting grid. Too many cells would see various descriptions of the same offender being split across a number of cells each with a highly specialized description. Too few cells would see cells formed containing a large number of different offenders potentially with a high degree of variability between descriptions. It was decided to construct a five-row-by-seven-column map. This allows for a potential of 35 different offenders each committing three crimes. If there were more than 35 offenders, it would force offenders with similar descriptions to be clustered together. If there are fewer than 35 offenders the SOM algorithm could place descriptions of the same

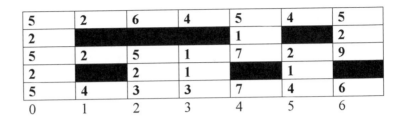

Figure 1.8
Derived cluster sizes.

offender across a number of cells. The SOM algorithm is free to put as many descriptions as it likes in a cell (i.e., more or less than three) depending upon how similar they are to each other.

1.15.5 Findings

The results produced by using the SOM option of Clementine can be seen in Figure 1.8. The cells in the table show the number of offenders placed in the cluster associated with the cell. The blacked-out cells indicate empty clusters. Their presence in the SOM tends to indicate large spatial differences between clusters on opposite sides.

In order to interpret this map, a symbolic description of each cluster was derived by finding the average value for each attribute in a cluster. Provided the average value was greater than 0.5, then that binary variable name was assigned as the cluster's attribute value. This interpretation of the SOM can be seen in Figure 1.9. Blank fields are due either to great variability in the values of the attribute or the absence of a description for that attribute in the crime report for the majority of cluster members.

1.15.6 Validation Process

The SOM-labeled map, together with the crime numbers apertaining to each description in a SOM cell, were passed to a police sergeant who was not part of the research team for independent verification. The sergeant had access to more information than had been made available to the SOM algorithm. This included full witness statements (often more than one for each crime), information on the *modus operandi* (MO), and information as to which crimes had been solved. Time permitted the sergeant to analyse 17 of the 24 nonempty clusters. The sergeant was given the brief to decide if there was sufficient evidence in the witness statements and for those crimes that had been solved to say whether there was a possible link between some of the crimes in each cluster. Clusters were analyzed individually with no attempt to look for links between neighboring clusters.

Figure 1.9 *Symbolic descriptions of clusters.*

	Attribute	0	1	2	3	4	5	6
4	Accomplices	0	0	1	1	1	1	2
	Race	IC1	IC1	IC1	IC1	IC1	IC1	IC4
	Height		5'4"	5'4"				4'10"
	Age	20		32			9	9
	Build							
	Hair Color	Dark	Dark					Dark
	Hair Length							
	Accent							
3	Accomplices	0				1		
	Race	IC1				IC1		
	Height	5'0"						4'11"
	Age	24				14		13
	Build					Slim		
	Hair Color	Dark				Fair		Dark
	Hair Length							
	Accent					Irish		
2	Accomplices	0			1	1	1	
	Race	IC1		IC1	IC1	IC1		IC1
	Height		5'8"	5'8"	5'8"	5'6"		5'0"
	Age	24	24	32		14	14	14
	Build		Medium	Medium				
	Hair Color			Dark	Dark	Dark	Dark	Dark
	Hair Length				Long			
	Accent							
1	Accomplices			1	0		0	
	Race	IC1			IC1		IC1	
	Height	5'5"		5'8"	5'6"		5'2"	
	Age	24		21	29		17	
	Build			Slim	Slim		Slim	
	Hair Color			Dark	Dark		Dark	
	Hair Length				Long		Long	
	Accent							
0	Accomplices	1	1	1			1	1
	Race	IC1	IC1	IC1		IC1	IC1	IC1
	Height	5'4"	5'6"	5'6"	5'6"	5'4"	5'4"	
	Age	24	23	19	19	17	17	17
	Build		Slim	Slim	Slim			Slim
	Hair Color	Dark	Dark	Dark	Dark			Dark
	Hair Length	Long			Short	Long	Long	Short
	Accent			Local				Local

Of the 17 clusters analyzed, one contained insufficient details to make a judgement; five had no apparent links between offenders in them.

The remaining 11, in the judgement of the sergeant, contained subsets of offender descriptions that could be linked based on the extra sources of information.

An example of a description provided by the sergeant is cluster (6,0).

> 6 crimes; 3 with 1 male and 1 female, 2 with 2 female and 1 with 1 female and 2 males. One crime was detected to Mr. X. The female ages range from 13 yrs to 25 yrs across the cluster, only one not being described as slim/thin. The heights range from 5'2" to 5'5." Short hair. In three crimes the MO was very similar in that social services and food parcel were mentioned, but this did not occur for the detected crime

The independent evidence provided by the social services MO provides suggestive evidence for linking three of the six crimes. The descriptions for these three crimes could be consolidated to form a composite picture of the female offender.

These results are encouraging, as links between crimes have been established that had not been previously made. However, the sergeant mentioned two negative aspects that need addressing. First, many of the cells analyzed contained members that were in his opinion clearly different from the majority of members of the cell. Second, some of the solved crimes pertained to offenders appearing in widely differing cells on the map. He suggested one possible cause being the wide variance in descriptions of the same offender (in those case where a definite link can be made, this is contrary to Barber's findings). To illustrate, he provided the following example again for cluster (6,0):

> 2 crimes in this cluster were committed next door to each other 3 1/2 hours apart on the same day. The same MO was used, and 1 male and 1 female were the offenders. In the first crime the offenders were described as female, IC1, 18 yrs, local accent, 5'5" thin build with blond bobbed hair; male IC1, 25 yrs, 6' thin build with short ginger hair. In the other crime the offenders were described as female, IC1, 20 - 25 yrs, 5'2", slim build with short dark hair; male, IC1, 25 - 30 yrs, 5'8", robust build with fair hair. In the case papers, the officer who attended the scene commented that the victim, in the second crime, was confused and forgetful and could not be regarded as a reliable witness.

1.15.7 Discussion and Further Work

While generally encouraging, the validation process indicated a number of areas where there is room for improvement. One would be to consider removing descriptions from the analysis where there are a number of incomplete values. This was the main contributor to the clusters where the sergeant could not find any links. This does not mean these crimes would be ignored. Once the SOM is derived from the more complete descriptions, the less complete descriptions can be matched against the stereotype description for each cell and then ranked in terms of the goodness of the match. Possibly, these vague descriptions could be considered as "secondary" members of more than one cell.

Another possible improvement is to merge some of the neighboring clusters to make allowance for slight variations in descriptions. The five-row-by-seven-column SOM was an arbitrary selection. Possibly it is too big. One way of merging clusters suggested in [8] is to use the vector of average values representing each cluster and apply hierarchical agglomerative clustering [7]. This basically means sequentially merging clusters based on their distance apart (distance can be measured in many ways; here we used the standard squared Euclidean distance), recalculating the new cluster average, and then merge the next two nearest. The agglomerative clustering was performed using the SPSS statistical package. The results are displayed in the dendrogram in Figure 1.10. (A dendrogram is a graphical way of showing the hierarchical merging process.)

This dendrogram shows that cluster (3,4) should be the first to be merged with (4,4). As these both had the same symbolic description in Figure 1.9, this is no surprise. The next two clusters to be merged would be (4,0) and (5,0). This process could be continued indefinitely until there is only one cluster. Ripley [7] suggests stopping the merging process when a merging is suggested between two clusters that are not contiguous on the map. This occurs when (0,2) is suggested as being merged with the (2,4), (3,4), and (4,4) supercluster.

The effect of applying hierarchical clustering on the SOM can be seen in Figure 1.11.

Merging to avoid missing possible links with neighbors will undoubtedly mean merging some unrelated crime descriptions together. However, the numbers are still at a tractable level for manual analysis. Also, it is possible to apply a splitting criteria (e.g., race) to members of the specific supercluster. Different superclusters might use different splitting criteria.

The above merging will address some of the problems where descriptions vary slightly; however, for more radical variations, it will not help. These are best addressed outside the context of software tools. If an indication of the reliability of the witness statement could be obtained, then only reliable data

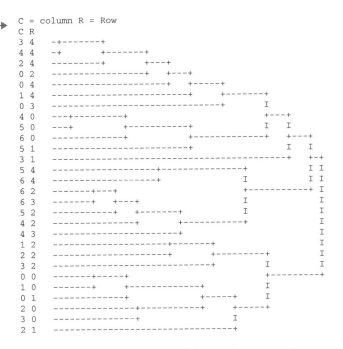

Figure 1.10
Dendrogram for hierarchical agglomerative clustering of SOM cluster centres.

```
C = column R = Row
C R
3 4   -+--------+
4 4   -+        +-------+
2 4   ---------+        +---+
0 2   -----------------+    +---+
0 4   -----------------------+  +-----+
1 4   -----------------------+  +-------+
0 3   -----------------------------+          I
4 0   ---+---------+                     +---+
5 0   ---+         +----------+          I  I
6 0   -------------+          +-----------+  +---+
5 1   -----------------------+            I  I
3 1   ---------------------------------------+  +-+
5 4   --------------------+-------------------+    I I
6 4   -------------------+              I      I I
6 2   -------+---+              +-----------+ I
6 3   -------+   +---+          I            I
5 2   -----------+   +-------+  I            I
4 2   ---------------+       +-----------+   I
4 3   -----------------------+            I
1 2   ---------------------+-------+      I
2 2   -----------------------+     +---------+  I
3 2   -----------------------+         I      I
0 0   -------+-----+                +---------+
1 0   -------+     +-------------+   I
0 1   -------------+             +-----+   I
2 0   -----------------+---------+     +-----+
3 0   -----------------+             I
2 1   -------------------------------+
```

could be used. Also some variability is due to the time span. The data used in this study covered a three-year period. During that time, the appearance of one particular teenage offender, who was convicted for a number of the crimes, changed radically. When dealing with larger collections of data (e.g., male offenders), crimes committed within a smaller time window should be used.

A valuable source of information not included in this study is the *modus operandi* (MO). The diversity of MOs, together with the variety of ways of describing them, precluded their use within the time scales and budget of the current study. However, this information was utilized for validation purposes by an independent police officer.

Figure 1.11
SOM map following merging of spatially near neighbors.

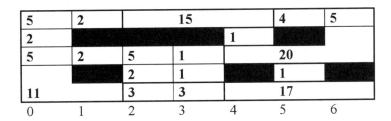

The loss of this information initially appears restrictive, but it does lend extra generality to results obtained as they would be applicable to descriptions for crimes other than bogus official burglaries. An illustration of the type of information available, but omitted, can be seen in Table 1.1.

Table 1.1   *Illustrative Examples of the Modus Operandi Free-Text Field.*

MO Field
PERSON UNKNOWN POSING AS COUNCIL WATERBOARD WORKER GAINED ENTRY TO PREMISES. KEPT IP ENGAGED IN KITCHEN WHILE SECOND MALE ENTERED PREMISES AND MADE SEARCH OF FLAT AND STOLE PROPERTY (2ND PERSON NOT SEEN IN PREMISES), BOGUS WORKER MADE EXCUSES AND LEFT PREMISES.
OFFENDER ATTENDED PREMISES. SHOWED "HOUSING DEPARTMENT" ID CARD WITH PHOTO ON IT AND SAID HE NEED TO CHECK THE WATER. OFFENDER WAS ALLOWED IN BY ELDERLY IP, WHO WAS THEN TOLD TO RUN THE KITCHEN TAPS. OFFENDER STAYED FOR A FEW MINUTES BEFORE LEAVING DURING WHICH TIME HE WAS ALLOWED ACCESS TO ALL ROOMS UNACCOMPANIED. AFTER OFFENDER HAD LEFT PREMISES, IP DISCOVERED PROPERTY MISSING.

A further use of the SOM could be to link crimes based on pairing offenders. For example, if a crime was committed by two offenders and the description of one offender is in, say, cell $(0,0)$ and the description of the other offender is in cell $(4,4)$, then look for other crimes committed by pairs belonging to these two cells or their near neighbors. This will be the subject of further investigation.

1.15.8 Conclusions

We have described how the SOM algorithm can be used to cluster offender descriptions for a particular type of crime, the bogus official burglary. Independent validation has shown that interesting links have been found within clustered descriptions. Some problems have been identified and solutions suggested. Some of these problems are to do with the data and the need for cleaner fuller descriptions being selected before being used by the SOM algorithm. Others are to do with modifying the final map in order to facilitate the search for links with descriptions belonging to neighboring clusters.

References

1. Adriaans, P. and Zantinge, D. *Data Mining*, Addison-Wesley, 1996.

2. Adderley, R. and Musgrove, P.B., General Review of Police Crime Recording and Investigation Systems, Submitted to *Policing: An International Journal of Police Strategies and Management*.

3. R. Lucas, "An Expert System To Detect Burglars Using a Logic Language and a Relational Database," *Fifth British National Conference on Databases*, Canterbury U.K., 1986.

4. Charles, J., "AI and Law Enforcement", *IEEE Intelligent Systems* Jan/Feb 1998 pp. 77–80.

5. Kohonen, T., "The Self-Organizing Map," *Proceedings of the IEEE*, Vol. 78, No. 9, 1990, pp. 1464–1480.

6. Baber M. and Brough P., "Identification Evidence of Elderly Victims and Witnesses," *Police Research Group, Home Office:* 1997.

7. Gordon, A.D., *Classification*, Chapman and Hall, 1981.

8. Ripley, B.D., *Pattern Recognition and Neural Networks*, Cambridge, U.K.: Cambridge University Press, 1996.

1.16 The Future

The above is one of many case studies that will be provided in subsequent chapters. In each, the reader will be shown how data mining technologies are being used by innovative investigators, criminalists, and analysts to detect and deter crime and terrorism. These case studies will demonstrate first-hand how link analysis, software agents, text mining, neural networks, and machine-learning are being used for everything from signature detection of illegal drugs to alerts of bio-terrorist attacks. As we said in the beginning of the chapter, the world has changed and so have the weapons, expanding the application of AI technologies for detecting and deterring criminals.

In the aftermath of 9/11, the director of the FBI, Robert S. Mueller, acknowledged that the bureau might have prevented the attacks. "Putting all the pieces together, who is to say?" Mueller said, noting that warning signs amounted to "snippets in a veritable river of information." As part of a major reorganization, the director announced, "The Bureau needs to do a better job of analyzing data and put prevention ahead of all else." With that the FBI took a new strategic focus and a key near-term action to "substantially enhance analytical capabilities with personnel and technology and expand the use of data mining, financial record analysis, and communications analysis to combat terrorism." The future, it appears, has arrived.

1.17 Bibliography

Turvey, Brent. (1999) *Criminal Profiling: An Introduction to Behavioral Evidence Analysis*, San Diego: Academic Press.

Vellani, K., and Nahoun, J. (2001) *Applied Criminal Analysis*, Boston: Butterworth-Heinemann.

2

Investigative Data Warehousing

2.1   Relevant Data

One of the most difficult and frustrating phases of data mining is getting access to the right data. In government there are always issues between agencies and agreements to be sorted out, not to mention formats that need to be reconciled, all of which require several meetings before arrangements can be made. In private industry, there are the issues of privacy and cost. These are some of the minor, but very real, obstacles that accompany most data mining projects. Of greater significance are the issues revolving around what data is required for the desired objective. However, in the aftermath of 9/11 a new sense of urgency has evolved, in the face of which these obstacles pale in comparison to failing to resolve these data integration issues.

The value of any data mining model is very much dependent on the quality of the data used to construct it; for this reason it is critical that some creative discussions be held and consideration be made about what data is available at the start of the project. Aside from the data that is internally available, thought should be given to what external data sources could provide valuable insight to the data mining analysis. In this chapter we will discuss the closed and open sources of data available both online and offline and how to integrate and prepare the data prior to its analysis.

Data mining is about predicting behavior or profiling individuals; as such, it is critical to have access to timely and relevant information. Without it, the whole process is doomed to failure. For example, in order to construct an accurate link analysis chart of phone calls made by targeted suspects, it is critical to have access to the most current wireless toll records. Similarly, in order to construct predictive models for the profiling of fraudulent transactions or other criminal or terrorist activities, it is equally important to be able to construct a centralized database or to query multiple networks with very relevant and current data. In order to construct a good fraud model, for example, it is critical to have an adequate sampling of all the types of illegal transactions that have been uncovered by, say, an insurance provider, an e-commerce site, or a wireless carrier.

2.2　Data Testing

It is highly recommended that the initial analysis start with a subset of the entire data that is available. Using this subset an initial model can be constructed and tested on a specific segment to evaluate its functionality and accuracy. Start the project by constructing a model with a small sample of a database, rather than the entire population. Tests can be conducted using a particular region, date segment, district or office, dollar range, region, and the like. So, one of the first decisions will be what segments and samples of the entire data set will be used for the initial analysis and testing.

For example, to detect and profile vehicles likely to be used for smuggling contraband or weapons, an initial analysis can be started with the data from a single point-of-entry or limited to trucks only. Once the initial model has been developed and tested on this specific segment, then the project can be expanded so that multiple models, if necessary, can be developed to cover jurisdictions across an entire department or agency or, as in this case, to cover all of the points-of-entry along a border for all types of vehicles.

In data mining, it is important to start with a clear objective. This will guide the project and lead to the selection of the data that will be accessed and used. To a very large extent, the success of any data mining project depends on the quality of the data. Once the data can be accessed or is received, the next challenges are its integration and preparation for mining and modeling for purposes of configuring a composite of individuals and companies and analyzing them for investigative applications. There are commercial, financial, medical, demographic, utility, telecom, real estate, vehicle, licensing, credit, criminal, Internet, retailing, etc., data sources, as well as tools for preparing and integrating them. Unfortunately, data is usually housed in databases for applications other than data mining; it is commonly stored for processing, billing, tracking, and reporting. Seldom is the data created with the intent of modeling and analysis. There are many sources of information on individuals and companies and many formats that this data is likely to be in.

2.3　The Data Warehouse

The concept of data warehousing—that is, assembling a cohesive view of customers from multiple internal databases coupled with external demographic data sources—has been an accepted practice for several years by large companies, especially retailers. The idea of the data warehouse is to have a multidimensional picture of customers, mixing information about their spending habits with insightful lifestyle demographics. While the concept of this type of consumer data warehouse is not directly applicable to law enforcement and counter-intelligence, its data architecture does have merits: the assembling of information about individuals from disparate databases into a composite to gain a comprehensive view of their identities and behaviors.

The most common analyses that data warehouses in the private sector are subject to are online analytical processing (OLAP) and data mining. OLAP tools are used to extract data cubes, which are reports segmenting customer or sales information by area—for example by zip code, city, state, and region. They are a fairly straightforward, analysis-driven type of reporting. While OLAP reports are valuable in summarizing of customer activity, data mining is more valuable because it often identifies the hidden patterns of customer behavior.

The ability for companies to use these types of analyses on their data warehouses has led to the practice of customer-relationship management (CRM). In CRM, firms integrate all point-of-contact customer data, including Web site forms, e-mail, dealership sales data, phone call site data, and transactional data, in order to provide better service and retain their customers. While the concept of CRM also does not apply to law enforcement either, the lessons about integrating data from multiple sources in order to assemble a picture of an individual is applicable, because, again, a cohesive view of perpetrators and suspects can be obtained.

September 11 demonstrated the need to share and access multiple data sets containing critical strategic information, as well as to be more effective in the use of data mining techniques normally used for profiling individuals in marketing, call centers, insurance, telecommunications, utilities, retailing, and e-commerce. The same type of CRM analysis, which uses data warehousing and analytic techniques, can be applied to counter-intelligence and criminal detection applications. This is not to suggest the use of the simplistic type of racial profiling that has been used in the past, but a more effective methodology of using data mining as a modeling tool for sorting through vast databases to identifiy perpetrators based on behavioral patterns and socioeconomic, Internet, consumer, credit, criminal, lifestyle, and other commercial and government data sources.

As was mentioned in the preceding chapter, individuals cannot exist without leaving a trail of digital data in commercial and government databases and online and offline information. Appendix A includes a partial listing of several hundred Web sites that provide links to some of these files. However, the sites listed in Appendix A are just a start; there are many more potential data sources for enhancing the value of an investigative data mining analysis. Users of data mining tools and techniques from industries in financial services, retailing, marketing, and the like have long employed the concept of *overlaying* information about their customers and prospects with external lifestyle, socioeconomic, and demographic data.

For example, an e-commerce site can mine not only the clickstream data of its most loyal and profitable online customers, but it may also look at their zip-code and geo-code demographics in an attempt to obtain a profile about them. It can also look at the geo location of their Internet provider address. Using a similarly method, perpetrators may be profiled via data appends from diverse and unrelated databases. Unexpected results may occur when this is done; for example, the German authorities used utility-power usage records to identify potential dormant terrorists: foreign students who rented (safe) houses and used no electricity.

2.4   Demographic Data

As we mentioned, demographics have long been used by marketers to segment and target consumers. Based on census population data, private firms such as Acxiom, CACI, ChoicePoint, DataQuick, Experian, Equifax, Polk, Trans Union, and others aggregate this data with additional lifestyle and socioeconomic information, reselling it at the zip-code or specific physical-address levels and matching it by various keys, such as an address telephone or Social Security number. To gain an understanding of the type of data that these aggregators provide, we will look at the InfoBase product from Acxiom.

Acxiom, like others in this industry, offers a wide variety of U.S. consumer, business, and telephone data. Their main product, InfoBase, includes mailing lists, database or file enhancement, analytical services, and telephone and e-mail data. InfoBase provides demographic, socioeconomic, and lifestyle data on individuals, households, geographic levels, and businesses. Acxiom, for example, can match household information to an address and return the data attributes listed in Table 2.1.

Acxiom InfoBase basic data profile

Using public sources gathered from applications, registrations, and licenses for new corporations with secretaries of state, fictitious business names, business licenses, and trade names filed with either state or counties, Acxiom also aggregates information on companies. For business entities, Acxiom can provide the type of information listed in Table 2.2.

As with other data providers, Acxiom also offers analytic services, including a data profile analysis offering, which does a comparison of one set of businesses with another set. This profile service enables the user to perform a statistical comparison of a firm against other companies in the same industry from the Infobase reference group or file. For example, using this type of profiling service, money-laundering investigators might ferret out dummy business entities set up as fronts, which appear legitimate but are in fact producing no revenue.

Table 2.1 *Acxiom Infobase Basic Data Profile*

Truck/motorcycle/RV owner	First and second individual age ranges
Aggregate value of vehicles	
Adult age ranges	Working woman
Children's age ranges	Mail responders
Occupation-first and second individual	Credit card indicator
	Presence of children
Homeowner/renter	Age range of individual
Length of residence	Number of adults
Dwelling size	Estimated income code
Marital status	New car buyer/leased car
First and second individual name and gender	Known number of vehicles owned
	Dominant vehicle lifestyle
Verification date	Apartment number
Mail order buyer	DMA do not mail/phone flags
Household status indicator	

Neighborhood profiles are also available from these demographic data providers, such as CACI, which at the zip-code level offer an ACORN (a classification of residential neighborhoods) database, a geodemographic segmentation system. ACORN classifies U.S. households into 9 groups and 40 distinct consumer clusters, profiling by demographics, such as median age, socioeconomic (median household income), residential (median home value), and preferences in their spending patterns and lifestyle choices. The major groups include the following consumer clusters:

- Group 1: Affluent families
- Group 2: Upscale households
- Group 3: Up-and-coming singles
- Group 4: Retirement styles
- Group 5: Young mobile adults
- Group 6: City dwellers

- Group 7: Factory and farm communities
- Group 8: Downtown residents
- Group 9: Nonresidential neighborhoods

Table 2.2 *Partial List of Type of Information or Companies Provided by Acxiom*

Business Name	Ethnicity
Tradestyle and Mailing Street Address	Sales Volume Code at Location
Primary SIC Code	Location Employee Size Code
Census Tract	Actual Location Employee Size Code
MSA Code	Sales Growth Range
Mailing Address Lines	Line of Business
DSF Delivery Type	Headquarters. Subsidiary Indicator
State & County Code	Business/Government Indicator
Population Code	Public Company Indicator
Phone Number (w/ area code)	Business Filing Type/Sort Code
Fax Area Code & Phone	Year Business Established/Start Date
Contact Name/Title	Business Filing Date
Self-Employed Flag	Professional Flag
Standard Industry Market Title	Secondary SIC Code
Standard Industry Market Function	Import/Export Flag
Age of Contact	Estimates of telecommunication and utility purchases
Gender of Contact	
Marital Status of Contact	Products Manufactured
Suffix of Key Contact (i.e. CPA. MD)	Fortune 500
Owner Type	Building Square Feet Actual
Owner Home Phone Number	Number of Stories
Owner Birthday	Unit Count
Number In Family	Projected Utility Expenses
PC Owner	Type of Heating
Owner Gender	Type of Cooling
Type of Company	Year Built
Individual or Firm Identifier	Plant Size
Owner Occupied	Assessed Property Value

These types of neighborhood demographics provide lifestyle information about individuals at the zip-code level, which traditionally has been used by marketers. The following is a partial description of Group 7, Factory and Farm Communities:

Demographic data: The demographic profile of these communities is similar to the U.S. population: family-oriented and predominantly white (but also including blacks, American Indians, and Hispanics). The median age is between 33 and 45 years. Most are married couples with children.

Socioeconomic data: Their median household income ranges from $27,000 to $40,400. Employment is average; unemployment below average. Most work in manufacturing, farming, mining, or construction.

Residential data: These households are in rural neighborhoods located in the Midwest and South and also in urban areas throughout the United States. Occupants live in single-family and mobile homes. Their homes are owned-occupied and valued between $52,800 and $86,600.

Preferences data: This market style is rural, but not remote. Commuting long distances to work is a way of life. Most of the households own vehicles. They hunt, fish, and listen to country music. They also enjoy eating fast food and renting videos. They own pets, have personal loans, and watch TV.

Group 7, Factory and Farm Communities, consists of seven lifestyle clusters:

1. *Middle America*: top vegetable gardeners, high cat ownership, country music, campers, chain saws

2. *Young frequent movers*: loans, trucks, SUVs, videos, country music, pets (cats and dogs), hunt, fish

3. *Rural industrial workers*: top dog owners, high used–American truck buyers, country music

4. *Prairie farmers*: top cat owners, top used-car buyers, high home improvements, high borrowers

5. *Small-town working families*: hunt and fish, trucks, videos, diets, country music, women's magazines

6. *Rustbelt neighborhoods*: needlework, movies, sitcoms, soap operas, bifocals, lottery, news tabloids

7. *Heartland communities*: high vegetable gardeners, large American cars, campers, chainsaws, tools

Typically, marketers use these types of demographics for segmenting their customers and prospects in order to construct composites or profiles of their most profitable and loyal clients. However, these same types of demographics may be applied to overlay additional information about suspects in order to develop composites for investigative data mining applications.

2.5 Real Estate and Auto Data

DataQuick sells real estate–related information, which it captures directly from county assessors and recorder offices. The company also captures and makes available detailed information about property owners. Sales and loan information is entered within 72 to 96 hours of receipt. DataQuick coverage spans real estate information on 800 jurisdictions in 47 states and nearly every metropolitan area. Table 2.3 lists the type of information they provide.

For auto-related information, Polk is the best source in the industry, while Experian, Equifax, and Trans Union, the three major credit report companies, also provide demographics as part of their services. All of the companies that provide these types of demographics offer different options for purchasing the data—by tape, CD, dedicated line, or the Web.

Table 2.3 *Type of Information Provided by Data Quick*

Structure age/year	Homeowner/renter
Dwelling unit size	Length of residence
Property type	Dwelling size œ single/multi
Home size range Œ sq. ft.	Purchase date of home
Lot size range Œ sq. ft.	Year home was purchased
Insurance X-date	Month home was purchased
Presence of pool	Minority census tract
Year built	CRA income classification

2.6 Credit Data

Access to credit information in the United States is regulated by the Fair Credit Act. These reports are matched most commonly by Social Security numbers or a combination of addresses and are broken down into these main sections.

1. The identification section contains the individual name, date of birth, current and previous addresses, and employer information,

when available. This section of a credit report is available to anyone because it does not contain any credit information, and each of the three national bureaus bundle and sell these "short" reports for such applications as skip-tracing.

2. The grantor section contains information on account balances and monthly payment amounts. For every grantor listed in the report, there is also detailed information regarding the credit payment history for at least one year. A credit report will also display all inquiries that have been made by grantors; generally, the more inquiries, the higher the credit risk assigned to an individual.

3. The last section of a credit report contains detailed information for contacting all of the grantors listed in an individual's report. Investigators attempting to locate an individual or his or her assets can use this third-party contact information.

2.7   Criminal Data

Criminal records and statistics are also available through various sources. For example, aggregated crime data is available for analysis to develop a picture of potential criminal activity, risk, and security for a particular location. This type of crime data includes calls for service (CFS) consisting of every report of crime, suspected crime, and activity called into the police via the 911 emergency system and other channels. CFS includes incidents reported, along with the location, date, and time the event was reported.

The CFS data is generally quite useful, especially for security situations involving preventive measures against property crimes. The CFS data allows for temporal and spatial analyses of trends and patterns in crime activity, enabling countermeasures to be developed. CFS data can be used in conjunction with local law enforcement agency offense or incident reports, as well as the FBI's Uniform Crime Report (UCR) codification system.

CFS data and offense or incident reports can be mined in order to forecast criminal activity and for the clustering of unsolved crimes. This will be covered in depth in Chapter 12. Other aggregated crime data includes the FBI's National Incident-Based Reporting System (NIBRS) which will expand the (UCR) data available on the following eight primary crimes:

Violent:

1. Murder

2. Rape

3.   Robbery

4.   Aggravated assault

Property:

1.   Burglary

2.   Larceny theft

3.   Motor vehicle theft

4.   Arson

Another criminal data set is that of the National Crime Victimization Survey (NCVS), containing the characteristics of crime victims, including their age, sex, race, ethnicity, marital status, household income, years at their residence, and relationship to the offender. NCVS data is compiled via surveys of approximately 60,000 U.S. households. The NCVS, like the CFS, can be used for analysis of patterns and crime risk assessment, which, in this case, is crime against individuals rather than property. NIBRS is also being developed for collecting data on crimes focusing on 22 offense categories:

1.   Arson

2.   Assault offenses: (aggravated assault, simple assault, intimidation)

3.   Bribery

4.   Burglary/breaking and entering

5.   Counterfeiting/forgery

6.   Destruction/damage/vandalism of property

7.   Drug/narcotic offenses: drug/narcotic violations, drug equipment violations

8.   Embezzlement

9.   Extortion/blackmail

10.   Fraud offenses: false pretenses/swindle/confidence game, credit card/automatic teller machine fraud, impersonation, welfare fraud, wire fraud

11.   Gambling offenses: betting/wagering, operating/promoting/assisting gambling, gambling equipment violations, sports tampering

12.   Homicide offenses: murder and non-negligent manslaughter, negligent manslaughter, justifiable homicide

13. Kidnapping/abduction

14. Larceny/theft offenses: pocket-picking, purse-snatching, shoplifting, theft from building, theft from coin-operated machine or device, theft from motor vehicle, theft of motor vehicle parts or accessories, all other larceny

15. Motor vehicle theft

16. Pornography/obscene material

17. Prostitution offenses: prostitution, assisting or promoting prostitution

18. Robbery

19. Sex offenses, forcible: forcible rape, forcible sodomy, sexual assault with an object, forcible fondling

20. Sex offenses, non-forcible: incest, statutory rape

21. Stolen property offenses (receiving, etc.)

22. Weapon law violations

Aggregate crime statistics exist at the following levels: national, state, metropolitan statistical area (MSA) consisting of the core cities with over 50,000 people, city and county, beat, district or precinct, crime statistical reporting area, census tract, and individual property. There are also security reports (SR) maintained by private industry for all major buildings, which contain detailed information on crime for their premises with usually the following data:

- Incident reported
- Date of incident
- Time of incident
- Location of incident
- Victim(s), if any
- Witness(es), if any
- Modus operandi (MO)
- Follow-up investigation
- Outcome

Some of these statistics are available from the Department of Justice site at

```
http://www.ojp.usdoj.gov/cmrc/weblinks/welcome.html
```

Other criminal databases and networks include the following:

- *National Law Enforcement Telecommunications Systems (NLETS)*: NLETS is a nationwide network that links all states and many federal agencies together for the exchange of a criminal justice information. In each state, an interface agency is responsible for maintaining an in-state law enforcement telecommunication systems that delivers messages throughout the state. Through those connections, any criminal justice agency on a state law enforcement telecommunications systems in one state can communicate with any criminal justice agency on a law enforcement telecommunications system in any other state. This includes all major police agencies and most smaller ones. In addition, many prosecutors, probation departments, parole offices, and the like communicate with each other and with local, state, and federal law enforcement agencies through these systems.

Information Available from Other States Via NLETS

- Vehicle registration information
- Drivers license information
- Criminal history records
- Boat and snowmobile registration[1]
- Parole and probation information[1]
- Corrections information[1]
- Sex offender registration information[1]

National Files Available to NLETS Users

- ATF gun tracking data
- FAA tracking information
- FAA aircraft registration data
- National impounded vehicle file
- National drug pointer index
- Hazardous material information
- INS's law enforcement support center

Data Available From Canada Through NLETS

- Wanted persons
- Stolen and registered vehicles
- Drivers license files

---

1.   Information not available from all states

- Stolen articles files
- Stolen guns files
- Stolen securities files
- Stolen boats files
- Criminal history records

- *National Crime Information Center (NCIC)*: Another source of criminal data for each state law enforcement telecommunications system is the FBI's Network. The system has been in operation since its inception in 1967. Its current, enhanced version, NCIC 2000, came online in July 1999. NCIC is a national index of theft reports, warrants, and other criminal justice information submitted by law enforcement agencies across the country. It provides real-time information regarding persons and property to police officers by the side of the road, case investigators, booking personnel, prosecutors, probation and parole officers, and others. Through NCIC, almost all police departments in the country share their theft reports, warrants, missing-person reports, and the like with each other in an online, real-time mode. At present, users generate more than 2,000,000 transactions per day.

Information Regarding Property Available from NCIC

- Stolen vehicles
- Vehicles used in felonies
- Stolen license plates
- Stolen boats
- Stolen articles
- Stolen securities
- Stolen guns
- Recovered guns

Information Regarding Persons Available from NCIC

- Wanted person reports (warrants)
- Foreign fugitive reports
- Missing-person reports
- Protective order data
- Persons of possible danger to secret services protectees
- Sex offenders registration data

- Persons on supervised release
- Violent gang and terrorist organization (and members) data

The NCIC Network also provides inquiry access to the FBI's Interstate Identification Index (III). The III index points to the criminal history record residing either in the FBI or the particular state's holding information. It utilizes the telecommunications systems of the FBI, the individual states, and NLETS to respond to requests for criminal history information. This decentralized system promotes the use of state records, which are more complete, and reduces the FBI workload in maintaining and disseminating the records.

The FBI's Criminal Justice Information Services Wide Area Network (CJIS WAN) connects the states to the FBI's Integrated Automated Fingerprint Identification Systems (IAFIS). This WAN has a connection in each state, which allows for the electronic submission of arrest fingerprints to the FBI from the state criminal history repository. That submission causes the creation of a criminal history record in III. The CJIS WAN also provides for the electronic submission of latent fingerprints for the investigation of crimes and for submission of the fingerprints of noncriminal justice applicants for national background searches.

With IAFIS, those states that have built, or are building, in-state AFIS systems capable of accepting electronic submission of fingerprints from local arresting agencies will be able to forward those electronic fingerprints to the FBI and receive a response as to that person's national identification and criminal history within two hours. Plans for the CJIS WAN call for expanding its use to include non-CJIS services. The first major addition is to use the WAN for the delivery of certain FBI laboratory services, such as the DNA information shared among the states and FBI. Long-terms plan call for the NCIC 2000 Network and the CJIS WAN to be consolidated into a single network.

Other systems and telecommunications networks providing criminal-related data include the following:

- *CODIS*: the Combined DNA Index System, a national index of DNA profiles limited to convicted offenders and crime-scene evidence

- *NIBIN*: the National Integrated Ballistics Information Network, an attempt to unify BATF and FBI firearms databases

- *NDPIX*: the National Drug Pointer Index, a pointer system that allows state, local, and federal agencies to determine if a suspect is under investigation by any other participating agency

- *UCR/NIBRS*: the National Uniform Crime Reporting System, a statistical system based on crime reporting by state and local police agencies not intended to include personally identifying information

- *NICS*: the National Instant Criminal Background Check System for presale firearm background searches by licensed firearms dealers

- *LEO*: the Law Enforcement On-Line, a public safety intranet for research and training

Other federal criminal data systems that support the justice activities of one or more agencies at the federal level only include the following:

- *TECS*: the Treasury Enforcement Communications Systems

- *DRUGX*: a common FBI/DEA drug intelligence database intended to allow coordination of investigative activities for both federal agencies

- *JABS*: the Joint Automated Booking System, a federal booking capability that enables federal agencies to share arrest data and provides linkage between the booking systems of federal law enforcement agencies and the FBI's IAFIS

- *NIPC*: the National Infrastructure Protection Center database

- *IDENT-INS*: two print AFIS capability for searching aliens entering the country

- *FinCEN*: the Financial Crimes Enforcement Network

There are also multistate networked databases containing additional criminal data, such as:

- *RISS*: the Regional Information Sharing System

- *WIN*: the Western Identification Network, an AFIS consortium of western states

- *SWBS ADIS*: the Southwest Border States Anti-Drug Information System

Figure 2.1   *Sample record extract (criminal record detail).*

Nevada criminal search			
2 charges for Nevada criminal detail records found			
Name: DOE JAMES			
Birth MM/YYYY:	02/23/1963	Release Date:	
Sentence Date :	11/8/1994	County Name:	
Offense :	SEXUAL ASSAULT	Statute:	114
Sentence:		Cause Number:	989561
Disp Date:		Disposition:	
File Date:		Fine Amount:	
Name: DOE JAMES			
Birth MM/YYYY:	02/23/1963	Release Date:	
Sentence Date :	11/8/1994	County Name:	N/A
Offense :	SEXUAL ASSAULT	Statute:	114
Sentence:	N/A	Cause Number:	976251
Disp Date:		Disposition:	N/A
File Date:		Fine Amount:	

- *GREAT*: the Gang Reporting, Evaluation, and Tracking system, an investigative database of suspected gang members maintained by the Los Angeles Sheriff's Department, accessible to agencies nationwide

Aside from criminal statistics, there are of course individual criminal records, some of which are available on the Web, at such sites as criminalfiles.info, which provides instant searches from its databases of criminal

Table 2.4   *Criminalfiles.info available jurisdictions.*

Alabama	Arkansas	Arizona
Colorado	Connecticut	Florida
Florida-Duval County	Florida-Pinellas County	Florida-Dade County
Florida-Hillsborough County	Florida-Palm Beach County	Georgia
Idaho	Illinois	Illinois-Cook County
Indiana	Kentucky	Michigan
Minnesota	Mississippi	Missouri
New Jersey	New York State	New York City
North Carolina	Nevada	Ohio
Oklahoma	Oregon	South Carolina
Tennessee	Tennessee-Shelby County	Texas
Texas-Dallas County	Virginia	Washington State

records covering the most populous U.S. states and some U.S. counties. This site maintains databases containing felony, and misdemeanor dispositions and traffic violations. In general, search results from these databases show name, date of birth, race, sex, offense, disposition, date of disposition, county, and case number. The site charges a $10-per-search fee. Figure 2.1 provides a sample of a record extract.

Appendix A contains additional websites with criminal data.

2.8   Government Data

There is also a vast amount of government statistical data available from portals, such as FedStats.gov, enabling the search of information via keyword across agency sites. There is also an immense amount of aggregate and statistical information from FirstGov.gov, a portal to 30 million government pages. Appendix A lists additional sites with government data.

2.9   Internet Data

With the advent of the Web, a new kind of data is being generated and made available for analysis. This includes both Internet server data in the form of log files, as well as other mechanisms known as cookies and Web bugs, also known as invisible graphics. When a browser visits a Web site server, multiple transactions get recorded, both in the server log files and in the browser's hard disk. This kind of data can provide a trail of what sites a computer user has visited.

2.9.1 Log Files

Almost all Web servers generate log files as ASCII comma-, space-, or tab-delimited text files. This is where every transaction between the server and browsers is recorded with a date and time, the domain name or IP address of the server making the request for each page on a Web site, the status of that request, the number of bytes transferred to that requester, the location from which a visitor arrived at a Web site (such as a search engine and the keywords used), the browser type used, and a cookie field. The breakdown of these log files usually follows this format:

1.   Internet provider IP address, such as the following:

      `prominer.com or 204.58.155.58`

2.   The identification field, usually a hyphen or a dash:

      `-`

3.   The `AuthUser` field, usually the ID or password required for accessing a protected area:

      `:prominer :secreto`

4.   The date, time, and GMT [Greenwich Mean Time] of the transaction, such as the following:

      `Thu July 1712:38:09 2001`

5.   The method of transaction, usually as follows:

      `"GET /index/products.html`

6.   The status or error code of the transaction, usually as follows:

      `200 (successful transaction)`

7. The size in bytes of the transaction:

    4565

8. Location where visitor came from, such as the following:

    ```
    http://search.google.com/bin
    /search?p=profiling+criminals -> /index.html
    ```

9. The agent log, which identifies the browser type, such as:

    ```
    Mozilla/2.0 (Win98; I)
    ```

10. Lastly, the cookie field, such as the following:

    ```
    secure.webconnect.net    FALSE   /cgi-bin    FALSE
    1234117888      C113      010218233632550410021001
    ```

2.9.2 Cookies

What is important about the cookie is that a server will write it to a browser's hard disk and store it in a cookies.txt file under the Windows directory as a small text file for purposes usually of identification, tracking, and personalization. This Internet mechanism allows the server Web site to follow visitors and recognize returning browsers; however, it also creates digital tracks on the browser's PC. For example, the following cookies.txt file shows what Web sites this user has visited; it also shows the unique identification numbers each server assigned to this machine.

```
# Netscape HTTP Cookie File
# http://www.netscape.com/newsref/std/cookie_spec.html
# This is a generated file!  Do not edit.

secure.webconnect.net  FALSE  /cgi-bin  FALSE  1234117888  C113
010218233632550410021001

www.3dfiles.com  FALSE  /board  FALSE  1010723160  LastLoginDT  01-10-
2001%2011%3A25%20PM

.snap.com  TRUE  /  FALSE  2145916832  u_edition_0_0  clubvaio

.doubleclick.net  TRUE  /  FALSE  1920499321  id  80000000e6fc269

.flycast.com  TRUE  /  FALSE  1293753789  atf  1_49546875499

.avenuea.com  TRUE  /  FALSE  1279843247  AA002  964545236-17582523/965764864
```

```
.yahoo.com   TRUE   /   FALSE   1271361644   B   dhvvr4ksnrn98&b=2&f=s

.acxiom.com   TRUE   /   FALSE   2051222650   SITESERVER
ID=5032d01e60ae1b242a1ab0f7dc7fddc5

.mediaplex.com   TRUE   /   FALSE   1245628800   svid   96695507215933387491061573154

www.landsend.com   FALSE   /   FALSE   1597685661   cust_ck   63.70.82.34.6268966965538269

63.236.54.72   FALSE   /   FALSE   1577837100   NewChannel   C158693-166.204.10.196

63.236.54.72:80   FALSE   /   FALSE   1577837101   NewChannel   C158699-166.204.10.196
```

For an investigator, a cookies.txt file from a suspect's PC or laptop provides a clear map of the sites visited by that individual. In addition, most cookies are also assigned a unique value, which is placed in the last field of the cookie and can potentially be matched against the server log files to recreate what paths and items were viewed and purchased by that individual. The following is a breakdown of the cookie standard data format:

Table 2.5   *Anatomy of a Cookie*

.acxiom.com TRUE / FALSE 2051222650 SITESERVER ID=51e60ae15	
.acxiom.com	This is the domain of the Web site that created and issued the cookie.
TRUE	Cookie was created by HTTP header, if FALSE it was by JavaScript.
/	Path variable allows Acxiom to modify cookie.
FALSE	This is an unsecured cookie, HTTPS, SSL cookies are encrypted.
2051222650	Expiration date in seconds from January 1, 1970.
SITESERVER	Name of the cookie.
ID=51e60ae15	Value of the cookie, usually a unique ID number.

In Table 2.4, for example, by going to the acxiom.com server and doing a look-up for the ID-51e60ae15, a synopsis of what this browser looked at while at that site can be reconstructed.

2.9.3 **Web Bugs**

Yet another Internet mechanism used by Web sites to track visitors, usually used in conjunction with cookies, is clear GIFs, or Web bugs. Web bugs are bits of code that are invisible to the visitors of Web sites or recipients of e-mail; however, they are present and broadcast important information about a browser, such as IP address, time of visit, and some demographics when visitors complete a form (gender, age, zip, etc.). Web bugs can also be placed in e-mail so that a site or a marketing company can report on when messages are opened or when recipients click on embedded links. Web bugs and cookies are just a couple of Internet mechanisms used by Web sites to track and identify visitors, with each generating important information about their browsing behavior.

2.9.4 **Internet Forms**

Still another Internet technique used by Web sites to capture and store information about their visitors is the online form. These forms may be as simple as the prompt on a search engine for a keyword, or one involving the collection of an assortment of information from a visitor via a series of questions for everything from an application to a contest to a survey about preferences. Forms are used in conjunction with programs that store all the information completed by visitors into databases. Again, if an examination of a cookie.txt file identifies the sites visited, it is possible that if they use forms on their site and important information might have been captured. For example, if it can be determined that the user of a PC went to the American Airlines site based on a line in the cookie.txt file, it is possible that the user completed a form and purchased tickets online and important information may be found about that user's itinerary.

2.10 **XML**

The data sets that have been discussed so far are but a few of those available. There are certain to be other data sets that have not been covered, but are likely to be needed. This brings us to the next step in the investigative data mining process, the accessing and preparation of the data. Because so much of the data being created today is Web-based, a brief discussion of XML is appropriate, for it represents the standard by which different data sets can be merged and used for analysis.

XML can play a central role in allowing agencies and departments to share information. XML, or the extensible markup language, is a standard that can provide interoperability among disparate systems. It is designed to improve the functionality of the Web by providing more flexible and adaptable information identification. It is called extensible because it is not a fixed format like HTML, which is a single, predefined markup language.

XML is actually a *metalanguage*; a language about languages, which lets the user design customized markup languages for limitless different types of documents. Theoretically, XML can be used to link disparate databases and could be used to develop composites from different data sources for investigative data mining analyses. The following are six key items about XML, a technology that can facilitate greater collaboration of data for interoperability among multiple government agencies and private industry:

1. *XML is for structuring data.* Structured data includes objects, such as spreadsheets, most-wanted lists, configuration parameters, financial transactions, and technical drawings. XML is a set of rules, guidelines, or conventions for designing text formats that let users describe their data. XML is not a programming language; it is a standard for generating, reading, and structuring data. XML is extensible and platform-independent.

2. *It is not HTML.* Like HTML, XML makes use of *tags* (words bracketed by < and >) and *attributes* (of the form *name="value"*). While HTML specifies what each tag and attribute means and often how the text between them will look in a browser, XML uses the tags only to delimit pieces of data and leaves the interpretation of the data completely to the application that reads it. So, for example, a <p> in an XML file is not a paragraph; it could be a price, a parameter, or a person.

3. *XML has a family.* XML 1.0 is the specification that defines what tags and attributes are. Beyond XML 1.0 is a growing set of modules that accomplish other tasks. *Xlink* describes a standard way to add hyperlinks to an XML file. *XPointer* and *XFragments* are syntaxes under development for pointing to parts of an XML document. An XPointer, instead of pointing to documents on the Web, points to pieces of data inside an XML file. *XSL* is the advanced language for expressing style sheets. It is based on XSLT, a transformation language used for rearranging, adding, and deleting tags and attributes.

4. *XML leads HTML to XHTML.* There is an important XML application that is a document format: World Wide Web Consortium's XHTML, the successor to HTML. XHTML has many of the

same elements as HTML. The syntax has been changed slightly to conform to the rules of XML. A document that is XML-based inherits the syntax from XML and restricts it in certain ways (e.g., XHTML allows <p>, but not <r>); it also adds meaning to that syntax (XHTML declares that <p> stands for "paragraph," and not for "price," "person," or anything else).

5. *XML is Modular.* XML allows the user to define a new document format by combining and reusing other formats. Since two formats developed independently may have elements or attributes with the same name, care must be taken when combining those formats (does <p> mean "paragraph" from this format or "person" from that one?). To eliminate name confusion when combining formats, XML provides a namespace mechanism.

6. *XML is the basis for RDF and the Semantic Web.* W3C's Resource Description Framework (RDF) is an XML text format that supports resource description and metadata applications, such as a set of mug shots, playlists, or bibliographies. For example, RDF might allow a user to identify certain suspects in a set of photos using information from a wanted list; then a mail client could automatically start a message to investigators alerting them that these photos are on the Web. Just as HTML integrated documents, menu systems, and forms applications to launch the original Web, RDF integrates applications and agents into one Semantic Web. Just as people need to agree on the meanings of the words they employ in their communication, computers need mechanisms for agreeing on the meanings of terms in order to communicate effectively. Formal descriptions of terms in a certain areas, such as manufacturing or law enforcement, are called *ontologies* and are a part of the Semantic Web envisioned by W3C, the governing body of standards for the Internet (www.w3.org).

More information will be provided about how such an ontology would work via a Web service in the context of a real-time data mining system proposed in Chapter 11.

2.11 Data Preparation

The following are some basic steps and issues likely to be considered during the course of normalizing a data set prior to analysis; they are by no means all-inclusive. Adequate time needs to be provided for this process, as it is not uncommon for data preparation to take up to 80% of the effort during a data mining project:

1. *Clean*: Prior to any data analysis, the removal of extraneous characters from the data stream might be required, such as the removal of ($) from a string field that represents an actual monetary variable, which will be analyzed as a numeric value. Other characters warranting similar cleaning and removal include @, #, %, *, <, >, " as well as such strings as Mr., Mrs., unk, n/a, etc.

2. *Convert*: The data needs to be converted into a standardized format, (e.g., YYYYMMDD for dates) so that other temporally related fields can be compared. The objective is to have a single uniform standard of conversion for fields that represent currency, weight, distance, time, and other methods of measurement and comparison. Some algorithms, such as CART, can work only with numeric fields; this may require converting string fields, such as MALE to 1, FEMALE to 0, or LEGAL to 0, FRAUD to 1, etc.

3. *Concatenate*: Transactional data is usually organized and stored in discrete fields, such as lastname, firstname, address, city, state, and zip. These units can be combined into a single data object that represents an individual or suspect. In some instances, some of these fields can be excluded altogether. For example, in most cases, the price of a ticket purchased has no measurable impact on a profile or a model.

As part of the data preparation process, the data will need to be split into training and testing data sets when you are constructing and evaluating a predictive model. Most of today's data mining tools use a random number selection feature, which automates this process. The idea of course is to construct a model using a subset of the data to train it and then use an unseen section of the data to test it. Moving the data from original sources to the system used for preparing and converting the data for mining should be identified, and the whole process should be well documented.

As part of this process, ad hoc standard query language (SQL) extracts from relational databases of host systems may be performed, developing discrete tables for the actual analysis. In some instances the assistance of a database administrator (DBA) will be available or required. Most mature data mining tools support various data formats or allow for ODBC connection to various tables. As part of the data preparation process, an analyst or a team of analysts may first generate a summary count of every value of every field in a file. This may require simply loading the data into a spreadsheet such as Excel or a statistical software package such as SAS or SPSS. It is important to remember that numbers are not always numeric, such as zip or vehicle ID numbers. They represent category values, which at times can be clustered into segments of pseudo-categories, such as suspects versus nonsuspects, or low, moderate, or high alert.

Consideration of the structure of the data is a very important issue that may influence how the data mining process will evolve. A study (STATLOG) conducted by several universities in multiple countries during the 1990s with a diverse number of data sets from different industries was designed to compare the accuracy of various classification algorithms, such as regression, neural networks, machine-learning algorithms, etc. The four-year study concluded that the structure of the data was the most critical factor in determining the most accurate classification system. The STAGLOG findings can be summarized to these two observations: Use a symbolic classifier, such as CART or other machine-learning-algorithm–based tools if categorical fields outnumber the continuous value fields in a file, and use neural networks if continuous value fields outnumber categorical fields.

2.12 Interrogating the Data

As previously mentioned, it is recommended that any analysis start with a sampling of all the data that will eventually be used for the construction of a model or profile. Data mining is exploratory by its very nature in that it is not a process of creating reports. The analyst is commonly searching for clues, ratios, attributes, patterns, characteristics, features, trends, and other telltale intelligence stored in large databases.

The process is iterative, leading to correlations and insights often leading to further mining. Once a particular area or finding is discovered, additional information may be required to confirm a hypothesis. Data mining is an interactive process that often leads to more interesting findings. As we mentioned in Chapter 1, it is very much like the process of criminal profiling, requiring some heuristics skills. It is not an exact science. One of the key items to consider during the data interrogation process is documenting how it was conducted. The process may need to be duplicated by other investigators or analysts. In addition, as with other forensic analyses and findings, the results may end up in court.

2.13 Data Integration

Data derived for criminal detection and security deterrence in most instances will be from distributed locations—from miscellaneous internal databases and third-party sources. Prior to the development of a profile or a model, the data will need to be sampled, extracted, moved, integrated, and converted into a format that can be imported into a data mining tool. During these processes, certain data mining preparations will need to be performed. Most of the data in today's databases is not designed for analysis, profiling, or modeling. It is generally maintained for reporting and queries or billing and accounting. There are also some data integration issues most data mining projects must cope with, such as the following:

- The location of the data
- The computer platform
- The level of security
- The access process
- The type of media
- The type of query
- The data format
- The data source

A key issue during the data integration process is how the connection to the data will take place: Will ODBC or CORBA be used? How will access to the tables residing in Sybase, Oracle, Informix, SAS, Excel, or IBM servers take place? Will the data be found in flat or fixed-length files? Even flat files have different features that need to be resolved. Some are delimited by commas while other are not. There is the issue of multiple formats, such as relational databases, hierarchical structures, free-text (such as e-mail data), ASCII, field-delimited, or fixed-length format. All of these data integration issues must be considered at this juncture, prior to any data mining analyses.

As part of the data integration process, it may be necessary to deal with multiple operating systems, such as UNIX, Linux, and NT as well as multiple platforms, such as PCs, workstations, servers, and mainframes that support different access protocols. All of this will require dealing with different interfaces. Additionally, the structure of the data can be affected by the operating system, such as with end-of-line characters. These data-integration issues can often constitute the bulk of the effort and time put into some data mining projects. Some of these issues can be further complicated when dealing with proprietary, customized information systems, such as those used by large governmental agencies.

The data required for analysis may reside in multiple locations, which may mean that these sources must be accessed via LANs, WANs, Intranet, dial-up, wireless, Internet, or proprietary closed, secured networks. This may mean that control and access is by a third party and the data is not in a centralized repository or data warehouse. This is yet another data-integration issue that may limit the type of information available for some investigative data mining projects.

Most data mining projects typically involve the use of structured data in relational tables or flat-file formats. However, there may be situations where data has to be retrieved from terminal screen captures using special scripts or table creation software. Although uncommon, this may well be another integration issue, which requires the use of schemes for submitting multiple queries in order to retrieve all of the desired information, such as, for example, capturing the screen data from a point-of-entry terminal used by immigration or customs personnel.

Last is the thorny issue of integrating multimedia formats, involving unstructured free-text data, as well as images, audio, video, e-mail, wireless data, and other binary objects. For counter-intelligence analyses, which need to deal with these types of information objects and formats, this is a very real data-integration and analysis issue. The single best way of dealing with this obstacle is to ensure there is a consistent framework established for this type of data mining project so that all objects with a given class are consistent with each other. This can be a real challenge when dealing with time-sensitive analyses and a need to implement solutions in real time.

2.14 Security and Privacy

A major concern is the possible misuse of all of this information and the need to ensure that the models that evolve from it are correctly applied and are rigorously tested before being implemented. Any profiles require that ample tests be performed prior to widespread deployment. The American Civil Liberties Union (ACLU), for example, is raising concerns about plans for the Transportation Safety Administration's CAPP II (computer-assisted passenger prescreening) system to pull in data from banks, and other data providers mentioned in this chapter. Care must be taken to ensure the security and privacy of personal data is protected and the rights of citizens are not violated.

Issues involving security, especially when it comes to Internet, financial, credit, and government data, will also influence any data-integration efforts. Copyrights, personal and medical records, and other sensitive data will likely also restrict what information can be used. Above all, the privacy and security of individuals must be protected, and any access to private information, such as unlisted telephone numbers, must be done with the proper legal instruments, such as subpoenas or summonses. Note that some data mining models can be constructed without specific identification information, such as names, addresses or other unique identification numbers. To further protect the data, it can be classified using a variety of methods from unrestricted to a special compartmentalization-restricted security level.

2.15 ChoicePoint: A Case Study

One of the largest providers of information is ChoicePoint, whose customers include federal, state, and local government agencies; the FBI; the Drug Enforcement Administration (DEA) and the U.S. Immigration and Naturalization Service (INS). It provides access to various types of records in several formats. Its AutoTrackXP and ChoicePoint Online provide Internet access to more than 14 billion current and historical records on individuals and businesses and allow users to browse through those records instantly.

With as little information as a name or Social Security number, ChoicePoint provides access and cross-referencing of public and proprietary records, including identity verification information, relatives and associates, corporate information, real property records, and deed transfers. In addition, access is available to a staff of field researches who perform county, state, and federal courthouse searches.

Subscribers can use AutoTrack Wireless to access some of ChoicePoint's most widely used public-record databases through a variety of wireless platforms. Through their SQL Direct, batch processing can provide access to multiple databases include the following:

- Credit header (identification section)
- Real property records
- Corporations and limited partnerships
- Uniform Commercial Code filings
- Bankruptcies, liens, and judgments
- Telephone directory (includes reverse directory)
- Business directory listings

- SEC significant shareholders
- FAA aircraft and pilots
- US Coast Guard watercraft registrations
- Physician reports
- Address inspector
- Federal employer identification (FEIN) listings
- OSHA filings
- Professional licenses
- Fictitious business name registrations

ChoicePoint's National Comprehensive Report can provide the following data items:

- Date of birth
- Possible AKAs for subject
- Possible other Social Security number
- Possible other names associated with SSN
- Possible addresses associated with subject
- Possible real property ownership
- Possible deed transfers
- Possible vehicles registered at subject's addresses
- Possible watercraft
- Possible FAA aircraft registration
- Possible UCC filings
- Possible bankruptcies, liens, and judgments
- Possible professional licenses
- Possible FAA pilot licenses
- Possible DEA controlled substance licenses
- Possible business affiliations
- Possible relatives
- Other people who have the same address as the subject

- Possible licensed drivers at subject's addresses

- Neighbor phone listings for subject's addresses

At the end of the report the user is provided with the following notification:

```
The following databases were searched but data for the subject was
not found:

ABI Business Directory, Active U.S. Military Personnel, Broward
County Felonies/Misdemeanors, Broward County Traffic Citations,
Federal Firearms and Explosives License, Florida Accidents,
Florida Banking and Finance Licenses, Florida Beverage License,
Florida Boating Citations, Florida Concealed Weapon Permits,
Florida Day Care Licenses, Florida Department of Education,
Florida Felony/Probation/Parole, Florida Fictitious Name, Florida
Handicap Parking Permits, Florida Hotels and Restaurants, Florida
Insurance Agents, Florida Marriages, Florida Money Transmitter
Licenses, Florida Salt Water Product Licenses, Florida Securities
Dealers, Florida Sexual Predator, Florida Tangible Property,
Florida Tobacco License, Florida Unclaimed Property, Florida
Worker's Compensation Claims, Marine Radio Licenses, Significant
Shareholders, Trademarks / Service Marks, and state-specific
databases. *** End of Report SS_009/01 ***
```

Lastly, ChoicePoint offers through its CORE service the ability to pull public-records data directly into the investigative databases of subscribers for data and link analysis (www.choicepoint.com).

2.16   Tools for Data Preparation

Because multiple data sets may be used that are in various transactional formats, extensive data preparation may be required. There are various commercial software products that are specifically designed for data preparation, which can facilitate the task of organizing the data prior to importing it into a data mining tool. The following is a list of some of these vendors:

Amadea

Amadea from ISoft supports a methodology that splits up a data transformation process into several steps: extraction, cleansing, loading, and reporting. Once the user is connected to data source tables, the tool supplies all the functions predefined for cleansing, such as replacing missing values and putting aside outlying values. The transformation step in itself is supported by a library of operators for normalization, denormalization, binarization, verticalization, aggregation, join, union, selection, etc. Operators are graphically compiled so that the user does not need to type code lines. The resulting tables can be

Figure 2.2 *The iManageData interface.*

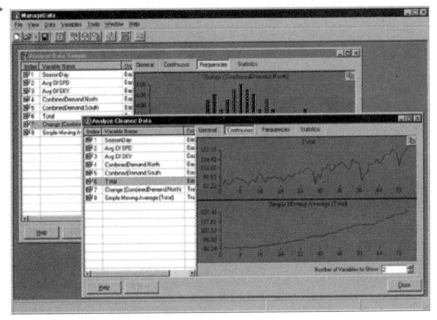

exported under most data formats now available on the market. The tool can be used to create data marts or to develop existing data warehouses according to ISoft.

BioComp

BioComp *i*ManageData supports access to delimited text files, Microsoft Excel workbooks, Microsoft Access databases, Oracle, SQL Server, and other relational databases. Comprehensive arrays of mathematical preprocessing functions are available, including trig functions, moving averages, logs, ratios and many more. The tool can create new binary variables based on ranges and thresholds.

DataManager

DataManger is an inexpensive program, that allows the user to process and manipulate data via a graphical interface. DataManager reads and writes delimited files, such as comma-separated files (CSV), and also can read data from ODBC data sources. It allows the user to construct a conceptual design for how to process and transform the data. For example, this tool could be used to prepare massive Web server log files.

Data-Audit

Data-Audit is a diagnostic tool for market research and database evaluation. Key indicators reported are as follows:

1. *Information content (quality of data representation)*: What is the information level contained in the dataset?

2. *Data efficiency (real versus potential redundancy of variables)*: How many variables are needed to represent the information?

3. *Information representation (univariate and multivariate)*: What variables can be used to represent the information contained?

Datagration

Datagration is a data cleansing tool that finds and uses data patterns. Datagration finds and fixes data errors at the source system. A configurable Data Discovery Message Gateway can be taught to identify common error patterns and then automatically fix them at the record or field level before moving the data to other enterprise systems or into a data mining tool.

Dataskope

Dataskope is a department-level tool to map, transform, alarm, output, and view high volumes of binary or ASCII input data. Dataskope allows users to convert, decipher, and view any kind of event record, such as call data records or comma-separated variable records. It can also interact with the converted data to set triggers on particular events and execute actions. These actions include replacing or modifying values, showing a dialog box, changing color, and the like. Dataskope can read from files or directly from the telephone switch using a serial link or the API it comes with. The files can be read one by one or by using the polling features, which will poll a directory and start reading files automatically when new files are discovered. The converted files will then transfer automatically into a backup directory for redundancy. This kind of tool can be used in investigations involving call-site files and toll-usage records.

Datawash

Datawash provides online access to data enhancement services and cleans and dedupes databases for increased deliverability and professional presentation. Datawash is a service requiring no purchase of software and may fit the needs of some ad hoc investigations.

Digital Excavator

Digital Excavator simplifies and speeds up the preparation of data for modeling using an intuitive GUI for data assembly, exploration, and the transformation of data from multiple sources into a single analysis set. The analysis set consolidates the relevant data into a form required by the modeling techniques. The format consists of one row per object being modeled (e.g., suspect) and numerous columns that represent the variables the miner desires the model to consider in developing its prediction. The tool processes several activities:

- *Cleansing* or implementing the desired approach to address the identified quality problems.
- *Consolidating* or integrating the various raw data sets into a single set. This may involve joins or merges and denormalization. In addition, various aggregations may be calculated to summarize multiple events (represented as multiple records in different sets) to a number of variables represented on a single row.
- *Calculating variables*, which are sometimes more useful in producing a good model than the individual components that exist in the raw data. The tool automates the process of creating ratios.

GritBot

GritBot is a data preparation tool that tries to find anomalies in data as a precursor to data mining. It can be thought of as an autonomous data quality auditor that hunts for records having "surprising" values of nominal (discrete) and/or numeric (continuous) attributes. Values need not stand out in the complete dataset. GritBot searches for subsets of records in which the anomaly is apparent.

IBM Datajoiner

IBM Datajoiner allows the user to view IBM, multivendor, relational, nonrelational, local, remote, and geographic data as local and access and join tables without knowing the source location. With a SQL statement, the user can access and join tables located across multiple data sources, such as IBM DB2, Informix, Microsoft SQL Server, Oracle, Sybase SQL Server, Teradata, and others.

Princeton Relational Tools

Relational Tools is a testing toolset that allows the user to move, edit, and compare complex sets of related data. These tools support the leading database management systems in both the mainframe and client/server environments and always respect the data-access rights defined in the database. With Relational Tools the user can extract and move data between production and test environments. The user can edit and browse complex relational data and compare images of relational data.

Sagent

Sagent provides a suite of data transformation and loading tools that can implement both Extract, Transform, and Load (ETL) and Extract, Transform, and Present (ETP) on large SMP servers running Solaris and Windows 2000. It includes a component-based development model that connects analytic objects together to easily develop scalable, reusable algorithms that perform address standardization, geo-coding, and spatial determination.

SyncSort

SyncSort is a sort and data manipulation product that provides speed, efficiency, the ability to handle a wide variety of data and file types, and a full set of versatile features. It speeds ETL applications and facilitates data mining and the processing of clickstream data from Web sites.

2.17   Standardizing Criminal Data

One of the obstacles to data preparation, integration, and analysis is dealing with unstructured free text data as captured in crime reports. As we saw in the case study in the previous chapter (1.15.3 Data Selection, Cleaning, and Coding), crime reports may contain fields, which make automated data analysis difficult. Police officers and investigators may use widely varying styles and formats in describing criminal scenes and modus operandi. Spelling errors and abbreviations may vary in these criminal reports using free-text fields making it difficult to structure the data they contain into categories for importing into data mining software.

In order to reduce this inconsistency, police departments and agencies may want to standardize their crime reports by eliminating or reducing free-text form fields and instead use reports using checklist and categorical fields. So that for example, rather than allowing investigators to enter in free-form word sequencing data such as "Southern acent," "Southern accent," "accent southern," "local accent," "accent: Southern," or "not local accent," etc. the crime report would use a table checklist format, such as this:

```
CRIME REPORT
Perpetrator Accent
[  ] Local
[  ] Not local
[  ] Southern,
[  ] etc.,

Perpetrator Race
[  ] White
[  ] Black
[  ] Hispanic
[  ] Asian
[  ] etc.,

Perpetrator Height
[  ] 5'
[  ] 5' 2"
[  ] 5' 4"
[  ] 5' 6"
[  ] 5' 8"
[  ] 5' 10"
[  ] 6'
[  ] etc.,

Perpetrator Age
[  ] 14
[  ] 16
[  ] 18
[  ] 20
[  ] 22
[  ] 24
[  ] 26
[  ] 28
[  ] 30
[  ] etc.,
```

```
Perpetrator Build
[  ] Slim
[  ] Medium
[  ] Heavy
[  ] etc.,

Perpetrator Hair Color
[  ] Dark
[  ] Light
[  ] etc.,

Perpetrator Hair Length
[  ] Short
[  ] Long
[  ] etc.,
```

Another possible method by which free text descriptions from crime reports can be standardized is through the use of a text mining tool. Text mining software can extract free form text summaries as found on crime reports and create major categories. This is one possible solution in situations where there are a voluminous number of historical crime reports.

2.18 Bibliography

Business Week, (June 5, 2002) "The Intensifying Scrutiny at Airports."

Mena, J. (1999) *Data Mining Your Website*, Boston: Digital Press.

Mena, J. (2001) *WebMining for Profit*, Boston: Digital Press.

Pyle, D. (1999) *Data Preparation for Data Mining*, San Francisco: Morgan Kaufmann Publishers, Inc.

Stout, R. (1997) *Web Site Stats*, Berkeley: Osborne McGraw-Hill.

St. Laurent, S. (1998) *Cookies*, New York: McGraw-Hill.

3

Link Analysis: Visualizing Associations

3.1   How Link Analysis Works

Seeing the criminal associations hidden among all of the commercial and government databases is like finding the proverbial needle in the haystack. And that is where data mining technologies like link analysis can be employed by law enforcement investigators and intelligence analysts to help them examine graphically the anomalies and inconsistencies and connect networks of relationships and contacts hidden in the data. Link analysis is the first level by which networks of people, places, organizations, vehicles, bank accounts, telephone numbers, e-mail addresses, and other tangible entities can be discovered, linked, assembled, examined, detected, and analyzed.

Effectively combining multiple sources of data can lead law enforcement investigators and government analysts to discover patterns to help them be more proactive in their investigations. Link analysis is a good start in mapping terrorist activity and criminal intelligence by visualizing associations between entities and events. Link analysis often involves seeing via a chart or map the associations between suspects and locations, whether physical or on a network or the Internet. The technology is often used to answer such questions as *who knows whom and when and where have they been in contact?*

3.2   What Can Link Analysis Do?

Link analysis can be used to expose the underlying patterns and behaviors pertaining to national security and homeland defense related to such areas as terrorism and narcotics trafficking. The intelligence community can use link analysis to sift through vast amounts of data looking for connections, relationships, and critical links among their suspected targets. In the private sector, link analysis can be used to monitor online and offline transactions by fraud specialists. Link analysis is but the first data mining technique used to assist investigators and analysts in investigating such areas as money laundering, narcotic trafficking, and terrorism. Link analysis is already used to detect fraud by specialists in the insurance and telecom industries, as well as in the area of e-commerce.

Intelligence analysts and criminal investigators must often correlate enormous amounts of data about entities in fraudulent, political, terrorist, narcotics, and other criminal organizations and is a critical first step in the visualization of the data. This is accomplished by organizing it in a cohesive manner, in terms of relationships between people and organizations under investigation. One of the challenging aspects, unique to the intelligence community, is discovering patterns derived from nontraditional data sources ranging from free-text documents and message intercepts to video clips and audio streams. The data mining systems typically used by the intelligence community are comprehensive and extremely specialized, customized for their unique needs. In these situations, link analysis is but one component and technique used by these intelligence analysts.

3.3   What Is Link Analysis?

Link analysis is a data mining technique that reveals the structure and content of a body of information by representing it as a set of interconnected, linked objects or entities. Often link analysis allows an investigator to identify association patterns, new emerging groups, and connections between suspects. Through the visualization of these entities and links, an investigator can gain an understanding of the strength of relationships and the frequency of contacts and discover new hidden associations. For this reason, link analysis is typically used by criminal investigators in such fields as fraud detection and money laundering, as well as by intelligence analysts in the study of terrorist networks. Link analysis is the first level of data mining. It is a manual interactive technique for forming and examining a visual network of relationships (see Figure 3.1).

Link analysis begins with data that can be represented as a network and attempts to infer useful knowledge from the nodes and links of that network from which an investigator or analyst can discover associations. Many of the current link analysis tools are highly specialized, interactive graphical software —with some having the capability of incorporating multimedia and some interactive *what-if* scenarios. While these visual-link networks have proven useful to investigators, their manual construction has proven difficult when it involves hundred of thousands of transactions.

Linkage data is typically modeled as a graph with nodes representing suspects of interest to the analyst and the links representing relationships or

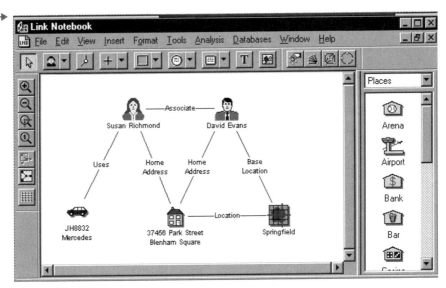

Figure 3.1 *A financial link analysis network.*

transactions. Examples might be a collection of telephone toll data with phone numbers, times of calls, and durations of calls subpoenaed for a criminal investigation; a collection of cash transactions to and from certain domestic and foreign bank accounts; a collection of sightings of individuals' meetings and their addresses, trips to foreign countries, points of entry, wire transfers, schools or churches attended, Web sites visited, and other related commercial or social interactions. The events can be a few meetings or conversations or a large number of toll calls or bank deposits or withdrawals. However, if the observations are very voluminous, the value of link analysis will begin to deteriorate.

3.4 Using Link Analysis Networks

Before links can be constructed to yield valuable associations, the analysts must have a complete understanding of the data they are working with. As with all data mining projects, extracting and preparing the data for analysis is commonly a major task. Transactional databases more often than not contain incomplete or inconsistent information, or multiple instances of the same entities because they are designed and built for speed not analysis. For example, a database of airline ticket purchases may have different names or account numbers for the same person or different individuals with the same name. In order to map associations correctly it is necessary to first identify accurately the right individuals in a database. This process of disambiguating and combining unique identification information into a unique entity is the task of data consolidation and preparation and must take place before any link analysis can be undertaken. (This was discussed in the preceding chapter, under section 2.11 on data preparation.)

Applying domain-specific knowledge is a very important component of this task. An investigator or analyst must know the nuances of the databases that she or he is working with. In data mining it is critical that the analyst know what every field in a database or column in a spreadsheet contains and what each value represents. For example, in a database of financial transactions a single, specific family, gang, cell, group, unit, or company may represent the desired level of granularity for analysis. Knowing and working at the right level of granularity is a very important part of preparing the data for link analysis.

Representing and configuring suspects who underlie the transactions and are reflected in various identifiers in the data involves two operations: *consolidation* and *disambiguation*. For example, it is often necessary to *consolidate* multiple transactions in order to evaluate the activities of targeted entities. On the other hand, a process of "merge-purge" for correcting errors in data (which may be intentional misrepresentations) is the process of *disambiguation*. Striking the proper balance is the task of data preparation prior to analysis. Data mining is a mixture of science and art, much like cooking: It requires experience, and, like every meal, no two projects are ever exactly the same.

Profiling entities and discovering anomalies that may indicate fraud or other criminal activity often requires assembling transactions in order to uncover patterns of unique behavior. Before any analysis can be conducted, the essential, initial activity of data preparation must, be undertaken prior to generating a link analysis chart. The data must be formatted to identify relevant entities from transactional formatted data; for example, deposits into a bank account should be organized in terms of that individual entity to look for structuring activity in a money-laundering scheme. *Structuring* is the practice of making multiple deposits under the $10,000 maximum that requires their reporting to the IRS.

3.5   Fighting Wireless Fraud with Link Analysis: A Case Study

Wireless fraud is by nature reactive in that a carrier can't detect it until it takes place. One way that carriers are reducing fraud is by identifying and stopping repeat offenders via link analysis. Using link analysis, fraud investigators gather and correlate subscriber information that can associate new customers to fraudulent activities. Various types of subscriber data can be used for this type of analysis. One method, known as a dialed-digit analysis, scrutinizes the records of who's calling whom. Using a link analysis tool, a large volume of call detail records (CDRs) is used to reveal correlations between records. The strategy is to identify fraud and potential suspects by association.

Using link analysis techniques an investigator can track a new subscriber's 10 most frequently called numbers. For example, alarms are set to activate when the dialed numbers match those associated with ongoing or previous fraud case phone number accounts. This enables the carrier to identify a previously banished criminal by his or her most frequently dialed numbers. Expanding the fraud circle of association, accomplished by including the criminals' incoming calls, is another way to perform a dial-digit analysis. The system tracks not only the people the fraudulent phones dial, but also those who call the fraudulent phones.

Because the analysts can visually represent the calling patterns, they can find numbers to investigate that may not have popped up through other methods. In some cases, returning criminals may not call numbers that can be linked to past crimes, but they might call a number called by another fraudulent subscriber, which can alert the fraud analyst of possible criminal activity by association. Using link analysis, an analyst creates a web of *who calls whom* and represents those associations in a digital map, which from an analyst's perspective makes it a lot easier to recognize patterns of behavior that may not be evident through other traditional analyses.

Another way that carriers use link analysis to detect potential bad accounts is by analyzing call-pattern usage information in combination with billing information. The objective here is to understand usage information better in the context of a subscriber's billing profile. For example, if a new customer subscribes to the least expensive plan a carrier offers but starts making 300 calls a day, there's a problem. Link analysis is also used to detect potentially fraudulent new subscribers, primarily by looking at their provided credit-card information and its association with other bad accounts. The analyst marks accounts that have used fraudulent credit cards before and looks for new accounts that use the same credit-card information.

Link analysis is also used to catch subscription fraud by detecting suspicious changes early in the life of a new account; for instance, a subscriber who changes the account address within the first week would raise suspicion. Sometimes fraudulent subscribers change the account address early to prevent the legitimate credit-card owner from receiving welcome information from the wireless carrier. A series of link analyses are also performed on other identity data, such as Social Security numbers and home telephone numbers, again the objective being to find associations with previously tainted, bad accounts.

3.6 Types of Link Analysis

Link analysis is the process of building up networks of interconnected objects or items over time and the use of special techniques and software tools for forming, examining, modifying, analyzing, searching, and displaying these patterns of behavior, especially for the investigative data miner. These objects or items may consist of *entities, events,* and *associations.* Typically, the *entities* of interest include:

- *Places,* such as a physical or IP address, or geo code coordinate, such as latitude

- *Organizations,* such as cells, gangs, governments, commercial or military units

- *Facilities,* such as factories, airports, hotels, schools, warehouses

- *Individuals,* such as names, titles, or identification numbers

- *Components,* such as chemicals, fertilizers, masks, acids

- *Documents,* such as passports, driver licenses, e-mails

- *Money,* such as cash, wire transfers, money orders

- *Weapons,* such as guns, knifes, rifles, bombs

- *Vehicles,* such as planes, trucks, boats, cars

- *Drugs,* such as type, weight, source

Additionally, for *entities,* such as a suspect, other more detailed dimensions may be available, such as name, aliases, gender, membership, affiliation, religion, marital status, citizenship, race, date of birth, occupation, country of origin, hair color, eye color, height, weight, countries visited, among other things.

For *events* the nature of the investigation is the determiner of the dimensions in the data. For example, for counter-drug analysts, this may include processing, purchasing, transportation of drugs, planning, meeting, cartel association, region affiliation, training or educational background, military background, and communication about drugs. On the other hand, for counter-terrorist intelligence analysts those events may include the dimensions of training in weapons and tactics, affiliations to groups, place of birth, bombing, hijacking, killing, hostage-taking, countries visited, buying and stealing of weapons, the sending and receiving of money, and the purchases of materials for the assembling of weapons of mass destruction.

3.7 Combating Drug Trafficking in Florida with Link Analysis: A Case Study

By its very nature, drug trafficking involves some organization—transportation, distribution and sales "channels"—all of which try to keep themselves hidden. Investigating such organizations may require correlating apparently unrelated information and finding submerged links between people and organizations. The growing amount of online data could make this work easier if access to it were automated.

Florida's St. Petersburg Police Department had more online data than could be known or effectively used by detectives in the course of routine investigations. They had 10 years of data in a fairly sophisticated database from which they could extract fields and look up information. The department had been sharing the data with the Pinellas County Sheriff's office for five years. They had not, however, been able to extract information from the narratives of crime reports. Under the department's system, officers entered basic information about an incident into an online form. This form included such things as the names of involved parties, the time of the incident, etc.

Officers did not, however, type the narrative descriptions of the incident. Instead, they dictated the narratives, which were later transcribed. This method saved officers time and had proven much more cost-efficient. When the narratives were later transcribed, they were electronically associated with the basic data entered by the detectives. Although the narrative data had technically always been available online, the existing software couldn't search the narratives, let alone do link analysis.

Development of a system to access narrative data began when representatives of the federal Counterdrug Technology Assessment Center (CTAC) approached the department. CTAC falls under the Office of National Drug Control Policy and is the central counterdrug enforcement research and development organization of the U.S. government. CTAC interviewed 30 narcotics detectives, asking them, if they could have a computer do anything for them, what would it be? Following the initial meetings, the University of Tennessee got involved to do the application development. Rather than suggesting theoretical solutions from afar, the university took the time to find out what was really needed by the field investigators. They worked with them in the field to understand their information needs.

What came out of this design phase was a plan for several applications, collectively known as the West Florida Counterdrug Investigative Network

(WFCIN). The first application to be implemented gives officers the ability to query the information contained in the online narrative reports. This is done using a Web interface that talks through a backend process to the existing database system: The University of Tennessee developed both the interface and the backend. For example, if a detective receives a report of an incident in which a drug dealer used a specific type of gun, he can enter the gun type and get back a standard HTML page with links to narrative reports in which that type of gun is mentioned.

A second application to be implemented will stores images—surveillance photographs, evidence photographs, or scanned newspaper articles—linking them to criminal cases. The application automatically stores and links images to cases; so, say there are 100 images on a case, and one is a photograph of a gun under a bed. The user can go into the comments section and type in "gun under bed." The application links the comments to the photo and stores that information. The comments become part of the case file; so, if another investigator types in "gun under bed," it will not only search the narratives, but also the associated photos. Searches will return links to both the text-based narrative and the images associated to that case.

The network's image-carry capacity extends to real-time audio and video for teleconferencing—or for sharing video monitoring tapes with law enforcement officers in other jurisdictions. Another application will provide "link analysis" for graphically displaying connections between individuals, groups, and organizations. This kind of functionality can help locate associations that otherwise would have gone unnoticed, and that may be key to developing a case or directing an investigation.

The data mining applications being developed and used by the St. Petersburg Police Department are still in the beginning stages, but they show the promise of things to come. A complete, integrated package that allows investigators to search across jurisdictions for common characteristics and to build link analysis charts to help identify key culprits and their associates will help bring crime investigation and prosecution into the twenty-first century.

3.8   **Link Analysis Applications**

Associations of networks created via link analysis may be grouped into such categories as entity-to-entity, entity-to-event, or event-to-event. Entity-to-entity associations between individuals may include blood relative, spouse, employees, friend, acquaintance, neighbor, etc. Associations between individuals and an organization may include labels such as leader, owner, member, head, and employee. Association networks between an individual and a place may include place of birth, point of entry, residence, current location, country visited, and place of training. Entity-to-event association networks may include labels for bomber, victim, object, visits, meetings, enrollment, weapon, or place. For these events, the roles for any date and time are a factor. Event-to-event association networks include tying communications, such as phone calls, e-mails, physical meetings, or planning events, to each other.

Links, as well as nodes, may have attributes specific to the domain or relevant to the method of collection. For example, link attributes might indicate the certainty or strength of a relationship, the dollar value of a transaction, or the probability of an infection. Some linkage data may be simple, such as a meeting, or voluminous, such as phone calls, wire transfers, or e-mails, with a uniformity of node and link types and a great deal of regularity. On the other hand, data may be extremely rich and varied, though sparse, such as clandestine meetings common with law enforcement investigative data, with elements possessing many domain-specific attributes, as well as confidence and value, which can change over time.

The ability of link analysis to represent relationships and associations among objects of different types has proven crucial in assisting human investigators to comprehend complex webs of evidence and draw conclusions that are not apparent from any single piece of information. Link analysis often raises the following questions for a criminal investigator and intelligence analyst:

- Which nodes are the main leaders of a network?
- What are the underlying relationships in the network?
- What are the relevant sub-networks in a large network?
- Are there undetected links or hidden nodes in the data?
- What level of aggregation best reveals the links in a network?
- Which links can be severed to impede the operation of the network?

Fortunately, link analysis tools have the capability of answering these and other types of questions the investigative analysts may want to interrogate from the data. Many more applications exist for link analysis techniques in the areas of fraud prevention and criminal analysis, as we shall see in the following chapters.

3.9 Focusing on Money Laundering via Link Analysis: A Case Study

NETMAP is used extensively by several government agencies including the U.S. Treasury Department's Financial Crimes Enforcement Network (Fin-CEN), which is involved in the proactive detection of financial crimes such as money laundering. Money laundering usually involves the conversion of large amounts of cash from illegal activities into legitimate funds. Current estimates are that $100 to $300 billion are laundered annually; obviously, this involves massive amounts of transactional data, which cannot be manually analyzed. Just in one day more than $1 trillion is wired through New York City alone.

Financial crime analysts and investigators use tools like NETMAP to begin to define the important parts of financial transactions as they relate to individuals, organizations, and locations, including dates, amounts, institutions, sources, and ID-numbers (see Figure 3.2). When NETMAP is used for money-laundering investigations, the tool is used to expose and associate indirect relationships of bank accounts, home and business addresses, and identification numbers by multiple filers of required forms with the financial organizations. For example, a reliable method of detecting wrongdoing is the use of the same address by several individuals conducting transactions in excess of $10,000 that require reporting to the IRS. The related gang member or terrorist cell operative may be using the address of a dummy or vacant safe house.

Analysts use NETMAP in money-laundering investigations to search for links between individuals and organizations, such as car dealerships, wire transfer companies, and *casas de cambio* (houses of exchange) for buying and selling dollars that are prevalent in the border cities between the United States and Mexico.

Recently, FinCEN completed the first phase of a data mining study. They piloted three tools: Darwin from Oracle, Clementine from SPSS of Chicago, and SGI's MineSet, along with two data mining contractors, Visual Analytics of Poolesville, Md., and Nautilus Systems of Fairfax, Va. Not surprisingly, they quickly found a problem in the quality of the data. Since 1996, Treasury also has required financial institutions to use a three-page form called the Suspicious Activity Report to describe potential embezzlement, money laundering, check kiting, loan fraud, or other crimes. The form has a space for an account of the suspect activity, a category of information not present on other Bank Secrecy Act reporting forms. The free-format data—which can be cryptic, detailed, or nearly unintelligible—presented a huge challenge to the data miners.

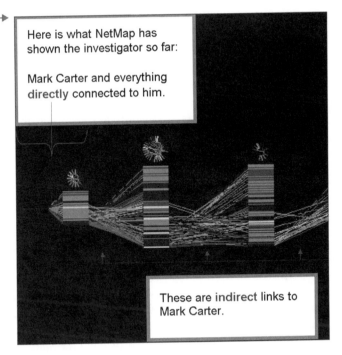

Figure 3.2 *A NETMAP link chart displaying financial relationships.*

Cleaning the raw data turned out to be a crucial first step. Not only did the researchers have to fix the usual typographical errors and misspellings, but they also had to resolve data inconsistencies among the free-format text fields. For example, bank officials would describe a suspect's occupation with terms such as "worked," "worker," "working at," "works on," or "worked for." Ultimately, the data mining software must lump the variations under one term, "employment." To find data correlations—say, between suspects' job titles and their crimes—the researchers tested several standard mining approaches. A clustering algorithm sought to group data from a given field into natural clusters. Ultimately, the broad patterns of criminal activity detected in the forms could help filter the suspicious cases out of Treasury's database of more than 12 million in annual currency transaction reports. In the next phase, the agency plans to define specific data abstraction routines and train FinCEN analysts. Ultimately, the form for capturing the data needs to be redesigned in order to make it easier for mining via neural networks and machine-learning algorithms.

3.10   Link Analysis Limitations

Link analysis is a very labor-intensive method of data mining. In investigations involving a high volume of transactions, such as those in money laundering, link analysis requires an extensive amount of data preparation. Even then, the results of link analysis are often quite limited when compared to other more powerful methods of data mining designed to discover the needles hidden in the haystacks.

Link analysis works best in situations where there is a limited number of observations, such as events (meetings) and entities (suspects). Its functionality begins to deteriorate once a large number of observations or transactions begins to populate a case file. Keep in mind that the key functionality of this technology is to organize the data in the form of a graph or chart. Link analysis is primarily a visualization technology, as are the tools covered in this chapter. This is not to say that these tools are not valuable and essential to investigators and analysts in resolving open criminal cases and identifying potential threats from dangerous entities.

Link analysis is distinct from other data mining technologies and tools that construct models via neural networks or extract association rules from databases via decision trees employing statistical and machine-learning algorithms. These data mining technologies discover and represent associations based on the aggregate statistical characteristics of a sample of instances drawn from large databases. For example, given the millions of vehicles that enter the United States via its various points of entry along the Southwest border, which makes and types of vehicles are most likely to be used to smuggle contraband? This is a question that a neural network or a machine-learning–based tool is ideally suited to solve, but one that a link analysis tool would be hard pressed to solve.

As mentioned earlier, one of the users of link analysis in detecting crime (money laundering) is the U.S. Treasury Department's Financial Crimes Enforcement Network. FinCEN analysts do not construct profiles of money laundering using conventional data mining tools. Instead, they use a variety of unconventional and largely manual methods to form profiles of money laundering. They use a form of iterative concept refinement—formulating initial profiles, querying FinCEN databases, evaluating the results using their own domain knowledge, and then refining the profile and iterating again. They use historical cases as prototypes, generalizing incidental aspects and finding similar cases. They also devise and test hypothetical schemes, based on domain knowledge and their own conjectures about likely methods for laundering money. Though profile generation is largely manual, two technical approaches do greatly aid analysts' reasoning: data restructuring techniques and link analysis.

FinCEN's data restructuring focuses on three relatively simple operations on local databases: *disambiguation* identifies when a single token (e.g., Bill Smith) refers to two or more individuals; *consolidation* identifies when several tokens (e.g., Bill Smith, Bill J. Smyth, and William Smyth, Jr.) refer to the same individual and builds a record of that individual; and *aggregation* provides useful summaries of transaction-level data.

Disambiguation, consolidation, and aggregation are simple in principle, but they are more difficult in practice. Disambiguation must make use of multiple identifiers (e.g., name, address, phone, account number) that are often misentered at the Detroit IRS Center or change over time. Disambiguation also makes considerable use of low-level domain knowledge about national and cultural conventions of name ordering and spelling. Consolidation is also surprisingly difficult given that different overlapping consolidations are useful for different analytical purposes. Similarly, useful types of aggregation depend strongly on the inferences they are meant to support.

FinCEN's use of consolidation and aggregation mirror related techniques used elsewhere for fraud detection. Consolidation can be viewed as a form of clustering, a common technique for understanding data in the absence of class labels indicating the correct inference (e.g., moneylaundering or notmoneylaundering). Similarly, aggregation is used in other fraud detection applications to build a profile of a "normal" use (e.g., for a credit card or a cell phone account). Deviations from this profile can then be used to indicate fraud. As we shall see, similar techniques exist for intrusion detection systems (IDSs) for identifying hackers.

As we have seen, the analysis of a network of associations is a visualization technique to reveal structure in sets of related records. Linkage data are typically modeled as a graph with nodes representing entities of interest in the domain and links representing relationships or transactions. As shown, these examples might be a collection of cash transactions to and from bank accounts, a collection of telephone toll data (e.g., numbers, times, and duration) subpoenaed for a criminal investigation, or a collection of sightings of individuals' meetings, their addresses, and other related commercial or social interactions.

Links, as well as nodes, may have attributes specific to the domain or relevant to the method of collection. For example, link attributes might indicate the certainty or strength of a relationship, the dollar value of a transaction, or the probability of a connection. Some linkage data may be simple but voluminous (e.g., telephone calls), with a uniformity of node and link types and a great deal of regularity. Other data may be extremely rich and varied, though sparse (e.g., law enforcement data), with elements possessing many domain-specific attributes, as well as confidence and value, which may change over time.

FinCEN analysts search for patterns of financial transactions and other events and facts that are indicative of money laundering. They sift through millions of reports by banks, tips from law enforcement agencies, and records of cooperating federal agencies to discover patterns that reveal illegal activity. FinCEN receives and processes over 10 million currency transaction reports (CTRs) and thousands of suspicious activity reports (SARs) submitted by banks and other financial institutions. FinCEN can also access dozens of remote, structured databases of postal, business, and travel records, as well as many remote, unstructured databases of news stories and other textual data. However, at present, inducing profiles from link charts is largely a manual process, although methods such as inductive logic programming and other techniques could be used to draw inductive inferences from these types of data.

As we shall see in subsequent chapters, link analysis is distinct from other data mining techniques that construct predictive models from neural networks and rules or decision trees from machine-learning algorithms. These techniques use networks as a *model* representation and discover associations based on the aggregate statistical characteristics of a sample of uniform instances drawn from some population. In contrast, link analysis uses networks as a *data* representation and infers useful knowledge based on the relations present in a network of heterogeneous records.

The main drawback to link analysis is that the aggregate number of data records that can be presented in most diagrams is limited. The human eye can only see so much, even for very experienced investigators and analysts. However, a number of AI technologies have the potential to assist investigators in constructing complex networks of voluminous entities and events, as we shall see in the following chapters. These techniques involve the use of intelligence agents for information retrieval, text mining software for sorting and organizing content from thousands of documents, neural networks for pattern recognition, and machine-learning algorithms for constructing profiles and extracting rules from large databases, all technologies covered in the following chapters.

3.11 Link Analysis Tools

Link analysis tools are increasingly used by law enforcement investigators, insurance fraud specialists, telecommunications network researchers, counter-intelligence analysts, and a host of other detection and deterrence professionals. As we have seen, link analysis explores associations among large numbers of objects, commonly between different entities and events. Typically, a law enforcement application might examine relationships among suspects and victims, the addresses at which they reside, and the telephone numbers that they called during a specified period of time.

The following are some of the most popular and dominant link analysis tools, which can vary tremendously in price and functionality, with some being nothing more than simple graphical organizing software, while others are very expensive high-end systems capable of incorporating audio and video streams in their charts and graphs.

ATAC

http://www.bairsoftware.com/atac.htm

The Automated Tactical Analysis of Crime (ATAC) is a unique criminal information analysis tool designed to isolate, identify, track, and view crime patterns, trends, and series. Its Trend Hunter utility can find trends hidden in data using an artificial neural network; it can compare combinations and permutations of tens of thousands of crime records, finding hidden links and similarities, then generating a report of results. The use of a pattern-recognition component, such as a neural network, is a unique function for a link analysis tool. ATAC can export and interact with almost any other software program, such as desktop GIS products like ArcView or MapInfo, or statistical and data mining systems, such as SPSS, SAS, or MathSoft, and tactical analysis software, such as TimeScan, GeoGenie, AutoLog, and Trend Tracker.

Analyst's Notebook

http://www.i2.co.uk/home.html

The Analyst's Notebook includes two main software products for different types of criminal investigative analysis—the *Link Notebook* and the *Case Notebook*. This is one of the most popular link analysis tool on the market and is used by securities, investigative, intelligence, and law enforcement analysts. In fact, i2 Ltd., which developed the software, recently announced a multiyear contract to provide its software and training to the FBI.

The **Link Notebook** tool supports various methods of organizing and viewing entity relationships, including the following components:

- Link analysis charts, also called association charts
- Network or high-volume link charts
- Commodity flow charts
- Activity charts

Figure 3.3 *The Link Notebook supports zoom in features.*

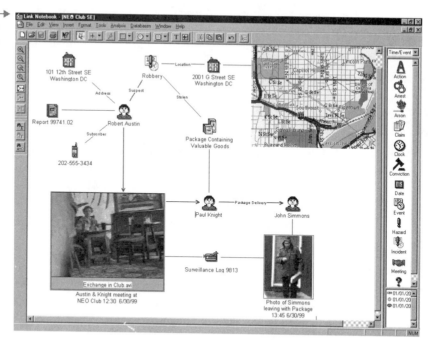

The structure of the *Link Notebook* allows the user to control and select options from a sidebar menu, from which icons representing different entities can be dragged-and-dropped to construct the chart. It also allows users to select and arrange graphical elements into position (see Figure 3.3).

The *Case Notebook,* on the other hand, supports a somewhat different method of organizing and viewing events. This includes the following graphs:

- Case flow or transaction charts
- Timeline or sequences-of-events charts
- Combined charts showing events and flows

The *Case Notebook* is specifically designed to enable an investigator or analyst to organize and view the progressive state of an ongoing case. The *Case Notebook* can set events in a timeline, thereby enabling an investigator to quickly locate significant times and dates, such as special meeting or trips by suspects. Timeline charts can be used to show the significant events where information is inconsistent or where accounts diverge. The *Case Notebook* charts can be used in drug, terrorist, fraud and other criminal investigations where events with associated dates and times are significant (see Figure 3.4).

Figure 3.4
*A timeline
displaying time-
related events.*

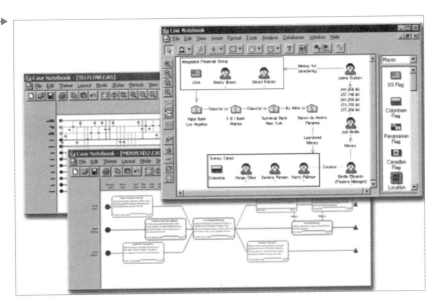

The *Analyst's Notebook* tool from i2 supports a wide range of analytical conventional graphical link standards, including the following methods of creating charts.

Confirmed/unconfirmed lines Solid lines are used where the analyst is confident about the information that validates a link and wishes to indicate it is "Confirmed" (see Figure 3.5).

Figure 3.5
*Confirmed links
are shown as
solid lines.*

Dashed lines are used where the analyst believes further action is required to confirm the validity of a link, and so it is "Unconfirmed" (see Figure 3.6).

Organizations shown inside boxes The method for grouping entities on a chart is to draw a box around related entities. For example, those individuals who are principal players in the same organization, such as a gang, a cartel, or a terrorist cell, are organized inside of a box (see Figure 3.7).

Figure 3.6
*Unconfirmed
associations are
dashed lines.*

Figure 3.7
*Members of an
organization are
grouped inside a
box.*

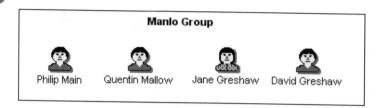

Where there are many organizations on a chart, a common convention is to simplify the graph by showing the less significant organizations as icons (see Figure 3.8).

Figure 3.8
*An organization
can be
aggregated as an
entity.*

Chart clarity Another standard in link analysis is where possible to avoid crossing lines on a chart since it confuses the eye of the viewer (see Figures 3.9 and 3.10).

Figure 3.9
*The central
contact is
unknown.*

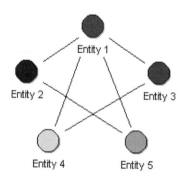

Figure 3.10
Here Entity 1 is ID.

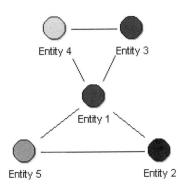

However, it is impossible to avoid crossing lines completely in larger, more complex charts, and in these instances the link types used in a chart are deliberately different.

Link types A chart may be organized to use different link styles (single, directed, and multiple) in order that links actually represent multiple associations (see Figure 3.11).

This use of multiple the type of links can drastically reduce the size of a chart, while still avoiding crossed lines. However, they should not be used excessively because they are not as visually clear as straight lines.

Figure 3.11
The links are the intelligence.

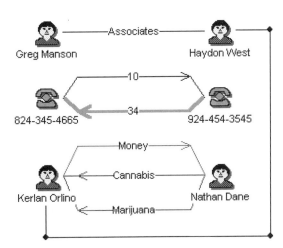

Figure 3.12
*A sample of a
chart with a
legend.*

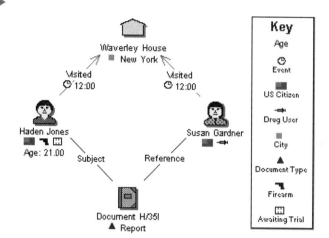

Legend A chart may also incorporate a legend to indicate the meaning of visual items on the diagram, including link types and attributes (see Figure 3.12).

Telephone toll analysis For these types of unique diagrams, investigators and analysts commonly create link analysis charts directly from toll usage data or other billing structured data to discover volumes of calls and common numbers called (see Figure 3.13).

Figure 3.13
*A telephone toll
analysis chart.*

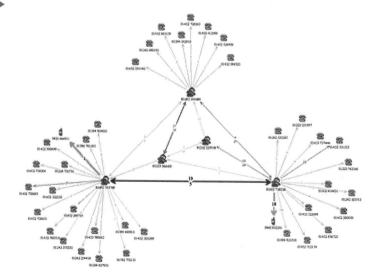

Figure 3.14
*Voluminous
amounts of data
can lead to
vague charts.*

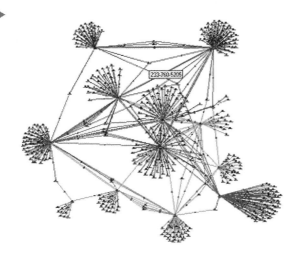

High volume data In situations where there is a large number of instances, observations, contacts, or transactions, the limitations of this type of technology begins to become apparent, as the granularity of individual records begin to get lost (see Figure 3.14).

The i2 link analysis tool also supports Timeline Analysis, the conventions of which are several, including the following:

- *Time axis.* A time axis graph can be labeled to show the passage of time, be it in minutes, days, or years. Time axes can grow or shrink to reflect a large volume of data on the chart, thereby reducing the length of the chart (see Figure 3.15).

Figure 3.15
*An analyst can
move events and
change the chart
as needed.*

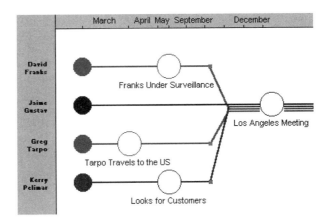

Figure 3.16
*Events are
placed on the
theme they relate
to.*

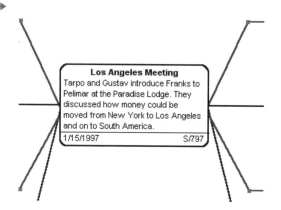

Los Angeles Meeting
Tarpo and Gustav introduce Franks to
Pelimar at the Paradise Lodge. They
discussed how money could be
moved from New York to Los Angeles
and on to South America.

1/15/1997   S/797

- *Events.* Although the precise graphical representation of events varies,
  a complete event usually includes a title, description, date, and information source (see Figures 3.16 and 3.17).

Figure 3.17
*Several events
can also be
combined.*

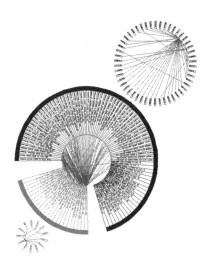

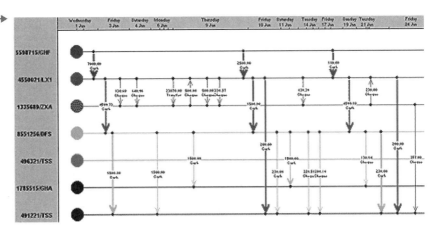

Figure 3.18
*Multiple events
and transactions
can be mapped.*

- *Transaction flow analysis.* Investigators also frequently analyze telephone-call and financial data to create transaction flow charts (see Figure 3.18).

As demonstrated by these charts, the i2 link analysis tool is a very robust and highly developed software system for investigators and analysts.

Crime Link

http://www.crimelink.com/

Crime Link is yet another link analysis tool designed specifically to assist the law enforcement investigator and counter-intelligence analyst in compiling data and putting case information into a graphical, cohesive, comprehensible, and actionable format. Crime Link also allows for the display of photos and the attachment of documents and audio and video files to entities on its graphs. Manipulation of links on the graph is easily done with Crime Link with individuals associated to organizations, gangs, terrorist cells, and any other group displayed inside rectangles.

A unique feature of Crime Link is its ability to generate a two-dimensional association matrix that basically shows *who knows whom, who has done what, who has been where,* etc. (see Figure 3.19). The association matrix is also the primary user interface for entering and maintaining information from an ongoing investigation case into Crime Link. The cells of the matrix contain and display the symbolic relationship types via columns and rows, so that, for example, a solid circle represents a known and confirmed association link, while a hollow circle signifies a suspected and unconfirmed association link. It is a very basic, yet effective, method of displaying and examining associations between entities and events. It is clearly an effective manner of providing a

Figure 3.19
*The association
matrix in Crime
Link.*

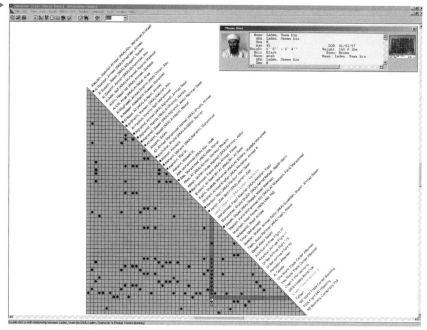

presentation to other investigators or for use in court or other judicial
proceedings.

The link analysis diagrams are used in Crime Link to graphically represent
complex relationships and to make comprehension of associations easier.
Because Crime Link generates its link association diagrams directly from the
information entered into its association matrix, it ensures that the integrity of
the diagrams is maintained at all times (see Figure 3.20).

Crime Workbench

http://www.memex.com/cwbover.html

Crime Workbench is a tool for intelligence management with the option of
creating databases on virtually any entity type; this application is relevant to
all types of criminal and fraud investigation. Crime Workbench offers
enhanced searching capabilities by utilizing the Memex Information Engine.

The Action Management module allows users to task items and actions to
other users on the system. For organization wide communications, there is a
bulletin board option for disseminating findings via a department intranet.
Differing intelligence records relating to the same topic can now be grouped
together for ease of locating and searching with the Case Management module in Crime Workbench. The main Workbench tool has also incorporated a

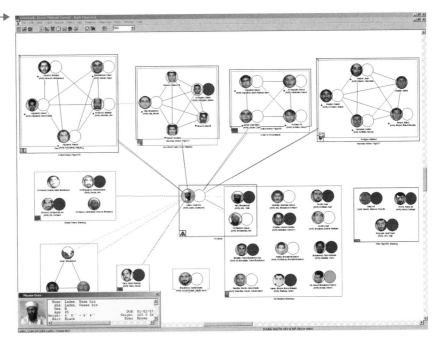

Figure 3.20
From the matrix Crime Link generates its diagrams.

Link Management module for graphical analysis. A search that returns one record plus all other records linked to that original record, in a cluster diagram, highlights in an instant the major players and events in any investigation. Crime Workbench can integrate with the i2 Link Notebook version 5, one of the main link analysis products.

Entering data into Crime Workbench is simple with the intuitive forms and forms builder. The Entity Manager allows administrator users to create new entities and forms on virtually any topic. Searching Crime Workbench databases can be carried out several different ways:

1. *Query by form*: useful for searching data in a specific field

2. *Structured query*: simultaneous searching over one or more database types

3. *Free-text search*: the easiest method of searching, utilizing query capabilities

Crime Workbench Web is a scaled down version of the main intelligence management product, which allows for the interaction of analysis via a Web browser. The requirement for this Web product stemmed from the number of

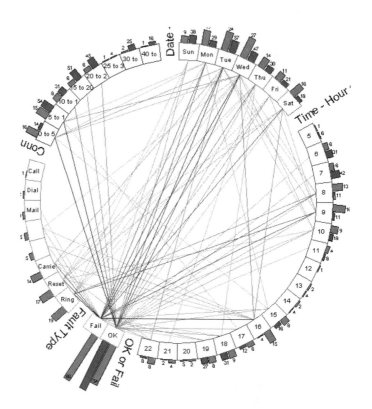

end users who require only basic input and search functionality. With Crime Workbench Web, the end user can gain access from any location via an intranet or the Internet. Crime Workbench Web is aimed at the intelligence analyst and law enforcement investigator on the move who requires a tool to collect information and access to up-to-the-minute data from any location via a Web browser.

Daisy

http://www.daisy.co.uk/daisy.html

Daisy, which stands for Data AnalysIS InteractivelY, is a very intuitive link analysis tool, which like i2 is also from the United Kingdom, available from Daisy Analysis. Daisy supports a circular layout of nodes that are interconnected with linkages to represent entity or event associations (see Figure 3.21). In addition, each node can be associated with histograms to display frequencies and intervals. The Daisy display can be manipulated by zooming, panning, and fitting it to the viewer screen, with any node capable of being profiled by simply clicking on it to get a summary of its content. A profile

Figure 3.22
The formats supported by NETMAP.

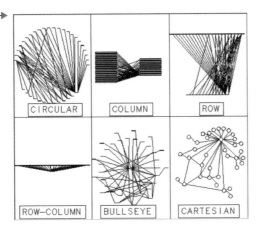

window displays the name of the node and its associated groupings, the number of records and links it represents, such as duration, distance, amount, and number of meeting.

Daisy provides the user a quick menu for setting up a new chart through the use of templates. The menu options are extensive, with options for allowing an inexperienced user to develop a link analysis chart quickly. The menu provides five general options for generating a chart, including standard, duplicate, circular, date/time, and summary. A submenu is provided for selecting the fields that will be used to generate the link analysis chart. Daisy is relatively inexpensive and is well suited for users with little to no experience in link analysis, working with a small case data set.

NETMAP

http://www.altaanalytics.com/

NETMAP is a very mature link analysis tool from ALTA Analytics that basically uses vectorization to map its displays; that is, everything is represented as a line, including all text and shapes. NetMap is an enterprise system that employs data marts to help organize information and that can query a wide range of databases using SQL. NetMap decomposes data, such as a name or bank account number, to its simplest form, called a node. Then, it seeks common links among nodes. The primary method of manipulating the NETMAP display is through a pair of node and link menus for filtering and displaying the data. The main shapes of NETMAP link charts are those of a wagon-wheel format, with color conveying very important factors; for example, bank accounts may be displayed in green, individuals in blue, and the links between them in red. NETMAP, however, also supports some additional layouts, including circular, column, row, row/column, bullseye, and Cartesian charts (see Figure 3.22).

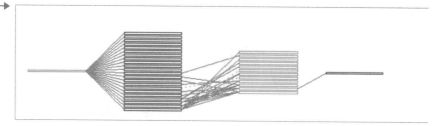

Figure 3.23
This chart shows the link between the nodes at both ends.

As previously mentioned, investigators can use link analysis tools such as NETMAP for identifying suspicious financial transactions and identifying hidden relationships between criminal and terrorists entities. All of these values can be assembled and represented as objects in sections of circular charts with the linking nodes used to identifying relationships. For example, in NETMAP a graph can be created using the column format, which is a fairly compact way of stacking data elements (e.g., addresses, phone numbers, vehicles, banks, wire transfers) and then exploring their relationships via a step-link format (see Figure 3.23).

NETMAP allows all data to be traced back to their original sources; data imported into the software can be tagged with such attributes as time-of-load and other user information.

NETMAP can also be configured to allow for multiple security levels to allow analysts to filter out the source of the data, agency, department, or classification level.

ORION

http://www.orionsci.com/productinfo/Magic.html

ORIONInvestigations is yet another tool for tracking and analyzing crimes based on case-related information compiled from different events, groups, entities, and associations. This tool is specifically an application for populating a database with details about known facts and leads relating to a crime scene; it is more of a criminal case data organizer. It uses a series of forms to interact with an investigator and is configured with three general levels—supervisor, clerk, and data entry—to control security data access within the system. Another feature of ORIONInvestigations is a filter wizard that looks for related records based on similar selection criteria. A reporter component generates various outputs related to a specific investigation.

ORIONInvestigations can be integrated with ORIONLink, the actual link analysis component from ORION. ORIONLink represents entities as circles connecting them via other circles, or squares, diamonds, and triangles (see Figure 3.24). This link analysis tool also uses colors to represent shared

Figure 3.24
*An
ORIONLink
sample
diagram.*

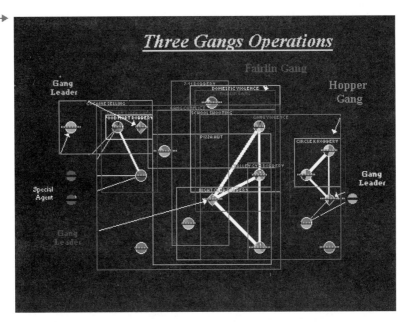

attributes for entities, such as event associations or group membership. Every individual who is a member of multiple groups or who has attended an event or a meeting will have several different colored pie-wedges on the ORION-Link chart display. Objects sharing the same color share the same value of an attribute.

ORIONLink can be used to draw boxes automatically around nodes to display specific terrorist cells, gangs, intragroups, or incident functions and relationships. The tool supports complete interactive displays so that objects can be moved and grouped in diagrams annotated with text and symbols. A special feature of ORIONLink is its *what-if* mode, which allows objects and their connections to be hidden or restored on the fly, allowing for the viewing of their impact on the total organization, such as a terrorist cell or criminal gang.

ORIONLink provides several interactive analytic features with the ability to change the data attributes and their impact on the diagram. This can be done by a pop-up dialog box associated with any node. All of the associations of a particular individual can also be highlighted interactively. A Show Articulations mode can automatically highlight all "keynodes" in a diagram, which, if removed, would cripple or severely damage the total group structure. This way individuals who are critical for organizational cohesiveness, strength, or communications can be easily identified for higher levels of attention.

VisuaLink

http://www.visualanalytics.com/

VisuaLink is a high-end link analysis software suite with multiple data preparation components designed to assist investigators and analysts in the identification of terrorist threats, money laundering, insurance fraud, and other criminal activity. For example the suite can be used to track different types of "criteria" technologies used in international transactions, such as specific material components for manufacturing terrorist weapons.

As with other link analysis tools, VisuaLinks can be used to evaluate group behavior, funding resources, communication networks, recruiting methods, organization locations, etc. The software was designed specifically with the law enforcement user in mind and was not intended for the corporate world.

VisuaLinks can also be used to analyze and diagram systemic suspicious financial activity and filing compliance, including the analysis of the real assets of suspected money laundering enterprises. The tool allows the investigating agency or task force to uncover different types of transactions (deposits, withdrawals, wire transfers, and currency conversions) used by suspected money launderers.

For drug investigation, VisuaLink can be used to examine subtle connections between individuals, organizations, vehicles, facilities, locations, accounts, and incidents, as well as transportation routes and communication lines. For insurance fraud investigations, the tool can be used to uncover connections between individuals, organizations, incidents, and claims.

Using a special software component it calls DIG, for example, an insurance investigator can retrieve and analyze data from both in-house and industry-wide claims databases to uncover suspicious activities. The program allows for the indexing, searching, and managing of large numbers of databases, text sources, and Web sites concurrently. VisuaLink can visually display the retrieved data and assist in identifying possible fraudulent claims activity with the frequency of connections displayed by varying link thickness.

3.12 Bibliography

AAAI (1998) Symposium on Artificial Intelligence and Link Analysis.

Chabrow, E. (January 14, 2002) "Tracking The Terrorists," *Information Week*.

Grady, N., Tufano, D., and Flanery, R. (1998) "Immersive Visualization for Link Analysis," Oak Ridge National Laboratories Publication.

Picarelli, J. (1998) "Transnational Threat Indications and Warning: The Utility of Network Analysis," Pacific-Sierra Research Corporation Publication.

Westphal, C. and Blaxton, T. (1998) *Data Mining Solutions*, New York: Wiley Computer Publishing.

Wong, R. (1998) "Financial Crimes Enforcement Network," U.S. Department of the Treasury Publication.

4

Intelligent Agents: Software Detectives

4.1   What Can Agents Do?

In a networked environment such as ours, a new entity has evolved: *intelligent agent software.* Over the past few years, agents have emerged as a new software paradigm; they are in part distributed systems, autonomous programs, and artificial life. The concept of agents is an outgrowth of years of research in the fields of AI and robotics. They represent concepts of reasoning, knowledge representation, and autonomous learning. Agents are automated programs and provide tools for integration across multiple applications and databases, running across open and closed networks. They are a means of retrieving, filtering, managing, monitoring, analyzing, and disseminating information over the Internet, intranets, and other proprietary networks.

Agents represent a new generation of computing systems and are one of the more recent developments in the field of AI. Agents are specific applications with predefined goals, which can run autonomously; for example, an Internet-based agent can retrieve documents based on user-defined criteria. They can also monitor an environment and issue alerts or go into action based on how they are programmed. In the course of investigative data mining projects, for example, agents can serve the function of software detectives, monitoring, shadowing, recognizing, and retrieving information for analysis and case development or real-time alerts.

Agents can be used by investigators and analysts to work on their behalf; for example FinCEN, the U.S. Treasury agency set up to detect money laundering, must review all cash transactions involving dollar amounts of above $10,000. This amounts to roughly 10 million transactions a year, which cannot be manually monitored. The FinCEN Artificial Intelligence System (FAIS) uses an agent to weed through this large data space and search for abnormalities and fraud through the use of neural network and link analysis.

However, before continuing, a definition should be established regarding what comprises an intelligent software agent.

4.2 What Is an Agent?

An intelligent agent is software that assists users and acts on their behalf. Agents autonomously perform tasks delegated by their creators and users. Agents can automate repetitive tasks, remember events, summarize complex data, learn, and make recommendations. For example, an agent can be used to monitor and search for a suspect's name from multiple government and commercial databases, or it can be set up to assemble evidence for use in a prosecution case.

Intelligent agents continuously perform three main functions, which differentiates them from other software programs:

1. They are capable of *perceiving* dynamic conditions in an environment.

2. They can *take action* to affect conditions in an environment.

3. They can *reason* to interpret findings, solve problems, draw inferences, and determine future actions.

For example, agent software can act on behalf of investigators and, thus, reduce their workload by sifting through large amounts of data for evidence gathering. Agents have the capability to interact with the external environment and perceive changes in it; hence, they can then either inform investigators of changes, such as that a suspect on the INS list has entered the country. Or, they can be set up to react dynamically to findings, issuing an alert at the point-of-entry station, once a match of a suspect on the INS list is found. While there are multiple definitions of intelligent agents, this is their essential characteristic: *a software agent is a computing entity that performs user-delegated tasks autonomously.* An agent can perform many tasks; however, for investigative data mining the most dominant ones are likely to be information monitoring, retrieval, organization, and reporting.

Agent technology is not a single, new technology, but rather the integrated application of a number of network, Internet, and AI technologies. As such, developers normally do not set out to construct an agent; more commonly they set out to add new functionality to a new or existing application that posses agent-like features. These agent programs possess various forms of learning, creating, and modifying rules of behavior and developing strategies for collaborating among other programs, databases, networks, and users and even other agents. As you will come to see in subsequent chapters where we discuss other data mining technologies, agents can be integrated with other applications, enabling investigators and analysts to automate many tasks. In Chapter 11 we will propose a system using agent technology for the integration of human investigators and machine-learning algorithms to create a new type of evolutionary investigative system resulting in a fusion of human and machine intelligence.

4.3 **Agent Features**

In order to define the characteristics of an agent further and to distinguish them from any other type of program, the following list ennumerates the attributes and features required of them:

- *Autonomy.* Being able to carry out tasks independently is the most important feature of an agent; this differentiates an agent from any other computing technique or program. Traditional computer applications only respond to direct manipulation via user instructions. On the other hand, intelligent agents can perform actions without human intervention. An agent principally operates without direct intervention, typically in the background, to the extent of the user's specified delegation. The autonomous ability of an agent can range from being able to initiate a lookup in a database to issuing alerts or collecting and assembling a file from multiple networked sources. The search agent will take the input and perform the search independently without user intervention. With the widespread use of the Internet, intranets, and other electronic and wireless networks, stationary and mobile agents can be used for investigative data mining applications for detection and deterrence. Stationary agents can send scripts and receive data via networks, but cannot themselves move. While all agents are not mobile, there have been significant trends toward developing nimble and mobile agents. Mobile agents have the capacity to navigate through networked architectures in the performance of their tasks and to report their findings to various wireless devices or appliances.

- *Perception.* The agent needs to be able to affect its environment via some type of programmed mechanism for autonomous operation. It needs to be able to monitor its environment in order to be able to perform its task independently. An agent must be able to perceive events in the environment and react to them as necessary in an appropriate fashion. Agents almost never operate in isolation. They work within a system or in a network. Its environment includes other agents, systems, human users, and, in certain cases, external objects, such as sensory devices on factory floors or robots. An agent receives inputs or requests from its environment and sends information back to it. For example, an agent can be programmed to monitor a network system for erratic behavior, signaling a hacker attack. This is a common function of some intrusion detection systems (IDSs) the topic of Chapter 10. An agent with special sensors may also monitor an environment for anthrax or other type of virus attacks, coordinating data from various inputs and issuing alerts to designated personnel, which, as we will soon see, is a system envisioned by DARPA for countering bio-terrorist attacks.

- *Purpose.* Agents perform a set of tasks on behalf of a user or other agents that are explicitly approved and programmed by users or organizations. Agents essentially need to be their own bosses and have clearly defined goals that they seek to accomplish. Being goal-driven also entails that an agent be proactive rather than just reactive to an environment. Some of the most sophisticated agents can learn as they perform their tasks, with new dynamic rules of behavior evolving as they learn user preferences and users' needs for specific types of information or actions. For investigative data miners, this means agents can be used for the retrieval of specific suspect- or case-related information at predefined intervals and ranges.

- *Communications.* An agent needs to be able to interact with the user, receive task delegation instructions, and inform the user regarding task status and completion through an agent-user interface or through an agent communication language. Agents need to be able to communicate with other agents and humans. Agent and human communication can be via terminal input, such as keyboards, or more sophisticated technologies, such as natural language processing and speech recognition. Multiagent communication can take place using standard or defined protocols. Agents allow for scalability, permit software reuse, and can handle software evolution and promote open systems. For an agent to work in this environment, it should be able to cooperate with its peers and also coordinate efforts. Agents operate continuously; upon achievement of their goals they continue to run in the background and monitor the environment. In this context an agent-based application is not supposed to terminate.

■ *Intelligence.* Lastly, an agent needs to be able to interpret monitored events to make appropriate decisions for autonomous operation. Agents need to possess a certain degree of intelligence in order to perceive the working environment and be autonomous when performing their programmed tasks. The level of intelligence exhibited by an agent will depend on its function. The dimension of intelligence equates to the degree to which the agent employs reasoning, learning, and other techniques to interpret the data to which it has access. The intelligence of agents equates to the degree to which they are able to perceive their environment and change it dynamically. Some agents can incorporate expert systems with predefined rules; however, dynamic rules generated from machine learning can make them even more intelligent by instilling them with the ability to learn and evolve. For this reason, the intelligence of an agent—that is, the rules that it follows to complete its designated tasks—can evolve either from the developer or independently from its environment and built-in algorithms.

4.4 Why Are Agents Important?

One of the most compelling uses for agent technology is in the area of information retrieval; the explosion of information about individuals and companies on the Internet and the databases connected to it is huge. Based on studies from Forrester Research and the Yankee Group, there are over 1 billion documents on the visible Web, with 7 million documents being added on a daily basis. What is more important is that the Web is becoming increasingly database driven, and records in these databases cannot be indexed or retrieved using typical search engines. This is due in part to the rise of new technologies like XML and Active Server Pages (ASP), which conventional search engines omit simply because they cannot retrieve the records from these dynamic databases.

These same studies indicate that this dynamic Web is 500 times larger than the visible Web of 1 billion pages. Agent technologies, which support special scripting capabilities, have the capability to correspond to different information types and, thus, to retrieve much more information than normal search engines. In other words, agents can sense the type of data source and adjust and convert the parameters into a query that can be understood by the information source. Of course, these types of agents can negotiate and extract information, not just from Web-connected databases, but also from local databases, intranets, extranets, and other proprietary networks.

Agents are needed to help analysts and investigators deal with and leverage a tremendous amount of data in the course of their work. Agents are sophisticated programs that, as we have discussed, possess human-like attributes, such as the ability to work independently, communicate, coordinate, learn, and accumulate knowledge to conduct their assigned tasks. When used in conjunction with other data mining technologies, such as those that will be covered in subsequent chapters, agents can assist investigators in accessing, organizing, and using current and relevant data for security deterrence, forensic analysis, and criminal detection.

As we have seen, agents are designed to perform in a particular environment, such as a closed network or the Internet; they can also be categorized according to their functionality, such as information retrieval, information filtering, monitoring and alerting, etc. They can also be classified according to their core architecture; for example, there are learning agents that employ internal neural networks to acquire knowledge as they work or machine-learning algorithms to generate their own rules for behavior and action. For the most part, there are two major categories of agent that lend themselves to investigative data mining applications: Internet (open sources) and intranet (secured sources) agents.

4.5   **Open Sources Agents**

These Internet agents provide search services over the Web. There are also server-specific agents that provide services, such as security, at the server level. There are Internet agents that can serve as information-filtering agents, so that, based on the security level of users, only certain information is passed to them. There are also notification and special services agents and even mobile agents for executing specific tasks, like special alerts to wireless devices. Internet agents are computer programs that reside on servers performing specific data detection, retrieval, and delivery tasks to designated users based on preset parameters, behaving very much like intelligent robots. In this context, intelligent agents can play an integral role in the overall process of investigative data mining.

These Web robots operate using different Boolean or vector-space strategies when following links and retrieving documents, based on different prioritized methods and schemes. In fact, search agents are the most widely used Web services. Using keyword query forms, they are easy to use and provide the user an instant response and a hierarchical list of sources of information. Their indexing provides users a universe of information in an instant. In addition, some metasearch engines incorporate the knowledge of where to look for information depending on the attributes of the data, such as searching for individuals, phone numbers, physical and e-mail addresses, technical reports, public record fillings, and foreign news stories in their native language.

4.6 Secured Sources Agents

Intranet agents can serve as database service providers. They can also automate workflow processes and collaborate communications to intranet or proprietary closed network users; for example, they may be programmed to issue special alerts to designated need-to-know analysts or investigators. There are intranet agents that can perform resources allocation services, which are IT-specific, such as updating a data set or deleting a database. These intranet agents can also be programmed to perform a variety of reports and conduct ad hoc analyses of databases across a network. As with Internet agents, intranet agents can perform similar data-organization tasks for users in closed proprietary secured agency and departmental networks.

An intranet agent is a software program that resides on an internal agency or departmental server or cluster of servers in a private proprietary network. These types of agents are designed to focus on information dissemination among a team of users involved in special task forces or focusing on specific type of data aggregation and analyses. Typically, these intranet agents are programmed to assist in accessing internal databases, data marts, and data warehouses or proprietary networks. Some can also provide support via wireless devices to field investigators. They enable information sharing within a designated and authorized group of users. They can also be set up to shield and protect unauthorized access to some users and provide alerts when changes to the data occur.

4.7 How Agents Work

Regardless of whether it is an open or a closed type of agent, or of the function that it performs, its benefits are usually in automating some type of repetitive behavior that is either time-based or event-based. They can automate repetitive tasks, such as performing a common query against a database. More advanced agents can notify specific users of the arrival or creation of new data ready for their analysis; they can assist users with more advanced analyses, guiding them in processes they are not knowledgeable about; and lastly, they can perform messaging tasks, such as notifying users when a model has been completed. Some data mining tools incorporate agents to automate the process of model construction and analysis.

Specialized database or network agents can, on the basis of user requests, go out and perform queries, assemble the data found into a predesigned template, or process the data through a designed analysis. Database agents provide valuable functions in making information available to users in the most useful form and context. Once the data has been retrieved and assembled or the analysis is complete, such as the creation of a data cube or a data mining model, the results can be transmitted to a designated group of users. The entire process can be done in real time or overnight; the agent can be programmed to perform the task as required by the agency or department needs. The benefits are clear: agents reduce the workload of investigators, lead to faster decision making by the analysts, and increase the productivity of everyone involved.

4.8   **How Agents Reason**

Men and machines such as agents reason through simple to elaborate networks of rules:

```
IF    X,    AND    Y,    THEN       Z
```

Some of these rules are codified from the domain of experts; hence, the development of expert system in the early 1990s. However, these systems fell out of popularity after some initial enthusiasm when they proved to be expensive to maintain and brittle in deployment. Expert systems represented a set of rules in such areas as making soup or configuring systems or auditing tax returns. Some expert systems still exist; for example, the TriPath medical system uses rules that it developed from pathologists to examine Pap smears to diagnose for cervical cancer in its FocalPoint system.

The FBI and IRS both set up AI labs with the intent of developing expert systems to assist field agents with working cases and developing good prosecutions. The idea was to codify the experience of seasoned FBI agents who had worked and solved specific types of criminal cases. These expert systems would subsequently aid younger agents in working cases to prosecution and eventual conviction.

The IRS had various applications under development, most of which never left the lab, due in part to the high maintenance cost of the expert systems. For example, one application was to automate the audit examination process; unfortunately, the tax code and forms change every year, with Congress cranking out new legislation, meaning the rules of the expert system would need to be constantly changing. Audits can involve multiple years, meaning the expert system would have to incorporate hundreds of rules from each of those years. In the end, the task proved to be expensive to maintain.

However, there is a different method by which rules can be constructed; this involves data mining. Replacing expert systems as reasoning engines was the development of neural networks and machine-learning algorithms in the area of AI. Rather than developing rules from experts and taking a top-down approach to knowledge acquisition, rules can be extracted from observations in large databases. This is the inductive method of data analysis, now known as data mining, which uses machine learning and is a bottom-up approach to knowledge acquisition.

These processes of rule creation are not mutually exclusive; in fact, a hybrid system is probably the ideal solution for investigative data mining applications, in which some rules are drawn from years of investigators' experience, coupled with rules extracted from hundreds of thousands of cases from large databases. This type of man-machine hybrid system is the topic of a proposed data mining architecture in Chapter 11. Agents, as engines of inference, can use both types of rules. To develop intelligence in agents, certain steps can be taken. Briefly, they involve the following type of rule sequencing and construction:

1. The user or developer provides a set of rules that describe a desired behavior: When X happens, then do Y. This can be done using a plain-text editor and then transcribed to code-such as C or Java.

2. The reasoning system is next provided with a set of conditional input events, such as When a match of Entity Z898R from List DEA-01/02/04 happens, do Y.

3. The reasoning system is provided with interfaces to perform or initiate various desired actions; for example, do Y may require that an alert be made by sending a message to a system object, by writing a file, or by other system action that a program can perform.

4. After the reasoning system is initiated, it can wait for an event to arrive. It will extract facts from the event and then evaluate its rules to see if the new facts cause any of them to fire. If one or more rules fire, it may cause additional action to be initiated or a record to be written or updated.

The above process follows a set structure, leading to the creation and use of conditional rules and logic, which can be coded in a variety of ways. Here is an example:

```
IF      (Condition 1)
OR      (Content A)
AND     (Condition 3)
THEN (Action Z)
```

This can be demonstrated by the example of a system for issuing alerts to, say, customs agents at point-of-entry stations, based on conditions gleaned from a plate number input into a network system using models developed from both human investigators' experience and machine-learning-generated rules. These data mining rules could well have been developed from an extensive analysis of prior convicted cases of contraband prosecutions:

```
Condition fields:
    IF INSURER is None (Condition 1)
        Source: Human Domain
    OR YEAR is 1988 (Content A)
        Source: DMV Registration Record
    AND MAKE is CADILLAC (Condition 3)
        Source: Data Mining Model
    Prediction # 1: THEN ALERT is Medium (Action Z)
        Inspect Trunk
```

4.9   Intelligent Agents

Unlike an expert system, an agent is embedded in its environment and can perceive and react to it using inputs of conditions. It can dynamically construct new rules as it works; in other words, some agents are capable of using sensors to monitor their surroundings, develop new rules, and then take action independently. For example, Doppelgaenger is an agent developed at MIT's Media Lab that uses sensors that provide many kinds of information about the user population in its computing network environment. These sensors can include active badges that provide location information about users, along with login information that detects their arrival and departure from the MIT computer network.

This agent can gauge user actions that reflect the frequency and duration of the use of applications, programs, and workstations and telephones. The system monitors what applications and data sets users tend to access in order to construct a profile of user preferences so that as it monitors their behavior, it dynamically creates new rules. Doppelgaenger uses this user information to construct profiles into statistical clusters; this type of intelligence is used by the agent to provide users with network-specific information likely to be of interest to them. It also uses this behavioral information to provide them with notification about databases and applications that meet their profile interests. It can also alert specific users about changes to data sets they have an interest in.

4.10 A Bio-Surveillance Agent: A Case Study

Through the use of these types of sensors, for example, agents could be used for the construction of a real-time bio-surveillance system for monitoring bio-terrorist attacks. DARPA recognized this and solicited applications for such an agent-based system, citing a covert release of an infectious disease as one of the most insidious threats to civilian and military personnel within the United States. DARPA believes that in addition to traditional threats to our national security, our adversaries now possess the ability to disable our nation's infrastructure and inflict casualties on U.S. citizens at home and abroad, as was made evident by the 9/11 attacks.

According to the Department of Defense (DOD), if effectively executed, such an attack could go unnoticed and infect a large number of our forces with a fatal disease. For the individuals that survive, the quality of life, burden on the medical system, and impact on the local government and economy would be immeasurable. For this reason, DARPA believes surveillance for covert biological warfare and biological terrorist activities is needed to counter this type of threat. If an event occurs, surveillance is needed to identify the presence of the pathogen or the initial indicators of disease as soon as possible so that a rapid response can be implemented.

DARPA envisioned the development of an integrated bio-surveillance system capable of very early detection of a covert release of biological agents (see Figure 4.1). In its solicitation, it called for a system that would do the following:

- Receive and correlate data from heterogeneous databases
- Glean applicable data from these databases, while maintaining patient privacy privileges
- Analyze the data to discern abnormal biological events from normal epidemiology patterns
- Classify abnormalities and identify specific pathogens, as well as determine the release event and location
- Provide alerts to the appropriate DOD emergency response infrastructure

Figure 4.1
*Bio-terrorism
system using
agents with
sensors.*

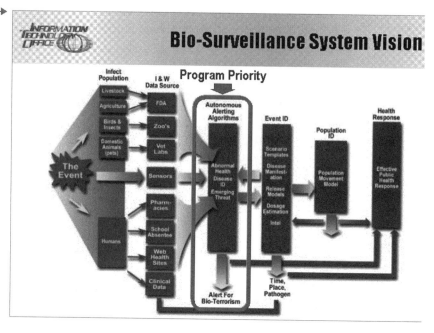

This type of bio-terrorist system would obviously not only make use of agents equipped with an assortment of sensors to monitor various environments; the system would also make use of expert system technology, as well as data mining models constructed with neural networks and machine-learning algorithms designed to recognize the signatures of deadly viruses, all of which would need to be networked over a secured, fail-safe infrastructure, providing 24/7 support to medical, disaster recovery, and DOD personnel.

The objective of this program in bio-surveillance is to develop, test, and demonstrate the technologies necessary to provide an early alert to the appropriate continental U.S. DOD emergency response elements regarding a release of biological agents, involving both natural and unnatural pathogens, against military and civilian personnel. Specifically, the system would reduce the existing probable alert period for a nominal pathogen from four days after release to two days (see Figure 4.2).

DARPA specifically wants a bio-surveillance system using autonomous altering algorithms for monitoring multiple sources of data that would do the following:

- Determine relevant sentinel data sources

- Develop appropriate data correlation and analysis software for anomaly detection, pathogen classification, and epidemiology

Figure 4.2
Agent system would serve to provide early detection.

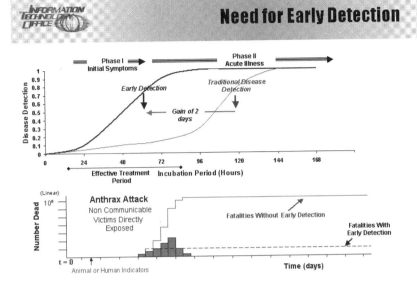

Integrate information, using heterogeneous databases and traditional and nontraditional data sources

Detect pathogens despite masking by normal infections [similarily of symptoms of bio-warfare attack to other diseases (e.g., flu)]

Collect incident-specific information with adjustable privacy constraints

DARPA is calling for a system that would use agents to retrieve, monitor, and assemble the data, enabling other AI-based components to use models to conduct analyses, issuing alerts to the responsible DOD personnel. A modified system could be used to provide public health agencies and corporate offices of multifacility providers with early warning of biological or certain chemical incidents. Surveillance is accomplished through (1) broad-based, large-scale agent sensors monitoring for patient symptoms, and caseloads by type, therapy, and intervention or diagnostic procedures, and (2) the rapid retrieval of key documents and information for suspect cases from strategic clinics and hospitals.

A combination of agents and data mining models could be used to construct a bio-terrorism system so that, for example, the reporting of certain symptoms such a rashes or sore throats by regional health clinics, hospitals, and emergency-planning agencies, or certain increases in school absenteeism or frequencies of over-the-counter sales of cold medicine that exceed certain thresholds, may signal a potential attack. More sophisticated sensors might monitor water supplies or air samples. All of this in combination with data mining techniques and tools could be used to recognize an epidemic. Using agents, a computerized system could use emergency room data to monitor the frequency rates of rashes, fevers, coughs, and intestinal problems and the location of patients to identify potential biological attacks. The agents would work in unison with expert systems and other data mining tools in this anti-bio-terrorism system. Farther in the future are agents with the capability to detect bio-agents like aflatoxin in actual detection devices.

4.11   Data Mining Agents

Investigative data mining represents a powerful new approach to criminal monitoring detection and alert dissemination. In private industry, data mining has primarily been applied to very large corporate databases for such applications as identifying potential customers. While data mining was originally conceived of as a way of extracting hidden associations from large databases, when coupled with agent technology it can be used to monitor events, extract important information via the Internet, intranets, and other proprietary networks, discover new patterns, assemble profiles, and deliver alerts to military, medical, law enforcement, and intelligence agency personnel. Using sensors, agents can work in tandem with other systems to analyze collected data and then issue real-time alerts to systems or personnel via the Internet, to proprietary networks, even to wireless devices.

For example, IBM developed an agent to work with its Intelligent Data Miner suite. The system consists of five agents:

1.   A user interface agent that provides a Web interface for users to interact with the data miner and help them perform data mining analysis and display results

2.   A coordinator agent that is responsible for delegating and managing various tasks that need to be performed for problem solving

3.   A data-set agent that is responsible for keeping track of what data is stored in which data mart or data warehouse and actively maintaining metadata information

4.   A data mining agent that executes the user-defined algorithms, performs on-line analytical processing (OLAP) analysis, and communicates the results to users or other agents

Figure 4.3
*Agentland.com
provides agent
software for
downloading.*

5.   A visualization agent that allows for ad hoc and predefined reporting capabilities and a wide array of graphical reports

As we shall see in some of the following chapters, other data mining software tools are already incorporating agents into their products to assist the user in minimizing the effort of extracting, preparing, modeling, and delivering the results of their analyses. In the next chapter, we will explore how agent technology can be used with text mining technologies to monitor and retrieve specific information via the Web and other networks for criminal and terrorist detection and case development.

4.12   Agents Tools

Agent software is readily available from various sources, including the Web, from such sites as agentland.com (see Figure 4.3).

Agents that perform different functions can also be downloaded from agentland (see Figure 4.4). There are information retrieval agents, monitoring agents, and development kits for constructing agents.

Figure 4.4
*A menu of
development
agent software
available.*

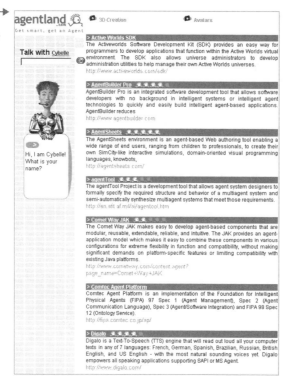

To illustrate how some of these agents work, we will use InfoGIST, an information retrieval agent to search and aggregate a set of Web pages on the basis of keywords we provide: *the search will be for "investigative data mining."* The agent is instructed to retrieve all pages with all of these words in them and to prioritize them in a list (see Figure 4.5).

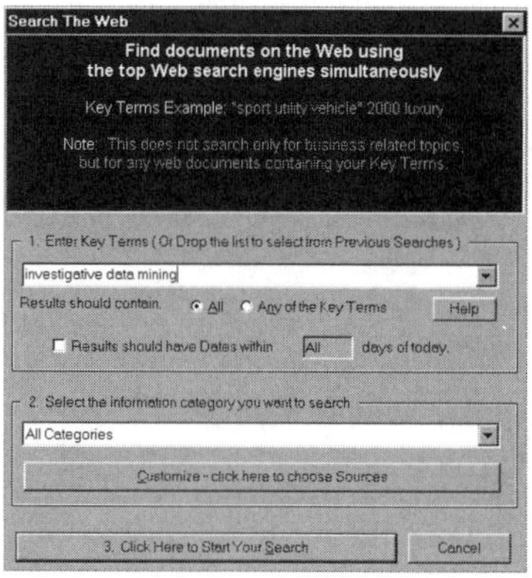

Figure 4.5
*The completed
agent form.*

Figure 4.6
A list is generated with scores of relevance associated with them.

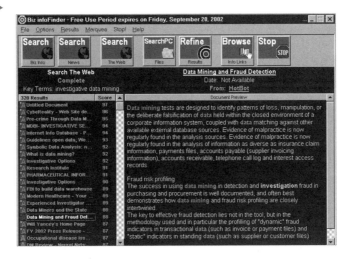

Figure 4.6 shows the results of the agent's search.

Using an agent, as opposed to a search engine, has the advantage that all of these links can be viewed at any time. The links are also scored for relevance. This particular agent also assigns a grade to each item it retrieves, with the most relevant earning an A. Portions of the documents are shown on the right screen, with links and the search engine used presented in the upper right window. Analysts can use agents routinely to search for relationships between new data, update old data, perform specific calculations, etc.

4.13   Bibliography

Caglayan, A. and Harrison, C. (1997) *Agent Sourcebook*, New York: Wiley Computer Publishing.

Franklin, S. and Graesser, A. (1996) "Is It an Agent, or Just a Program?: A Taxonomy for Autonomous Agents," *Proceedings of the Third International Workshop on Agent Theories, Architectures, and Languages*, Springer-Verlag.

Kotz, D. and Gray, B. (May 1, 1999) "Mobile Agents and the Future of the Internet," *Workshop Autonomous Agents*, Seattle, WA.

Wooldridge, M., and Jennings, N. (1995) "Intelligent Agents: Theory and Practice," *Knowledge Engineering Review*, Vol. 10, No. 2.

Text Mining: Clustering Concepts

5.1 What Is Text Mining?

The explosion in the amount of data generated from government and corporate databases, e-mails, Internet survey forms, phone and cellular records, and other communications has led to the use of several data mining technologies, including the need to extract concepts and keywords from unstructured data via text mining tools using unique clustering techniques. Patterns in digital textual files provide clues to the identity and features of criminals, which forensic investigators and intelligence analysts can uncover via the use of a special genre of text mining tools.

Based on a field of AI known as natural language processing (NLP), text mining tools can capture critical features of a document's content based on the analysis of its linguistic characteristics. NLP attempts to analyze, understand, and generate languages that humans use naturally. This goal is not easy to reach. Understanding language means, among other things, knowing what concept a word or phrase stands for and how to link those concepts together in a meaningful way. It's ironic that natural language, the symbol system that is easiest for humans to learn and use, is hardest for a computer to master.

NLP development may take place in attempting to understand the optimal ways in which natural language can be incorporated into multimedia interfaces, such as software agents, or in integrating linguistic processing with speech recognition, both to make speech recognition more accurate and to use the results of speech recognition in practical applications. Much of the work of NLP focuses on the development of a natural language parsing and semantic interpretation system based on unification grammar for such applications as retrieving airline schedules, fares, and related information from, say, relational databases or the development of a spoken-language interface to synthetic forces in military battlefield simulations. However, in the context of forensic data mining, NLP is most applicable in the involvement of interpreting and extracting information from written text, such as online newspaper articles or other types of evidence documents.

Text mining tools use a variety of search methods that combine lexical parsing and clustering techniques to extract phrases from gigabytes of text to organize their content and key concepts. Text mining allows the investigator and analyst to discover hot keywords and key concepts within documents and groups of similar documents without having to read an entire database of documents. Text mining tools eliminate up-front manual categorization, tagging, or building of tree topics and documenting of indexes. They provide automatic identification and indexing of concepts within the text. Some text mining tools enable users to make new associations and relationships, offering three-dimensional charts, paths, and links for further analysis by forensic investigators.

5.2   How Does Text Mining Work?

One of the obvious applications for text mining is in its use to monitor multiple online and wireless communication channels for the use of selected keywords such as *anthrax* or the names or aliases of individual or groups of suspects. Text mining has typically been used by corporations to organize and index internal documents, but the same technology can be used to organize criminal cases by police departments to institutionalize the knowledge of criminal activities by perpetrators and organized gangs and groups. This is already being done in the United Kingdom using text mining software from Autonomy. More importantly, criminal investigators and intelligence analysts can sort, organize, and analyze gigabytes of text during the course of their investigations and inquiries using the same technology and tools. Most of today's crimes are digital in nature, requiring the coordination and communication of perpetrators via channels that leave text trails investigators can analyze. As we shall see, there is an assortment of tools and techniques for discovering key information concepts from narrative text residing in multiple databases in many formats.

As with some of the other data mining technologies covered in this book, text mining is one of many new tools for combating digital crimes in today's world. Almost all of these technologies have their roots in the field of AI, and almost all have been developed to amplify and assist human endeavors in the fields of science, commerce, and now forensics. There have been some recent developments and applications in the field of mining text-based data using an assortment of algorithms and various statistical and visualization schemes.

Text mining is similar to data mining because both deal with automating the analysis of large volumes of data and can be used for the purposes of profiling individuals, groups of entities, and companies. The techniques differ in the types of data they analyze and the methods they use to conduct their analyses. Data mining is primarily intended for analyzing and discovering relationships or ratios in *structured* data, both numeric and categorical. Conversely, text mining analyses specifically work with *unstructured* textual information in searching for concepts and clusters in thousands of documents or Web pages.

Data mining uses technologies like neural networks for detecting patterns or extracts predictive rules using machine-learning algorithms to automate the process of data analysis and profiling. However, a key differentiator between data mining and text mining is that the latter makes extensive use of lexical processing and analysis, word/phrase parsing, and other NLP techniques in order to highlight key concepts and relationships between words and clusters of documents, based on their content. In addition, text mining applications typically rely on advanced visualization to present an overview of document content; they also use XML and HTML to link large numbers of similar documents, which users can drill back through. Depending on the type of investigation and the format of the data, different tools will be required, including those based on text analysis.

5.3   **Text Mining Applications**

In the context of investigative data mining, text mining techniques and tools can be used to sort and organize large collections of text-based data, such as licenses, registrations, airline tickets, credit-card transactions, point-of-entry passport records, criminal files, transcripts of investigations, and any other type of text-based data set for which a name, word, or concept needs to be identified and tracked. However, as with every data mining project, the results returned from text mining are very much dependent on the quality, relevance, and objective of the analyst.

For text mining to be effective, the content and focus of the documents and databases is very important. For example, applying text mining to a collection of random e-mail files probably won't generate much in the way of relevant findings or lead to an ongoing investigation or counter-intelligence analysis unless the e-mail files are specifically those of confirmed suspects. However, using text mining to analyze the e-mails of a group of individuals related to or who have had some contact with a group of suspects in a wide area is likely to provide some important leads to an ongoing discovery-and-detect investigation, where the objective is to identify, for example, unknown associates in a criminal ring or terrorist cell.

Text mining software can also be used to construct investigation dossiers or internal intranet directories by classifying hundreds of thousands of documents based on multiple, inherent concepts found in the source text. For example, criminal files can be organized based on modus operandi by applying NLP techniques and other advanced algorithms. Text mining software can automatically identify and extract key concepts from investigation-related documented records. These concepts can be automatically linked to a taxonomy that can meet an agency's, department's, or specific investigative team's information requirements. These taxonomies provide users with a directory structure for exploring further via link analysis tools or by browsing or searching for the information through an intranet.

Because text mining extracts the key concepts in the documents rather than a single keyword, the taxonomies make it easier for investigators and analysts to find relevant case-related information existing in multiple, linked documents. Such concept-based indexing also eliminates the need to force documents into predefined categories. Text mining software also replaces manual categorization and tagging efforts that add to the costs and deployment/update times for agency- or department-wide portals. This type of organization of crime-related information allows for the institutionalization of modus operandi and of criminal detection procedures.

Text mining software uses the source text itself to automate portal taxonomy creation by extracting multiple key concepts from the documents, mapping the interrelationships between these concepts in the document collection, and creating a taxonomy database that references and links these concepts. For example, criminal cases can be organized by a text mining tool into distinct categories based on the type, time, location, modus operandi, rate, cost, and any other characteristics or feature the user decides, or they can be organized and clustered automatically by the software.

5.4   Searching for Clues in Aviation Crashes: A Case Study

NASA developed a suite of data mining tools called Perilog designed to retrieve and organize contextually relevant data from any sequence of terms. Perilog has used to sort through thousands of narrative reports in order to extract key terms for identifying the root causes of air crashes. The software measures the degree of contextual association for large numbers of term pairs in text or any sequence to produce models to measure their degree of similarity to a query model. It also develops a ranking of relevance and presents the search results in a table format.

Perilog was originally designed to support the FAA's Aviation Safety Reporting System (ASRS). The NASA software was used to analyze thousands of aviation accident incident reports, which typically contain free-form narrative descriptions written by participants, such as flight or ground crews, air traffic controllers, and other professionals. Perilog was used to sort through a voluminous number of incident reports in order to extract the dominant causes of airline crashes, such as mechanical failure or pilot error. Perilog relies on four methods for text mining:

1.   Keyword-in-context search which retrieves narrative that contains one or more user-specified keywords in typical or selected context and ranks the narratives on their relevance to the keyword in context

2.   A flexible, model-based phrase search that retrieves narrative that contains one or more user-specified phrases and ranks them on their relevance to the phrases

3.   Model-based phrase generation, which produces a list of phrases from documents that contain a user-specified word or group of words

4.   Narrative-based phrase discovery, which finds phrases that are related to topics of interest by generating a list of narratives similar in meaning to the keyword or phrase query

Relevance ranking is a process of sorting a list of items so that those likely to be of greater relevance to one's concerns and interests appear closer to the top of the list. Relevance ranking can help an analyst to read and interpret efficiently very large collections of narratives, reports, and text. Perilog can be used to sort through thousands of pages and rank and prioritize phrases in pairs by a relational metric value that is highest when there is a match:

```
Probe Term    Term in Context    Relational Metric Value
FBI           crash              205
```

Perilog's manipulation of patterned or sequential symbols, data, items, objects, events, causes, time spans, actions, attributes, entities, relations, and representations allows for searching of any type of information repository, not just text. What is interesting about this NASA-developed software is that it can perform smart retrieval of sound, voice, or audio data making it an ideal context search and retrieval tool for investigative monitoring analysis of multimedia. NASA is looking for a commercial developer to bring the government-developed software to market.

5.5   Clustering News Stories: A Case Study

We all have access to lots of information, but are seldom in a position to exploit it effectively for decision making. In times of crisis, this problem can be especially severe. Imagine you are a senior analyst besieged with news and intelligence reports of a hostage situation at an American embassy. Who is in charge of the terrorists? Is their group likely to attack other embassies?

How can computers help this process, which relies so critically on collective human understanding and insight, in the midst of the furor of a crisis? Genoa, a project of DARPA, is aimed at improving analysis and decision making in crisis situations by providing tools that allow analysts to collaborate in developing structured arguments in support of particular conclusions and to help predict likely future scenarios. Genoa also provides knowledge discovery tools to mine the information in these sources for important patterns, trends, and anomalies to discover nuggets of valuable information.

One of the challenges Genoa faces is to make it easy for analysts to take knowledge gleaned with the use of these discovery tools and embed it in a concise and useful form in an intelligence product as evidence in support of structured arguments. The MITRE Organization developed a console of various text mining software units that allows the analyst to select various text mining tools from a menu and, with just a few mouse clicks, assemble them to create a complex filter that fulfills whatever information discovery function is currently needed. A filter here is a tool that takes input information and turns it into some more abstract and useful representation. Filters can also weed out irrelevant parts of the input information.

For example, in response to the crisis situation discussed earlier, an analyst might use these mining tools to discover important nuggets of information in a large collection of news sources. This use of data mining tools can be illustrated by looking at TopCat, a MITRE-developed system that identifies different topics in a collection of documents and displays the key players for each topic. TopCat uses association rule mining technology to identify correlations among people, organizations, locations, and events, shown in Figure 5.1 in different shades and boxes. Clustering these correlations creates topics like the three in the following figure, built from six months of global news from several print, radio, and video sources—over 60,000 news stories in all.

Figure 5.1
Topics derived from clustering 60,000 news reports.

This allows the analyst to discover, say, an association between people involved in a bombing incident, which gives a starting point for further analysis (e.g., do McVeigh and Nichols belong to a common organization?). This, in turn, can lead to new knowledge that can be leveraged in the analytical model used to help predict whether this terrorist organization is likely to strike elsewhere in the next few days. Similarly, the third topic reveals the important players in an election in Cambodia. This discovered information can be leveraged to help predict whether the situation in Cambodia is going to explode into a crisis that affects U.S. interests.

Now, suppose an analyst wants to know more about the people in the last topic. Instead of reading more than 6,000 words of text from 10 articles on the topic, the analyst can compose a topic detection filter like TopCat with a biographical summarization filter that gleans facts about key persons from the topic's articles. The result of the composition is a short, 86-word summary, shown in Figure 5.2.

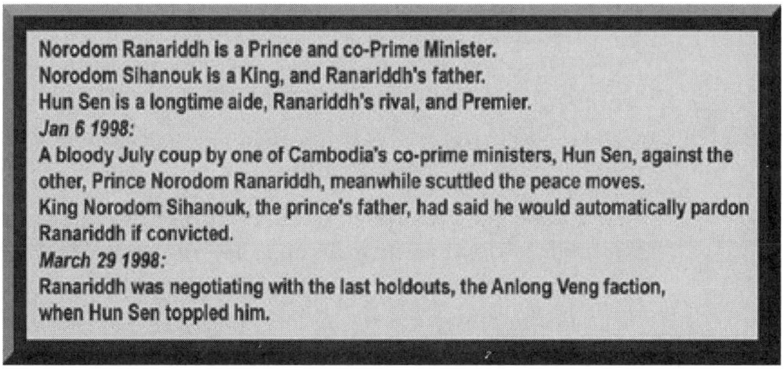

Figure 5.2 *An 86-word summary of the news stories.*

Norodom Ranariddh is a Prince and co-Prime Minister.
Norodom Sihanouk is a King, and Ranariddh's father.
Hun Sen is a longtime aide, Ranariddh's rival, and Premier.
Jan 6 1998:
A bloody July coup by one of Cambodia's co-prime ministers, Hun Sen, against the other, Prince Norodom Ranariddh, meanwhile scuttled the peace moves.
King Norodom Sihanouk, the prince's father, had said he would automatically pardon Ranariddh if convicted.
March 29 1998:
Ranariddh was negotiating with the last holdouts, the Anlong Veng faction, when Hun Sen toppled him.

This summarization filter, developed under DARPA funding, identifies and aggregates descriptions of people from a collection of documents by means of an efficient syntactic analysis, the use of a thesaurus, and some simple natural language generation techniques. It also extracts from these documents salient sentences related to these people by weighting sentences based on the presence of the names of people, as well as the location and proximity of terms in a document and their frequency among other things.

TopCat and a summarization filter perform a function to collect broadcast news continuously in order to extract named entities and keywords and to identify the transcripts and sentences that contain them. The summarization filter includes a parameter to specify the target length or the reduction rate, allowing summaries of different lengths to be generated. For example, allowing a longer summary would mean that facts about other people (e.g., Pol Pot) would also appear in the summary.

This example illustrates how mining a text collection using a composed summarization filter can reveal important associations at varying levels of detail. The component-based text mining console allows these filters to be integrated easily into intelligence products such as reports and briefings. To help analysts present structured arguments and supporting information to decision makers, Genoa provides an electronic notebook briefing tool. Summarization filters can be associated with regions on a page in a briefing book that can be shared across a community of collaborating analysts. When a document or a folder of documents is dropped onto a region associated with a filter, the filter applies, and the textual summary or visualization appears in that region (http://www.mitre.org).

5.6　**Text Mining for Deception**

Text mining software developed by Dr. James W. Pennebaker from The University of Texas can be used to detect whether someone is lying or not by keying in a selected number of words. Lying often involves telling a story that is either false or one that the teller doesn't believe. Most research has focused on identifying such lies through nonverbal cues or physiological activity. Dr. Pennebaker's work and software are investigating the linguistic styles that distinguish between true and false stories.

When people attempt to deceive another person, several possible clues to their anxiety—and to their deception—must be controlled at the same time. However, people do not possess the resources required to monitor all possible channels of communication. As a result, deceivers must attempt to control a smaller number of channels. Deceiving another person usually involves the manipulation of language and the careful construction of a story that will appear truthful. In addition to constructing a convincing story, the deceiver also must present it in a style that appears sincere. Although the deceiver has a good deal of control over the content of the story, the style of language used to tell this story may contain clues to the person's underlying state of mind.

The FBI trains its agents in a technique called statement analysis, which attempts to detect deception based on parts of speech (i.e., linguistic style) rather than the facts of the case or the story as a whole. Suspects are first asked to make a written statement. Trained investigators then review this statement, looking for deviations from the expected parts of speech. These deviations from the norm provide agents with topics to explore during interrogation. Before Susan Smith was a suspect in the drowning death of her children, she told reporters, "My children *wanted* me. They *needed* me. And now I can't help them." Normally, in a missing-person case, relatives will speak of the missing person in the present tense; the fact that Smith used the past tense suggested that she already viewed them as dead. Human judges may be more accurate at judging the deceptiveness of a communication if they are given time to analyze it and are trained in what to look for. But which dimensions of language are most likely to reveal deception? As seen in the case of Susan Smith, statement analysis works by identifying stylistic features of deception that are context-dependent.

Dr. Pennebaker's approach has been influenced by the analysis of linguistic styles when individuals write or talk about personal topics. Essays that are judged more personal and honest (or, perhaps, less self-deceptive) have a very different linguistic profile than essays that are viewed as more detached. This suggests that creating a false story about a personal topic takes work and results in a different pattern of language use. Extending this idea, Dr. Pennebaker's software can predict that many of these same features would be associated with deception or honesty in text-based communication, such as e-mail. Based on his research, at least three different language dimensions can be associated with deception:

1.   Few personal self-references

2.   Few markers of making distinctions

3.   More negative emotion words

The idea is that deception is a cognitively complex undertaking. From a cognitive perspective, truth tellers are more likely to tell about what they did and what they did not do. That is, they make a distinction between what is in the category of their story and what is not. Individuals who use a higher number of exclusive words are generally healthier than those who do not use these words. Similarly, deceivers might also want to be as imprecise as possible. Statements that are more general are easier to remember, and the deceiver is less likely to be caught in a contradiction by keeping his or her story as simple as possible. In everyday interactions, little or no attention is paid to these linguistic dimensions, but if the appropriate elements of linguistic style could be identified, they might serve as a reliable marker of deception.

The linguistic profiles of Dr. Pennebaker have led to the development of the Linguistic Inquiry and Word Count (LIWC) software, a text-analysis program that computes the percentage of words within various categories that writers or speakers use in normal (i.e., nonclinical) speech or writing samples. The program analyzes written or spoken samples on a word-by-word basis. Each word is then compared against a file of words that are divided into 74 linguistic dimensions. LIWC operates under the assumption that a person's psychological state—in this case, attempting to deceive another person—will be reflected to some degree in the words that are chosen.

In an analysis of five independent samples involving hundreds of writing examples, the LIWC text analysis program correctly classified liars and truth tellers at a rate of 67% when the topic was constant and a rate of 61% overall. Compared to truth-tellers, liars used fewer self-references, other-references, and exclusive words and more "negative emotion" and "motion" words. The lie-detection text analysis software is available from simstat.com. The LIWC program analyzes text files on a word-by-word basis, calculating the percentages of words that match each of several language dimensions. Its output is a text file that can be opened in any of a variety of applications, including word processors and spreadsheet programs. Table 5.1 shows the LIWC 2001 table of dimensions and word examples.

Table 5.1   *LIWC 2001 Dimensions and Sample Words*

Dimension	Abbreviation	Examples	Number of Words
I. Standard linguistic dimensions			
Total pronouns	Pronoun	I, our, they, your	70
1st person singular	I	I, my, me	9
1st person plural	We	we, our, us	11
Total first person	Self	I, we, me	20
Total second person	You	you, your	14
Total third person	Other	she, their, them	22

Table 5.1 *LIWC 2001 Dimensions and Sample Words (continued)*

Dimension	Abbreviation	Examples	Number of Words
Negations	Negate	no, never, not	31
Assents	Assent	yes, OK, mmhmm	18
Articles	Article	a, an, the	3
Prepositions	Preps	on, to, from	43
Numbers	Number	one, thirty, million	29
II. Psychological processes			
Affective or emotional processes	Affect	happy, ugly, bitter	615
Positive emotions	Posemo	happy, pretty, good	261
Positive feelings	Posfeel	happy, joy, love	43
Optimism and energy	Optim	certainty, pride, win	69
Negative emotions	Negemo	hate, worthless, enemy	345
Anxiety or fear	Anx	nervous, afraid, tense	62
Anger	Anger	hate, kill, pissed	121
Sadness or depression	Sad	grief, cry, sad	72
Cognitive processes	Cogmech	cause, know, ought	312
Causation	Cause	because, effect, hence	49
Insight	Insight	think, know, consider	116
Discrepancy	Discrep	should, would, could	32
Inhibition	Inhib	block, constrain	64
Tentative	Tentat	maybe, perhaps, guess	79
Certainty	Certain	always, never	30
Sensory and perceptual processes	Senses	see, touch, listen	111
Seeing	See	view, saw, look	31
Hearing	Hear	heard, listen, sound	36
Feeling	Feel	touch, hold, felt	30

Table 5.1   *LIWC 2001 Dimensions and Sample Words (continued)*

Dimension	Abbreviation	Examples	Number of Words
Social processes	Social	talk, us, friend	314
Communication	Comm	talk, share, converse	124
Other references to people	Othref	1st-per pl, 2nd-, 3rd-per prns	54
Friends	Friends	pal, buddy, coworker	28
Family	Family	mom, brother, cousin	43
Humans	Humans	boy, woman, group	43
III. Relativity			
Time	Time	hour, day, oclock	113
Past-tense verb	Past	walked, were, had	144
Present-tense verb	Present	walk, is, be	256
Future-tense verb	Future	will, might, shall	14
Space	Space	around, over, up	71
Up	Up	up, above, over	12
Down	Down	down, below, under	7
Inclusive	Incl	with, and, include	16
Exclusive	Excl	but, except, without	19
Motion	Motion	walk, move, go	73
IV. Personal concerns			
Occupation	Occup	work, class, boss	213
School	School	class, student, college	100
Job or work	Job	employ, boss, career	62
Achievement	Achieve	try, goal, win	60
Leisure activity	Leisure	house, TV, music	102
Home	Home	house, kitchen, lawn	26
Sports	Sports	football, game, play	28
Television and movies	TV	TV, sitcom, cinema	19

Table 5.1   *LIWC 2001 Dimensions and Sample Words (continued)*

Dimension	Abbreviation	Examples	Number of Words
Music	Music	tunes, song, cd	31
Money and financial issues	Money	cash, taxes, income	75
Metaphysical issues	Metaph	God, heaven, coffin	85
Religion	Relig	God, church, rabbi	56
Death and dying	Death	dead, burial, coffin	29
Physical states and functions	Physcal	ache, breast, sleep	285
Body states, symptoms	Body	ache, heart, cough	200
Sex and sexuality	Sexual	lust, penis, fuck	49
Eating, drinking, dieting	Eating	eat, swallow, taste	52
Sleeping, dreaming	Sleep	asleep, bed, dreams	21
Grooming	Groom	wash, bath, clean	15
Appendix: Experimental dimensions			
Swear words	Swear	damn, fuck, piss	29
Nonfluencies	Nonfl	uh, rr*	6
Fillers	Fillers	youknow, Imean	6

The program has 74 preset dimensions (output variables), including linguistic dimensions (e.g., percentage of articles, pronouns), word categories tapping psychological constructs (e.g., positive and negative emotions, causal words), and personal concern categories (e.g., sex, death), and it can accommodate user-defined dimensions as well. The LIWC 2001 Dictionary is composed of 2,290 words and word stems. Each word or word stem defines one or more word categories or sub-dictionaries.

Each of the 74 preset LIWC 2001 categories is composed of a list of dictionary words that defines that scale. Table 5.1 provides a partial list of the LIWC 2001 dictionary categories with sample scale words and relevant scale word counts. The WordStat software has the ability to look at the frequency analysis on words, phrases, derived categories or concepts, or user-defined codes entered manually within a text (see Figure 5.3). The present studies in

Figure 5.3
*WordStat
univariate
word-frequency
analysis.*

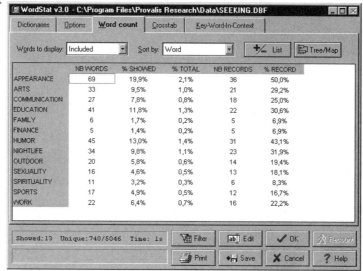

this area suggest that liars can be reliably identified by their words—not by what they say, but by how they say it.

5.7   Text Mining Threats

Most of what people do with computers centers on text. Individuals, including criminals and terrorists create, transfer, read, search, edit, and otherwise transform textual information in myriad ways. Text mining technology integrates multiple strategies, including statistical, keyword, grammar-based, and pattern-based, as well as diverse information sources, including linguistic, conceptual, and domain knowledge, to develop text analysis quickly and efficiently for investigations and analyses. As we have seen text mining uses NLP and proprietary algorithms in some cases, coupled with neural-network or vector analyzers for mapping, clustering, and organizing concepts from unstructured documents and other textual data sources.

Information technology, and especially the Web, has changed the concept of war, forensics, defense, and security. The new concepts of cyber crime and terrorism have altered criminal investigations and counter-intelligence. Before, the major task for any criminal investigation and intelligence activity was first to gather the information; today, that information is available. In fact, analysts and investigators are drowning in it. The new enemy of any intelligence activity is the daily avalanche of information that analysts have to collect, read, filter, and report on. Text mining technology offers a solution to this otherwise impossible task. Text mining allows the collection and analysis of raw data from diversified sources within few seconds, sources such as the following:

- The Web
- News agencies
- Press reports
- CDs
- E-mails
- Chat rooms
- Databases
- Forums
- Newsgroups

Using different text mining tools and techniques, it is possible to identify the context of the communication, the thematic relationships between documents. This approach not only allows the capture of the opinions, tastes, truth, and emotions embedded in the data, but also allows the analysts to monitor trends and significant dynamics within the information flow.

It is clear that text mining will become a fundamental tool for any investigative and counter-intelligence activity. The Pentagon's 100-page document called *Response to Transnational Threats* describes how the military should respond to the threat of saboteurs and bombers aiming for violence, not victory. The solution is to develop a set of agent-based tools that includes micro-robots, bio-sniffers, and sticky electronics, coupled with text mining technology and capabilities. The Office of Advanced Information Technology at the CIA is tackling the information overflow issue with a set of intelligent software agents using tools like Oasis which can convert audio signals from television and radio broadcasts into text, or FLUENT, which enables a user to conduct computer searches of documents that are in a language the user does not understand. The user can put English words into the search field, such as "nuclear weapons," and documents in languages such as Russian, Chinese, and Arabic will pop up.

There is a definite distinction between how text mining tools work with unstructured textual information and how data mining tools work with structured data sets; however, both types of technologies attempt to extract some insight that can be used by forensic investigators and analysts. Most text mining tools and techniques use all or some of the following processes:

- *Natural language processing* for capturing critical features of a document's content based on the analysis of its linguistic characteristics
- *Information retrieval* for identifying those documents in a document collection that match a set of criteria
- *Routing and filtering* for automatically delivering information to the appropriate destination according to subject or content
- *Document summarization* for producing a compressed version or summary of a documents or collection of text, such as e-mails, with a summation of its content
- *Document clustering* for grouping textual sources according to similarity of content, with or without predefined categories, as a way of organizing large collections of documents

There are various applications related to the forensic criminal detection and intelligence-gathering fields that lend themselves aptly to text mining technology, including the surveillance and identification of terrorists. For example, terrorist groups using chemical weapons, biological weapons, explosives, or other nonconventional weapons will have experts with specific knowledge. These individuals will have had to study, perform research, and attend technical seminars and conferences. All of these activities would leave electronic traces scattered across the Web, universities, and other organizations' networks and the registration databases of organizers. Using a text-clustering tool, these connections can be uncovered and the names or aliases detected.

Frequently, the only traces available after a terrorist attack are the letters or the communications claiming the act. The ability of text mining to analyze the style and the concepts expressed in the communications can be very helpful in establishing connections and patterns between documents. By finding similarities between the styles of these anonymous letters, groups of individuals or people can be identified and linked. Text mining analyses can spot connections, similarities, and patterns in declarations or statements that could suggest links between individuals that officially don't have any connection.

Good applications for using this type of technology are situations where a large volume of text-based data needs to be read, organized, and analyzed. In fact, investigators having to sort through any large unstructured text data sources, such as e-mail, word processing files, PowerPoint presentations, Excel and Lotus spreadsheets, PDF files, Lotus Notes archives, intranet and Internet server log files, Web pages, chat files, newsgroup files, interrogation scripts, investigation questionnaires, live chaVIRC files, and online news feeds can benefit from the use of text mining tools and techniques.

For counter-intelligence analysts working with documents containing a high level of focused content, such as scientific, technical, and other research documents, are excellent sources for text mining because they are highly informative in extracting only the most important content. These tools can be used to search, sort, and discover key clues in large collections of textual databases. They can also be used by agencies and departments to organize internal investigation–related case files in order to distribute it effectively to field investigators and intelligence analysts.

5.8   **Text Mining Tools**

The market for text mining products can be divided into two groups: text mining tools and kits for constructing applications with embedded text mining facilities. They vary from inexpensive desktop packages to enterprisewide systems costing thousands of dollars. The following is a partial list of text analysis software. Keep in mind, this is not an all-encompassing list; however, analysts need to know what these tools do and how they may want to apply them to solve profiling and forensic needs.

Autonomy

http://www.autonomy.com

Autonomy offers a number of products that use text mining technology for developing internal department or agency networks, intranet, or Web site portal applications. Autonomy's knowledge portal application also provides a unified view of disparate data sources across an organization. Such sources include e-mail, word processing files, PowerPoint presentations, Excel spreadsheets, PDF files, Lotus Notes archives, intranet file servers, SQL/ODBC databases, live chat/IRC, news feeds, and the expertise profiles of other employees. A user-profiling system automatically identifies an employee's area of expertise based on the user's search patterns and document and e-mail content.

For example, users of the Autonomy technology include the Defense Evaluation and Research Agency (DERA), an agency of the U.K. Ministry of Defence responsible for non-nuclear research, technology, testing, and evaluation. The U.K. police forces are also using Autonomy to categorize and tag criminal information stored within police stations. Police officers use the Autonomy Server™ as a central police information repository, categorizing and tagging live information from various sources.

The U.S. DOD is using Autonomy's Portal-in-a-Box™ to make personalized portals available to all of its personnel. The portals automatically draw information from thousands of Internet and intranet sites and create personalized sites for each individual to deliver specific information that the user either explicitly requests or has previously shown an interest in.

Clairvoyance

http://www.claritech.com/

Formerly Claritech, this company was founded in 1992 to commercialize text-analysis technology developed at the Laboratory for Computational Linguistics at Carnegie Mellon University. Clairvoyance's tools employ NLP capabilities, which enable it to carry out in-depth automated analysis of unstructured information. For example, the technology can recognize that different words or phrases can have the same meaning in certain contexts, such as determining that "go for a car" and "really like a car" express similar attitudes. It can also identify "probelm" as a misspelling of "problem" and discern an individual's feelings, attitudes, and intentions by distinguishing the subtle differences among words such as "prefer," "lean toward," and "like a lot" in text-based e-mail messages or call records. It can also differentiate among time expressions such as "soon," "immediately," and "in a few weeks." The ability to gauge the attitudes in the textual content that it analyzes makes this particular software useful for monitoring the communications of suspects in an investigation.

Claivoyance has put a lot of effort into packaging its technology into an application development environment that mainstream developers can use with the following functions:

- NLP (for morphological analysis and phrase/sub-phrase identification)

- Automatic document indexing

- Information retrieval

- Routing/filtering of streaming texts

- Subject classification

- Summarization of documents

- Automatic thesaurus discovery

- Spell-checking (empirically based, without a reference lexicon)

- Information extraction (identification of entities and relations)

Figure 5.4
*ClearForest
taxonomy
graphical view
of an
individual.*

- Virtual hypertext—automatic linking of content "on the fly"

- Document and concept clustering

- Compound-document management (combining text and page images)

This text mining technology clearly can be applied to a wide range of monitoring and reporting capabilities for detection and deterrence of a wide variety of criminal and terrorist activities.

ClearForest

http://www.clearforest.com/

Formerly ClearResearch, this text mining software can be used for the analysis and visualization of a large collection of documents. ClearForest can read vast amounts of text, extract relevant information specific to users' requirements, and provide visual, interactive, and executive summaries. ClearForest extracts and delivers knowledge snapshots from structured and unstructured information repositories, allowing investigators and analysts to gain rapid and valuable insights from massive amounts of textual files. This saves end users significant time, enabling them to be more productive and, ultimately, to make better analytical decisions in less time.

As ClearForest's name implies, its software is designed to allows users to obtain a "clear" view of the textual and document "forest." ClearForest's technology assimilates text data of any size and structure, extracts key terms,

Figure 5.5
*Dynamic view
of relationships.*

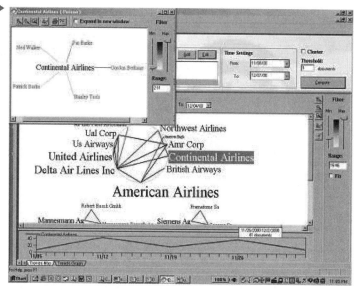

assigns them to meaningful categories (a taxonomy), and establishes their inter-relationships (see Figure 5.4).

The output of this tool is a highly structured map of the information that users can slice as needed, generating within seconds patterns in a variety of visual forms, such as maps, tables, and graphs. Information specifically relevant to each user's needs is extracted and displayed in a variety of simple, visual maps that the user can interact with as associations, patterns, updates, and trends are identified (see Figure 5.5).

Dynamic browsers allow users to drill down and roll up the visual maps as needed in order to focus on the relevant results. Throughout, the system maintains links to the original documents, allowing the user to back up and access the actual documents that contributed to the discovered pattern.

Copernic

http://www.copernic.com/company/index.html

Using agent technology, this firm provides a group of desktop text mining, indexing, and organizing products. Their Copernic 2001 software allows users to find exactly what they want on the Internet by simultaneously accessing the best search engines on the Web. Copernic uses its own technology to query hundreds of specialized and multilanguage Internet sources, including some business databases. Copernic can aggregate and integrate search results from scores of information sources, including intranets, extranets, proprietary networks, and the Web. It uses statistical and linguistic algorithms to retrieve key concepts and extracts the most relevant sentences from the original text. This particular tool combines agent technology for content retrieval and text mining capabilities for concept aggregation, making it a good forensic instrument for investigators and analysts.

DolphinSearch

`http://www.dolphinsearch.com/`

DolphinSearch provides a text-reading robot, mainly for law-related organizations, powered by a computer model mimicking the object-recognition capabilities of a person. The software is based on neural-network and fuzzy-logic technologies that allow the program to read documents and to know the meaning of the words in their native context. A person solves the problem of understanding the meaning of written sentences by forming vast interconnected networks among the words and their meanings.

These vast networks allow people to make inferences, understand analogies, and do a myriad of other things with words; it is the basis of a theory of semantic projection, which is at the core of this text mining software. Each piece of text (e.g., a document or a paragraph) is translated into a vector for neural network input. One neural network learns the pattern of word relations in the organization's documents and learns to represent the meaning of those words in terms of these vectors. The result of this learning is a semantic profile for each word in the vocabulary. These semantic profiles can be used to compare queries with documents, to compare documents with documents, or to compare documents to serve the interests of the organization or individuals.

DolphinSearch believes organizations differ in the way they understand words. They evolve their own jargon and their own patterns of discourse. Consequently, the software first learns the meanings of words used by a community by reading an authoritative *training* text. By the way, this concept of *training* is a key process when using neural networks to recognize patterns in data. The same patterns of word use that allow the members of the community to understand one another can be learned by DolphinSearch so that it can recognize new documents that are relevant to the community and can understand their content. Later, when a community member enters a query, DolphinSearch understands the meaning of the words in that query in the same way that human community members would and finds relevant documents that contain the corresponding concept.

dtSearch

`http://www.dtsearch.com/`

dtSearch provides several versions of its text mining software for the desktop, Web sites, remote servers, and for embedding in other applications. dtSearch software has over two dozen search options and can work with PDF and HTML files with highlighted hits, embedded links and images, and multiple hit and file navigation options. It can convert XML, word processor, database, spreadsheet, e-mail, zip, Unicode, etc., to HTML for browser display with highlighted hits and multiple navigation options. Most indexed searches take less than a second; indexing, searching, and display do not affect original files. This particular text mining tool is ideally suited for rapid indexing by forensic investigators.

As computer crimes continue to increase, law enforcement and corporate security personnel require new technology to fight this battle. The Forensic Toolkit™ (FTK), from AccessData is a password recovery and forensic file decryption product. FTK offers users a suite of technologies for performing forensic examinations of computer systems. The Known File Filer (KFF) feature can be used to automatically pull out benign files that are known not to contain any potential evidence and flag known problem files for the investigator to examine immediately. The FTK uses the text search engine of dtSearch for all of its searching of text strings; the dtSearch technology is incorporated into the FTK product.

HNC Software

http://www.hnc.com/

HNC's text-analysis technology uses both mathematically-based context vector data modeling techniques and HNC's proprietary neural-network algorithms to automate a number of text-processing applications. Together, these technologies provide the ability to read and learn the content of unstructured, text-based information and to discover relationships between words and documents. This learning capability serves as the foundation for a line of products that provide both interactive and automated decision making based on the text and its internal relationships, as well as predictive modeling of future patterns, trends, and analysis. HNC calls this process context vector modeling.

Context vector modeling is a form of machine learning that employs neural-network techniques to analyze text-based information to automatically discover similarity of usage at the word level. Context vector modeling systems break down a document. They function by translating free text into a mathematical representation composed of vectors. Any text-based object (such as a word, document, or document cluster) is assigned a vector in a multi-dimensional space, referred to as a document universe. A learning algorithm then automatically adjusts word vectors so that the words that are used in similar context will have vectors that point in similar directions. Because the vectors encode the contexts in which the words appear, they are referred to as context vectors. Vectors representing larger bodies of text are derived from the vectors for the individual words occurring within them. As a result, vectors for documents with similar subject content have vectors that point in similar directions. Their proximity (closeness) in the document universe is equivalent to closeness or similarity in subject content.

One of the most important functions of context vector modeling is clustering documents by similarity of meaning. Because documents with similar information content possess context vectors that point in similar directions, it is possible to use a clustering algorithm to find clusters of documents with similar concepts. Moreover, because each document cluster can be represented by a context vector, any operation that can be performed on word or document clusters can also be performed on cluster vectors. For example, the meaning of the clusters can be explained automatically by summarization. This operation consists of determining the words whose vectors are closest to each cluster center.

In addition, the clustering operation can be applied recursively on the cluster centers. The result is a hierarchy of clusters called *cluster trees*. Because a cluster tree is organized by similarity of meaning, it provides a hierarchical subject index for all the textual information modeled as context vectors. Consequently, cluster trees provide the basis for efficient context vector storage. Once stored as context vectors, words, documents, predefined categories, and naturally occurring document clusters can be directly compared and contrasted. The resulting representation serves as the basic model for conducting a range of text-processing operations, including document retrieval, routing, document summarization, query-by-example, and keyword assignment.

Because the context vector technique is based on a mathematical model, it is language-independent. Thus, this technique can be applied to any language without the need to resort to external dictionaries or thesauri, as is necessary with NLP-based text mining systems. Context vector modeling provides the base technology for most HNC products. Because this type of text mining technology is language neutral, it is especially attractive to government agencies responsible for monitoring foreign textual data.

IBM

http://www-3.ibm.com/software/data/iminer/fortext/index.html

IBM Intelligent Miner for Text offers system integrators and application developers several text-analysis tools, full-text retrieval components, and Web-access tools. IBM's Intelligent Miner for Text is a developer toolkit containing several components, including a text-analysis, feature extraction, clustering, summarization, and categorization set of tools. A free 60-day evaluation of this text mining application development kit is available from IBM.

Figure 5.6
TextRoller
summary results.

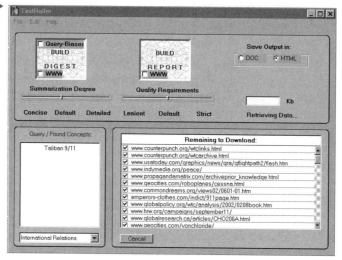

iCrossReader

`http://www.insight.com.ru`

iCrossReader lets a user automatically build an on-demand survey from excerpts of documents without the need to first search for the texts and conduct a visual review. Created in Russia, InsightSoft combines text processing technology with text-retrieval and text-analysis techniques. The principal of the firm is professor Martin Subbotin, who has over 30 years of experience with intelligent text-processing technologies, having written over 150 scientific papers in the field of text mining. Running on a desktop, the software captures and builds a document corpus or collection on your hard disk, on-the-fly, as it searches. This process requires extensive CPU power because at the same time that it's locating and downloading Web documents, the computer is doing brute-force processing, and analyzing the text streams within each document to determine their relevance to the query. This requires an enormous amount of RAM.

A new agent-based product called TextRoller can retrieve and summarize the content of documents or Web pages in real time. It is available free from this firm's Web site. This is a very impressive little information-retrieval tool. The user simply fills in the small form with some key words, clicks on the WWW window button and TextRoller starts compiling a little folder with relevant Web sites that is placed on the user's desktop or in a predefined directory. A Word file is also created, which extracts the core content of the HTML pages retrieved. What is amazing is the accuracy of the content that is retrieved, the speed with which it performs these tasks, and the fact that the demo of TextRoller is free!

TextRoller can conduct searches on the Web or on internal computer systems for DOC or HTML text. Different settings can be set by domain specificity, such as international relations, scientific, business, economy, etc. In addition, the search parameters can be controlled through some simple sliding controls.

The software does not seek to assemble or create lists of documents that are potentially relevant to a user's query. There's no pre- or post-coordinate indexing or characterizing, no analyzing of the document to create a surrogate record, no attempt to describe or classify the content. Instead, the software uses pure computer power to pour through a document text meticulously to find and extract segments of relevant text information. It uses natural language scanning to identify potentially relevant material and linguistic and semantic text analysis algorithms to extract highly relevant information. In comparison to search engines such as Google, it by far outperforms them in seeking, organizing, and summarizing relevant content on the user's desktop. One word of caution: TextRoller can bring a PC to a grinding halt as it requires a high amount of RAM. All other applications should be closed when using it.

Klarity

http://www.klarity.com.au

Klarity learns, recognizes, analyzes and labels any textual information for subsequent recall; it is an application development text mining tool kit.

Kwalitan

http://www.gamma.rug.nl

Kwalitan uses codes for text fragments to facilitate textual search and display overviews, which can be used to build hierarchical trees.

Leximancer

http://www.leximancer.com

Leximancer makes automatic concept maps of text data collections. First, it creates a map of the documents it collects. Then it constructs concept keys. Leximancer can be used to discover ideas or names linked to an initial concept, such as whether two suspect names refer to the same thing—for instance aliases or a group of closely linked corporations. The technology behind Leximancer is based on Bayesian theory, meaning that by examining the bits and pieces of evidence, it can predict what associations exist.

Leximancer examines the words that make up a sentence in order to predict the concepts being discussed in a document or a collection of text, such as newsgroups, chat files, e-mails, etc. (see Figure 5.7). One of the most impor-

Figure 5.7 *A Leximancer concept map of 155 Internet news groups.*

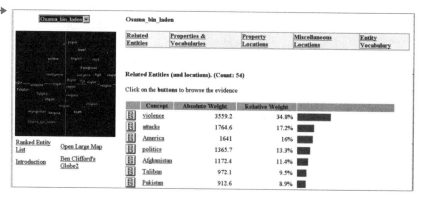

tant innovations of this system is its ability to learn automatically and efficiently which words predict which concepts for a wide range of concepts across large groups of documents. A very important characteristic of these concepts is that they are defined in advance using only a small number of seed words, often as few as one word.

Lextek

http://www.languageidentifier.com

Lextek basically provides a text-profiling engine that can sort through large amounts of data looking for keywords and trying to discern if someone is up to something nefarious. The tool kit could be used either by police departments (for sorting through data on someone's hard drive) or by agencies such as the FBI, CIA, and NSA for watching traffic on the Internet or for scanning other communications. The text mining tool kit can be integrated into an application using C/C++ or other similar programming language. Lextek provides the underlying text-searching technologies, allowing other developers to build their specific forensic application around them. Lextek offers a wide range of document management systems using text-indexing technologies. Its products include the following:

- Onix Toolkit for adding full-text indexing search and retrieval to applications

- Lextek Profiling Engine for automatically classifying, routing, and filtering electronic text according to user-defined profiles

- LanguageIdentifier for identifing what language and character set a document is written in (it supports 260 language and encoding modules)

Other Lextek text mining tool kits include the following:

- RouteX Document Classifier which uses rules to route documents
- Brevity Document Summarizer which generates summaries of documents for users
- SpellWright Spellchecking and PhonMatch Phonetic Toolkits

Typically, building text-search technologies that are competitive speed-wise and that have more than basic functionality is a huge process. For this reason, developers and companies that need this kind of functionality typically license the text-search and categorization technologies from a vendor, such as Lextek. A user requiring text-indexing and search technology would use the Onix engine, while the technology used to locate documents by their subject matter would require the licensing of their Profiling Engine kit.

The main difference is that Onix is better for a specific set of data (such as a database, file system, etc.) where multiple searches are going to be performed. The reason for this is that it takes time to build the index where all the words are. On the other hand, the Lextek Profiling Engine is better suited for filtering and categorizing documents that are in a stream of data. An example of this would be an e-mail stream, scanners watching Internet traffic, etc., where this is done once on a document and not performed on that same document again. Either would be appropriate for integration into criminal analysis software, though this would probably depend a lot on the specific application.

Semio

`http://www.semio.com/`

Semio offers taxonomy-building and content-mapping tools for automating the process of creating searchable, hierarchical directories for intranets and portal applications. Semio's text mining toolkit consists of a core concept-mapping engine, lexical tools and utilities, client visualization software, and administrative tools and utilities. Semio also provides a text mining tool that features a GUI front end coupled with a back-end, server-based, concept-mapping engine that users can deploy across multiple platforms.

Semio's concept-mapping engine features automatic text processing, including lexical extraction in English, French, Spanish, and Italian. It also has a Java front end to display the engine's text mining results visually in a browser. Semio can process a wide variety of document formats, including text-only, PDF, HTML, Microsoft Office documents, Lotus Notes databases, Web pages, XML, and other sources. Semio uses four automated processes to analyze and categorize text in real time:

1.   Text indexing and extraction

2.   Concept clustering

3.   Taxonomy generation

4.   Graphical display and navigation

Semio's lexical technology is based on research in linguistic semiotics. It functions by extracting phrases instead of keywords from text, and it tracks the co-occurrences of extracted phrases. The extractor is customizable for particular applications; for example, for a particular type of investigation, analysts can modify the taxonomy to build or create their own set of keywords. The Semio client component uses data visualization techniques to display key concepts and relationships graphically. This three-dimensional "concept map" lets the user move through related concepts, drill down to different levels of detail, or jump to the referenced documents.

The document categories, which are dynamically generated, are presented based on their relationship to one another in a graphical map. This map allows an investigator or analyst to navigate quickly through the key phrases and relationships within a body of text and drill down and back up to specific documents as desired. Investigators can explore and view a variety of documents, e-mails, articles, chats, and any other textual data using this type of text mining tool.

Temis

http://www.temis-group.com

The Temis Group provides a text mining tool using a combination of components for information extraction, categorization, clustering, and creating automatic reports enabling users to understand and visualize the content of text documents in a multilingual context. Temis also offers its Insight Discoverer and Skill Cartridge text mining engines and software components. Temis can cluster, categorize, and extract text using its Insight Discoverer Clusterer, Categorizer, and Extractor components.

Another application is its Online Miner, which crawls the Web and online databanks, using text mining techniques in any of seven languages. Using their Temis Skill Cartridges, a user can "model" the language (with its grammars, slangs, and vocabularies), defining the target the user wants to monitor. In business applications, this capability allows companies to analyze their customers' and prospects' interactions, such as e-mails, chat lines, newsgroups, forums, and call center transcriptions, in order to recognize similar groups of customers with common interests and feelings. In forensic applications, this

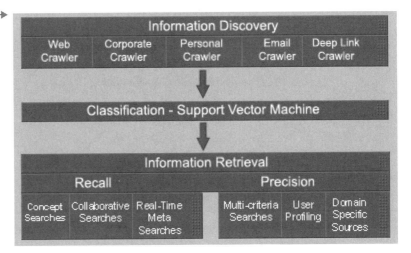

Figure 5.8
TripleHop's three-layer architecture.

allows the detection of "invisible colleges," groups using the same language and styles, and having the same attitudes.

Online Miner can also gather information from large collections of documents in different languages. It can organize the documents by topics through the analysis of clusters; it can group documents by similar content and main themes or by categories. The tool provides content-based navigation by establishing relationships between documents and between topics. It also highlights the strategic content hidden in documents. Online Miner can be used to gather intelligence as described by the definition of objectives, monitoring directions, and targets of interest.

Text Analyst

http://www.megaputer.com

Text Analyst offers semantic analysis of free-form texts, summarization, clustering, navigation, and natural language retrieval with search dynamic refocusing. Text Analysts is one of several data mining components offered by Megaputer, a data mining firm originating in Russia.

TripleHop

http://www.triplehop.com/ie

Formerly *Matchpoint*, this product collects information from corporate documents, e-mails, Web pages, proprietary network servers, and other data sources; it simultaneously classifies the data and delivers content to specific users based on preset profiles. It uses three levels of information processing (see Figure 5.8):

1. *Information Discovery.* This layer captures both structured
    and unstructured data located on the Internet, corporate net-
    works, e-mail servers and internal databases stored in differ-
    ent formats including text, html, Word documents, PDF
    files, spreadsheets, and database tables.

2. *Classification.* This layer uses a proprietary algorithm based
    on a statistical method called support vector machine (SVM)
    to organize and associate the text.

3. *Information Retrieval.* This layer routes the retrieved docu-
    ments by relevance to users.

This software could be used to collect, organize, and route specific content
to members of law enforcement agencies and police departments.

Quenza

```
http://www.xanalys.com/quenza.html
```

Quenza automatically extracts entities and cross-references from free-text documents and builds a database for subsequent analysis. Their PowerIndexing
component applies a set of rules called a grammar to extract information from
text. Grammars are specialized for particular domains; for example, for
money-laundering investigations you might need to identify companies,
financial information, and commercial activities. Alternatively, you might
need to identify people, vehicles, and property in a drug or weapons criminal
investigation. The type of investigation would determine the type of grammar
an investigator would use with this tool.

Quenza's visualization tool, *Watson,* can be used to support the development and presentation of prosecution or defense arguments by validating and
illustrating patterns, alibis, links, and relations. Watson has been used to find
and track individual criminals and criminal gangs, pinpoint and trace the
areas and origins of criminal activity, as well as trace and document Internet
crimes such as child pornography.

Readware

```
http://www.readware.com
```

Readware information processor for intranets and the Internet classifies documents by content and provides literal and conceptual searches. It includes a
ConceptBase with English, French, or German lexicons.

VantagePoint

```
http://www.thevantagepoint.com
```

VantagePoint provides a variety of interactive graphical views and analysis tools with the ability to discover knowledge from text databases. Including document categorization and utilities for cleaning data, VantagePoint has also the ability to create a thesaurus for data compression and scripting capabilities to automate knowledge gathering. The tool can be configured to text mine most forms of structured bibliographic data.

VisualText™

http://www.textanalysis.com/

VisualText by TextAI is an excellent text mining toolkit for developing custom text analyzers with multiple functions, such as generating rules from text or documents. For those agencies or departments with an IT staff wishing to customize and build its own text analyzer, this kit is ideal. Some functions that this kit supports include the following:

- Information extraction: systems that extract, correlate, and standardize content

- Shallow extraction: systems that identify names, locations, and dates in text

- Indexing: systems for indexing text from the Internet and other sources

- Filtering: systems that determine if a document is relevant

- Categorization: systems that determine the topic of documents

- Test grading: systems for reading and matching prose

- Summarization: systems for building a brief description of contents in text

- Automated coding: systems for coding documents, such as police reports

- Natural language query: systems for interacting with a computer using plain text

- Dissemination: systems for routing documents to people who require them

Figure 5.9 *The VisualText GUI interface.*

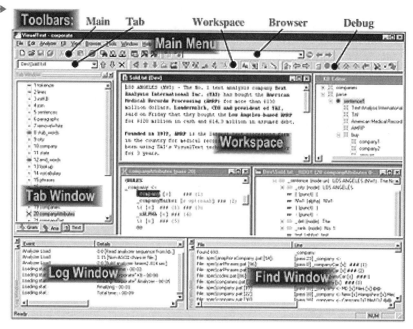

VisualText provides a comprehensive interface for quickly building a text analyzer (see Figure 5.9).

Wordstat

http://www.simstat.com/wordstat.htm

Wordstat is a tool for mining textual information contained in responses to open-ended questions; for example, it may be used to analyze interrogation transcripts, criminal interviews, etc., in any text stored in several records of a data file. It supports several optional features, including the following:

- Optional exclusion of pronouns, conjunctions, etc., by the use of user-defined exclusion lists

- Categorization of words or phrases using existing or user-defined dictionaries

- Word and phrase substitution and scoring using wildcards and integer weighting

- Frequency analysis of words, phrases, derived categories or concepts, or user-defined codes entered manually within a text

- Interactive development of hierarchical dictionaries or categorization schema

- Ability to restrict the analysis to specific portions of a text or to exclude comments and annotations

- Ability to perform an analysis on a random sample of records

- Integrated spell-checking with support for different languages, such as English, French, Spanish, etc.

- Integrated thesaurus (English only) to assist the creation of categorization schema

- Record filtering on any numeric or alphanumeric field and on code occurrence (with AND, OR, and NOT Boolean operators)

- Ability to define a memo field linked to individual records to write annotations, side notes, comments, or codes

- Ability to print presentation-quality tables (word count, cross tabs, or KWIC lists)

- Ability to save any table to ASCII, tab-separated or comma-separated value files or HTML files

- Option to perform case-sensitive content analysis

- Option to use disks for the storage of temporary files or the analysis of large files

- Flexible keyword highlighting (the text editor can display all categories using different colors)

5.9 Bibliography

Caruana, R. and Hodor, P. (August 20–23, 2000) "High Precision Information Extraction," *Sixth ACM SIGKDD International Conference on Knowledge Discovery and Data Mining*.

Jensen, L. and Martinez, T. (August 20–23, 2000) "Improving Text Classification by Using Conceptual and Contextual Features," *Sixth ACM SIGKDD International Conference on Knowledge Discovery and Data Mining*.

Manning, C. and Schutze, H. (1999) *Foundations of Statistical Natural Language Processing*, Cambridge, MA: MIT Press.

Neural Networks: Classifying Patterns

6.1 What Do Neural Networks Do?

Neural networks are software systems modeled after the human process of learning and remembering. They mimic the cognitive neurological functions of the human brain. As such they are capable of predicting new observations from historical samples after executing a process of learning. A neural network can be used to detect a fraudulent transaction, a computer intrusion, and an assortment of other criminal activities, so long as examples of observations are available for training it.

Neural network software comprises programmable memories designed to make predictions. Neural networks were introduced to the marketplace in the mid-1980s and became practical commercial software products only after advances in computing power at the desktop and server level became a reality. They have been used in private industry to do one or more of the following:

- *Classification*: discriminating between two things based on similarities, such as separating loan applications into good or bad risks or distinguishing a legal from a fraudulent transaction. They can also be used to discriminate between criminal and legal activities. Chapter 8 illustrates how neural networks are used to detect Internet fraud on an e-commerce site.

- *Clustering*: organizing observations into groups with similar features or attributes—for instance identifying groups of customers who buy the same type of products, also referred to as affinity market-basket analysis; they can also be used to group criminals who perpetrate the same types of crimes. This involves using a special type of Kohonen neural network (named after its creator, Dr. Tevo Kohonen). They are also known as self-organizing maps (SOM). Several case studies demonstrating this type of analysis are provided further in this chapter, and book.

- *Generalizing*: generalizing from examples about new cases or problems just as humans can learn to model relationships from examples. This same process can be used to model criminal signatures. A case study is provided in this chapter illustrating how neural networks are used to recognize the signature of kerosene in arson investigations.

- *Forecasting*: looking at current information and predicting what is likely to happen. Prediction is a form of classification into the future. Neural networks can also be trained on observations in order to predict (with some probability), for example, who is likely to be a smuggler. A demonstration will be provided in this chapter illustrating this process.

6.2   What Is a Neural Network?

Neural network softwares are programs designed to do what human brains have evolved to perform: learn from examples and recognize patterns. As a neural network is trained, it can gradually learn, for example, the patterns of behavior and the attributes of criminals; this is actually done through an adjustment of mathematical formulas that are continuously changing, eventually converging into a model.

This model, in most instances, is the end product of neural networks and is usually in the form of a formula or a series of equations, representing a set of input values and a predictive output. For example, Table 6.1 shows a model designed to predict fraud at an e-commerce Web site. When given the number of visits a person makes to a site (input 1), coupled with a dollar range (input 2) and a particular type of product bought (input 3), a network would then create a formula to compute a probability score (output) for classifying that transaction as being either legal or fraudulent.

Table 6.1   *Model with Three Inputs, a Set of Formula Weights, and One Output*

Input Types	Values	Network (Weights) Formula
Number of visits	2	Input => *.08766 x
Dollar range	(567–879)	Input => *.00934 x
Product category	4	Input => *.4956 x
		Output = 68% fraud probability score

Neural networks are software systems designed to do what a human brain does, which is to figure out how to find patterns in the environment in order to survive. Neural networks deal with the basic problems that our ancestors had in hunting, finding paths, knowing the seasons, recognizing prey and predators, and identifying threats to the tribe and village: pattern recognition.

6.3   How Do Neural Networks Work?

There is no universally accepted definition of a neural network. Most definitions, however, agree that they are networks of many simple processors or units that are connected and process numeric values. Neural networks are models of biological learning systems; in fact, much of the inspiration in all the fields of AI comes from the desire of researchers to emulate with software the human capacities of recognition, learning, remembering, and evolving. Thus, neural networks were developed as analogs of human brains. They were proposed 50 years ago in theory, motivated by a desire by scientists to understand how the human brain works. Similar to the way brain cells learn, neural networks work through a process of excitation and connection, depending on the weighted functions of the inputs from many other cells to which they are wired.

A neural network software system is an information-processing program inspired by the heavily interconnected structure of the human brain. They are collections of mathematical models that emulate some of the observed properties of biological nervous systems and draw on the analogies of adaptive biological learning. Learning in biological systems involves adjustments of the synaptic connections that exist between the neurons. This is the basic process that neural networks attempt to replicate; evenly distributed observations are required for the network to learn the patterns of different types of behavior. Learning occurs by example through exposure to a set of input-output data where the training algorithm iteratively adjusts the connection weights (synapses). These connection weights store the knowledge necessary to solve specific problems, which, for investigative data mining, involve recognizing the patterns of various types of cybercrimes, fraud, system intrusions, and other digital crimes (Fausett, 1994).

Knowledge, then, for a neural network is reduced to a set of weights between its internal connections. Learning comes down to what gets encoded in the wiring and the weighting factors of the various neurons. For example, to construct a fraud-detection model with a neural network, samples of fraudulent and non-fraudulent transactions are required for it to distinguish the different features and behavior of each. For this reason, when working with neural networks, the selection of samples in the training is extremely important. Adequate effort must be made to ensure that a balanced number of observations are presented to a network.

6.4   Types of Network Architectures

There are literally hundreds of neural networks architectures, which set the way internal connections and learning occur. However, the most dominant ones are the multi-layer perceptrons (MLP), also known as back-propagation, for classification and the Kohonen network or SOM for clustering. Most networks are trained via a feedback mechanism, which gradually adjusts and trains with the data by the testing and correction of errors. This is by most estimates the most common type of architecture in use for all neural networks.

While the majority of neural networks are classified as feed-forward (adjustment of errors), there are some that are recurrent, implementing a feedback scheme, depending on how data is processed through the network. Yet another way of classifying neural network types is by their method of learning or training. Most neural networks employ supervised training, while others are referred to as unsupervised, such as the SOM or Kohonen network. A SOM does not need training; its task is, instead, discovering clusters of similarity in a database, which it does through a concept of distance measurements unique to its architecture.

Supervised training is similar to a student being guided by a teacher or mentor. This type of back-propagation neural network is used when a sample of cases, profiles, or crimes is available for training a network to recognize the patterns of criminal behavior. For example, an auction site such as ebay.com could use this type of network to detect the probability of criminal activity because it probably has in its servers records of transactions where fraud was perpetrated.

The popular MLP networks have found their way into countless commercial and marketing applications requiring pattern recognition, classification, profiling, and prediction. It is estimated by industry analysts that 75% to 90% of most of today's applications use MLP schema networks. The MLP networks, main advantage is that they are easy to use and that they can approximate any input/output map. Their disadvantages are that they train slowly and require an adequate sample of training data.

In order to address some of the inadequacies of the MLP, other architectures exist, such as generalized feed-forward networks, which are a generalization of the MLP. These networks often solve problems much more efficiently and quickly. Yet another architecture is the modular feed-forward networks, which are a special class of MLP. These networks process their input using several parallel MLPs, and then combine their results. These networks tend to speed up training times and reduce the number of observations required for training. In situations such as fraud detection or terrorist profiling, this architecture may be ideal.

A rather unique architecture is the principal component analysis (PCA) network which combines unsupervised and supervised learning in the same topology. PCA is an unsupervised linear procedure that finds a set of uncorrelated features from the input. An MLP is next deployed in a supervised format to perform the nonlinear classification from the features discovered from the unsupervised procedure.

As noted, most networks require supervision; that is, they need samples of what the user is trying to classify to recognize, for example, a potential fraudulent transaction. However a Kohonen neural network also known as SOM, is different. This class of network does not need samples. A SOM basically creates clusters of similar records in a database without the need for a training output. This type of network, as we shall see in some case studies, has been used by some ingenious police investigators to cluster and associate crimes and criminals based on their modus operandi. Other neural network architectures include learning vector quantization, radial basis function, and hopfield, just to name a few.

6.5   Using Neural Networks

To construct a model for detecting perpetrators using an MLP neural network, samples of criminal observations and their attributes are required. It is through the training of these samples that connections among the various layers in the network can be made to converge. This enables a model to be created for recognizing future perpetrators, so that whenever the features of a criminal are input, an alert output is produced, since a network will associate and recognize a profile of similarity.

The neural network is then said to have learned to recognize the features of criminal perpetrators. Once training is complete, the neural network uses these learned patterns to predict the probability that a new individual will exhibit the modeled transaction patterns. Moreover, the trained network is able to recognize new perpetrators that are similar, but not identical to, those used in its training sessions.

This application of training and modeling for profiling and prediction to investigative data mining can be applied in criminal investigations, fraud detection, internal corporate investigations, cybercrimes, system intrusion detection, criminal profiling, and criminal analysis and prevention. The challenge, as some of the case studies will illustrate, is in the encoding of the data.

Most law enforcement departments and government agencies have not adequately digitized their criminal records into a structured and uniform manner. Many still use free-form text narrative entries in documenting their criminal cases; this impedes the use of neural-network techniques. The top law enforcement agency in the United States, the FBI, has made great strides in gathering criminal data for its investigations and for reports; however, by its own admission, it has been remiss in its analysis of this data.

If a standardized system of recording crimes can be developed, data mining techniques can begin to be deployed in order for crime to be analyzed, modeled, and to an extent predicted. For this to happen, effort on the parts of the local, state, and federal law enforcement agencies must begin to structure in a machine-readable format how crimes get reported and documented. Once the crime data is standardized and warehoused, it becomes a much easier task to analyze it to extract predictive models from it.

6.6   Why Use Neural Networks?

Neural networks have been demonstrated to be very effective in dealing with noisy input data, such as handwriting and speech recognition and various forms of image processing, which are very difficult to process with the rigid reasoning techniques of statistical systems. The pattern-recognition ability of neural networks has proven extremely effective in predicting and recognizing patterns of consumer behavior and can be used similarly to detect criminal activities. Some neural networks, in conjunction with other technologies, are being used for retina, thumb, and facial recognition applications; they are the "reasoning engines" to these proprietary identification systems.

Neural networks provide solutions to a variety of classification problems, such as speech, character, and signal recognition, as well as functional prediction and system modeling, where the physical processes are not understood or are highly complex. So far, neural networks have not been widely applied to profiling criminals, aside from detecting fraud. However, crime and terrorism in our time cannot exist without generating digital trails and transactions, all of which are subject to scrutiny and evaluation by neural network models. In fact, after 9/11, there were calls in the media for development of this very type of analysis to be accelerated by the government and private industry to foster homeland defense.

The advantage of neural networks lies in their ability to deal with samples of input data and learn quickly from these training sessions. They are often good at solving problems that are too complex for conventional technologies but that a human is able to recognize and learn. However, rather than taking years to train a good fraud specialist to recognize when a crime is being com-

Figure 6.1 *This is the suspect the police are searching for.*

mitted, a neural network can be trained in a few minutes, if examples of fraudulent observations are available to create a model. From that point, when a red flag or possible criminal scenario is raised, expert human analysis can be implemented to assess the credibility of the program's alert.

Another distinct advantage of neural networks is that they can be used to process and score hundreds of thousands of records or transactions in milliseconds. Once trained, a neural network tool can generate code that can be used in real-time productions systems. Neural networks are highly accurate, portable, and fast, which when coupled with an investigator's knowledge and intuition can be a hybrid deterrence to future threats from criminals and terrorists.

6.7   Attrasoft Facial Recognition Classifications System: A Demonstration

Attrasoft is a neural network company selling various systems in the areas of image and facial recognition. For this demonstration, we are using the facial recognition systems and a database of images of known criminals. The Attrasoft system is first trained to recognize a perpetrator and then search for a specific photograph(s) or sketch(s) of the matching suspect. Figure 6.1 shows a photograph of a suspect the police are searching for.

The image database of known criminals is passed through the system; this database can contain an unlimited number of suspect photographs. Attrasoft can search this database at a rate of 10 photographs per second. The first step is to have the Attrasoft system trained to recognize the face of the suspect. This is the ImageFinder interface (see Figure 6.2).

Next, the user clicks on the Train button and waits for one second until in the status text area the message "Training End!" appears. The user can modify the setting parameters, like blurring, sensitivity, external weight cut, image type, segment size, etc. Once training is complete, the system can be directed to go out and look for images that match the training sample, with the output having an integer, representing a similarity value. The higher the score between the training image(s) and the retrieved images, the better the match. Figure 6.3 shows high matching similarity translation symmetry and is, in fact, a photograph of the suspect.

Figure 6.3
*System
recognized the
suspect wearing
a hat.*

Figure 6.4
System recognized suspect with a beard.

However, the system also matched the following photograph based on the original training image (see Figure 6.4).

All three images are of the same person. The facial recognition system was able to make a match despite the fact the other photographs had the suspect wearing a hat and a beard.

Facial recognition software works by measuring a face according to its peaks and valleys—such as the tip of the nose, the depth of the eye sockets—which are known as *nodal points*. A human face has 80 nodal points; however, facial recognition software may require only 14 to 22 to make a match, concentrating on the inner region of the face, which runs from temple to temple and just over the lip, called the "golden triangle." This is the most stable area because if an individual grows a beard, puts on glasses, gains weight or ages, this region tends not to be affected. The relative positions of these points are converted into a long string of numbers, known as a face print.

This type of facial recognition technology can be incorporated into the Transportation Safety Administration's planned computer-assisted passenger prescreening system (CAPPS II), enabling it to recognize potential hijackers and terrorists from existing databases of photographs. Currently, most facial recognition systems are in use by casinos, with more than 100 across the United States using them in their daily operations.

6.8 Chicago Internal Affairs Uses Neural Network: A Case Study

The Chicago Police Department's (C.P.D.) Internal Affairs Division used neural networks to study 200 officers who had been terminated for disciplinary reasons and developed a model for predicting current officers with a likelihood of having similar disciplinary problems. The model, when compared to current department officers, produced a list of officers who it determined were "at risk" of having some future problems

The C.P.D. Internal Affairs Division used the model to study the records of 12,500 current officers. These personnel records included such information as age, education, sex, race, number of traffic accidents, reports of lost weapons or badges, marital status, performance reports, and frequency of sick leaves. The model was able to produce a list of 91 at-risk officers. Of those 91 people, nearly half were found already to be enrolled in a counseling program founded by the personnel department to help officers guilty of misconduct. The Internal Affairs Division wanted to use the neural network model to supplement the counseling program, because the sheer size of the Chicago police force makes it nearly impossible for all at-risk officers to be identified by their supervisors.

The motivations cited by the developers for wanting to use neural networks was that the software could be effective for two reasons: (1) they observed that as the number of variables increased, so did the accuracy of the predictions, and (2) they found that neural networks could effectively deal with missing data, which for this application was often the case, as some of the personnel files contained text narratives and were not uniform. This is an important feature of neural networks: their ability to perform with incomplete data. The importance of training the networks with good examples should also be noted.

Despite the ethical discussion raging over whether a neural network should be used to monitor human beings, an issue raised by the brotherhood union, the model can not be accused of being subjective and personally biased, as can human-based evaluations. Clearly, the software can hold no personal grudges and seeks only to identify patterns and examine behavioral characteristics that could spell trouble. The alternative system, being human-based, cannot avoid subjectivity and bias at some level. It is worth noting that the Fraternal Order of Police "vehemently opposed" the department's old system for that very reason.

To counterbalance the inherent "dispassion" of the neural network, the department closely examined the software's findings to ensure that officers who are clear anomalies, and thus don't warrant being on the list, are removed from consideration. This combination of objective technology and subjective humanity does not necessarily spell perfection, but it demonstrates that hybrid systems that incorporate machine and human intelligence are clearly the optimal methodology for investigative data mining; care, however, must be taken as, often, the use of data mining will raise the issues of privacy and human rights.

6.9   Clustering Border Smugglers with a SOM: A Demonstration

Dr. Kohonen's SOM is one of the most popular artificial neural network algorithms in the world. This type of neural network can be used to discover clusters of similar records in a database; for example, a case study will be provided in which investigators use a SOM to associate MOs to a network of criminals. The learning process of SOMs is competitive and unsupervised, meaning that there is no teacher to define the correct output, as there is with most of the other types of neural networks. A SOM is, thus, most commonly used to find hidden clusters in databases automatically. Applications abound in finance, marketing, and medicine, and we will see how it can be used in the context of investigative data mining in this demonstration.

The architecture and function of a SOM is like that of a fabric wrapping itself around database records with similar features. A SOM, for example, can transform a database of, say, fraudulent and legal transactions into a two-dimensional, discrete color map so that the illegal transactions are red and the legal ones are blue. This neural network works by performing tests for similarities in the data in order to identify distinct clusters of fraud versus legal records and organize them accordingly. In a two-dimensional graph from which further explorations can be performed. Another way this type of clustering network might be used is in the detection of potential smugglers at a border crossing. Envision an immigration inspector keying in the plate number of an auto at a point-of-entry border station, relaying the information to a centralized system containing a model that uses data from INS, the Departments of Transportation, the Treasury, and the Social Security Administration. In this scenario, important data relating to this visitor's activity can be used to develop a clustering profile, which may warrant issuing an alert, resulting in the inspector taking further steps in questioning a particular driver. There are several ways such a model could be constructed, including through the use of a neural network, either an MLP or a SOM, or through the use of machine-learning algorithms, as we shall demonstrate in the next chapter.

To demonstrate how a SOM-based system would perform and could be used to extract distinct features from a database in a totally autonomous and automatic method, we will use a data set we will call *Border Profile*, containing the following values:

```
AGENCY DATA SOURCES
Transportation_(Truck_License_1=Yes_0=No):
    A 1 increases the alert
```

Figure 6.5 *This is how the data looks in our Border Profile database.*

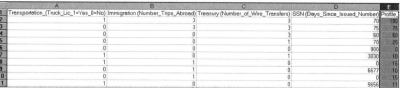

	A	B	C	D	E
1	Transportation_(Truck_Lic_1=Yes_0=No)	Immigration (Number_Trips_Abroad)	Treasury (Number_of_Wire_Transfers)	SSN (Days_Since_Issued_Number)	Profile
2	1	3	3	70	100
3	0	3	3	75	75
4	0	0	3	60	50
5	0	0	1	70	25
6	0	0	0	900	0
7	1	0	1	3030	10
8	1	1	0	0	15
9	0	1	0	6677	10
10	0	1	0	0	15
11	1	0	0	5656	11

```
Immigration (Number_Trips_Abroad):
    A high number increases the alert

Treasury (Number_of_Wire_Transfers):
    A high number increases the alert

SSN (Days_Since_Issued_Number):
    A lower number increases the alert

Profile_Score: Range from 0-100, the higher the number
increases the ALERT
```

The data itself would look like that in Figure 6.5 in a spreadsheet format. Note the profile score is the rightmost cell, with 100 representing instances of a detection at a border point-of-entry culminating in an arrest.

For example, the first record is a high-risk target; its parameters are as follows:

```
Transportation Truck License is Yes = 1
Immigration Number of Trips is = 3
Treasury Number of Wire Transfers is = 3
Social Security Number Days Since Issue is = 70
Profile is = 100 (High Alert)
```

On the other hand, for record 7 the values are quite different:

```
Transportation Truck License is Yes = 1
Immigration Number of Trips is = 0
Treasury Number of Wire Transfers is = 0
Social Security Number Days Since Issue is = 3030
Profile is = 10 (Very Low Alert)
```

After importing the data, the SOM tool is allowed to train itself and discover key clusters; the error rate starts dropping after a few minutes. Once the

Figure 6.6 *The different colors represent different stages of alerts.*

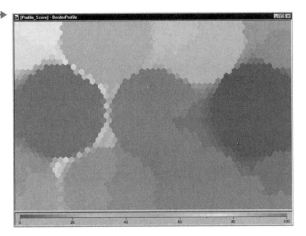

training is complete, a two-dimensional map is generated by the SOM tool and is reviewed with the objective of looking at those occurrences where inspections led to the apprehension of illegal entries and eventual arrests. Different clusters are created by the SOM ranging from low- to moderate- and high-alert status. Those instances were scored in a scale from 0 to 100 with the higher values indicating arrest (see Figure 6.6).

This tool, called SOMine is from Eudaptics, a data mining company from Austria (http://www.eudaptics.com/home/index.html). It supports the further exploration of the clusters it discovered. For example, the dark cluster on the left side of the map, which represents illegal detentions, can be marked and extracted as a text file (see Figure 6.7).

Figure 6.7 *The cluster of arrests can be marked and exported to a file.*

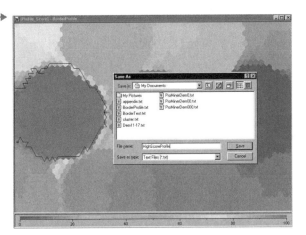

In other words, a sub-set of the data can be cut out and pasted as a separate database. This new data set will represent only the dark cluster of detections that led to "arrests."

The user can mark and extract the dark cluster, exporting it into a spreadsheet for further analysis. In the spreadsheet of highly scored smugglers, we can further explore a range of factors about these individual accounts, such as their average number of days (84) since the Social Security Administration issued a number to them or the average number of trips abroad (3) and average number of wire transfers (5), etc.

However, this would only be the start of this type of investigative data mining analysis. Additional information can be associated to these records to further develop a profile of these individuals. For example, there are a host of other demographics from commercial data providers. There are also additional attributes that could be matched from other government databases, such as vehicle records and license information that could be associated to them. For example, what are the demographics of their neighborhoods at the zip-code and geo-code level. Are these individuals students? What are their median ages? What is the dominant gender? What are their income ranges? Through the use of a SOM, further clues and features can be developed for the creation of a profile about potential smugglers and their lifestyle and socioeconomic features.

6.10 Neural Network Chromatogram Retrieval System: A Case Study

During the course of researching this book, many ingenious and dramatic uses of data mining technologies were found. The following case study (presented in its original version) is a very important and new application of neural networks in the analysis of physical evidence as part of a forensic search for the signature of chemicals in an arson investigation. The criminalist that developed this quantitative analysis readily admits that it could not have been performed without the assistance of neural network technology. It represents a unique use of advanced-pattern recognition technology in the context of traditional forensics analysis. In this case study, a neural network is used to detect and discover from a clinical chemical forensic analysis the distinct profile of ignitable kerosene.

NNCRS

Developed by Matt Vona, Criminalist, Bureau of Forensic Service, California Department of Justice

Summary

This research will develop a Neural Network Chromatogram Retrieval System (NNCRS), an automated means of chromatogram profile (or chemical fingerprint) comparison and retrieval unlike any that currently exists. This technology will be used in the comparison and retrieval of ignitable liquid profiles. Ultimately, this technology could be applied to more than arson analysis. The technological advances made here could lay the groundwork for applications used for explosives, other chemical profiles, impression evidence, infrared spectrometry, near infrared, and even biological protein or macromolecular signature analysis. The ability of neural networks to judge degrees of similarity based on pattern recognition while remaining independent of scaling, rotation, or symmetry will allow us to comprehensively reference an unlimited database of chemical signatures. Neural networks have already been applied and tested elsewhere in mainstream industry. It is now time that forensic applications are able to gain from these advances.

This white paper details a research proposal for exploring the application of NNCRS to volatile liquids analysis. We will develop this neural-network–based system of chromatographic signature comparison and retrieval. Simultaneously, through a co-operative, we will develop a system of collecting and redistributing a standards database from a large number of laboratories for use in case work comparison. Ultimately, we will have developed a deliverable NNCRS product, capable of being plugged into many applications across many forensic disciplines.

Background

The number and variety of ignitable liquids encountered in case work is increasing, as new and varied petroleum products enter the market place. The matrixes, or background materials, are often manufactured using the same volatile/ignitable liquids analysts detect. New adhesives, plastics, flooring, and other products are among many being introduced to the market place, which contain trace amounts of ignitable liquids. Recently a study presented at the Technical Working Group for Fire and Explosives (TWGFEX) symposium in Orlando, Florida demonstrated that some forms of newsprint contain ignitable liquid components.

The significance of an ignitable liquid being present in any fire debris sample is becoming increasingly unclear to the forensic analyst. In volatile liquid proficiency tests administered to 44 arson analysts located around the nation by the Proficiency Test Program of the International Forensic Research Institute at Florida International University in May of 2001, 18 of 44 analysts reported the presence of an ignitable liquid when none was present. These errors occurred largely because many analysts detected trace components of a miscellaneous ignitable liquid in an unadulterated sample of linoleum. While the matrix present in the sample may have contained these components, the analysts were not able to differentiate between a background contaminant and the presence of an additional ignitable liquid.

An NNCRS would allow analysts to compare the ignitable liquid signature produced by their unknown to an exhaustive external reference database for comparison. The NNCRS would be capable of sorting through thousands of standard submissions collected on any number of analytical systems from around the world. The neural network could then alert analysts to the possibility that their unknown profile is similar to the pyrolysis products of a particular type of matrix or even the low weight profile of a little known mixture. Analysts taking the proficiency mentioned above would have been alerted to the potential contribution of the linoleum matrix to their results and, thus, avoided writing a misleading report.

The laboratory analysis of fire debris typically involves the following steps:

1.   Obtain a sample of the fire debris, which is believed to contain residues of an ignitable liquid.

2.   Use one of several methods to extract the ignitable liquid from the debris.

3.   Analyze the extracted ignitable liquid on a gas chromatograph, mass spectrometer.

4.   Interpret and classify the unknown ignitable liquid through comparison of the results to a comparable standard.

Because of variations that could occur in steps 1 to 3, the data produced from any one standard or unknown is never identical from one laboratory, analyst, or instrument to another. Neural networks, like analysts, are able to recognize similarities. This unique ability allows them to recognize patterns independent of slight changes in instrumentation or despite the presence of pyrolysis products. Because they are automated, neural networks are simultaneously able to comb through a very large number of possible references and return a small number of likely matches to the analyst.

Research History

Our research began as part of the California Methamphetamine Signature Program. Chromatograms, unlike mass or infrared spectra, cannot easily be searched using conventional technology. Because of retention time changes, impurities, and variations in column length, two chromatograms of the same mixture of substances will often differ. This difference confuses conventional technology. Thus, a computer program was developed which was capable of

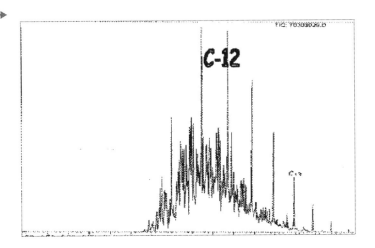

Figure 6.8
Example given to the neural network. The C-12 denotes the position of dodecane.

searching a large database of chromatograms versus an unknown chromatogram.

Arson was chosen as the field with which to initiate this research because of the large amount of readily available data. Neural networks were explored because of their ability to match patterns despite a large amount of actual difference and signal noise. A neural network application was developed, specifically to look for matching chromatograms. The neural network was tested by giving it an exemplar chromatogram and having it search a reference database of over 400 reference chromatograms. The preliminary results were very exciting. Figure 6.8 illustrates the exemplar chromatogram, Figures 6.9 and 6.10 illustrate the matching reference chromatograms, and Figure 6.11 illustrates the next closest nonmatching reference chromatogram.

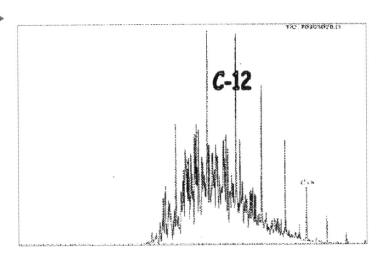

Figure 6.9
One of the two matches found by the neural network. The C-12 denotes the position of dodecane.

Figure 6.10
A second match found by the neural network. The C-12 denotes the position of dodecane.

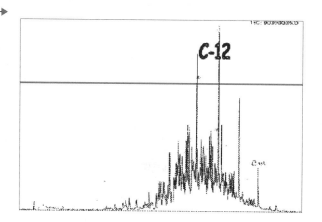

The neural network found an identical chromatogram and a very "closely related" chromatogram as possible matches out of 400 other unrelated chromatograms. By "closely related," we mean that the unknown's profile was very similar to the example. This is important, because other variations due to different instrumentation and sampling techniques from lab to lab will not be masked from the computer. The neural network can identify all "closely related" chromatograms and give the analyst a chance to further evaluate a smaller list of possible matches more thoroughly.

Notice that the second matched chromatogram (Figure 6.10) only extends out to C14. One may see this variation in different samples, but also in the same sample analyzed at two different labs. The neural network has demonstrated the ability to recognize similarity. Most computer programs could only match a chromatogram to an identical chromatogram. Further, the network's next closest nonmatch (Figure 6.11) was also a kerosene petroleum distillate type, but it was sufficiently different to be excluded from any further serious consideration.

The positive impact of the neural network's ability to make subtle distinctions without relying on identically formatted digital information is far reaching.

One of the first logical consequences for arson analysis is that the neural network could recognize a weathered sample as being similar to a nonweathered sample. For instance, the "unknown" chromatogram on which the network was trained (Figure 6.8) shows a distillate distribution with the highest peak of C11. The second matched chromatogram (Figure 6.10) shows a distillate with the highest peak at C12. Such variations can occur with weathering and other variations and could be readily explained or excluded by a trained analyst. It is important to note that while this technology will assist an analyst

Figure 6.11
The closest non-match found by the neural network. The C-12 denotes the position of do-decane.

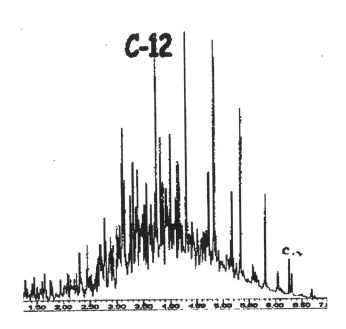

Figure 6.11
The closest non-match found by the neural network. The C-12 denotes the position of dodecane.

in comparing the sample to a large database, it can never operate independently of an experienced analyst.

A second consequence could be that the neural network could recognize that two samples are similar, even though different techniques were employed to collect data from one volatile liquid. As an example, the first matched chromatogram (Figure 6.9) shows a slightly left-tilted Gaussian peak distribution with a hydrocarbon peak distribution from about C9 to peak C17, and the highest peak at C11. The second matched distillate (Figure 6.10) doesn't extend out quite this far. Such variations can occur with differences in sampling techniques. Remember that the neural network's purpose is merely to narrow down a much larger list of chromatograms for the analyst to review, so it would preferably include too many exemplars, as opposed to too few.

This preliminary assessment has demonstrated a basic proof of concept. A neural network can recognize the subtleties in patterns generated by volatile substance analysis. While this test is not in any form a complete study, it has demonstrated a capability, which must be further evaluated by this research project.

6.11   **Neural Network Investigative Applications**

For the investigative data miner the power of neural networks comes from their ability to learn from experience, from samples of historical evidence collected in a criminal scene or instance. A neural network learns how to identify patterns by adjusting its weights in response to data input. This learning, as we have seen, can occur with a neural network via a supervised or an unsupervised setting. With supervised learning, which is the most typical, every training sample has an associated known output value. The difference between the known output value and the neural network output value is used during training to adjust the connection weights in the network (Hecht-Nielsen, 1990).

With unsupervised learning, which usually involves a SOM or Kohonen neural network, clusters are found in the input data that are close to each other based on a mathematical definition of distance. Self-organizing feature maps (SOFMs) transform the input of random values into a two-dimensional discrete map subject to a topological (neighborhood-preserving) constraint. In either case, after a neural network has been trained, it can be deployed within an application and used to make decisions or perform actions when new data is presented. For the investigative data miner, this means new crimes can be detected and patterns of crimes can be discovered. This does not mean that networks can replace investigators or criminalists; they are simply a new set of forensic tools.

Empirical studies have shown that neural networks can be paired with other techniques and technologies, such as genetic algorithms and fuzzy (continuous) logic, to construct some of the most powerful tools available for detecting and describing subtle relationships in massive amounts of seemingly unrelated data. As more and more crime is committed in our digital, interconnected environment, the criminal investigators and intelligence analysts of the future will need to rely on powerful new tools, such as these, that capture the nuance of criminal acts and potential threats to our security.

System intrusion, fraud, and other cybercrimes are just new types of digital crime spawned by the Internet and computers. In the following case study, a SOM is used by an innovative investigator to cluster the criminal modus operandi of perpetrators, which could apply to any type of criminal activity. We present the case study in its original version and would like to thank Inspector Rick Adderley for its contribution and permission to use it. It is worth noting that prior approaches, both manual review of cases and the use of an expert system, did not yield the type of success that resulted from the use of this data mining analysis.

6.12   Modus Operandi Modeling of Group Offending: A Case Study

By Richard Adderley and Peter Musgrove[1]

This paper looks at the application of data mining techniques, principally the multi-layer perceptron, radial basis function, and self-organizing map, to the recognition of burglary offenses committed by a network of offenders. After progressing through the data preparation stages, it is possible to suggest a list of currently undetected crimes that may be attributed to those offenders.

The data was drawn from four years of burglary offenses committed within an area of the West Midlands Police. The data was encoded from text by a small team of specialists working to a well-defined protocol and analysed using the multilayer perceptron (MLP), radial basis function (RBF), and Kohonen self-organizing map (SOM) tools of SPSS/Clementine. Three months of undetected crimes were analysed through the Clementine stream, producing a list of offenses that may be attributed to the network of offenders. The results were analyzed by two police sergeants not associated with the development process who determined that 85% of the nominated crimes could be attributed to the network of offenders. To produce a manual list would take between 1.5 to 2 hours and be between 5% and 10% accurate.

Introduction

Today, computers are pervasive in all areas of business activities. This enables the recording of all business transactions, making it possible not only to deal with record keeping and control information for management, but also via the analysis of those transactions to improve business performance. This has led to the development of the area of computing known as data mining (Adriaans and Zantinge 1996).

The police force like any other business now relies heavily on the use of computers, not only for providing management information via monitoring statistics, but also for use in tackling major serious crimes (usually crimes such as armed criminality, murder, or serious sexual offenses). The primary techniques used are specialized database management systems and data visualisation (Adderley and Musgrove 2001). However, comparatively little use has been made of stored information for the investigation and detection of volume crimes, such as burglary. This is partly because major crimes can justify greater resources on grounds of public safety, but also because there are rela-

1.   Inspector Richard Adderley, West Midlands Police, West Bromwich Police Station, West Bromwich, B70 7PJ, England, e-mail: r.adderley@west-midlands.police.uk. Dr. Peter Musgrove, University of Wolverhampton, School of Computing and Technology, 35/49 Lichfield Street, Wolverhampton, WV1 1EL, e-mail: P.B.Musgrove@wlv.ac.uk.

Figure 6.12
The CRISP-
DM
methodology.

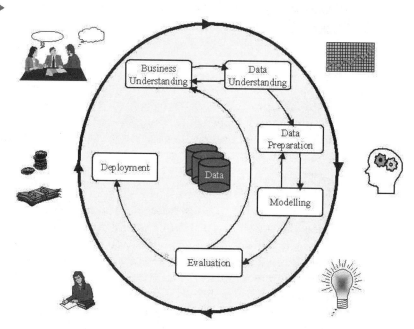

tively few major crimes, making it easier to establish links between offenses. With volume crimes, the sheer number of offenses, the paucity of information, the limited resources available, and the high degree of similarity between crimes render major crime analysis techniques ineffective.

There have been a number of academic projects that have attempted to apply AI techniques, primarily expert systems, to detecting volume crimes, such as burglary (Lucas 1986 and Charles 1998). While usually proving effective as prototypes for the specific problem being addressed, they have not made the transfer into practical working systems. This is because they have been stand-alone systems requiring the duplication of data inputting as they do not integrate easily into existing police systems. They tended to use a particular expert's line of reasoning with which the detective using the system might disagree. Also, they lacked robustness and could not adapt to changing environments. All this has led to wariness within the police force regarding the efficacy of AI techniques for policing.

The objective of the current research project is, therefore, to evaluate the merit of data mining techniques for crime analysis. The commercial data mining package SPSS/Clementine is being used in order to speed development and facilitate experimentation within a Cross Industry Platform for Data Mining (CRISP-DM) methodology (see Figure 6.12).

Clementine also has the capability of interfacing with existing police computer systems. The requirement for purpose-written software outside the Clementine environment is being kept to a minimum.

In this paper, the authors report the results from applying three specific data mining techniques: the multi layer perceptron (MLP), radial basis function (RBF) and the Kohonen self-organizing map (SOM) to the building descriptions, *modus operandi (*MO), and temporal and special attributes of crimes attributed to a network of offenders for a particular type of crime, domestic and commercial burglaries.

An MLP (Swingler 1996) is a supervised classification technique, which has the ability to form categories based upon learning from examples within the data. Using known data (for example, detected crimes) which are separated into a training set and a testing set, the network is trained on the former and tested on the latter, which it has not seen. An RBF (Broomhead and Lowe 1998) is similar, but operates on more localized data using a two-stage approach. The first stage recognizes patterns, and the second places those patterns in clusters of similar data. An SOM (Kohonen 1982) is an unsupervised technique that uses the many variables in the data set (multi-dimensions) and recognizes patterns to form a two-dimensional grid of cells. This technique has similarities to the statistical approach of multidimensional scaling. The output from all of these techniques is a confidence level between zero and one; the greater the value, the greater the confidence in the classification process.

The benefits of extracting a formal structure from the free-text MO field and using this structure in the mining process are discussed together with the stages of data selection, coding, and cleaning. The results achieved by this process were independently validated by two police sergeants, who were not part of the research team; they are discussed, together with further areas for research.

The two validating sergeants are Community Safety Bureau staff in the area of the West Midlands Police in which the target network of offenders mainly operates. These bureaus are the focal points on each command unit for strategic planning, operational tasking, and intelligence. The two sergeants have been working in this environment for a number of years and are highly experienced.

Business Understanding

The traditional view of offenders operating together revolves around the hierarchical gang structure, having a leader, several lieutenants, and a number of lower operatives. This may hold true for the more serious structured crime, such as illegal importation of drugs, but when this percolates to the street level, the formal gang structure no longer exists. For a whole range of crimes,

Figure 6.13
*Primary
network of
offenders.*

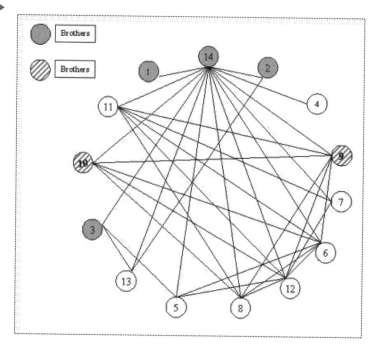

groups of offenders work together for a common purpose; they form a network of people that more resembles an organic structure than a hierarchical gang structure. There is no "Mr. Big" for the entire network.[2] Figure 6.13 illustrates a group of 14 offenders who have worked extensively together. The numbered circles represent individual offenders and the connecting lines represent codefendant instances [people who have been arrested and charged for the same offense(s)]. It is interesting to note that family membership (blood ties) appears to be important in these networks.

Within the network illustrated in Figure 6.13, offenders 2, 3, 4, 7, 8, 9, 10, 11, and 14 all have burglary offenses recorded against them, and it appears that they commit their offenses together in different combinations of people. For example, 14 has committed six offenses with 2, four with 7, eight with 10 and 11, etc. None of the offenders have a standard MO; however, they do favor particular types of buildings, use a finite variety of methods to gain entry to most of those buildings, and have a slight preference for an individual day of the week for committing their crimes.

When an offender has been arrested for an offense and brought into custody, the person is interviewed regarding that offense and any other similar offenses that may, as yet, be undetected. The interviewing officer will request

2.   Diagram produced courtesy of the West Midlands Police, Force Linked Intelligence System (FLINTS).

from the intelligence department a list of offenses that are similar to the one for which the person has been arrested with a view to questioning the offender and clearing further crimes. That is, the offender will admit his or her part in committing the crime, and it is recorded as being detected to that offender. The intelligence department will examine the base individual crime and then search through the crime system to locate those that have similar spatial, temporal, and MO features. This process can take between one and two hours depending on the complexity of the base crime. It is a semi-manual task requiring a SQL search and then manual reading of the retrieved documentation. The intelligence staff estimate that they are about 5% to 10% accurate in supplying a list for interview. This figure is based upon the actual number of offenses attributed to the offender during the interviewing process.

In preliminary previous work by the authors (Adderley 2001), it was shown that by examining a series of crimes committed by an individual offender, 11 previously unseen random crimes from this person could be recognized in the top 285 from over 3,500 detected crimes in the South of Birmingham. This was without using spatial or temporal variables. By using these additional variables and examining the working practices of a group of offenders, it was believed that the accuracy would improve.

Offender Behavior

Before the results of the encoded offender behavior can be utilized it is important to understand the current research relating to criminology and its relevance to the data set in question.

Routine activity theory (Cohen and Felson, 1979; Felson 1992; Clarke and Felson 1993) requires that there be a minimum of three elements for a crime to occur: a likely offender, a suitable target, and the absence of a suitable guardian. Offenders do not offend 24 hours a day committing crime. They have recognizable lives and activities, for example, go to work, support a football team, and regularly drink in a public house. They have an awareness space in which they feel comfortable, which revolves around where they live, work, socialize and the travel infrastructure that connects those places.

It has been stated that crimes against the person, such as rape, homicide, and assault, occur closer to the offender's home than property crime, such as burglary (Brantingham and Brantingham 1991; Rhodes and Conly 1991). However, the authors have established that offenders who commit sexual crimes commit their crimes further from home than burglary offenders (Adderley and Musgrove 2001). Based on two years of burglary crimes in a district of the West Midlands Police area, the average distance that a burglary offender traveled from his or her home address varied between 1/2 mile and 2 1/4 miles, depending upon age (see Figure 6.14). Sampling a random 60% of

Figure 6.14
Distance chart.

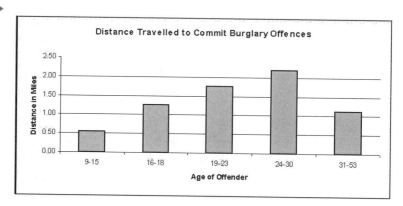

recorded offenders from the major crime (sexual offenses) Violent Crime Linkage Analysis System (ViCLASS) database who only commit offenses within the borders of a single force, the average distance from their home address was 4.11 miles.

The rational choice perspective (Clarke and Felson 1993) states that committing a crime is a conscious process by the offender to fulfil his or her commonplace needs, such as money, sex, and excitement. For example, an offender within the system has committed 22 offenses of burglary, the MO being indecent assault of the female occupant, but not theft. By these actions, he is fulfilling two of the stated needs, sex, and excitement.

Data Understanding

The burglary database used in this study contained 23,382 recorded offenses that occurred between January 1997 and February 11, 2001. Table 6.2 shows the specific crime categories and the numbers of offenses associated with each.

There are a total of 4,159 offenses that have been detected to a variety of offenders representing 17.79% of total crime. This includes 214 crimes attributed to a known network of offenders (Primary Network) representing 0.92% of the total crime and 5.15% of all detected crime. When compared to the detected crimes, Table 6.2 clearly shows that the Primary Network offenders' profile is to target shops and petrol filling stations, but not to attack sheds and offices.

There are limitations with the data set that should be recognized prior to the research:

Table 6.2   *Classification of Burglary Offense*

	Drinking Places	Dwellings	Factories	Garages	Offices	Sheds	Shops	Other	Total
All Offenses % of Total	642 2.75%	11,394 48.73%	1,387 5.93%	406 1.74%	939 4.02%	4,004 17.12%	1,640 7.01%	2,970 12.70%	23,382 100%
All Detected % of Total	77 1.95%	2,294 58.15%	195 4.94%	70 1.77%	143 3.62%	306 7.76%	361 9.15%	499 12.65%	3,945 100%
Primary Detected % of Total	5 2.34%	126 58.88%	10 4.67%	11 5.14%	4 1.87%	2 0.93%	48 22.43%	8 3.74%	214 100%

- Even though the data set is complete, it contains all reported offenses of burglary; it is possible that unsolved crimes held within the database may be attributed to one of the known offenders.

- Although people who have received the same training have input the crimes, there are inconsistencies in the transcription process, which will be discussed later in the paper.

- It has to be assumed that the known offenders have actually committed the crimes that have been attributed to them.

Data Preparation

The quality of the data is directly proportional to the results of the mining process. With a small number of persons responsible for transcribing and entering the data, it was assumed that the quality of the data would be high. However, there are inconsistencies within the subsequent transcription particularly within the MO entries. Table 6.3 illustrates an example of free-text MO information.

Number 3 does not state how the doors were forced, what rooms were searched, or the mode of search. Numbers 2, 3, 4, and 5 do not state whether the premises were occupied. Number 4 does not state the location of the room in which the computers were located, whether the removal was tidy, or whether the room was ransacked.

When a paper crime report is completed, the MO is written in unstructured free text, which is subsequently entered into a computerized recording system. From each of the 21 operational command units (OCUs) within the

Table 6.3   *Modus Operandi Text*

1	OFFENDER APPROACHED SECURE UNOCUPPIED DWELLING IN RESIDENTIAL AREA WENT TO REAR OF PREMISES AND FORCED REAR ROUND FLOOR PATIO DOOR BY BENDING METAL FRAME WITH JEMMY TYPE INSTRUMENT REMOVING DOOR FROM FRAME ENTERED AND MADE UNTIDY SEARCH OF ALL ROOMS DEFECATED IN FRONT UPSTAIRS BEDROOM CARPET STOLE ITEMS AND MADE OFF EXIT AS ENTRY
2	OFFENDERS UK APPROACHED SEMI DETACHED HOUSE AND KICKED FRONT DOOR FORCING ENTRY ENTERED AND SEARCHED ALL ROOMS OFFENDERS HAVE STOLEN TV VIDEO CASH CHEQUE BOOKS OFFENDERS HAVE LEFT PARCEL SHELF FROM AN UK CAR A CHILDS PRAM CHILDS BIKE AND BLANKET OUTSIDE FRONT OF HOUSE OF DRIVEWAY MAKING GOOD ESCAPE
3	BTN STATED TIMES OFFENDER FORCED FRONT DOORS ENTERED AND STOLE PROPERTY LEFT VIA WAY ENTERED
4	PERSONS U/K WENT TO REAR OF FACTORY PREMISES CUT THROUGH METAL BARS SMASHED INNER GLASS ENTERED OFFICE AND STOLE COMPUTERS
5	SMASHED GLASS IN FRONT DOOR REACHED IN & RELEASED RIM LOCK ENTERED MADE UNTIDY SEARCH OF BEDROOM STOLE PROPERTY

West Midlands Police, there can be up to 200 police and civilian personnel writing the text and a further five persons entering the data onto the system. With no guidelines indicating the language to be used, the variety of wording and spelling is vast. A structured encoding method would aid automatic investigation and detection methods. However, to introduce such encoding would incur a cost to alter the existing paper and computer recording systems. In this paper, software has been used to encode certain aspects of free-text data fields. Due to the nature of these fields, even after the encoding process, the data was not 100% clean. It would be preferable if such data was encoded at the time of inputting as encountered in a previous study involving serious sexual assaults (Adderley & Musgrove 2001). This study will demonstrate the benefits of using suitably encoded volume crime data.

Missing Data

There are a number of fields that do not contain data that are stored in the database as "$null$" or as an empty string. These mainly relate to location information. If an address is incorrectly entered into the system an 'unconfirmed location' is registered, which permits the crime to be recorded, but an operator will manually enter the correct information when time permits. These are often subsequently left blank.

It is not uncommon for data sets to have fields that contain unknown or incorrectly entered information and missing values. How should they be treated? Are those fields essential to the mining process? There are a number of methods (Weiss and Indurkhya, 1998) for treating records that contain missing values:

- Omit the incorrect field(s)

- Omit the entire record that contains the incorrect field(s)

- Automatically enter/correct the data with default values (e.g., select the mean from the range)

- Derive a model to enter/correct the data

- Replace all values with a global constant

Within this work, those crimes that did not contain post code or grid reference information were omitted from the spatial analysis.

Data Encoding

A critical step within the data mining process is the way in which data is encoded. It is suggested that the central objective of this stage is to transform the base data into a spreadsheet-type format where individual variables are identified or created/derived from combining or extracting information from the data set (Weiss and Indurkhya, 1998).

The data was encoded in four sections. Temporal analysis determined the times of day and particular days of the week for which the offenders showed a preference. Spatial analysis indicated the geographical base of the offenses. A large number of building types were analyzed and categorized into a small number of sets. The MO itself was sub-classified into a further three sections.

Temporal Analysis

Certain offenders have a propensity to offend within certain hours of the day and on particular days of the week. The detected crimes were compared against the crimes attributed to the Primary Network to ascertain whether there were similarities or differences between times and days.

Temporal analysis presents problems within the field of crime-pattern analysis due to the difficulty of ascertaining the exact time at which the offense occurred. There are generally two times that are relevant: the time that the building was secured and the time that the burglary was discovered, the from time/date and the to time/date. This duration of time may span two or more days, adding to the complexity. Analysis indicated that individual hours of the day did not appear to be relevant in determining a pattern of offending; it was more important to ascertain a time period. For example, many offenses

Figure 6.15
*Crimes by time
of day.*

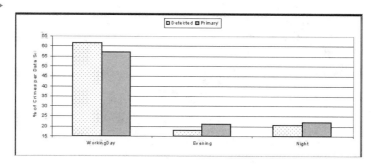

are committed during the working day when the occupier is not at the premises; however, the time period may be relevant to the type of premises attacked.

Figure 6.15 illustrates that the Primary Network has a slight preference, in comparison to the detected crimes, for offending during the evening and night-time periods. In this study, "Working Day" means between 0700 hours to 1900 hours, "Evening" means between 1900 hours and 2200 hours, and "Night" means between 2200 hours and 0700 hours.

Figure 6.16 shows the percentage of crimes that were committed by day of the week. It clearly demonstrates that the Primary Network has a preference for offending on a Tuesday, in comparison to the mass of detected crimes.

In order to weight the differences illustrated by Figures 6.15 and 6.16, the percentage rates of the detected crimes were subtracted from the Primary Network rates to give a figure that represents the importance of the temporal offending pattern relating to the Primary Network.

Figure 6.16
*Crimes by day of
week.*

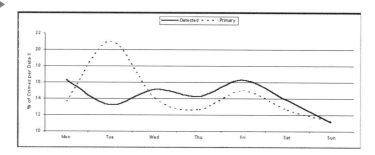

Figure 6.17
Spatial analysis.

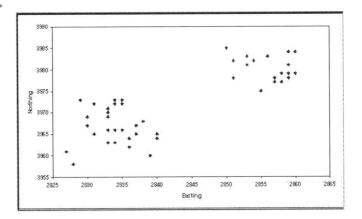

Figure 6.17
Spatial analysis.

Spatial Analysis

Using all past and present home addresses as anchorage points, the Primary Network commit 84.3% of their burglary offenses within 500 meters of their own or immediate coaccuseds' addresses. The spread of these addresses represents approximately 10% of the West Midlands Police Force area. Therefore, the geography of crime is an important factor in determining an offender's pattern of offending.

The six figure eastings and northings refer to the British Ordnance Survey grid referencing system, which is used by West Midlands Police and is accurate to one meter. The grid reference integer is truncated to four figures, reducing the accuracy to 100 meters, and that fourth digit is rounded up or down to either a 5 or 0, which reduces the accuracy to the required 500 meters. It is the 500-meter grid that is used in this work. The RBF network node was utilized to generate scores relating to the location of crimes according to their 500-meter grids. The function was able to identify and cluster areas of the map as illustrated in Figure 6.17, and the new field relating to the grid reference score was created combining individual variables into a single nominal category.

Building-Type Analysis

There are 72 individual building descriptions available for use. Many crimes are quite opportunistic (Clarke and Felson 1993), whether a motivated offender chooses a detached, semi-detached, or terraced house often depends upon the person's awareness space and the opportunities presented at the time. Within the current data set it did not appear that the specific type of premises was relevant, but by amalgamating groups of premises, those groups then became more relevant. Therefore, the 72 individual premise types were categorized into eight sets.

Comparing all detected crimes with those committed by the Primary Network, there is an indication that the Primary Network has a preference, in comparison to all detected crimes, for attacking factories, drinking places, and petrol filling stations. The new building-type field was created combining individual variables into a single nominal category.

MO Analysis

As stated in the "Data Encoding" section above, data encoding is a critical stage in the mining process. For this study, the MO was classified in three sections: which part of the building afforded entry; the method of entry to the premises; and whether the premises was alarmed, including how the alarm was circumvented. The first section derived four new fields: main entrance, rear door, front window and rear window. the second section derived six new fields: smashed glass, damaged lock, used vehicle (to gain entry, e.g., ram raiding), implement, forcing door, and insecure. The third section derived three new fields: premises alarmed, alarm disabled, and alarm activated.

It is during the data-preparation stage in the CRISP-DM cycle that a variety of encoding techniques may be utilized to provide additional fields for analysis and to enable fuzzy concepts.

Model Building

The 4,159 detected crimes, including those committed by the Primary Network, were separated into two sets, one for training and the other for testing. After removing the crimes that were not geo-coded, the training set comprised 916 crimes, 163 from the Primary Network and 753 from the remaining detected crimes. An MLP was used to create a model that recognized those crimes committed by the Primary Network. To test the efficiency of the network, the testing set comprised 44 unseen crimes from the Primary Network and 3,029 other unseen detected crimes. A measure of effectiveness was the number of Primary Network crimes that appeared in the top 20 index for the testing set—that is, the crimes with the highest confidence level. It was decided to use only 20 crimes, as this is the maximum amount that could be evaluated within a reasonable time by the two sergeants.

Building on previous work by the authors (Adderley and Musgrove 1999), a further level of refinement to the modelling process was used. Features of the MO, spatial, and temporal analysis from the Primary Network crimes were used in a Kohonen SOM algorithm to cluster the similarities. It has been suggested that the number of cells in the grid should be equivalent to the number of instances of the input data (Ripley 1996). If the clustering process was

Figure 6.18
Schematic data flow.

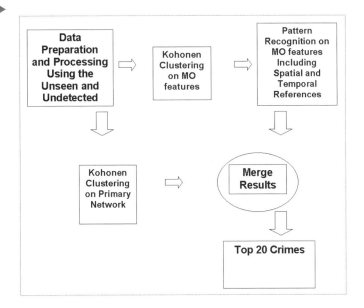

unsuccessful, there would be one crime in each of the cells. A 15 x 14 grid was used in this process, the resulting model producing a set of XY coordinates relating to the clusters.

Figure 6.18 illustrates the flow of data through the mining process. The new undetected crimes are preprocessed, as described in the "Data Encoding" section and assigned one of the 500-meter grid references. The data is then passed through the Kohonen model, assigning a cell XY coordinate for each new crime using the combination of the temporal, spatial, building, and MO analysis. The following MLP model assigns a confidence level as to the accuracy each crime achieves in relation to the Primary Network's detected crimes. Included within this model is the ability to assign a value of importance to the spatial attributes of each crime. This set of data is merged with a Kohonen network that has been trained on the detected crimes, thereby identifying all undetected crimes that are similar to those that have been committed by the Primary Network offenders.

A list of crimes was produced, together with the level of confidence for each crime as to its similarity to the Primary Network. Only the top 20 crimes that matched were utilized in the following process.

Validation

The "Business Understanding" section above describes the process of compiling a list of appropriate crimes that is required to prepare for interviewing suspects in custody. The results of the modelling process were a list of 20 crimes that were submitted to two sergeants who were involved in the supply of intelligence but were not part of the development process. Their remit was to ascertain whether any of the 20 crimes could have been committed by one of the Primary Network members. They had no other information. The sergeants researched the crimes already attributed to the offenders by examining the crime reports, case papers, and witness statements, and then examined each of the 20 submitted crimes in a similar way.

In their opinion, 17 of the 20 crimes could have been committed by one of the Primary Network offenders. Of the three remaining, one crime had a very similar MO, but the suspects' car did not contain any of the Primary Network members. The other two crimes had subtle differences in MO and type of property attacked.

The results are encouraging. After extracting the three-months crimes into Clementine, a list for interview could be prepared within five minutes, and 85% of the list was potentially relevant. This compares with manually researching recent crimes taking between one and two hours and only being between 5% and 10% accurate, as stated in the "Business Understanding" section.

To formalize the validation process, it would be ideal to give the two sergeants a set of randomly produced crimes for analysis, together with the top-20 list, and compare their results; however, time constraints on operational police resources prohibit this level of formality. The actual results obtained have been quite flattering, which indicate, at this stage, that formal experiment is unnecessary.

Discussion and Conclusions

The limitations identified in the "Missing Data" section, cannot be overstated; however, the results are not disappointing, and they have two practical uses in operational policing:

1. This process provides the ability to examine a number of currently undetected crimes with a view to targeting the intelligence gathering and investigative work toward a limited number of potential offenders.

2. Having arrested an offender, there is a requirement to collate information and intelligence prior to interviewing. From taking between one and two hours to provide a list for interview manually and only being 5% to 10% accurate, this process has reduced the time to approximately five minutes, providing an 85% accuracy rating.

The benefits of data mining software have been clearly demonstrated in operational police work.

How good are the two sergeants in assessing the crimes? Since the 20 crimes had been examined, three have now been detected. Of those three, the assessors originally stated that, in their opinion, one crime could not be attributed to the Primary Network and the other two could. They were correct in their assessment of that single crime. Of the two currently detected crimes that were originally assessed and attributed to the members of the Primary Network, one was committed by a member, the other was not. However, the MO used in the wrongly assessed crime was very similar to the other correctly assessed crime. This indicates that the two sergeants' assessment of the 20 crimes is quite accurate.

It is desirable to achieve a higher level of accuracy and widen the scope of practical implementation; the modeling process has been tailored to a particular network of offenders. Further work is required in the following areas:

- Using the types of property stolen within the modeling process
- From the free-text MO field, encoding a generic set of variables, which would cover the entire set of MO features
- Choosing a different network of offenders to ascertain whether the techniques are transferable

Data preparation, the use of a structured encoding method for MO analysis, was discussed, but the cost of altering computer-based systems has to be justified. This study used such a structured approach and was able to demonstrate time-saving benefits, together with aid in the crime investigation process.

The authors suggest this approach contributes to best value in policing.

References

Adderley, R. and Musgrove, P. B. (1999), *Data Mining at the West Midlands Police: A Study of Bogus Official Burglaries*. BCS Special Group Expert Systems, ES99, London, Springer-Verlag, pp. 191–203.

— (2001) "Data Mining Within the West Midlands Police: A Study of Bogus Official / Distraction Burglary Offenses." M.Phil. to Ph.D. Transfer Report, University of Wolverhampton.

— (2001), "General Review of Police Crime Recording and Investigation Systems. A user's view." *Policing: An International Journal of Police Strategies and Management* 24(1) pp. 100–114.

— (2001), "Data Mining Case Study: Modelling the Behaviour of Offenders Who Commit Serious Sexual Assaults," ACM Special Interest Group on Knowledge Discovery and Data Mining *Proceedings: Seventh ACM SIGKDD International Conference on Knowledge Discovery and Data Mining, August 26–29 2001, San Francisco*: Association for Computing Machinery Inc.

Adriaans, P. and Zantige, D. (1996) *Data Mining*: Addison-Wesley.

Brantingham, P.L. and Brantingham, P.L. (1991), "Notes on the Geometry of Crime," In *Environmental Criminology*, USA: Wavelend Press, Inc.

Broomhead D. S. and Lowe D. (1998), "Multi-variable Functional Interpolation and Adaptive Networks." *Complex Systems,* 2 pp. 321–355.

Chapman, P., Clinton, J., Kerber, R., Khabaza, T., Reinartz, T., Shearer, C., and Wirth, R., (2000), *CRISP-DM 1.0 Step-by-Step Data Mining Guide*, USA: SPSS Inc. CRISPWP-0800.

Charles, J. (1998), "AI and Law Enforcement," *IEEE Intelligent Systems,* Jan/Feb pp. 77–80.

Clarke, R.V. and Felson M. (1993), "Introduction: Criminology, Routine Activity, and Rational Choice" In *Routine Activity and Rational Choice: Advances in Criminological Theory, Volume 5*. Clarke, R.V. and Felson M. (eds.) New Jersey: Transaction Publishers.

Cohen, L.E. and Felson, M. (1979), "Social Change and Crime Rate Trends: A Routine Activity Approach." *American Sociological Review,* 44 pp. 588–608.

Felson M. (1992), "Routine Activities and Crime Prevention: Armchair Concepts and Practical Action." *Studies on Crime and Crime Prevention*, 1 pp. 30–34.

Kohonen T. (1982), "Self Organizing Formation of Topologically Correct Feature Maps," *Biological Cybernitics*, 43(1), pp. 59-69.

Lucas, R. (1986), "An Expert System to Detect Burglars Using a Logic Language and a Relational Database." In *Fifth British National Conference on Databases*, Canterbury.

Rhodes, W.M. and Conly, C. (1991), "*The Criminal Commute: A Theoretical Perspective in Environmental Criminology,*" USA: Wavelend Press, Inc.

Ripley, B.D. (1996) *Pattern Recognition and Neural Networks.* Cambridge University Press,

Swingler, K., (1996) *Applying Neural Networks.* San Francisco: Morgan Kaufman Publishers.

Weiss, S.M. and Indurkhya, N. (1998), *Predictive Data Mining: A Practical Guide.* San Francisco: Morgan Kaufman Publishers.

6.13   False Positives

In the movie *Minority Report* the mythical Precrime Department is able to foretell homicides before they occur and arrest perpetrators before they commit crimes through a process of previsualization. However, something goes wrong and the leading character (a precrime officer) becomes the wrongly accused suspect: he becomes a false positive. A *false positive* is a false alarm or false detection and is part of making predictions and classification. Models are not perfect and neither are the neural networks that they are constructed from. Care must be taken to ensure that rigorous testing takes place during the construction of predictive models from neural networks to ensure that false positives are minimized and innocent individuals are not wrongly accused of crimes.

In this chapter we have described several case studies demonstrating the ability of neural networks to predict at-risk police officers, identify potential smugglers, discover the signature of arson, and associate modus operandi to a network of criminals. While this is encouraging, many more applications await where neural network and other technologies can and will be used to intercept terrorists and discover patterns of criminal activity. Care, however, must be taken to ensure that the privacy and legal rights of individuals are not violated and that models are within the law of the land. The technology should be used to ensure that false positives are reduced, rather than increased, and that law-abiding citizens are protected from perpetrators.

As more and more information about individuals becomes available on-line, the need for robust and reliable means of verifying identity also increases. One of the technologies that is receiving considerable attention in the aftermath of 9/11 is biometrics—the use of the physiological traits or characteristics of individuals as a basis for recognizing and confirming a person's true identity. Neural networks are the core technology of these pattern-recognition engines used in fingerprint and facial recognition, retinal scanning, voice-prints, and even the monitoring of keystroke typing patterns or handwriting stroke patterns.

Man has from the beginning of time survived by recognizing the features and traits of his enemies, using the best available weapons, which today include neural networks. In addition to individual identification, ubiquitous Internet connections require that organizations whose internal computer systems connect to the Web also be prepared to prevent malicious or unwanted intrusion into internal systems or open public sites. Neural networks can be used to learn patterns of acceptable packet contents and arrival rates and, thus, serve as a dynamic security firewall.

6.14   Neural Network Tools

The current neural network tools are highly developed, unlike the software products of prior years, which were crude and required an extensive amount of labor to get the inputs and outputs out of them in a usable format. Today's commercial neural network products range from small, inexpensive programs to very sophisticated software suites costing thousands of dollars. Some of the current products have very intuitive interfaces, with most having the ability to generate code, such as C or Java, which can be incorporated into other applications. To obtain more information on these tools, the reader should go to Knowledge Discovery Nuggets (http://www.kdnuggets.com), a leading data mining portal. Today's neural network tools automate what once was a manual trial-and-error process of adjusting settings and preparing of the input and output data; a listing of some of these software products follows.

Attrasoft

http://attrasoft.com

Attrasoft is one of the most innovative neural network companies in the marketplace, providing a host of image recognition and pattern-recognition technologies. Its facial recognition product is highly accurate, versatile, and capable of searching millions of images, easily handling over a terabyte of data. Attrasoft has specialized in image recognition and pattern recognition since 1995. Their basic products are software components sold for licensing fees or complete software products sold as a package. Their core neural network software package is DecisionMaker.

DecisionMaker uses two files, the training data set, which it calls the problem database file, and a testing data set. The training file basically teaches DecisionMaker about the classification problem; the test file is then used to evaluate the model. Attrasoft also uses its proprietary algorithms to provide image, sound, and facial recognition products and services, all of which operate on the basis of their neural network technology.

BioComp

http://www.bio-comp.com

BioComp's *i*Model is a desktop tool for creating predictive models with automated optimization capabilities; using what it calls "mesh" technology. The *i*Model uses a genetic algorithm to optimize the model construction processes by performing searches through alternative model types, structures, and combinations of input variables. *i*Model works with delimited text files, Microsoft Excel workbooks, and Microsoft Access databases and has wizards for preparing and loading data. The *i*Model Professional and Enterprise versions support access to Oracle, SQL Server, and other relational databases. BioComp also sells modeling servers.

COGNOS 4Thought

http://www.cognos.com

4Thought is the neural network tool from Cognos, a company that primarily sells on-line analytic processing (OLAP) business reporting software. The tool supports every step of the analysis process, including data collection, transformation, exploration, and model creation. 4Thought can use data from the other Cognos data component including Impromptu, Powerplay, and Scenario, as well as external data sources like Microsoft Excel. It can automatically identify and omit anomalies and can also augment the data by creating new fields like ratios and percentages.

BrainMaker

http://www.calsci.com

NetMaker is a fairly solid product that has been around since 1985 and has sold over 25,000 copies; it is a very reliable back-propagation neural network tool. At its Web site, literally hundreds of applications are documented. NetMaker facilitates the building and training of neural networks by importing data from multiple formats, including ASCII, binary, and other text or numeric data. The spreadsheet-like interface allows the user to organize and preprocess raw data with column shifts, arithmetic operations, moving averages, moving medians, and more. The professional version of this tool has all the features of the standard BrainMaker, plus additional functions supporting larger data limits and providing the ability for more extensive automated training and tuning capabilities, plus a runtime license and more extensive graphics.

An optional component, the Genetic Training Option (GTO), applies a genetic algorithm to optimize the neural networks built with NetMaker. Following Darwin's theories of genetic mutation and natural selection, GTO automatically creates a large number of subtly different networks to do the

Figure 6.19
Panes allow the user to visualize the network training results.

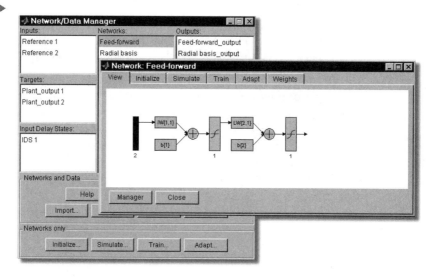

same job. GTO then trains, tests and ranks them to find the network that performs best overall. Once a good network is found, its "genes" are mutated to create another "parent" network. These two networks are then used as parents to create yet another "child" through genetic crossover techniques. When children perform better than their parents, they are saved as evolutionarily superior "beings" and are used for producing even better generations of networks. This represents one of the most advanced features of today's neural network tools.

MATLAB Neural Net Toolbox

http://www.mathworks.com/products/neuralnet/

This toolbox provides a complete set of functions and a GUI for the design, implementation, visualization, and simulation of neural networks. This tool allows for the construction of different neural network architectures, including multilayer perceptrons, radial basis function, and SOM via the use of simple tabs in a graphical interface. It supports a comprehensive set of training and learning functions. The *STATISTICA Neural Networks* can be purchased as a stand-alone application or as an add-on to the MATLAB main statistical product software package.

The tool contains a comprehensive selection of neural network methods with automatic wizards; a C-code generator add-on is also available for exporting the results into production applications. This tool, as with other more advanced neural network products, is entirely icon-based and has an extremely easy-to-use user interface (see Figure 6.19). MATLAB, as with other vendors such as NeuralWare and SPSS, offers on-site training services.

NeuroSolutions

`http://www.nd.com`

NeuroSolutions is NeuroDimension's base product. This neural network software combines a modular, icon-based network design interface with an implementation of advanced learning procedures, such as recurrent back-propagation and back-propagation time series. NeuroSolutions is a complete neural network package, currently in Version 4.2, that the company claims any novice can use for creating clustering or classification models.

The "feel" of NeuroSolutions is unique. The interface consists of electronic circuit components, such as resistors, capacitors, and transistors, which are laid out on a breadboard and wired together to form a circuit. NeuroSolutions provides a wizard to build a neural network "circuit" automatically. Neural components, such as axons, synapses, and gradient search engines, are laid out to form a neural network; input components are used to inject signals, and probe components are used to visualize the network's response. The tool provides a wide range of flexibility in designing models from scratch.

A demo shipped with the tool shows how a character-recognition problem can be developed in which the input to the network is a set of 24 x 18 images of handwritten digits. Each image has a corresponding desired output, the box on the right, which is an encoding of the digit that the image represents. The unsupervised portion of the network uses a principal component analysis (PCA) on the images. The features extracted from this preprocessing stage are then fed into a multilayer perceptron (MLP), which uses back-propagation to perform the image classification. This network has been trained to a relatively low error rate, such that the network closely matches the desired output. Note that the network classified the "5" correctly in the output box, but it also found that the image had some characteristics of the numbers "6" and "3" due to their similarity in shape (see Figure 6.20).

The wizard that comes with the software makes the creation of predictive models a process involving half a dozen clicks. Many features of this tool automate the process of data preparation and the selection of the appropriate neural network architecture. This is done through a NExpert component that automates the model creation process through a sequence of simple dialogs, which for the first-time data miner makes this tool very appealing.

NeuralWare

`http://www.neuralware.com`

Figure 6.20
Training to
recognize the
number 5.

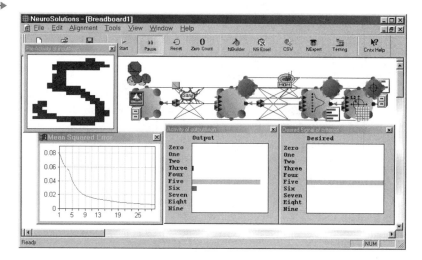

NeuralWare is one of the oldest neural network companies in the world. Founded in the mid 1980s along with HNC and Nestor, these three firms were the pioneers in the modeling software industry. Their *Professional II/ PLUS* is in Version 5.5, making it an established and comprehensive neural network development system. Professional II/PLUS is available for UNIX, Linux, and Windows operating systems on a variety of hardware platforms with data and network files being fully interchangeable. The Professional II/ PLUS package contains comprehensive documentation that addresses the entire neural network development and deployment process, including a tutorial, a guide to neural computing, standard and advanced reference manuals, and platform-specific installation and user guides. NeuralWare also provides considerable training for individuals interested in using their products. They also offer consulting services, as do most other neural network vendors.

NeuralWare's proprietary InstaNet facility allows quick generation of a neural network based on any one of 28 standard neural network architectures described in neural network literature. After a network is created, all parameters associated with it can be directly modified and customized to reflect more closely the classification or clustering problem of the user. Professional II/PLUS includes advanced features, such as performance-measure-based methods to inhibit over-fitting, automatic optimization of hidden-layer size, and the ability to prune hidden units.

As with the more advanced neural network packages in today's marketplace Professional II/Plus also contains an *Explain* facility that indicates which network inputs most influence a network output. These sensitivity reporting features and instruments allow today's software vendors to point out that neural networks are no longer the *blackboxes* that they were in the past. In addition to a wide variety of built-in diagnostic monitoring tools, Professional II/PLUS provides an interface through which user-written programs can supply input data and process neural network outputs. The *Designer Pack™* is an extension component to NeuralWorks Professional II/PLUS that can be used to generate C source code.

For beginners, NeuralWare also offers its Predict product, which can be run as an add-on to Microsoft Excel. Predict automatically analyzes input data to identify the appropriate data transform. It partitions the input data into training and test sets, selects relevant input variables, and then constructs, trains, and optimizes a neural network for a variety of classification problems. Predict allows for rapid creation and deployment of prediction and classification applications by combining neural network technology with genetic algorithms, statistics, and fuzzy logic for investigative and security small-scale or experimental applications.

ProForma

http://www.proformacorp.com

Founded in 1994 by mathematicians and programmers from Stirling University in Scotland and originally known as Neural Innovation, this firm's core neural network product is ProForma. To use ProForma, you follow this simple "by the numbers process" according the company:

1. Select a source of data, which will form the base of your solution.

2. Select the factors you wish to predict and those you wish to predict them with.

3. ProForma will now check the data, warn you of and help you to solve any problems, and build a solution that is capable of making the predictions you require.

4. You can then use this solution in a number of ways:
   - To make predictions from new events as they happen, or recognize new events as belonging to the same class as certain previous events
   - To perform dry runs of scenarios to see what would happen before you implement new plans
   - To calculate the set of actions required to optimize a given system
   - To analyze the relationships between the different variables and increase your understanding of the data

■ To embed the solution in another piece of software via an application programming interface (API) call to a dynamic link library (DLL) or Java program

In a sense, ProForma mimics the role of human experts, who learn that certain events lead to certain other events, make predictions based on what they have learned, and modify their behavior to try to improve the predicted outcomes. ProForma does this too, although this tool has exclusively been used in business intelligence and marketing applications. With some minor modifications, it can also be used for investigative analyses of criminal activity. For example, an insurance company client doubled its rate of detection of fraudulent claims using this tool, according to the company. The system also consistently detected 74% of fraudulent cases, with a similar system identifying the most risky 10% of policy holders.

SPSS Neural Connection

http://www.spss.com/spssbi/neuralconnection

Neural Connection is an SPSS stand-alone neural network package. It enables a novice user to build predictive models without training in statistics or AI. SPSS also offers neural networks components in its data mining flagship product Clementine, which will be covered in another chapter. Neural Connection includes the following architectures: Multilayer perceptron (MLP), radial basis function, Bayesian neural network, and the Kohonen (SOM) network. Neural Connection also provides the user with some of the standard statistical processes, such as multiple regression, closest class mean classifier, and principal component analysis techniques.

The tool provides data-management features, such as viewing descriptive statistics of a database to performing transformations (e.g., the creation of ratios or splitting a database into training and testing partitions). This interface, as with most of the advance generation of neural network tools, is graphically presented, requiring no programming or knowledge of statistics. A unique What If? utility enables the user to explore the results of the models interactively and graphically. It can also reposition two variables in the analysis to see how the change affects the model's outcome. The user can create specialized models for specific needs by combining the modeling and forecasting tools, such as the creation of committees of models for a combined set of predictions.

STATISTICIA Neural Networks

http://www.statsoftinc.com/stat_nn.html

This is a comprehensive, flexible, and powerful neural network package, featuring pre- and post-data processing, including data selection, nominal-value encoding, scaling, normalization, and missing value substitution, with interpretation for classification, regression, and time series problems. This neural network tool also comes with a wizard interface it calls the *Intelligent Problem Solver*, which can walk the user through a step-by-step process in creating a variety of different networks and choosing the network with the best performance. This is a state-of-the-art data mining product from a statistical software company with extensive experience in data modeling.

The tool also has an *Input Feature Selection* component for automating the selection of the right input variables for exploratory data analysis. The tool supports a wide variety of neural network architectures and combinations of networks architectures of practically unlimited sizes. It has comprehensive graphical and statistical feedback that facilitates interactive exploratory analyses. Because this tool is produced by a statistical software company, integration with the *STATISTICA* main system is supported, including direct transfer of data and graphs. As with most high-end neural network tools, code can be generated for integration with embedded solutions using other programming languages.

A Neuro-Genetic Input Selection component uses a genetic algorithm to automatically search for optimal combinations of input variables, even where there are correlations and nonlinear interdependencies. *STATISTICA Neural Networks* includes a Principal Components Analysis component to extract smaller numbers of dimensions from raw data inputs. The tool also includes automatic data scaling and recoding for both inputs and outputs. For classification problems, you can set confidence limits, which the tool uses to assign cases to classes.

Ward Systems

http://www.wardsystems.com

The NeuroShell tool from Ward Systems is another package that has been around since the mid-1980s. This tool has a very simple and clean interface, making the process of constructing a predictive model using neural network and genetic algorithms a very easy task. Ward System provides a variety of classification tools based on their neural network technology, including the following packages:

- *NeuroShell Predictor.* This is Ward Systems' core product for forecasting and estimation problems.

- *NeuroShell Classifier.* This professional system learns historical patterns to categorize or classify data.

- *GeneHunter.* This optimizer component uses genetic algorithms to find optimal solutions for many modeling problems.

- *NeuroShell Engine.* This is the package for creating an API from the Predictor and Classifier tools.

As seen in these product descriptions some of the more advanced neural network products incorporate yet another AI technique to optimize their design and performance: they use genetic algorithms (GAs). GAs are a programming mechanism based on a evolutionary method of computation founded by Dr. John Holland from the University of Michigan. GAs are an ingenious method of arriving at solutions and optimizing the performance of neural networks and are analogous to the way nature evolves by mutations and evolution in its "survival of the fittest" architectural design. GAs optimize their performance through a trial and error process by evaluating the correctness of their solutions to gradually improve their outputs.

6.15 Bibliography

DARPA (1988), "DARPA Neural Network Study," AFCEA International Press.

Fausett, L. (1994), *Fundamentals of Neural Networks: Architectures, Algorithms and Applications*, Upper Saddle River, N.J.: Prentice Hall.

Haykin, S. (1994), *Neural Networks: A Comprehensive Foundation*, New York: Macmillan.

Hecht-Nielsen, R. (1990), *Neurocomputing*, Reading, Mass.: Addison-Wesley.

McCord Nelson, M. (1991), *A Practical Guide to Neural Nets*, Reading, Mass.: Addison-Wesley.

7

Machine Learning: Developing Profiles

7.1   What Is Machine Learning?

As we have seen, there are a variety of AI technologies for combating crime. One of the most promising of them for the investigative data miner is machine-learning algorithms. These software programs can be used to develop profiles of perpetrators through a combination of decision trees and conditional IF/THEN rules. Unlike neural networks, which are at times difficult to decipher, using machine-learning and statistical algorithms like Classifier version 5 (C5.0), chi-square automatic interaction detection (CHAID), or classification and regression trees (CART), conditional constructs of criminal attributes and features can be extracted from large databases. For more information about the machine-learning technology go to http://www.mlnet.org.

The outputs from these and other machine-learning algorithms are highly descriptive in their classification of a desired solution, such as the conditions leading to criminal acts like fraud, or the attributes and features of criminals. For example, using one of these types of machine-learning algorithms, an analyst can generate a set of rules, such as the following one for profiling a potential smuggler at a point-of-entry border crossing:

```
IF Vehicle Make is CHEVROLET,
AND Year of Vehicle is 1998,
AND No Insurance Listed for Vehicle,
AND Lien Holder is Owned,
THEN there is
06.34% chance that Alert is Low
18.32% chance that Alert is Medium
75.33% chance that Alert is High
```

The rules are generated from an analysis of thousands of observations leading to a list of conditions (IF/AND) and a prediction (THEN) with a probability value associated to it (75.33%). The rules from these types of data mining analysis may be viewed as a ratio of conditions, which when combined lead to a predicted outcome with an associated probability. For investigative data mining, these types of machine-learning algorithms can lead to a wide range of criminal analyses and applications.

7.2   How Machine Learning Works

Machine-learning algorithms are engines of insight. They can be used by investigative data miners to predict the probability of crimes and to profile criminals from large databases into statistically significant clusters or segments. They automate the process of statistical operations and can provide a graphical breakdown of a database by mapping key clusters. Like neural networks they need to operate on samples of legal versus illegal transactions or criminals versus legitimate individuals. However, unlike neural networks, the output, in the form of either rules or graphical decision trees, is easy for humans to comprehend.

Each machine-learning algorithm operates somewhat differently on the data. The process, however, is basically the same: segment and classify the data based on a desired output. The operation is one of breaking down a data set through a process similar to the game of 20 Questions. For example, in the potential smuggler rule, a series of questions are posed against the data, so that the algorithm can begin to understand what attributes are the most important in determining a profile of a potential high alert. In this case, it is the vehicle type, along with the year of the vehicle, the lack of insurance, ownership, etc. How they interrogate the data differs somewhat; however, the end result is almost always the same. They cut down the features or conditions to a few precise clues.

Some of the most popular algorithms include CHAID, CART, and C5.0. CHAID was designed to detect statistical relationships between variables in a database and is restricted to the analysis of categorical types of data attributes, such as low, medium, and high, so that it might be used to rate the probability of a crime or the matching of a terrorist profile. CART was designed to measure the degree of diversity of variables in making its splits. CART looks to see which variable is the best splitter in a dataset. For example, it may look at all the makes of automobiles in order to find which models are most likely to be used to smuggle contraband at a border inspection point of entry. C5.0 measures the amount of information all the variables in a data set provide and ranks them in order of importance. The prominent Dr. J. Ross Quinlan devel-

Figure 7.1
Decision tree used to predict probability of smuggling by make of auto.

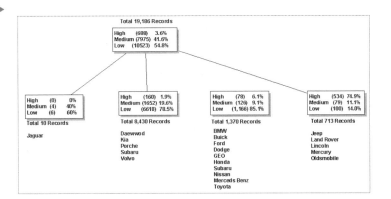

oped C5.0. The algorithm is one of the first learning systems capable of generating rules in the form of a decision tree.

7.3   Decision Trees

A decision tree is a graphical representation of the relationships between a dependent variable (output) and a set of independent variables (inputs), usually in the form of a tree-shaped structure that represents a set of decisions. The tree may be binary (only two branches) or multibranched, depending on the algorithm used to segment the data. Each node of the tree represents a test of decisions performed by the algorithm.

To demonstrate how this works, the following decision tree can be explained in this manner. In a database with 19,186 records, 10,523 instances where a search was made and nothing was found represents 54.8% of the samples and is classified as a low alert. There are also 7,975 instances where a search yielded some minor infraction after a search was conducted; this represents 41.6% of the samples and is classified as a medium alert. Lastly, there are also 688 instances where a search yielded a contraband arrest; this represents 3.6% of the samples and is classified as a high alert.

The top node of the tree represents all of these records, which show the total number of records (19,186). This then splits into multiple branches according to the model of the automobile in the database. This first branch indicates that of all the attributes (fields) in the database, the vehicle make is the most important one in predicting and targeting a potential smuggler (see Figure 7.1).

What is interesting from this decision tree is that the rate of high alerts, or arrest, increased from the 3.6% average to 11.1% when the make of the auto was Jeep, Land Rover, Lincoln, Mercury, or Oldsmobile. Conversely, when the make was Daewoo, Kia, Porsche, Subaru, or Volvo, the rate dropped to 1.9%. For Jaguar it was 0.0%. How could such a decision tree assist customs and immigration inspectors? Obviously, rather than inspecting 100% of the autos at a crossing, through this segmentation analysis, a more intelligent approach can be taken through the analysis of seized vehicles data and the investigative data mining techniques using machine-learning algorithms.

A decision tree partitions data into smaller segments called *terminal nodes* or *leaves* that are homogeneous with respect to a target variable, such as high alerts. Partitions are defined in terms of other variables, such as the vehicle make of an auto, and are called input variables, thereby defining a predictive relationship between the inputs (vehicle characteristics) and the target output the system is attempting to predict.

7.4   Rules Predicting Crime

The partitioning of data sets, such as this border alert sample, can be done autonomously by the software or by the user. For example, the analysts may want to split the data on the basis of a specific driver demographic or based on insurance coverage, rather than the vehicle type. Through this interrogation of the data, an investigator can create homogeneous groupings of potential smugglers and can learn to predict with greater certainty where conditions and the attributes of individuals increase the probability of a smuggling situation. More importantly, because the outputs of these types of algorithms are in graphical formats or rules, greater insight can be gained by analysts about smuggling conditions and smuggler attributes.

Machine learning by definition is rooted in AI and deals with the design, architecture, and application of learning algorithms. For the analyst, this translates to the use of proprietary and commercial data mining tools whose engines are based on machine learning for the segmentation and identification of crimes, such as fraud, as well as the construction of criminal profiles. Essentially, machine learning can be used to calibrate the probability of a crime, such as computer intrusion, money laundering, or smuggling, based on existing conditions. In the case of detecting automobiles with a probability of being used to smuggle drugs across a border point of entry, we demonstrated how decision trees can be used to detect these conditions. Machine-learning algorithms can also generate IF/THEN rules.

Envision this scenario: As an auto approaches an inspection point, the customs or immigration personnel key in the plate number, which is routed to a center where a set of IF/THEN rules resides, created using machine-learning algorithms. The rules themselves have been created using an assortment of information gleaned from department of vehicle registration and insurance records and even neighborhood demographics of individuals and automobiles that have been apprehended in the past attempting to smuggle various types of drug contraband.

```
Prediction Rule:
 HOUSEHOLD is LiveWithParents
 INSURER is 21stCentury
 YEAR is 1994
 OWNERSHIP is Owned
 MAKE is CHEVROLET


Prediction  # 1 : ALERT is High


Relevant rules:


1)    If  HOUSEHOLD is LiveWithParents
      and  INSURER is 21stCentury
      Then
      ALERT is High
      Rule's probability: 0.619
      The rule exists in 13 records.
      Significance Level:   Error probability <      0.01


2)    If  INSURER is 21stCentury
      and  MAKE is CHEVROLET
      Then
      ALERT is High
      Rule's probability: 0.944
      The rule exists in 68 records.
      Significance Level:   Error probability <      0.0001


3)    If  INSURER is 21stCentury
      and  OWNERSHIP is Owned
      Then
      ALERT is High
      Rule's probability: 0.755
      The rule exists in 253 records.
      Significance Level:   Error probability <      0.001


4)    If  INSURER is 21stCentury
      and  YEAR is 1994
```

Figure 7.2 *The Anti-Drug Network (ADNET).*

Stopping Traffic

Anti-Drug Network (ADNET)

```
Then
ALERT is High
Rule's probability: 0.625
The rule exists in 20 records.
Significance Level:    Error probability <        0.1
```

7.5   Machine Learning at the Border: A Case Study

This is a case study contributed by the MITRE Corporation.

A middle-aged man in a light blue Mustang is about to enter the United States from Mexico at one of numerous customs checkpoints along the southwest border. He's confident no one will suspect he's transporting more than 10 pounds of heroin in secret compartments within his vehicle; he's done it before and he plans to do it again—and again. But, a customs system operator at a site near El Paso, Texas uses the Anti-Drug Network (ADNET) system to access data on the driver and his car via his license plate (see Figure 7.2). It's just routine and takes a few moments.

The agent quickly learns—through a system that accesses a large data warehouse of information on crossings, seizures, and motor vehicles—that the driver makes this trip on a regular basis, at a regular time, but this trip is different. She decides it's worth her time and trouble to continue the inspection. Ten minutes later, she finds more than a dozen small packages of white powder; the drugs are seized and the driver is arrested.

Situations like this occur almost daily across the many ports of entry along the Mexican/U.S. border and other entry points into the United States. Sophisticated data-sharing systems developed by the ADNET community (i.e., Department of Defense, U.S. Coast Guard, Department of Justice, Department of State, Department of Treasury, Federal Communications Commission, and the intelligence community) give U.S. drug and law enforcement officials an arsenal of information needed to stem the flow of illegal narcotics and other dangerous substances into our country.

The MITRE Corporation is helping federal law enforcement agencies in the counter-drug community take advantage of the data that helps identify possible drug traffickers and trafficking activities. Through various mechanisms, the counter-drug organizations have access to an increasing amount of information. But the really difficult task is using that data to improve effectiveness. MITRE is providing data mining assistance for ADNET. The corporation cites the fact that what's needed now is a way for these groups to sift through all this data—most of it unimportant—and find the larger patterns, trends, and anomalies that ultimately lead to seizures.

To support this increased need for manageable information, MITRE computer scientists are providing high-level technical support in the areas of data mining and large-scale database management. In particular, MITRE is working on a now-fielded prototype targeting system that analyzes passenger vehicle crossing data and develops data mining rules and tools that help operators perform real-time analysis to identify potential counter-narcotics targets.

Today, this system is integrated into everyday enforcement as well as special operations. Data mining is being integrated into systems that automatically search through large amounts of data for meaningful and interesting patterns. The objective is to provide end users with a system that will quickly indicate if an individual coming into the United States is worthy of further inspection. The technology can be used to provide ways to search databases for links between individuals and organizations, which is useful for not only counter-drug operations but also counter-terrorism. The challenge for the counter-drug community is managing all this ever-increasing data—and developing the best ways to incorporate this technology into their operations.

The ADNET community uses high-performance workstations connected to the Secret Internet Protocol Router Network (SIPRNET) by routers or by secure data devices. There are approximately 140 sites and 350 workstations in the ADNET community. ADNET uses standard protocols (HTTP, SMTP, POP, etc.) to ensure interoperability across communities. More than 200,000 Web page hits per month occur among the 65 ADNETLINK servers (see Figure 7.3).

Figure 7.3
The ADNET control center.

7.6   Extrapolating Military Data: A Case Study

Using a rule-generating software package from WizWhy, a branch of the U.S. Navy developed intelligent applications for planning, discovery, and knowledge acquisition and recently received a grant from the Office of Naval Research. The grant gave this branch not only the ability to study new data surveillance and prediction software tools available on the market, but also the authority to determine their price/performance capabilities. Specifically, the Navy wanted to investigate a way to fuse volumes of data in a meaningful way in order to permit data cleansing, analysis, modeling, and prediction. However, the grant provided only a modest budget. This meant they needed to source a COTS product—the Navy's term for a commercial off-the-shelf product.

The Navy recognized that data mining is useful for condensing and extrapolating military information. Data mining helped them to make sense out of arrays of complex distributed heterogeneous sensors. As with many data mining analyses, their project began by collecting data and creating a database. Then, a data mining application was applied to reveal hidden patterns and relationships within the database. A set of rules was revealed explaining the data and issuing predictions for new cases. Based on the discovered rules, unexpected phenomena in the data were discovered.

WizWhy was used to mine those features and to explore, by feedback, the most important features. This in turn provided a better understanding of their working domain and, thereby, permitted the evolution of more complex systems that would otherwise have been impossible. Rule-based tools such as this one can be used to crack the knowledge acquisition bottleneck, which has impeded the growth and dissemination of knowledge-based technologies.

7.7   Detecting Suspicious Government Financial Transactions: A Case Study

The following data mining investigation describes work done under contract with the Federal Defense Financial Accounting Service by prime contractor EDS Corporation and subcontractors from the Federal Data Corporation, Elder Research, and Abbott Consulting.

As with most data mining projects, there were several steps undertaken by the analysts, starting with an understanding of the crime, followed by the establishment of goals. Next came the assembling of the data, an assessment of the challenges, the selection of a modeling strategy and algorithms, and the creation and testing of the models with the validation data set, culminating with some final observations and recommendations by the team of data miners.

7.7.1   Step One: Identify Investigative Objective

As with most data mining projects, the team begins by first understanding and clearly defining the scope of the criminal behavior and data mining problem. The client is well aware that there is a historical problem with intentional fraud in the vendor payment systems. Compounding the problem, however, as with most matters of criminal behavior, is that there is a limited number of known cases. Furthermore, the transaction data is incomplete for those known fraud cases. Then, there is the problem that fraud is often hidden in large sets of legitimate transactions.

7.7.2   Step Two: Establish Investigation Goals

The primary goal was to identify suspicious payments while maintaining a low false-alarm rate, a cost concern often associated with fraud detection models. This cost concern is due to a limited number of examiners to investigate suspicious payments. A secondary goal is to build a data mining process that can be generalized and reproduced for other applications and business questions within the agency. Lastly, the goal of knowledge transfer is desired, enabling the government to do the data mining process internally with its existing staff.

7.7.3   Step Three: Conduct Knowledge Discovery Process

This is the process in which the data miners spend time understanding the business methods involved. It is also the stage at which an understanding of

Figure 7.4
Eleven sets of training, testing, validation data (33 sets in all).

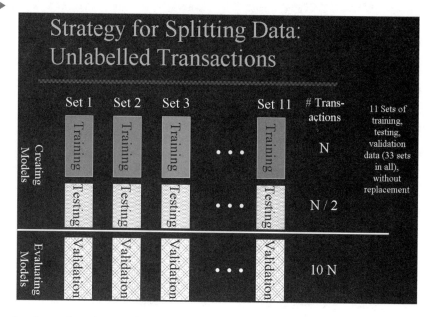

the data takes place and its preparation is performed. As part of this preparation, initial exploratory analyses are performed in order to refine the data preparation process for the creation of new models.

7.7.4 Step Four: Assess Investigation Challenges

In order to develop an effective data mining strategy, an assessment of the modeling challenges is performed at this juncture. First, the data set is a very large payment database with incomplete information in the vendor payment data file; this is a common problem when mining production data. In addition, payments are unlabeled and cannot be verified. Furthermore, there is a very small number of known fraud payments with instances of multiple payments from the same case. These conditions can lead to possible over-fitting or over-searching for models. To remedy these challenges, a three-stage process will be used for training, testing, and validation of the data sets. A cross-validation methodology will be used by creating several models with a variety of algorithms by different modelers who will use different data mining strategies.

7.7.5 Step Five: Set Strategy for Investigation

The main strategy was to create multiple structured and random samples for training and testing of fraud detection models. This called for 11 structured

Figure 7.5
*The data was
rotated in the
training, testing,
and validation
phases.*

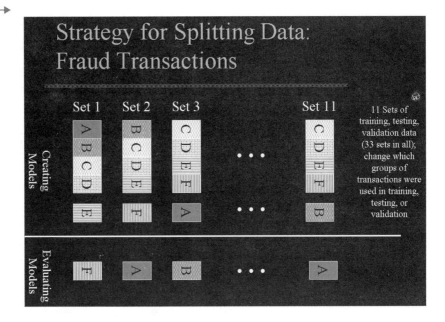

Figure 7.5
The data was rotated in the training, testing, and validation phases.

samples ("splits") for known fraud data, each with training, testing, and validation data subsets of 33 overlapping samples of fraud cases. In addition, 11 corresponding random splits were used with training, testing, and validation data subsets for non-fraud data of 33 non-overlapping samples of non-fraud (see Figure 7.4). The strategy employed used a small enough set of non-fraud data to make it unlikely that unlabeled "non-fraud" transaction were really being classified as "fraud"; this is a data balancing process. Next, multiple algorithms were used to construct the models using decision trees, rule induction tools, neural networks, and a priori rules. The strategy also called for use of multiple modelers, each assigned to work on different splits of the data. The objective was to generate hundreds of models and to keep the 11 best to create a model ensemble.

In addition to being split, the data was also rotated to ensure the validity of the models (see Figure 7.5).

7.7.6 Step Six: Evaluate Investigation Algorithms

Algorithms tend to have different error rates, based on the data sets in which they are used (see Figure 7.6). Empirical studies, such as StatLog, have demonstrated that the structure of the data influences the classification accuracy of algorithms, such as neural networks, regression, and decision trees.

Figure 7.6 *Five algorithms on six data sets yielded different results.*

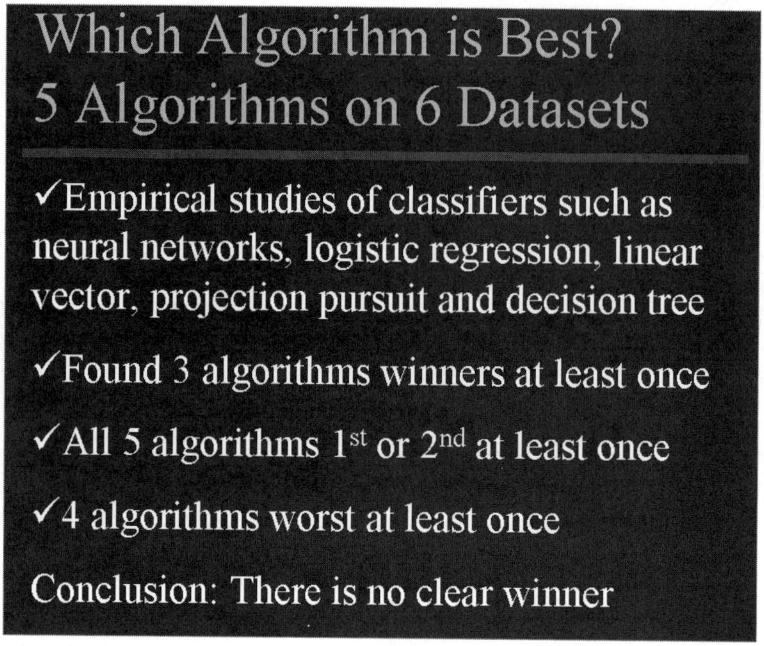

Which Algorithm is Best?
5 Algorithms on 6 Datasets

✓Empirical studies of classifiers such as neural networks, logistic regression, linear vector, projection pursuit and decision tree

✓Found 3 algorithms winners at least once

✓ All 5 algorithms 1st or 2nd at least once

✓4 algorithms worst at least once

Conclusion: There is no clear winner

7.7.7   Step Seven: Investigation Ensembles Are Selected

Because single-model synthesis can be difficult, algorithms search for the best model, but not exhaustively, either by decision trees, polynomial and neural networks, or logistic regression and because iterative algorithms converge to local minima, such as neural networks, the team agreed to use ensembles of models. Ensembles smooth out jagged decision boundaries and provide a means of eliminating errors from individual classifiers (see Figure 7.7).

Figure 7.7 *Model ensembles make decisions by committee of algorithms.*

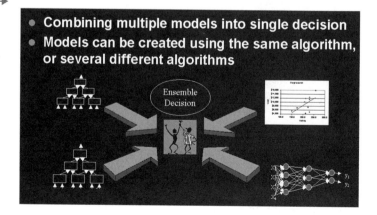

- Combining multiple models into single decision
- Models can be created using the same algorithm, or several different algorithms

Ensemble Decision

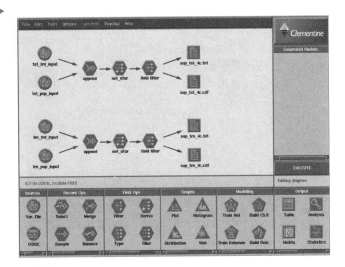

Figure 7.8
Data is prepared for mining.

7.7.8 Step Eight: Data Is Prepared

During the data preparation, some input and output data specifications are controlled via automated scripting. At the same time, some fields are removed prior to modeling, and some new features (ratios) are created (see Figure 7.8).

7.7.9 Step Nine: Models Are Created and Tested

Models are created on the basis of multiple criteria, such as fraud sensitivity and false alarm; they are assessed on the basis of their overall performance by weight, rank, and algorithm diversity (see Figure 7.9).

Figure 7.9
Model creation stream in Clementine.

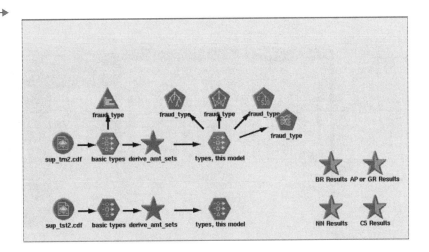

Figure 7.10
Results of final models.

Algorithms Used to Create Models Included in Final Combination		
Model #	Modeler / Split	Algorithm Type
1	Modeler 1, Split 8	Neural Network
2	Modeler 2, Split 5	Decision tree
3	Modeler 3, Split 7	Neural Network
4	Modeler 4, Split 9	Decision tree
5	Modeler 4, Split 8	Decision tree
6	Modeler 4, Split 11	Decision tree
7	Modeler 4, Split 11	Rule based
8	Modeler 5, Split 6	Neural Network
9	Modeler 6, Split 4	Neural Network
10	Modeler 6, Split 1	Neural Network
11	Modeler 1, Split 3	Rule based

Algorithm Performance Summary (Normalized, Higher is Better)			
Algorithm	Average Sensitivity	Average False Alarm	Average Total Score
Neural Network	2.9	1.1	6.9
Decision Tree	3.0	1.0	7.0
Rule Induction	2.3	3.1	4.2
Overall	2.9	1.4	6.4

The models are combined based on their scores in order to increase the robustness of their predictions (see Figure 7.10).

7.7.10   Step 10: Models Are Tested on Validation Data

The team found that the results were heavily dependent on which transactions were used for training, testing, and validation. Overall, however, the ensemble was the best classifier; the final result of the model was that 97% of known fraud cases were accurately detected in the validation data set sample (see Figure 7.11). The end result was that the models selected 1,217 suspicious payments for further investigation by the agency. Those inquiries are in progress.

Figure 7.11
Overall model score on validation data.

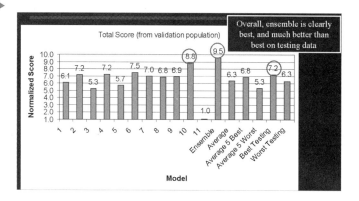

7.7.11   Conclusions of Investigation

In terms of performance, the team found that model ensembles mitigate risk compared to single-model solutions and that the ensemble, although not necessarily the best model, was always among the best, and rarely among the worst. They found that model ensembles were also able to identify key variables, attributes that are important for several models.

7.7.12   Future Directions

It was recommended that the data mining process be extended to include other operating locations through the reusability of these models. It was also suggested that prediction be prioritized on the basis of the dollar amounts of suspicious payments and that the results of examiners be improved in order to develop a methodology to integrate the entire process from data collection through examinations. Lastly, the team recommended that suspicious payment rules be deployed to prevent future fraudulent acts. The agency plans to convert the Clementine stream to C code.

As this case study demonstrated, it is very important to have the capability of developing and testing models using different algorithms in order to arrive at an optimum classification solution.

This case study was also presented at The Twelfth International Conference on Tools with Artificial Intelligence, Vancouver, British Columbia, November 13–15, 2000, by H. Vafaie, D.W. Abbott, M. Hutchins, and I.P. Matkovsky, under the title "Combining Multiple Models Across Algorithms and Samples for Improved Results." The author would like to thank and acknowledge Dean Abbott of Abbott-Consulting.com and Bill Haffrey of SPSS for sharing the material.

7.8   Machine-Learning Criminal Patterns

Digital crimes can take place in a variety of situations and through various methods of operation:

- Intrusion into computers or networks
- Insurance and health care crimes
- Money laundering
- Credit-card fraud
- Telecom fraud

- Identity theft
- NetFraud

Detecting these types of criminal activities follows a basic methodology, which, although they are not all inclusive, will generally follow these steps:

1. Evidence is gathered where criminal transactions have been discovered.

2. These transactions or observations are examined using a visualization tool.

3. Cross-referenced demographics or other third-party data that is relevant and appropriate is associated to these cases.

4. A link analysis or geo-mapping tool may be used to look for potential associations and trends in temporal and spatial dimensions.

5. A text mining tool may be used for the discovery of hidden concepts if large amounts of documents, HTML, e-mails, etc., are involved.

6. An intelligent agent may be used to retrieve and collate additional information to assemble with the criminal case from other networks or the Web.

7. A SOM network may be used to develop hidden clusters in the data, or a back-propagation network may be used to develop a model of the crimes.

8. The final phase of the process involves the use of machine-learning–based tools and techniques, as discussed in this chapter, for extracting rules and decision trees from the data for predicting crimes and profiling perpetrators.

One thing is certain. The process is rooted in pattern-recognition techniques and software tools with origins in AI. Not only are these tools ideal for combating these type of crimes, they can also be deployed to detect and deter terrorist attacks, such as those involving weapons of mass destruction and biological agents.

Detecting and deterring crime through data mining is particularly challenging due to several factors. First, although there is a vast amount of data available, there is usually only a small number of observations that represent criminal behavior, such as on-line fraud. In statistical terms, the distribution of the data is highly skewed. This fact is important to note because empirical studies of classification systems indicate that symbolic classifiers, such as those discussed in this chapter, are the most effective weapons for classifying highly skewed data sets.

Data mining is a tool for the human investigator. It does not replace the analyst responsible for the security of a system or for the detection of the criminal acts, although data mining assists analysts in sorting through hundreds of thousands of records enabling them to "connect the dots." For each type of crime, a data mining model has to be created in order for the analyst be able to detect its unique signature. Compounding this challenge is the fact that criminals are not stupid. They will intentionally modify their methods of operation; as such, a data mining detection system has to be adapted to recognize these new patterns constantly and continuously. Investigative data mining is a process, not a single-product solution.

Yet another challenge is that a data mining detection system needs to have a very fast response time in order to minimize the monetary losses and damages to systems and networks, individuals, and companies. For example, for the detection of credit-card and Internet fraud or system intrusion, real-time processing is necessary. However, this is not a problem that cannot be solved. Web mining for e-commerce is commonly done today for making real-time offers to consumers. The same type of Internet and wireless techniques and technologies can be used in conjunction with data mining models to detect and deter these types of crimes in real time.

Lastly, there are two types of errors in the detection and classification of these types of crimes: false alarms (false positives) and undiscovered cases (false negatives). Often an alert of a suspected crime needs verification by human personnel and may require special processing, such as putting a transaction in a special queue or status. A false positive needs special attention and time, while a false negative may cause further losses. In other words, the costs of both are different. However, in both instances, consideration must be given that doing nothing is the worst possible action and option facing a business, government agency, or law enforcement unit. The cost of doing nothing may, in time, be the most expensive option of all, especially in situations involving the destruction of trust, data, systems, property, and human life.

7.9   **The Decision Tree Tools**

Most machine-learning based software products are capable of generating decision trees or IF/THEN rules. Some are capable of producing both. The

Figure 7.12
*Alice decision
tree interface.*

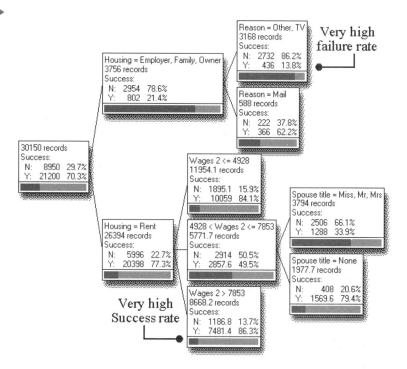

following software systems primarily produce decision trees. To obtain further information on these products, please proceed to their Web sites for white papers, demos, screen shoots, and evaluation copies of their software.

AC2

http://www.alice-soft.com

AC2 provides graphical tools both for data preparation and building decision trees. AC2 uses its proprietary machine-learning algorithm to tests all possible combinations from a data set to segment and discover the optimum criteria for converging on a selected variable (e.g., fraud versus legal). It ranks all relevant criteria along a graphical decision tree. An Example Editor allows the user to evaluate single data objects more closely. This software product is from France, but is available in the United States from its producer ISoft (see Figure 7.12).

Alice d'Isoft 6.0, a streamlined version of ISoft's decision-tree–based AC2 data mining product, is designed for individuals who are new to data mining (see Figure 7.13).

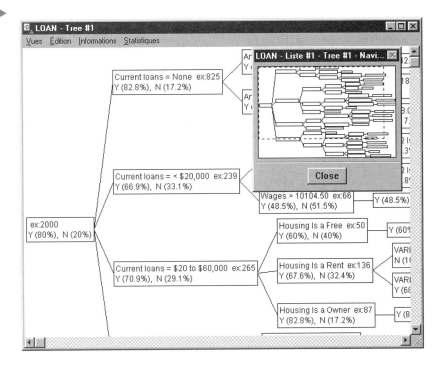

Figure 7.13
Alice d'Isoft 6.0 decision tree output.

Attar XperRule

http://www.attar.com/

XpertRule Miner provides graphical binary decision trees (two branch splits). The software is highly flexible and scalable, supporting workstation or server deployment. It can generate a variety of types of code from the trees it produces, such as COM+ Java, or XML for data exchange. Attar is a software firm from the United Kingdom, but all of its products have U.S. distributors.

Business Miner

http://www.businessobjects.com

Business Miner allows the user, with just a few mouse clicks, to build decision trees interactively that let them see the trends and relationships in any data set (see Figure 7.14). There's no complex algorithm tuning and no confusing technical terminology. The tool features a familiar, easy-to-use interface. Designed for the business analyst, it can be adapted for criminal investigation applications.

Figure 7.14
Business Miner decision tree interface.

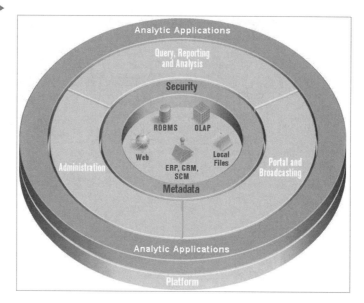

C5.0

`http://www.rulequest.com/`

C5.0 constructs classifiers in the form of both decision trees and rule sets. C5.0 includes the latest innovations, such as boosting for discovering patterns that delineate categories, assembling them into classifiers, and using them to make predictions. C5.0 has been designed to analyze databases containing hundreds of thousands of records and tens to hundreds of numeric or nominal fields. To maximize interpretability, C5.0 classifiers are expressed as decision trees or sets of IF/THEN rules, formats that are generally easier to understand than neural networks. C5.0 is available from its founder at the above site; it is also licensed to other vendors, such as SPSS and its Clementine data mining workbench, which is discussed later in this chapter.

CART

`http://www.salford-systems.com`

One of the most powerful data mining algorithms in the marketplace is CART, licensed and offered by Salford Systems. The algorithm was developed and refined over the years by several renowned statisticians, most notably Dr. Jerome H. Friedman from Stanford University. CART, like C5.0, can generate binary trees or IF/THEN rules. CART splits a node in its decision trees, which are exclusively binary, into two child nodes, always posing binary questions that have a "yes" or "no" answer. For example, the questions might be: is age <= 55? Credit Score <= 600? Or, Fraud <= 234?

Figure 7.15
*This is the
CART interface
for model setup.*

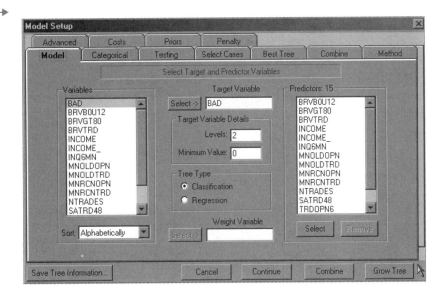

How does CART come up with the candidates for creating the splits in a data set for generating its rules? CART's method is to look at all possible splits for all variables included in the analysis. For example, consider a data set with 215 cases and 19 variables. CART considers up to 215 x 19 different splits for each variable in the data set for a total of 4,085 possible splits. Any problem will have a finite number of candidate splits, and CART will conduct a brute-force search through them all.

The CART algorithm has won the data mining contest for its accuracy; however, it is extremely demanding of computing power due to its brute-force search approach. One of the disadvantages of CART is that it works only with numeric data. This means categorical data, such as male or female, needs to be converted into something like male = 0 and female = 1, or high, medium, and low into high = 1, medium = 2, and low = 3. This requires some additional data preparation and rule deployment processing.

CART uses a software package DBMS/COPY, a data management utility to import data from virtually any format, which once loaded appears in the model setup screen. From there the target variable (the dependent field) that will be used to segment the data and all the other independent variables can be selected (see Figure 7.15).

Once the variables have been selected, tabs along the model setup can be selected so that, for example, the data can be split for training and testing via a random method or for partitioning according to a percentage of the file. This is how binary decision trees are generated by CART (see Figure 7.16).

Figure 7.16
The CART binary trees.

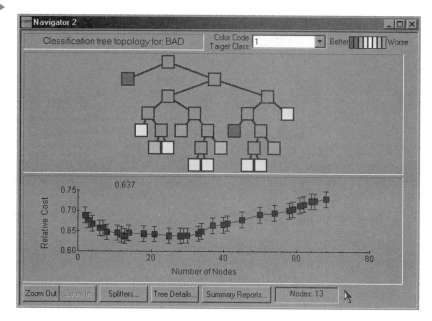

Once the decision trees have been created by CART, an assortment of charts and reports on the result of the analysis are available and accessible via tabs (see Figure 7.17).

The variables that are most important in the construction of a decision tree can also be prioritized and viewed (see Figure 7.18).

Figure 7.17
Lift charts for each class from the decision trees can be viewed.

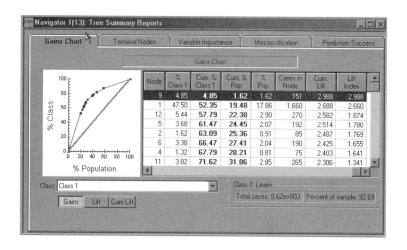

Figure 7.18
This instrument displays the variables of most importance.

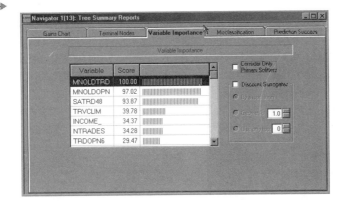

The tool can also report on the expected accuracy of the model, both on the training and test data sets (see Figure 7.19).

Rules can also be generated by CART directly from the data, the rules that CART is able to generate and export are in C programming format (see Figure 7.20).

Cognos Scenario

http://www.cognos.com/products/scenario/index.html

Cognos Scenario allows the user to quickly identify and rank the factors that have a significant impact on a database. The tool is specifically designed to spot patterns and exceptions in data and allows users to visualize the information being uncovered in graphs or classification trees. Scenario can also identify data variables that are not a factor for predicting such outcomes as fraud. The tool can also highlight data values that are unexpected and possibly incorrect, again a feature important for predicting fraud and data outliers. As with

Figure 7.19
The rates of prediction for training and testing classes can be viewed.

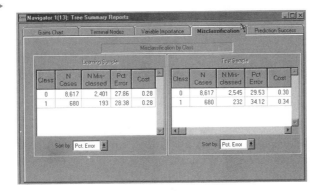

Figure 7.20
*Sample of
CART rules.*

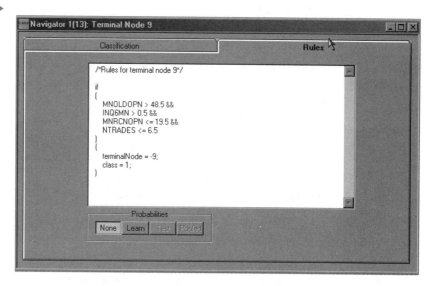

other software tools in this category, Scenario can be used to quickly and easily perform classification, segmentation, profiling, and outlier detection; it can also identify data points that are out of range, a key process in such criminal detection analyzes as money laundering. The user can drill down within factors to build a profile or choose from different views of the data: graphs, classification trees, etc. Query and reporting can be integrated with Cognos's other on-line analytic processing (OLAP) tools, Impromptu and PowerPlay.

Neusciences aXi DecisionTree

http://www.neusciences.com

Neusciences aXi DecisionTree uses ActiveX Controls for building decision trees. It can work with discrete and continuous data variables and can extract rules directly from the tree. The ActiveX component makes it easy to embed into other applications. It has four data preprocessing options, allowing the user to select the best one for his or her data. aXi has three different decision tree implementations and allows for the pruning and removal of unnecessary rules, which can be extracted in text format.

SPSS Answer Tree

http://www.spss.com/spssbi/answertree/

SPSS also offers their Answer Tree, an easy-to-use package that uses the CHAID algorithm as its decision tree engine; it includes decision tree export in XML format. SPSS also offers a decision tree component in its data mining suite, Clementine, based on the C5.0 machine-learning algorithm.

Free Trees

There are also some free decision tree software tools. Links to them may be found in the data mining portal kdnuggets.com (Knowledge Discovery Nuggets). They include the following:

- *C4.5*: the "classic" decision tree tool, developed by J. R. Quinlan. Available with restricted distribution from the master himself.

  `http://www.cse.unsw.edu.au/~quinlan`

- *EC4.5*: a more efficient version of C4.5; the predecessor of C5.0, which uses the best among three strategies at each node construction, made available from the University of Pisa.

  `http://www-kdd.cnuce.cnr.it`

- *IND*: Gini- and C4.5-style decision trees and more. It is publicly available from NASA with some export restrictions.

  `http://ic-www.arc.nasa.gov/ic/projects/`
  `bayes-group/ind/IND-program.html`

- *LMDT*: builds linear machine decision trees. Made available by Purdue University.

  `http://mow.ecn.purdue.edu/~brodley/software/lmdt.html`

- *OC1*: decision tree system with continuous feature values; builds decision trees with linear combinations of attributes at each internal node. Made available by Johns Hopkins University.

  `http://www.cs.jhu.edu/~salzberg/announce-oc1.html`

- *PC4.5*: a parallel version of C4.5 built with the Persistent Linda (PLinda) system. Made available by New York University.

  `http://cs1.cs.nyu.edu/~binli/pc4.5`

- *PLUS*: for constructing polytomous logistic regression trees with unbiased splits.

  `http://www.recursive-partitioning.com/plus`

7.10   The Rule-Extracting Tools

There are also tools for detecting crime and profiling that include the following software for classification using a rule-based approach. Keep in mind that some of these decision tree products, like CART, can also generate rules.

Figure 7.21
*SuperQuery
IF/THEN
dialog box.*

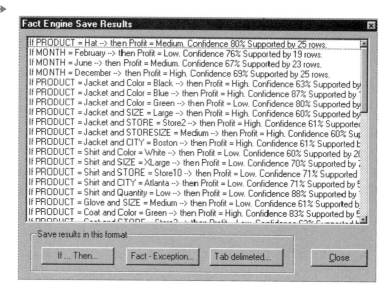

AIRA

http://www.godigital.com.br

AIRA from godigital is a rule discovery and visualization tool; it works as an add-on to Excel.

DataMite

http://www.lpa.co.uk/ind_top.htm

DataMite from Logic Programming Associate enables rules to be discovered in ODBC-compliant relational databases. DataMite will generate rules through a clustering process by combining elements using standard AND, OR, and NOT operators.

SuperQuery

http://www.azmy.com/

SuperQuery from AZMY Thinkware works with multiple data formats; this rule engine generator displays patterns in a database by reporting them as IF/THEN statements in a Fact Engine window (see Figure 7.21).

WizWhy

http://www.wizsoft.com/

WizWhy from WizSoft automatically finds all the IF/THEN rules in a database and uses them to summarize the data, identify exceptions, and generate predictions for new cases. This software can generate thousands of rules from a data set, so care must be taken in the setting of error rates. The higher the setting, the fewer rules the tool will generate. WizWhy uses a proprietary algorithm to generate its rules. Some additional features include the following:

- Performs Boolean as well as multivalue analysis

- Analyzes the data by discovering all the IF/THEN rules

- Reveals necessary and sufficient conditions (IF-and-only-IF rules)

- Calculates the error probability of each rule

- Calculates the best segmentations of continuous value fields

- Calculates the prediction power of each field

- Summarizes the data graphically by presenting the main rules and trends

- Reveals the interesting phenomena in the data by uncovering unexpected rules

- Predicts new cases on the basis of the discovered rules

- Explains predictions by listing relevant rules

- Calculates the prediction's conclusive probability

- Calculates the prediction's error probability

A session with WizWhy starts by importing a data set and completing a dialog box selecting the fields to be used in the analysis for generating the rules. In this case the BorderDemo.dbf data set has been prepared with IF/THEN rules used to predict the field ALERT. The fields that will be used to generate the rules are listed in the dialog box field grid (see Figure 7.22). Note that the

Figure 7.22
Alert is the field from which rules will be generated.

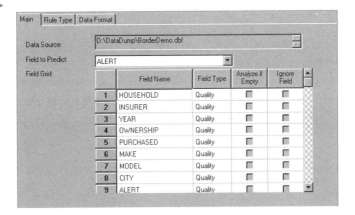

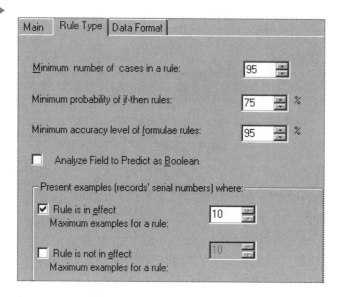

Figure 7.23
*This dialog box
in WizWhy
allows for the
setting of rule
parameters.*

user can exclude any field and can also analyze any field even if it is empty, an important feature in fraud detection analysis.

Next, some settings need to be set for the rules that will be generated. Note, however, that thousands of rules may be generated. With some trial and error, the user will begin to limit the rules that apply to the analysis (see Figure 7.23). Too few rules may yield little insight, while on the other hand thousands of rules will defeat the purpose of the data mining analysis.

Once the tool runs, the numbers of rules are shown and a report appears for the user from which various views can be performed. In addition, the rules can be exported via SQL statements or for use with a Predictor component that ships with WizWhy. This enables the user to analyze data, extract predictive rules, and then have an interactive application (see Figure 7.24).

WizWhy will provide the conditions for predicting a variable, as well as the rule's probability score, a count of how many records of this condition exist in the database, an error probability score, and the actual records in the database where this rule exists in the training database. WizWhy was originally created by a group of mathematicians from Israel; however, the product has been available in the United States for several years. It is a very powerful and accurate rule-extracting data mining tool.

Figure 7.24
*This is rule 6,
from a total of
214 rules. Note
the conditions
for a high alert.*

6)   *If* **INSURER** *is* <u>21stCentury</u>
      and **NEIGHBORHO** *is* <u>Young Frequent Movers</u>
      Then
      ALERT *is* <u>High</u>
      Rule's probability: **0.978**
      The rule exists in **131** *records.*
      Significance Level: Error probability < 0.00001
      Positive Examples (records' serial numbers):
      12, 43, 47, 52, 58, 62, 66, 70, 73, 74

7.11   Machine-Learning Software Suites

These data mining software products incorporate visualization, statistics, neural networks, and machine-learning algorithms in multiple and sometimes linkable components. These are high-end toolboxes that can be used for classification and segmentation. Other components can be used for clustering and visualization processes. These are the most advanced and expensive data mining software packages on the marketplace. Prices can range from $10,000 to $50,000 for a single license; these products can deal with very large data sets and take full advantage of multiple fast processors.

ANGOSS

http://www.angoss.com/

KnowledgeSTUDIO from ANGOSS, a Canadian firm, features multiple data mining models in an easy-to-use interface. This is a high-performance interactive decision tree analytical tool with neural networks and clustering components. Data can be imported from a wide variety of file formats including ASCII, dBase, Excel, ODBC, SAS, and all other major statistical packages. In a sufficiently powered data warehouse or data mart, the user can identify a table or view and mine it while the data resides in the database (known as "in-place" mining).

ANGOSS has one of the best decision tree components in the industry for exploring and visualizing relationships in a data set. The user has total control of how the decision trees can be developed and, once the data is split, even more flexibility to explore multiple views from any variable in the data set. The decision tree component has been under development and refinement for over 20 years and is a highly reliable software product for the investigative data miner.

The user has total flexibility in seeing how the data can be split on the basis of a desired output. For example, in a decision tree used to segment among

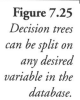

Figure 7.25
*Decision trees
can be split on
any desired
variable in the
database.*

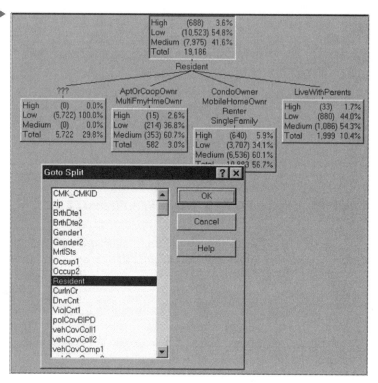

high, medium, and low alerts for our smuggler detection system, trees can be generated on the basis of any desired attribute in the database. Here, for example, we split the data on the basis of type of residence (see Figure 7.25). This is information collected by an insurance carrier. Note how Condo Owners and Mobile Home Owners have a higher probability of generating a high alert.

This tool, as with most decision tree software, makes it easy to ask such questions as Who is likely to be a smuggler? directly from the data. Here, for example, a decision tree is split on the basis of the make of the automobile, rather than the type of residence (see Figure 7.26).

The decision tree can be grown interactively or automatically; colored maps, reports, and graphics can also be inserted once the tree is built. KnowledgeSTUDIO can perform multiple types of analyses. All the user needs to do is select whether he wants a decision tree, a clustering analysis, or a neural network to be inserted (see Figure 7.27).

An assortment of instruments is available for viewing the results of the various machine-learning analyses this tool can perform, such as a lift report. A

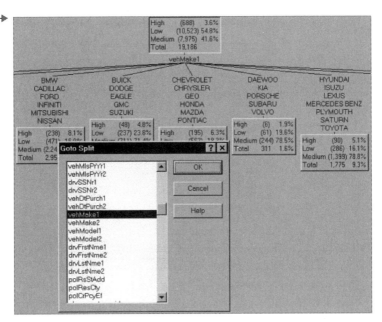

Figure 7.26
Decision tree split on the basis of vehicle make.

lift is the improvement on predicting a desired output, such as an event, action, or profile, over random chance. The straight line in Figure 7.28 is random chance, while the curve is the improved performance when the model (rules) is used.

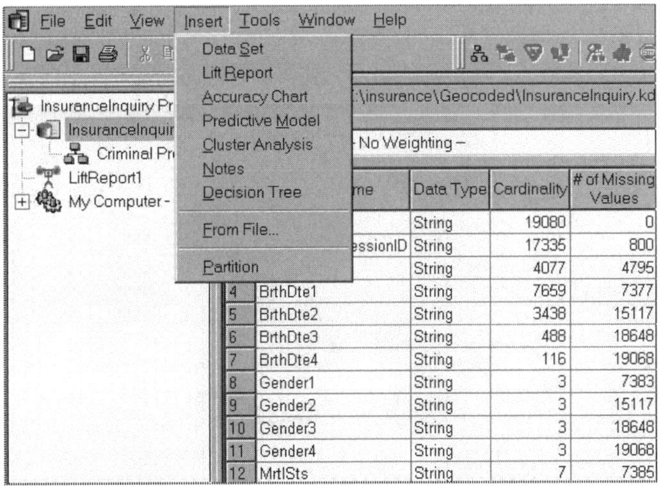

Figure 7.27
Multiple analyses can be performed by inserting them via a drop window.

Figure 7.28
*Note the
improved
performance at
70% of
population.*

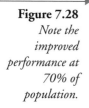
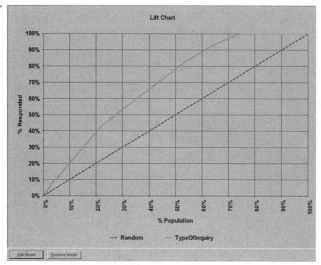

As with most of this class of data mining suites, simply constructing predictive classification analyses and models is not enough. The results need to be exportable to production applications, such as a profiling system for an alert system over a network. ANGOSS is able to export code in various formats (see Figure 7.29).

Code can be generated from the decision tree or neural network components. This is the output from the rules-type generator in Java code (see Figure 7.30).

Figure 7.29
*Rules can be
produced in
various formats.*

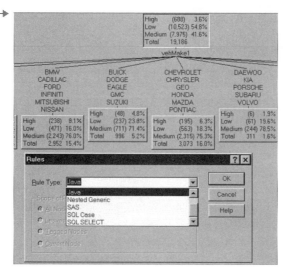

Figure 7.30
Partial view of rules generated in Java from this tool.

```
class DecisionTreeFilter extends DecisionTreeScorer {
    /**
     * Default constructor.
     */
    public
    DecisionTreeFilter()
    {
        this("DecisionTree");
    }

    /**
     * Construct a new decision tree scorer with a name.
     *
     * @param name
     *      the name of this filter.
     */
    public
    DecisionTreeFilter(String name)
    {
        super(name);
        dv = new FieldDescription("TypeOfInquiry", Value.STRING);
        dvType = Value.STRING;
        dvNames = new String[] {
            "TypeOfInquiry.High",
            "TypeOfInquiry.Low",
            "TypeOfInquiry.Medium",
        };
        ivDesc = new FieldDescription[1];
        ivDesc[0] = new FieldDescription("vehMake1", Value.STRING);
```

A neural network analysis can also be inserted once the data has been imported into the tool (see Figure 7.31).

Different types of neural networks can be constructed with Knowledge-STUDIO. The tool also has a clustering component using a Nearest Neighbor algorithm. The interface is fairly easy to navigate, enabling the user to create, test, and compare multiple analyses very quickly and easily.

Figure 7.31
The Neural Net Wizard interface.

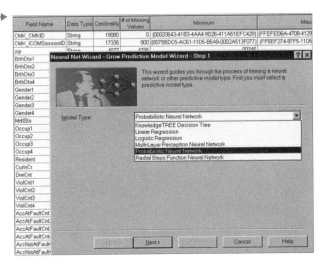

Figure 7.32
*This is
PolyAnalyst's
main window.*

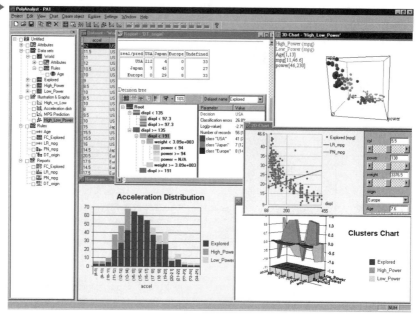

Megaputer

http://www.megaputer.com

PolyAnalyst from Megaputer is another machine-learning software suite. It includes an information gain decision tree among its 11 different modeling algorithms. Developed originally in Russia, PolyAnalyst has been on the U.S. market for several years and supports one of the largest numbers of modeling algorithms, including a text mining component.

A broad selection of exploration engines allows the user to predict values of continuous variables, explicitly model complex phenomena, determine the most influential independent variables, solve classification and clustering tasks, and find associations between events. The ability to present the discovered relations in explicit symbolic form is a unique feature of this tool. As with other high-end software suites, this program has a point-and-click GUI interface, which support versatile data import, manipulation, visualization, and reporting capabilities (see Figure 7.32).

PolyAnalyst can access data held in Oracle, DB2, Informix, Sybase, MS SQL Server, or any other ODBC-compliant database, including IBM's Visual Warehouse Solution or Oracle Express. PolyAnalyst includes a flexible Data Import Wizard that automates the task of accessing data in multiple locations and formats (see Figure 7.33).

Figure 7.33
This is the data import wizard interface.

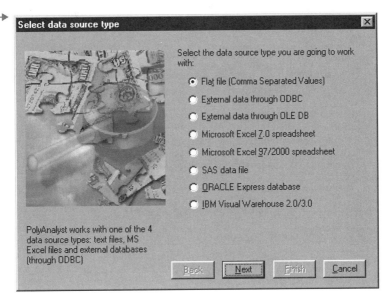

This software suite supports a wide array of data manipulations and mathematical transformation, so that rules, automatically discovered by PolyAnalyst or entered by the user, can be used to produce new fields, such as ratios (see Figure 7.34).

Figure 7.34
The Visual Rule Assistant simplifies rule generation.

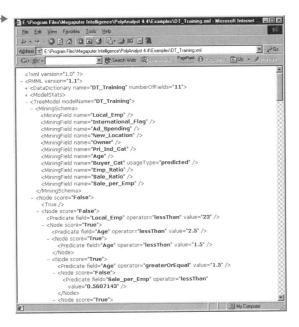

The machine-learning menu in this suite is extensive, supporting the following data mining processes:

- Memory case-based reasoning (CBR) for multiple group classification
- Multidimensional distribution analysis for finding dependencies
- Market basket analysis via transactional data processing
- Symbolic knowledge acquisition technology (SKAT)
- Discriminate analysis for unsupervised classification
- Clustering via localization of anomalies
- Multiple neural networks architectures
- Decision trees via information gain
- Stepwise linear regression
- Fuzzy-logic classification
- Summary statistics

The latest addition to this data mining suite is that of a decision tree exploration engine. It can assist in solving the classification of cases into multiple categories, such as high, medium, and low alerts. The decision tree component can work with up to 5,000,000 records and is very quick because it does not require loading all the data into the main memory of a server simultaneously. A decision tree report provides an assortment of statistics, such as the number of nonterminal nodes, number of leaves, the depth of the constructed tree, the classification statistics, etc. (see Figure 7.35).

Prudsys

http://www.prudsys.de/discoverer

The prudsys® DISCOVERER 2000 data mining is based on nonlinear decision trees. The system is suitable for individual qualification and the creation of profiles. The data and text import module automatically recognizes the structure of text files (see Figure 7.36).

A statistics module offers the user various options for statistically evaluating target databases. A classification module allows for the data to be visualized and evaluated in the form of linear or nonlinear decision trees.

Once the decision tree is created, the user can choose from various function classes:

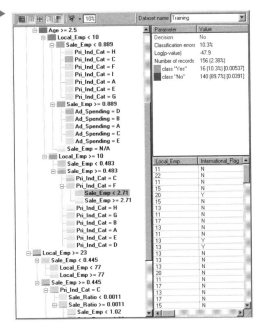

Figure 7.35
Decision tree interface with summary statistic window.

- Axis-parallel discriminant function

- Linear discriminant function

- Quadratic discriminant function

- Cubic discriminant function

- Discriminant function of fourth degree or higher

The most important feature of this tool consists of its continuous quality control through measurement charts (gains, lift, and ROC charts) during the entire computation and creation of decision trees. Problems, such as over-fitting, and over-training with a lack of generalizing, can be visualized and eliminated with the interactive charts.

Oracle

`http://www.oracle.com/ip/analyze/warehouse/datamining`
Oracle9*i* Data Mining suite, formerly Darwin, is a multiple-paradigm data mining software package, which has been embedded within the database, with all model-building and scoring functions available through a Java-based API. What makes this suite unique is that Oracle9*i* provides the infrastructure for application developers to build integrated business intelligence applications

Figure 7.36 *A schematic decision tree.*

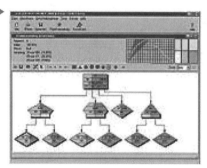 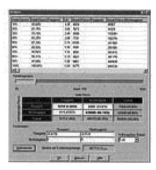

without having to extract the data and mine it in a specialized analytical server.

The tool supports an open standard for data mining via the Java Data Mining API. Since it is embedded in the database, Oracle9*i* Data Mining simplifies the process of extracting hidden intelligence from large data sets. This suite eliminates off-loading vast quantities of data to external special-purpose analytic servers for data mining and scoring. With this suite all the data mining functionality is embedded in the database, so the data, data-preparation, model-building, and model-scoring activities remain imbedded. Oracle9*i* Data Mining takes advantage of Oracle's parallelism for faster computing.

Quadstone

http://www.quadstone.com

Decisionhouse is Quadstones flagship software suite (see Figure 7.37). It provides data extraction, management, preprocessing, and very powerful visualization features. It supports segmentation, scoring and geographical display mapping. An analysis from one component such as a decision tree can be linked to charts and maps or a regression tool. This is a unique and very powerful feature of this tool.

Decisionhouse data mining suite features include the following:

- Data extraction
- Multidimensional visualization
- Data Enhancement and manipulation
- Geographical mapping display
- Data preprocessing
- webmaps

Figure 7.37
Decisionhouse graphical displays.

- Profiling
- Automated segmentation
- ScoreCard modeling

Decisionhouse can operate with two additional modules from Quadstone: ScoreHouse and HouseVision. ScoreHouse provides enhanced scorecard modeling capabilities to complement the segmentation, profiling, and visualization functions of Decisionhouse. HouseVision is a lightweight version of Decisionhouse that allows users to distribute their findings in a visual manner to a wider user community.

SAS

http://www.sas.com

Enterprise Miner is the data mining software suite from SAS, the world's largest statistical software company. Enterprise Miner uses what it calls a "Sample, Explore, Modify, Model, Assess" (SEMMA) approach to conducting data mining analyses (see Figure 7.38). SAS believes that beginning with a statistically representative sample of a data set, this methodology makes it easy to apply exploratory statistical and visualization techniques, select and transform the most significant predictive variables, model the variables to predict outcomes, and confirm a model's accuracy.

By assessing the results gained from each stage of the process, SAS believes its SEMMA process can determine how to model new questions raised by previous results, and thus return to the exploration phase for additional refinement of the data. Enterprise Miner incorporates decision trees and neural networks, as well as regression components, memory-based reasoning, bagging and boosting ensembles, two-stage models, clustering, time series, and association tools.

Figure 7.38
*Enterprise
Miner's
SEMMA
process.*

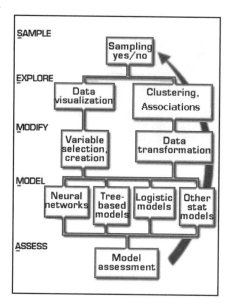

The complete scoring formula for all stages of model development is automatically captured in the form of SAS, C, and Java languages for subsequent model deployment. A reporter tool provides output in HTML for distribution and viewing via a browser. SAS emphasizes that with the Enterprise Miner's GUI and automated framework, users require little statistical expertise. Many corporations and large government agencies are already running the base SAS system and, thus, integration of Enterprise Miner facilitates the process of data mining.

SPSS

http://www.spss.com/spssbi/clementine

Clementine is SPSSs data mining suite. It is a totally icon-driven tool that supports a visual rapid-modeling environment for data mining (see Figure 7.39).

The interactive stream approach to data mining is the key to Clementine's power. Using icons that represent steps in the data mining process, the user can mine a data set by building a "stream"—a visual map of the processes the data flows through. Icons can represent data sources, such as variable types of flat files or ODBC connection. There are also Record Operational icons for excluding, merging, and sampling, records in a database. There are Field Operation icons for filtering and designating data types. There are also graphical icons for creating different types of visual reports. And of course there are

Figure 7.39
Clementine uses icons to perform data mining analyses.

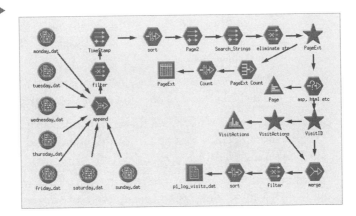

also Modeling icons for placing neural networks and machine-learning algorithms in the palette for mining the data. The user typically starts an analysis in Clementine by simply dragging a source icon from the object palette onto the canvas to access the data flow.

The user can start by exploring the data via a table or a graph icon to visually display the data prior to bringing to the canvas various algorithm icons to construct models, the results of which are represented as gold nuggets. SPSS provides Clementine users with prebuilt streams, which it calls Clementine application templates (CATs), and is planning on including a COP CAT for law enforcement applications.

The Clementine application template for crime and offender profiling (COP CAT) will be based on the existing work of the West Midlands, U.K. Police Department on extracting and using crime and offender profiles. This case study is described in more detail in Chapter 12. The COP CAT will include five modules:

1. Police resources and incident "hot spots" identify locations where requests for assistance from members of the public are likely to be high volume in a given time period, which will be based on a recent history of requests.

2. Patterns of individual offenders, given a number of offenses committed by the same individual, identify common patterns of MO and score unsolved crimes against this profile.

3. For patterns of groups of offenders, where the offenses are committed by a group of connected offenders rather than a single individual, a geographical component is used to identify hot spots for a particular group or network.

4.   Combining patterns of offenders and MOs and suspect descriptions: for those types of crime where suspect descriptions are often available (e.g., "bogus official" burglaries), this improves the accuracy of scoring.

Modules 1 to 4 are designed to use the type of information typically collected by police forces for all reported crimes.

5.   For patterns of offending for serious crimes (e.g., armed robbery) a more detailed description of the offense and circumstances is typically available.

In addition, SPSS is also planning to develop a CAT to target government fraud, which will be along two separate types of streams: one is the typical "train and test," while the other looks for outliers.

In the first stream, government agencies may be interested in identifying fraud, waste, or abuse in their vendor payment system, as in the case study in Section 7.7. They may have completed an audit of a small subset of the transactions and have identified only a very small percentage of these cases as actually incorrect or fraudulent transactions. Of course, the analysts will need to use this data in the best possible way to both train and test the model, then reapply that model to other transactions, hoping to find additional cases. There are various reasons identified to be the cause of vendor payment error, including multiple payments to the same vendor for the same cost, billing a cost center for a product that cannot be charged to that cost center, billing for more hours than normal/expected, and billing at much higher rates than expected. There are also a number of cases where the billing was deemed fraudulent, even though the line-item charges appear to be usual. Approaches to identifying fraud include profiling for the prediction of fraud based on historical cases of fraud. It will be clearly noted that fraud frequently transforms itself and other means of analysis are necessary to find "new fraud."

In the second stream, a government agency pays providers for service rendered. However, analysis in this case does not include any instances where fraud, waste, or abuse have been identified. In this situation the objective is to narrow the work down by identifying *abnormal* cases in the data set. Historically, claims have been reviewed at the claim level, with a series of audit checks performed to ensure that each claim meets the criteria for payment. The analysis performed in this CAT will aggregate each claim so that analysis can be performed at the provider and the customer levels in order to find unusual behavior. Approaches to identifying fraud can include the following:

- Data cleaning for removal of duplicate entries

- Application of Beneford's Law to find nonconforming groups

- Data aggregation for the identification of acceleration

- Provider clustering for identification of unusual cases of providers or cluster movement over time

- Customer clustering for identification of unusual customers and cluster movement over time

- Ping-ponging identification

- Unbundling and unusual sets of claims identification

SPSS is making a concerted effort to develop data mining application solutions in the areas of criminal and fraud detection, as well as developing CATs for countering bio-terrorism. Several case studies will illustrate how Clementine is being used in the detection of potential government agency fraud and the clustering of crimes and criminal MOs.

Teradata Warehouse Miner

http://www.teradata.com

NCR has developed Teradata Warehouse Miner a highly scalable data mining system for NCR's Teradata Relational Database Management System (RDBMS) software customers. Teradata Warehouse Miner complements traditional data mining software for Teradata customers by addressing the need to handle large volumes of data in a scalable manner. TeraMiner does this by providing data mining functions that operate directly on the data within the Teradata database via programmatically generated SQL. This facilitates data mining without having to move the data, and using as much of the data as desired, while storing the results directly in the database, and utilizing the parallel, scalable processing power of Teradata to perform data intensive operations. This is a unique data mining paradigm and is quite appropriate for analyzing very large data sets in data warehouses.

Models are represented in XML and are integrated inside the database warehouse system, SQL can be directly exported and integrated for real-time deployment. Teradata Warehouse Miner has a Windows-based user interface for model development, deployment and project management. A complete set of descriptive statistics are provided along with data visualization charts, plots, decision trees and graphs. Organization and partitioning functions are provided for data preparation, transformation and data reduction.

All of the major analytic algorithms are supported by Teradata Miner including linear and logistic regression, factor analysis, rule induction and decision tree, clustering and association/sequence analysis. This tool repre-

Figure 7.40
NCR's Data Mining Method and Teradata Warehouse Miner Technolgoy.

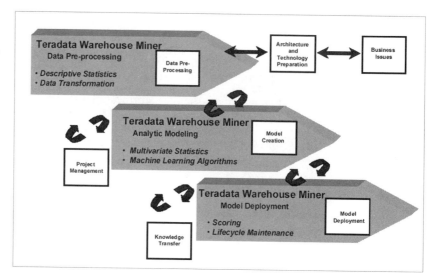

sents a next generation machine learning software suite in that the analytical model building, testing and deployment is constructed within the database itself. This design allows for leveraging the parallel processing of the RDBMS software, enabling for the analysis of large volumes of detailed data and quick deployment in such applications as fraud detection (see Figure 7.40).

thinkAnalytics

http://www.thinkanalytics.com

This vendor takes a unique approach to providing multiple data mining algorithms via its flagship product K.wiz, a suite designed specifically for integration into production applications. The suite is based on Java and XML, allowing its SDK to be integrated with messaging systems, application servers, and component technologies, as well as existing enterprise systems, such as those of IBM, SAS, and Siebel. K.wiz was designed from the outset to be embedded in other systems using a component-based architecture. The components can be any of several algorithms, including decision trees, regression, neural networks, naive bayes, KMeans, K-nearest neighbor, and Kohonen neural networks. thinkAnalytics is headquartered in Glasgow, Scotland, United Kingdom.

7.12   Bibliography

Shavlik, J. and Dietterich, T. (1990), *Readings in Machine Learning*, San Mateo: Morgan Kaufmann Publishers.

8

NetFraud: A Case Study

8.1   Fraud Detection in Real Time

Credit-card fraud detection is an extremely difficult problem to solve. Several factors compound the difficulty of this criminal pattern—recognition problem. First of all, the data provided in an authorization is extremely limited, such as the amount, location, and perhaps type of product or service being purchased. Second, the patterns of fraudulent use are very diverse. A person can use a credit card at millions of different places and thousands of Web sites, making it extremely difficult to match a pattern. Third, a thief can be using a credit-card number concurrently with an authorized user, making the pattern detection more challenging. A fraud detection model must determine a way to classify transactions made by the authorized party and those made by a non-authorized party. Finally, there is the issue of time and the anonymity of the thief. If he or she can get away with charging a few hundred dollars in a few days on a stolen card number, chances are the thief will never be tracked down. Therefore, fraud detection has to be done in real-time.

At a Web site, real-time fraud detection has to be done right at the virtual checkout counter, when the e-commerce site sends the information to Visa, which can be through several channels, and then as it arrives at the bank that issued the card. Before the bank sends an authorization back to the merchant through Visa, it will run it through a real time detection system. These fraud detection systems are almost always based on a combination of neural networks and rules, most which banks today outsource to HNC, a manufacturer of fraud detection software. HNC has developed neural network–based decision systems over the years because they provide a faster, statically robust, less subjective way to assess certain kinds of business risk.

Most banks have issued millions of credit cards, so using a non-neural network would be too slow for processing such a large database in real time. While real-time fraud detection can keep a thief from making one more illegal purchase on a card, it took several years for these systems to be effective. One of the early problems banks had with fraud-detection systems was that they were plagued with *false positives,* that is, situations where fraud is suspected on a legitimate transaction. This was expensive for banks, since they would use costly call centers to phone consumers to confirm questionable transactions. However, to the consumer, nothing could be more annoying than having a card declined simply because a transaction did not fit the profile created and maintained by their bank.

8.2   Fraud Migrates On-line

The same types of fraud schemes that have victimized consumers and merchants for many years before the proliferation of Internet are now beginning to migrate to the Web. Consumers are beginning to find fraud schemes in chat rooms, e-mail, message boards, and e-retailing and auction Web sites. The misuse of credit cards via identify theft was by far the biggest security problem on the Web and the leading consumer-fraud complaint, according to the Federal Trade Commission, which provided this breakdown:

- Credit card identity theft (42%)
- Internet auctions fraud (10%)
- Internet services scams (7%)

Complaints involving fraud on the Internet have jumped sixfold in the United States alone during 2001, according to consumer watchdog Internet Fraud Watch. The rising numbers are in line with the rapid growth of e-commerce, which has become a multimillion dollar business. Around 79 million U.S. citizens are now estimated to surf the Web, with many making purchases on-line or bidding in auction sites for goods and services. However, as e-commerce booms, more fraud is perpetrated.

8.3   Credit-Card Fraud

Years before the Web, credit-card fraud was already a big problem, where even the simplest instance of fraud was difficult to detect in light of the millions of transactions taking place every minute of every day. Credit-card issuers had been combating fraud for several years both by hiring teams of data miners and developing in-house detection systems employing pattern-recognition technologies, such as neural networks, or by outsourcing the problem to out-side experts.

Prior data mining analyses have found that certain variables contain telltale clues for detecting credit-card fraud. Citibank, for example, found that it could dramatically reduce fraud when it passed certain variables though a neural network. This included the following four information items:

- The Standard Industry Code of the product or service being purchased
- The number of transactions for that day
- The dollar amount of the transaction
- The zip code of the transaction

An amusing trend that Citibank discovered was that repeated purchases of expensive Italian shoes in New Jersey tended to indicate a high probability that they were being made with stolen credit cards. This example leads to some important lessons, which can be applied to the problem of on-line fraud. Features such as location, the type of product or service being pur-chased, the velocity of the transactions, and the dollar ranges are all key indi-cator for detecting and deterring on-line fraud. Another red-flag indicator for on-line sales is a transaction where the shipping address is different from the billing address. The experience of several e-retailers indicates that this type of transaction should be carefully monitored.

8.4   The Fraud Profile

Advances were made during the 1990s, enabling banks to be more effective in detecting credit-card fraud via detection systems consisting of a detailed trans-action-history database coupled with a sophisticated, real-time neural network and rule-based scoring system. A purchasing profile is built on each user, which is quite small, like a string of DNA chromosomes, using years of data. The detection system determines the patterns of a cardholder's shopping hab-its. These patterns include such information as frequency of purchases, aver-age purchases, location of purchases, and other transactional factors. All of this information is very compact; for example, a consumer's string can be 8 (number of purchases), $45 (average purchase price), 94### (location zip code of purchases), etc. Eventually, all of this transaction history is used to construct a knowledge base about each consumer.

Before a transaction can be authorized, the real-time detection system attempts to pattern match the transaction with the knowledge base of the cardholder's historical transactions. In addition, the system will attempt to pattern match the transaction with knowledge bases of known fraudulent transactions. Pattern recognition aims to classify data based on either a prior knowledge or on statistical information extracted from the patterns. The patterns to be classified are usually groups of measurements or observations. In this case, the pattern recognition attempts to put the transaction into either a legitimate or a fraudulent category.

8.5   The Risk Scores

Because of the broad profiles, however, a transaction is not so easily categorized into one of the two groups. Therefore, fraud-detection systems must also assign a risk score to each transaction. This score represents just how much the system felt the transaction was fraudulent. This is a continuous value number. Fraud profiles can be developed and evolved, providing a basis for fraud detection using artificial AI. Neural networks and machine learning are commonly used today to evaluate each transaction and assign this type of risk score.

This risk score is compared against a predetermined score threshold, thereby enabling acceptance or the firing of an alert rejection in real time. For example, a risk score of 90 might signal a fraudulent purchase, enabling any transaction with a score of 89 or below to be authorized. However, risk scores are also based upon previous risk scores for each individual. This means that a score of 89 will pass the test, but a subsequent score of 89 will be bumped up due to the previous score and the purchase will not be authorized. Also, the personal risk score of individuals who on average run up thousands of dollars on their cards each month may be significantly higher than those who average only a few dollars.

Seasonality can also hinder the detection of fraudulent purchases; credit-card fraud activity can increase 15% or more during the holiday season. High rates of purchase can put an extra load on a fraud-detection network system. Unusual purchases for a profile, such as those of gifts for relatives, can also affect the accuracy of the system. In effect, a consumer's purchasing profile is thrown out the window during the holiday season. Shopping patterns are unpredictable during this time, and thus, credit-card companies tend to treat this loss as a cost of doing business.

8.6   Transactional Data

One way of improving the accuracy of a fraud detection system is passing more data with each transaction, such as the Standard Industry Code (SIC) for the product or service being purchased. This data can be used to create a more detailed profile of a cardholder. For example, a $1,000 purchase at The Good Guys of a camcorder might score differently from the purchase of a TV for the same price. The difference between a $1,000 camcorder and $1,000 TV would result in a different risk score due to the fact a camcorder can be unloaded rather easily on an auction site while a large-screen TV cannot.

In addition, frequency of purchases for the same type of product would enable the fraud-detection system to score the transaction accordingly. Was another camcorder purchased this week? Another example where more data could be useful would be in airline tickets. A $500 charge from a travel site is not that suspicious, but a one-way ticket to Paris leaving tomorrow might affect the risk score. New data protocols, such as those based on XML, can enable the exchange of profile information at the time of a user visit and will make fraud-detection systems more accurate.

8.7   Common-Sense Rules

Before an e-business can spot and stop on-line fraud, however, it has to know what to look for. This commonly starts by developing a set of rules describing a fraud profile. A fraud profile summarizes the data characteristics that one would expect to find in questionable transactions. There are several common-sense rules that experienced fraud specialists look for in detecting and deterring this type of crime in the terrestrial business environment. They include orders with the following red-flag conditions:

- Multiple or single orders that fall just under the "review threshold" level
- Shipping addresses matching current or former employee's addresses
- All orders with different shipping and billing addresses
- Any returns, rejects, and for-credit orders
- All P.O. box address orders

These fraud rules can be coupled with models created with data mining software to detect and deter on-line fraud by e-businesses. As in the past, these types of tools gave merchants the ability to search quickly through millions of records in a matter of seconds in order to identify transactions in real or near real time that have the characteristics associated with fraudulent activity. Through the development of these common-sense rules and the use of predictive models created with data mining tools, merchants have the ability to reduce their losses and double-check certain orders before shipping them out.

8.8   Auction Fraud

The most damaging act that can be perpetrated against an on-line auction site like eBay.com is to tarnish its visitors' trust of the site. On-line auctions like eBay, Yahoo, and Amazon have started to attract situations where successful bidders pay for items, such as a camera or a laptop, and then never receive the goods after mailing their money. Interestingly, the large auction sites disclaim most of the responsibility for combating fraud that takes place in their marketplaces. For example, eBay says fraud accounts for a minuscule portion of its auctions—citing that less than 0.1%, or 1 out of every 40,000 listings, result in a confirmed case of fraud. Furthermore, it claims most items are covered by insurance for up to $200, less the $25 deductible. Despite its insistence that fraud is not a major problem, eBay created a new data mining unit designed to detect instances of crimes. It also developed a system called the Fraud and Abuse Detection Engine (FADE) to detect perpetrators at its site.

The Consumers League estimates most fraud takes place with large-ticket items that are not covered by insurance. Statistics from fraud.org confirm the magnitude of the on-line auction problem (see Table 8.1).

Table 8.1   *On-Line Auction Fraud Statistics*

2000 Top 10 Frauds		Jan.–Oct. 2001 Top 10 Frauds	
On-line auctions	78%	On-line auctions	63%
General merchandise sales	10%	General merchandise sales	11%
Internet access services	3%	Nigerian money offers	9%
Work-at-home	3%	Internet access services	3%
Advance fee loans	2%	Information adult services	3%

Ruben Garcia, assistant director of the FBI, defines Internet fraud as "Any instance in which any one or more components of the Internet, such as the Web sites, the chat rooms, e-mail … play a significant role in offering nonexistent goods or services to customers, in communicating false or fraudulent representations about schemes to consumers, in transmitting victims' funds or any other items of value to the control of the schemes' perpetrator."

Obviously, this can also be interpreted as including claims made about goods up for bidding in an on-line auction, which after payment is received, are never sent to the successful and unsuspecting bidder. Most large auction sites take some level of security to ensure that the identity and reputation of those participants in their site are legitimate and trustworthy; however, given the volume of bids placed on a daily basis, perpetrators are going to make their way into the marketplace.

Most victims of Internet auction fraud who contacted the FBI were males between ages 20 and 50. The most common frauds involved Beanie Babies (27%); however, more expensive items were also high on the list of scams, including video consoles, games and tapes (24%), and laptop computers (18%). The average victim lost $776, with most victims paying by money order or check and who typically only knew of an e-mail address or post office box number, according to the FBI. Of an estimated 500 million Internet auction sales last year, the bureau estimated about 5 million were fraudulent.

The biggest form of on-line auction fraud is where a seller takes payment and then fails to deliver the promised item. Alternatively, the item is delivered, but doesn't match the items description at the auction site. A seller might use flattering or deceptive photographs and "optimistic" descriptions, for example, to pass off damaged or second-rate goods as high in quality. In many cases, a mismatch between the item described in the auction and the item delivered may simply be a question of interpretation; one person's "good condition" may be another's "average condition." Sellers may overcharge buyers for packaging and shipping fees. Unscrupulous sellers are happy to make their money on inflated shipping charges for which they don't need to pay a percentage fee to the auction site.

One of the ways many auction sites attempt to regulate sales is through a feedback mechanism. When an auction is over, the winner/buyer can grade and comment on the seller and the transaction, and all grades and buyer comments are published for all to see. Obviously, buyers are more comfortable bidding on items from sellers who have received a lot of positive feedback and high grades.

Inevitably, then, sellers may attempt to fix their grades by submitting feedback about themselves or by getting friends and confederates to provide glowing reports. Fraud is not all one-way of course. Buyer collusion is where one buyer might make a low bid, and a second buyer then immediately makes a very high one, thus ensuring that nobody else makes any other bids. At the last minute, the second bidder retracts, allowing the first bidder to get the item for a very low bid.

The ability to disguise identity, revoke bids, and maintain multiple on-line identities may facilitate undesirable practices like *shilling*. Shilling is where sellers arrange for false bids to be placed on the items they are selling. Sellers place the bid themselves by using multiple identities or by using confederates. The idea is to force up the cost of a winning bid and encourage interest in the auction.

More stringent control over multiple identities and an analysis of the types of goods with a higher percentage of being fraudulent by these auctioneers could reduce the likelihood of criminal action on their site. Once an individual has perpetrated a fraud, an investigation into his or her identity, physical address, P.O. box, e-mail, IP address, and Internet provider should be aggressively pursued. Once identified, all this information should be collected in a centralized database in which queries from all major auction sites can be processed prior to the completion of auctions. Certain items, particularly dollar ranges, tend to attract fraud. These attributes, goods, and intervals are capable of being identified via data mining analysis. In the end, the solution to auction fraud is a combination of common sense, centralized access to a database of known criminals, and data mining models. As we have seen with eBay, concerns about protecting its bidders forced it to create a data mining Security and Trust Group to stem the flow of auction fraud.

8.9   NetFraud

In the situation of auction fraud, the individual bidder is left holding the bag. However, in the case where an e-business accepts a credit card and ships the goods out, it is the merchant that will be left to deal with the loss. Typically, e-retailers can expect that a certain percentage of their daily on-line sales are fraudulent. With already razor-thin margins, this is a very critical problem for on-line merchants. As e-commerce becomes more prevalent, there has been an increase in the use of credit-cards payments, from 11% in 2000 to 28% in 2001 and a parallel increase in fraud (see Table 8.2).

Table 8.2   *Top Three Payment Methods*

2000		2001	
Money Order	43%	Money Order	29%
Check	30%	Credit Card	28%
Credit Card	11%	Check	18%

In fact, this is a far larger problem for e-retailers than they are willing to admit. A popular seller of electronic products, for example, which on average makes about 6,000 sales a day, acknowledges that about 1,000 of those sales were made using stolen credit cards or fraudulent numbers. This popular e-retailer admits the amount of fraud can range from 14% to 20%, depending on the type of product being purchased.

This is further reflected in the statistics reported by fraud.org, which found that overall losses for 2001 were $4,371,724, up from $3,387,530 in 2000. The average loss per person also was on the increase from $427 in 2000 to $636 in 2001. There are significant differences in the per-person averages for each product category, with hardware and software being especially high targets of fraud (see Table 8.3).

Table 8.3   *Fraud Statistics Reported by fraud.org*

Top Fraud Product Targets	Average Loss Per Person
Computer equipment/software	$1,102
General merchandise sales	$845
Internet access services	$568
On-line auctions	$478
Information adult services	$234

Of course, hardware as well as other high-end electronic equipment is fairly easy for criminals to sell via auction sites. Compounding the problem for e-businesses is that because there are no shopper signatures with these fraudulent on-line transactions, they must absorb the bulk of the monetary deficit. The e-businesses are stuck with the entire loss because the credit-card companies only extend the $50 protection limit to the consumer cardholders and not to merchants.

8.10   **Fraud-Detection Services**

Several terrestrial services exist for flagging suspected credit-card transactions; one of the largest is that of the Falcon system by the HNC Corporation. The Falcon system incorporates proprietary and neural-network technologies and is the flagship service of HNC, a company that began as a neural-network company in the mid-1980s. Today, Falcon monitors over 240 million payment card accounts, or about 80% of all credit cards in the United States. Falcon uses neural-network–based cardholder profiling and real-time transaction-scoring techniques. HNC started out selling neural network software; however, it quickly found that companies were not interested in buying pattern-recognition programs. Instead, they were looking for business solutions based on the use of this technology. HNC decided to sell fraud-detection services to banks and other issuers of credit cards.

Financial firms found it difficult to administer and maintain their own neural-network models and instead opted to outsource via a subscription service to deal with their credit-card fraud problem. There are several advantages to this business model. For example, new scams can be recognized much more quickly by a fraud-detection expert than by an independent bank or merchant. Fraud detection service providers can also pool both data and technologies via a subscription consortium network, enabling them to detect criminal activity and patterns much more effectively. However, for those interested in learning about fraud-detection techniques, or at the least incorporating some preventive technology on their site, the following case study is provided.

8.11   Building a Fraud-Detection System

To demonstrate how a fraud detection system can be constructed using advanced data mining technologies and tools, this sample will be presented with the use of a data set from an actual e-business that sells electronic consumer products via its Web site. For this case study, we will go through several processes, including the following:

- Assembling samples of transactional data

- Enhancing the customer information with offline demographics

- Visualizing associations of fraudulent transactions with a link analyzer

- Mapping features of fraudulent transactions using a SOM

- Constructing predictive models for identifying fraud cases via neural networks

- Creating decision trees and extracting conditional rules via machine-learning algorithms

- Building an ensemble of models for detecting fraudulent transactions in real time

8.12 Extracting Data Samples

One of the first tasks is to aggregate an adequate sample of fraudulent and non-fraudulent accounts. As previously mentioned, it is critical to first create a *fraud profile*. This file should contain samples of on-line transactions by as many different types and categories of products lines for different dollar amounts and number of purchases made by legal and fraudulent shoppers. In order to create predictive models via data mining techniques, it is very important to have an adequate sample of observation for "training" a system such as a neural network to recognize the patterns of fraud. Additionally, a machine-learning analysis will be used to extract the features of fraudulent transactions. Typically, the transactional data variables collected and used for the modeling process include some of the following data items (see Table 8.4).

Table 8.4 *Transactional Data Variables*

Product Category	Number of Purchases	Vendor Name
Vendor ID number	Invoice number	Order date
Customer ID number	Billing address 1	Billing address 2
Phone number	SKU	Product name
Product price	Product quantity	Product description
Brand	File source	etc.

8.13 Enhancing the Data

In addition to transactional variables listed above, demographic information is associated to each customer account in a typical data warehousing technique. Demographic information is associated based on a zip code or a geo code matched against a shopper's physical address. This type of demographic data has typically been used for marketing purposes to segment potential prospects on the basis of their household and neighborhood features. In this situation, however, it is used for the profiling of perpetrators and the detection of criminal activity. Other data points can be included in the development of a fraud-detection model, incorporating additional clickstream information, which, again, is commonly used for marketing purposes but not fraud detection. This clickstream data can be created from such Internet mechanisms as Web bugs, cookies, and Web forms. The demographic data includes some of the following information; the following is a partial listing of over 150 lifestyle variables:

■ GEOCODE: A location code down to 200 household level

- MSA_CODE: Metropolitan statistical area
- LATITUDE: Location field
- LONGITUDE: Location field
- ZIP4: Zip plus four
- ACORN: A Classification of Residential Neighborhoods code
- POP_CY: 2000 population
- AVGHHSIZE: Average household size
- P_WHITE_CY: Percent White population
- P_AGE25_44: Percent 25–44 population
- MED_AGE_CY: Median age — total population
- P_COLL_GRD: Percent college graduates
- P_MANAGMNT: Percent in managerial positions
- P_POVERTY: Percent in poverty level
- P_URBAN: Percent urban residences
- P_SINGLE: Percent single
- P_WOM_LABF: Percent of women in labor force
- P_BLT_1980: Percent of buildings built prior to 1980
- MEDHOMEVAL: Median home value
- MED_RENT: Median rent
- P_INC_50: Percent of income $50,000–$75,000
- MED_INC: Median income amount
- MEDDISPINC: Median disposable income
- MEDNETWRTH: Median net worth

These types of demographics can be purchased from a number of companies, including Acxiom, CACI, ChoicePoint, Equifax, Experian, Trans Union, and others, as we discussed in Chapter 2. They can be purchased on a per-record basis, via disk, CD, tape, or in real time through secured networks or via the Web, directly from the companies or through third-party integrators. These demographics can reveal very interesting lifestyle information about on-line shoppers, including those likely to carry out fraud.

8.14   Assembling the Mining Tools

Using hundreds of these data attributes, several data analyses will be performed, including the construction of several predictive models using an assortment of data mining techniques and tools. We will first perform a visual inspection of fraud transactions and then move on to the construction of predictive models, decision trees, and IF/THEN rules, along with the associated code and final fraud-detection ensemble design. These data mining tools include some of the machine-learning software suites discussed in earlier chapters. They come from such companies as ANGOSS, SAS, SPSS, and others, all of which can be found at the data mining portal, Knowledge Discovery Nuggets (http://www.kdnuggets.com).

These data mining tools incorporate the technologies covered in preceding sections of the book, such as link analysis, SOM, neural networks, and machine-learning algorithms, technologies that are robust and proven. They have been around for years and are very intuitive to use. The objective, however, is not only to understand what the fraud profile looks like, but also to construct predictive models in the form of rules or formulas and code for deterring the criminal activity that takes place at e-commerce sites.

As we have learned, there are two basic types of data mining analyses. One is descriptive and designed to provide some insight into the user, such as a chart, graph, or decision tree, and we will incorporate these types of tools by starting the analysis using a link analysis program and a SOM neural network to discover, view, and explore the hidden associations and patterns related to fraudulent transactions. The second type of data mining analysis consists of creating predictive models. This is where a set of formula weights from a neural network in the form of code or conditional rules is extracted from a sample data set by a machine-learning tool and used to detect and deter fraud. For this second type of modeling analysis, we will use some neural networks and machine-learning algorithm tools. In the end, we will gain an insight into the profile of fraud at a given site and generate code that can be used to detect this criminal activity and for deterring it in real time.

8.15   A View of Fraud

We start with an initial exploratory look at the data by using a link analysis component that allows us to view the associations between various products, clickstream behaviors, and demographics as they relate to criminal activity. For example, after importing the data into a data mining tool, its link analysis component quickly finds strong associations between two main product lines and fraudulent transactions. The tool displays the strength of the associations

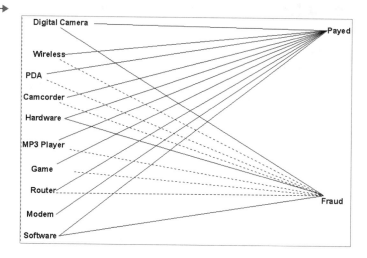

Figure 8.1
Associations between products and fraud. Note the bold line between hardware/software and fraud.

by the boldness of the links. The bolder the line, the stronger the association between the variables in the graph, and vice versa. The weaker relationships are displayed as broken lines, such as those between wireless and PDA units as they relate to fraud (see Figure 8.1).

This initial link analysis can display the associations between specific product lines and fraud for this e-business, which it is probably already aware of. However, using this same technique, other variables can be viewed and compared to see how fraudulent transactions relate to the time of day of the purchase, a visitor's operating system, median income, zip code demographics, and scores of other clickstream behaviors and demographic attributes. The objective of this first analysis is to begin the construction of a fraud profile prior to moving to deter the on-line criminal activity.

8.16   Clustering Fraud

We next move to another type of visualization analysis that at the same time performs an autonomous clustering of the data using a SOM neural network from SOMine, a data mining firm. As we found in Chapter 6, a SOM is a neural-network architecture that allows for unsupervised learning and is used to perform clustering of data, allowing it to organize itself around similar segments. For this situation, we wanted to discover the similarities of fraudulent transactions along different information factors. A SOM analysis is used most commonly in exploratory situations, where little is known about the data set. Using a binary value classification system, where a 0 (light) represents a paid transaction and a 1 (dark) is a fraudulent transaction, we are able to generate the two-dimensional clustering map shown in Figure 8.2.

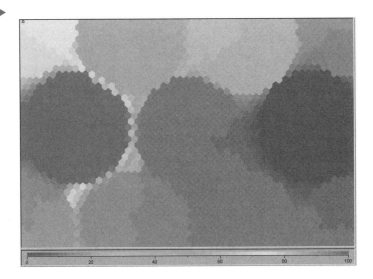

Figure 8.2 *A clustering map where light shades are legal and dark areas are fraudulent transactions.*

Using this SOM analysis, sections of the clustering map can be marked and extracted from the database into a subset for further analysis. In Figure 8.3 we marked the dark sections that represent fraudulent transactions at the right mid-section of the large map.

The section marked from the clustering map can now be cut and pasted into a spreadsheet for a more detailed review. For example, we may want to

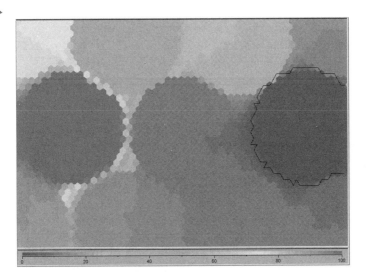

Figure 8.3 *We mark the section of fraudulent transactions.*

Figure 8.4
*Camcorders
with an average
price of $1,052
are a major
target for fraud.*

Product Category	prod.price	Average HsHldSize	% Age25_44	Median Age	% Migrants	%CollGrd	%Technicl	%Urban	%Married	MedRent
Digiatal Camera	722.67	2.0792133	31.785827	36.589089	45.450177	50.62208	36.22017	95.757	63.15397	541.1249
Digiatal Camera	987.56	2.9247686	39.572005	31.798267	39.671418	29.04112	38.61229	95.331	75.42773	804.8595
Digiatal Camera	875.58	2.086751	31.859704	36.51829	45.245663	50.2235	36.23002	95.93	63.16981	543.6992
Camcorder	756.59	2.995552	39.990908	30.126045	35.272557	18.88536	40.80722	99.68	78.66514	848.2572
Digiatal Camera	989.58	2.9248624	40.049134	31.726263	37.230475	31.75127	38.24802	96.404	73.67955	765.589
Camcorder	876.55	2.9974895	40.003409	30.095318	35.208483	18.76554	40.83007	99.758	78.6404	847.0295
Camcorder	897.87	2.9987434	40.287516	29.193465	39.142572	22.07258	42.32612	97.951	78.27173	745.8068
Camcorder	987.34	2.9985983	39.980205	30.073112	35.227765	18.54718	40.89139	99.781	78.69126	846.9009
Camcorder	1300.23	2.9989719	40.242219	29.186184	39.115365	21.88655	42.385	97.969	78.23744	744.5655
Camcorder	999.67	2.9975131	39.939706	30.084091	35.165646	18.51297	40.90467	99.778	78.58444	844.7445
Camcorder	987.66	2.9957119	38.08274	32.816921	19.770179	24.88277	40.88798	99.747	65.72718	858.9923
Camcorder	987.56	2.9874822	38.025357	32.845272	19.492674	24.93762	40.83213	99.687	65.36559	852.1032
Camcorder	1456.89	2.9835503	36.201447	35.554075	39.146537	22.35025	35.32541	99.705	62.57379	580.728
Camcorder	595.87	2.0773355	39.349648	31.480761	33.699794	35.31195	40.27734	99.585	59.16216	431.2564
Camcorder	987.56	2.7507151	39.564389	29.222042	27.05881	24.02758	35.79124	96.733	66.21069	424.8093
Camcorder	985.85	2.9817446	36.873561	33.366675	29.107659	25.47912	35.08664	99.68	66.04109	544.964
Camcorder	2219.85	2.9773953	40.391642	28.377331	19.809662	22.69282	35.47052	98.998	71.72961	408.6976
Camcorder	1335.87	2.8914004	33.388315	35.171243	22.495757	34.47703	34.51612	98.563	66.09068	620.6068
	1052.819									

view the fraud transactions according to products, average price ranges, or demographics (see Figure 8.4).

Through this clustering analysis, specific sectors of transactions related to fraud can be identified and extracted in order to develop a profile of shoppers likely to be responsible for criminal activity. For example, additional exploratory analyses can be performed by these types of visualization tools to discover associations between fraudulent transactions and other customer clickstream behaviors and demographic features. These types of analyses can yield actionable insights, enabling merchants to become more knowledgeable about the characteristics of criminals on their Web sites.

8.17　Detecting Fraud

Neural networks have been used to solve a variety of pattern-recognition problems, including the identification of prospects for offline and on-line offers by merchants. With an adequate sample of fraudulent observations, a neural network can also be trained to detect transactions where crimes are likely to take place. A neural network tool, such as SPSS Clementine's, can be used to construct a predictive model for detecting fraud. Figure 8.5 depicts a neural-network instrument monitoring a training session.

Figure 8.6 shows a *sensitivity report* generated from this neural network tool, which prioritizes the inputs into the network for predicting fraud for a model with an accuracy rate of 91.30%. This report provides a breakdown on the relative importance of the inputs into the model. Note that the Product Category was the most important variable (.39). Interestingly, the next highest input is the percentage of individuals ages 25 to 44 in the population

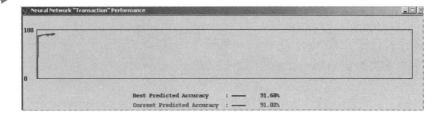

Figure 8.5 *The error rate is only about 8% for this neural-network model.*

(.32). This can be interpreted to mean that the type of product and the age of the shoppers are some of the most important characteristics in detecting fraud.

Figure 8.7 shows a view of a multilayered perceptron neural network during training for a second fraud detection model using another data mining tool, KnowledgeSTUDIO from ANGOSS.

Having the ability to detect and deter on-line fraud in rea ltime is critical. This is where the ability of these data mining tools to generate code directly from their models can prove to be useful. Both SPSS Clementine and

Figure 8.6 *This sensitivity instrument prioritizes the inputs for a fraud model.*

```
Neural Network "Transaction" architecture

Input Layer      : 62 neurons
Hidden Layer #1 : 8 neurons
Output Layer     : 1 neurons

Predicted Accuracy :  91.30%

Relative Importance of Inputs
Product Category   : 0.39466
P_AGE25_44         : 0.32042
pqty               : 0.17392
HU_90              : 0.15904
P_INC_75           : 0.15696
P_URBAN            : 0.13119
pprice             : 0.12313
P_INC_150          : 0.11154
MED_INC_CY         : 0.10924
MEDHOMEVAL         : 0.10461
P_HU_1_DET         : 0.10287
AGE_DEPIND         : 0.09579
P_AGE18_24         : 0.09495
PINC150PL          : 0.09457
P_MANAGMNT         : 0.08877
P_OO_HU            : 0.08689
P_BLACK_CY         : 0.08428
P_MARRIED          : 0.08423
P_OO_MORT          : 0.07869
P_TECHNICL         : 0.07863
MEDNETWRTH         : 0.07624
Purchases          : 0.07396
P_HU_10PLS         : 0.07322
P_INC_15           : 0.07288
```

Figure 8.7 A view of the training of the perceptron neural network.

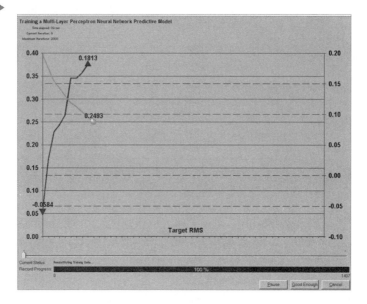

ANGOSS KnowledgeSTUDIO are capable of generating code for identifying potential perpetrators of fraud by scoring on-line transactions.

8.18   NetFraud in the United Kingdom: A Statistical Study

SAS, the world's largest statistical software company, recently commissioned a survey into fraud in the United Kingdom and uncovered some frightening statistics: 62% of the organizations questioned across the retail, telecommunications, finance, and public sectors have no measures in place against fraud over the Internet, a crime that grew by 20% last year alone, according to British officials. The survey showed that 84% of businesses feel the Internet is not secure, yet 72% plan to continue investing in e-business because they believe the benefits outweigh the dangers of Internet fraud.

While the benefits of e-business may induce corporations to forge ahead, cyber criminals are forging ahead as well, and "e-fraud" will continue to grow as e-commerce increases. Fortunately, Internet fraud can be detected and prevented. Analytical software can be used to model and predict suspicious patterns of behavior. Despite the potential return on investment, there is still some apathy among organizations about fraud.

Twenty percent of managers responsible for fraud prevention in U.K. businesses feel that Internet fraud is not a high priority at board level. This view is reinforced by the fact that 34% of those interviewed believe that fraud has little impact on their bottom line. However, four out of five people interviewed are concerned about the threat of fraud committed by other companies or subcontractors. An even higher 92% indicate concerns about the threat of fraud committed by customers or the public. The survey found that 90% had concerns about the threat of employee fraud.

Of those questioned, half feel that investment in technology is the only way to deal with fraud in the future. However, slightly more than 75% of those with fraud measures in place believe that they are sufficient for the company's needs. Despite the worries outlined in the survey, only 36% of the organizations questioned are planning to introduce new fraud measures in the next 12 months.

Fraud can be extremely difficult to detect, especially fraud perpetrated by insiders who know about a company's systems. The difficulty of detecting fraud grows proportionally to the size and complexity of the organization. But implementing anti-fraud systems and uncovering suspicious activity can improve working practices, erase security issues, and simplify e-business processes, making them more secure and reliable. These strategies are essential for any company wishing to operate both economically and efficiently in the digital age, while safeguarding the public's confidence and trust in its Internet operations.

8.19 Machine-Learning and Fraud

Data mining tools based on machine-learning algorithms allow for the extraction of rules directly from the data and the creation of graphical decision trees. A decision tree allows for the visual segmentation of various data components for predicting situations where fraud has a high probability of occurring. The core technology of these decision tree tools as we have learned are commonly machine-learning algorithms, which automate the process of segmenting important features and ranges hidden in a database. For example, these types of tools (ANGOSS and SPSS) can be used to discover situations in which fraudulent transactions are likely to increase, enabling e-retailers to take preventive steps to reduce their losses. ANGOSS uses CHAID and CART concurrently, while SPSS uses the machine-learning algorithm C5.0.

8.19.1 Decision Trees

The decision tree shown in Figure 8.8 demonstrates instances where the probability of fraud increases. For example, the upper node represents the total number of on-line sales for a single day (2,009) with 13.2% representing fraudulent transactions. However, when the product price was between

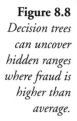

Figure 8.8
*Decision trees
can uncover
hidden ranges
where fraud is
higher than
average.*

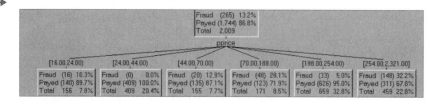

$70.00 and $188.00 (the fourth node from the left), the rate of fraud more than doubled to 28.1%; when the product price was over $254.00 (the node on the far right), it increased further to 32.2%.

Figure 8.9 examines the rate of fraud based on the type of products sold by an electronic consumer product site, which, on average, is 13.2%. As you can see, it increases on higher-price items, such as camcorders and PDAs to 22.4% and gets even higher with digital cameras and PCs to 34.9%.

Figure 8.10 shows a relationship between fraud and a specific demographic attribute, in this case the median rent of shoppers. This information is matched against their physical addresses, captured at the shopping cart on the site.

Interestingly, at this juncture, several clues on the profile of these on-line fraud perpetrators can begin to be assembled. They tend to be young, as the neural network model was indicating (25–44), and, as the decision tree tool discovered, they tend to live in apartments with rents in the range of $425 to $548. Through this type of data mining analysis, the user can interactively view the demographic features and dynamics associated with fraudulent transactions, enabling an e-business to begin to assemble a fraud profile.

8.19.2   Conditions for Fraud

Machine-learning–based data mining tools can also generate conditional and association rules directly from their segmentation analysis of a data set. Using a database with a sample of both legal and fraudulent transactions, rules can be extracted in order to anticipate and discover the conditions that are associated with fraudulent transactions.

These rules can be deployed to perform real-time alerts in situations where transactions and the associated demographics of on-line shoppers tend to indicate a high probability of fraud. From these analyses rules can be generated in many programming language formats, such as C or Java, enabling a Web site to incorporate them in its e-commerce application server software; for example:

Figure 8.9 *As fraud statistics show, computer equipment is high on criminals' lists.*

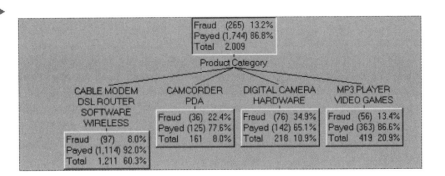

```
IF      PERCENT AGE_25-44 is      62.00
AND     MEDIAN RENT is            527.00 ± 74.00
THEN    TRANSACTION is            Fraud
        Rule's probability:       0.727
        The rule exists in:       320 records
        Significance level:       .001 error probability
```

These rules represent potential conditions where fraud is likely to occur, which can be integrated into an e-commerce system or outsourced to a Web service provider. The following is a sample of a rule written in SQL; other code formats include Visual Basic, C, and Java among others.

```
-- SQL Predictive Model
-- A separate nested case statement has been
-- generated for each predicted outcome.
--Block # 1: Calculates the probabality
--          that 'Transaction' equals 'Fraud'
--Block # 1: Calculates the probabality
--          that 'Transaction' equals 'Fraud'
```

Figure 8.10 *Fraud is highest in households where the median rent is $425–$548.*

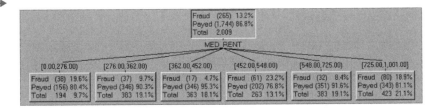

```
(CASE
WHEN (pprice >= 16 and pprice < 24) THEN
      0.102564102564
WHEN (pprice >= 24 and pprice < 44) THEN
      0
WHEN (pprice >= 44 and pprice < 70) THEN
      0.129032258065
WHEN (pprice >= 70 and pprice < 188) THEN
      (CASE
      WHEN (MED_RENT >= 0 and MED_RENT < 362) THEN
            0.274509803922
      WHEN (MED_RENT >= 362 and MED_RENT < 921) THEN
            0.139784946237
      WHEN (MED_RENT >= 921 and MED_RENT < 1001) THEN
            0.777777777778
      Else
            0.280701754386
      END)
WHEN (pprice >= 188 and pprice < 254) THEN
      0.0500758725341
WHEN (pprice >= 254 and pprice <= 2321) THEN
      (CASE
      WHEN (P_AGE5_17 >= 0 and P_AGE5_17 < 6) THEN
            0.0857142857143
      WHEN (P_AGE5_17 >= 6 and P_AGE5_17 < 12) THEN
            0.575342465753
      WHEN (P_AGE5_17 >= 12 and P_AGE5_17 < 14) THEN
            0.181818181818
      WHEN (P_AGE5_17 >= 14 and P_AGE5_17 <= 33) THEN
            0.314189189189
      Else
            0.322440087146
      END)
Else
      0.131906421105
END)
```

8.20   **The Fraud Ensemble**

For the final phase of this data mining project, we construct an ensemble from the multiple analyses, pooling the results from each algorithm. We partition the data into training, testing, and validating segments, then rotate them using the neural networks, decision tree, and rule generator to identify the fraudulent transactions, mixing and matching the resulting code to optimize the best possible performance from the multiple models. This is a time-consuming process that will require patience and experience, which can only be gained by working through the entire process of knowing the data, preparing it, enhancing it, and analyzing it with multiple algorithms.

8.21 **The Outsourcing Option**

Because of the dynamic and complex nature of detecting fraud in real time, some e-businesses may want to outsource the process, as banks have done with credit cards. A fraud-detection system enables an e-commerce site to counter criminal acts effectively via a subscription to a Web service provider that specializes in fraud detection via data mining or through a consortium network. One such fraud detection consortium is Retail Decisions, which works with card-not-present (CNP) transactions, primarily with operator-assisted credit-card payments over the phone, but also with e-commerce sites.

There is also CyberSource, which has an exclusive association with Visa U.S.A for matching fraud transactions. The CyberSource Internet Fraud Screen (IFS) system uses a combination of rules-based modeling and neural-network modeling techniques. It's IFS risk profile scores look at more than a dozen different information items, including the customer's local time and the risk associated with the customer's e-mail host. CyberSource also provides e-retailers with an IFS report that includes risk profile codes, address verification system (AVS) codes, and other relevant information to help e-merchants calibrate their risk thresholds and score settings. This enables the e-business subscribers to control the level of risk they want to operate under.

HNC, the long-time player in the area of credit-card fraud alerts, also provides its *eFalcon* detection consortium service geared toward telephone carriers and e-retailers. ProMiner is another Web service that can assist merchants in deploying advanced, scalable fraud detection without incurring large upfront capital costs for hardware, software, and implementation. The fraud-detection service allows an e-business to rely on data mining experts in the analysis of transactional, behavioral, and demographic databases. They mine an e-retailers' data, create the dynamic rules and code, and set up an alert system for a merchant with minimal impact.

A consortium or data mining fraud-detection Web service allows an e-retailer to focus on the core part of its business. These types of services typically use their own external servers, monitoring the transactional traffic that passes through a merchant site, matching the on-line behavior and profiles, so that anytime a potential fraudulent transaction is detected, alerts are sent directly to the e-business, which can then choose how to deal with the deviation.

8.22 The Hybrid Solution

Typically, a fraud-detection system employs a mixture of human domain knowledge and data mining technologies, such as machine-learning and neural-networks. Empirical studies have shown that hybrid systems, combining human insight and machine-learning rules with neural-network models, are the best for detecting fraud. They combine the better of two worlds and represent the strength of intuitive human instincts and powerful pattern-recognition technologies. It is the experienced hunter aided by the relentless hunting dog, searching for data clues and potential criminal activity.

For example, a fraud-detection specialist who is knowledgeable about what type of products tend to attract criminals would know that computer hardware is an item that can easily be unloaded at auction sites. However, a machine-learning algorithm can detect the range of transactions (3–5) and price intervals, out of thousands of transactions, that signal a potential fraudulent transaction. A data mining analysis can segment, in real time, several transactional and consumer variables, enabling the following type of real-time alert to be generated:

```
IF card expiration is 2 years from this month
AND number of purchases = 3 - 5
AND Standard Industry Code (SIC) of product = hardware
AND average price of purchases < $254 dollars
AND median rent = $425-548
THEN fraud probability score = 88%
```

One of the most difficult challenges to fraud detection is finding a new signature or pattern. For data mining to be used in the deterrence of fraud, samples of transactions that turn out to be fraudulent have to be used to train the system to extract either a scorecard, in the mode of a formula of weights from a neural network, or an array of rules created from a data mining analysis of fraudulent and nonfraudulent transactions extracted via a machine-learning algorithm such as C5.0 or a segmentation engine such as CART.

In addition to the use of data mining, coupled with a trained investigator's domain expertise, there are several deterrence techniques that can be used to detect and deter on-line credit-card fraud. For example, companies such as InfoSplit can provide the geo location of the IP address of a purchaser, which a merchant can compare against the shipping location to investigate all mismatches.

Other clickstream information, such as the time of day, browser type, operating system, and other on-line behavior data, such as the referring sites, can be included in the data mining process for developing a new set of models for detecting fraud. Unquestionably, the biggest obstacle to the future of successful e-businesses today is credit-card fraud, both for e-merchants and for consumers subject to auction fraud.

According to Meridien Research, without any technological investments in fraud detection and prevention, worldwide credit-card fraud will represent $15.5 billion in losses by 2005. However, if merchants adopt data mining technology now to help screen credit-card orders prior to processing, the widespread use of this technology is predicted to cut overall losses by two-thirds to $5.7 billion in 2005. Criminal analysts commonly work with statistics to determine trends and levels of threat to individuals and property, so it is not unrealistic to see how data mining, a technology rooted in the use of machine-learning and statistical algorithms, can be used to stem the flow of fraud in this emerging on-line marketplace.

The battle against on-line fraud is an unending one; e-merchants and Web auctioneers must be shrewd and use data mining technologies and experts to stay ahead of the scams of criminals, such as the gang, that had the audacity to invest in its own ATM machine, stock it with cash, and then wheeled it into a busy shopping mall for the purpose of *"skimming"* credit- and debit-card numbers, along with their associated PIN codes. This is a true story, and one where the perpetrators got away clean. Similar scams are rapidly evolving every day on the Web, where criminals are silently rolling out their virtual ATM machines in hopes of defrauding merchants of their money and consumers of their identities.

8.23 Bibliography

ZDNet AnchorDesk (August 30, 2000) "How to Protect Yourself From Auction Fraud."

ZDNet Tech Update (March 27, 2002) "The Paradox of On-line Fraud."

Criminal Patterns: Detection Techniques

9.1   Patterns and Outliers

In this chapter, we will explore some of the criminal patterns in several areas, such as financial crimes (fraud), as well as those in the insurance industry involving medical scams, and, most importantly, those being perpetrated in the telecommunications industry. The telecommunications carriers, as is the case with e-commerce, represent the type of business entities of the future, where identity theft through the combination of available credit and the absence of a physical presence can lead to financial losses in the millions of dollars. Some of these crimes may apply to other industries, but we will concentrate on these three sectors as they are by far the most common. The data mining investigative methodology remains the same across different industrial crimes.

Fraud is defined as "an act of deceiving illegally in order to make money or obtain goods" by the Oxford Dictionary. It is also known as "scams" or, more elegantly, as "economic offenses." By any definition, it is a crime, which in our networked environment can cost businesses billions of dollars a year. Fraud detection involves an assortment of deterrence activities: pattern recognition, profiling of perpetrators, early warning systems, prevention schemes, avoidance organization, minimizing false alarms, estimating losses, risk analysis, surveillance and monitoring, enhanced security, forensic analysis, evidence collection, prosecution of criminals, and notification of law enforcement officials.

We will first discuss some of the known MOs and some known indicators of these crimes, then move on to present a general methodology that can be applied to detect them via data mining. Every data mining project will be different because every database is slightly different for every company, Web site, and government agency. There are, of course, some processes that remain the same, such as the random sampling of records or the cleaning, enhancing, and preparation of the data prior to analysis. These steps are fairly standard and required of every project, and we will cite them in this chapter.

There is no single template for detecting fraud, just as there is no one methodology for data mining. Criminal perpetrators, whether hackers or thieves, are creative and opportunistic individuals, and attempts to catch them cannot be based solely on how they have behaved in the past. An investigative data miner must look for old patterns, as well as new ones that may signal a new type of criminal behavior or hack attack. For this reason, two typical analyses will be needed, one involving classification of known patterns and the other involving a clustering analysis in search of anomalies or outliers in the data. Additionally, link analysis might assist in detecting perpetrators and, in fact, is used in the detection of fraud in the insurance and telecommunications industries. The objective is fast and accurate fraud detection without undue burden on business operations, minimizing false positives, invasions of privacy, and discrimination.

9.2   Money As Data

In this era of interconnected networks, money represents information moving at the speed of light, where digital crime within the banking and financial services industry can cost billions of dollars each year—undetected and unreported. Using more sophisticated detection policies and procedures has become a necessity, and these include the use of investigative data mining. While some detection techniques are common to all frauds, the investigative data miner must understand the different nature of financial crimes in order to develop a methodology for uncovering them. Financial fraud often consists of repeated criminal incidents involving many transactions using methods of operation similar in content and appearance, but not quite identical.

Financial institutions should not rely solely on the experience and intuition of auditors, analysts, and fraud specialists to detect criminal transactions. In most cases, there is a history of audited fraudulent transactions that can be used to build models to predict future fraudulent activities. The goal of data mining for a financial institution is the development of rules and models enabling it to reduce the number of fraudulent-transaction alerts to a volume that can be handled and investigated by, say, an audit group in a bank. The problem is that the perpetrators of the crimes can learn the rules and procedures adopted by that audit group and take detection-avoidance action, such as changing their methods of operation, profiles, and dollar thresholds.

An effective analytic solution needs to capture the experience of fraud specialists, as well as incorporate the rules from analysis and predictive models. Together, a hybrid mechanism can be established in a flexible and sophisticated manner that makes avoidance by criminals difficult. We will describe a number of fraud scenarios and indicate similarities and some known signatures. It is very important to learn as much as possible about the nature of the crimes and the criminals' MOs. Fraud detection is a process; it never stops. It just evolves over time with new schemes, stings, scams, and MOs, but so do the weapons for detecting and deterring them.

9.3 Financial Crime MOs

9.3.1 Credit-Card Fraud

Credit-card fraud detection is especially challenging because the analyst needs to identify both the physical theft of a card, as well as an individual's identity; this means stolen cards, as well as cloned and personal identification number (PIN) thefts. This type of fraud can also be the result of the theft of an individual's identification, such as his or her Social Security number and home address, for the creation of new accounts under false or stolen identities.

MO: Credit-card theft will defraud the credit-card issuer or merchant. It has a profile of many small amounts, and an out-of-character purchasing pattern. The fraud activity is time-constrained. The card will be reported as stolen at some point and identity theft will be detected, at least by the next statement date. This time constraint forces perpetrators to use the card rapidly and for amounts normally out of pattern—this is the signature of this financial crime and a method to its detection. It is a crime where, inevitably, some loss will occur before detection. This crime is both highly organized and opportunistic.

Detection Technique: Look for lead indicators. Loss will inevitably occur before detection. Sequencing of purchases will change; the merchant mix will be out of character compared to previous consumer transactions. Frequency, monetary, and recency (FMR) techniques can be examined and employed. Time-sequence accumulated-risk scores may be used as an input to aggregated risk exposure. A change in location may indicate a ring operation. There are a number of leads that relate specifically to credit-card and debit-card fraud. They are common points-of-purchase (CPP) detection, particularly with regard to new merchant agents. The main method of detection is to look for outliers and changes in the normal patterns of usage. A SOM neural network can be used to perform an autonomous clustering of patterns in the data.

9.3.2 Card-Not-Present Fraud

Internet and phone-order transactions are the classic card-not-present (CNP) sales and, as we saw in the preceding chapter, are subject to higher than average dollar amounts and big-ticket items. They are also time-sensitive crimes, where the thieves are racing to beat the credit-card monthly statement mailing date.

MO: Internet credit-card thieves do leave characteristic footprints. For example, many businesses see fraud rates increase at certain times of the day, and orders coming in from certain countries exhibit a higher percentage of fraud. Thieves also gravitate to certain types of products, such as electronics, which are easy to sell via Web auction sites. Other clues to these perpetrators are the use of Web-based e-mail addresses and different shipping and billing addresses.

Detection Technique: This subject was covered in detail in Chapter 8; however, other indicators include looking for repeated attempts with slight variations of card numbers or the use of different names and addresses. Another possible indication of trouble is an IP address at variance with other data. If demographics are available, a model may be developed, as was demonstrated in the preceding chapter. The absence of certain data, such as activity in a credit report, are also signals of possible identify theft and fraud.

9.3.3 Loan Default

This type of financial crime involves the manipulation and inflation of an individual credit rating prior to performing a "sting," leading to a loan default and a loss for the financial service provider.

MO: This financial crime relies on creating a false identity and takes time to develop. Once an account has been created with a stolen or false identity, the marketing initiatives employed by the bank or credit-card issuer assist the perpetrator in building a portfolio of credit-cards, loan accounts, and a viable credit-rating and history—before defaulting on them.

Detection Technique: There are many lead indicators available. There is often only one "pot" of money that is cycled through the various accounts—a pattern of cash withdrawals from credit cards, and then at the end of the credit cycle, a similar amount repaid, usually using a cash withdrawal from another credit card. Lead indicators include credit cards that are rarely used to make actual merchant purchases and have small outstanding credit balances. Another pattern to look for is a loan account that is left unused. These techniques inflate a centrally controlled credit rating, providing a false impression that the account is deemed responsible. Detection has to occur before the "sting," which is a use of the credit and loan accounts very rapidly within a credit cycle. This financial crime can result in high losses. Detection must occur before the loss, because the sting has a short execution time.

9.3.4 Bank Fraud

This financial crime involves the creation of fictitious bank accounts for the conduit of money and the siphoning of other legitimate accounts. It may also be for fictitious account purchases, particularly in association with investment accounts and bond and bearer bond transactions.

MO: Many of the methods of executing internal fraud are similar to money laundering, except there is an obvious attempt to defraud the bank, whereas in money laundering the objective is simply to hide the funds. In addition, this fraud often works in conjunction with the establishment of creditworthy accounts, lines of credit, and fictitious accounts. The sting is often a single or small number of large-volume transactions, often related to real estate purchases, business investments, and the like.

Detection Technique: The method of detection relies on out-of-pattern transactions or anomalous account use. As with other financial crimes, detection must occur before any loss is sustained. There are lead indicators like the "manipulation of credit" described above and in the lack of references, high associations of matching attributes, and dubious acceptance criteria.

The critical factors for detecting all of these financial fraud crimes is knowing the behavior of credit, bank, and loan accounts and developing an understanding of the categories of customers. Data mining can be used to spot outliers or account usages that are normal and out of character. Sometimes the account seems "too good to be true," and it often is. The absence of telephone numbers or other contact information may indicate a "ring." These rings enable fraudulent activities to be distanced from their sources and add complexity to criminal detection. Another clue is the multiple use of the same address or phone number for different accounts.

9.4 Money Laundering

Money generated in large volume by illegal activities must be "laundered," or made to look legitimate, before it can be freely spent or invested; otherwise, it may be seized by law enforcement and forfeited to the government. Transferring funds by electronic messages between banks—"wire transfer"—is one way to swiftly move illegal profits beyond the easy reach of law enforcement agents and at the same time begin to launder the funds by confusing the audit trail.

To launder money is to disguise the origin or ownership of illegally gained funds to make them appear legitimate. Hiding legitimately acquired money to avoid taxation, or moving money for the financing of terrorist attacks also qualify as money laundering activities. United States Treasury officials estimate that as much as $300 billion is laundered annually, worldwide, with from $40 billion to $80 billion of this originating from drug profits made in the United States.

MO: Law enforcement officials describe three basic steps to money laundering.

1. *Placement*: introducing cash into the banking system or into legitimate commerce

2. *Layering*: separating the money from its criminal origins by passing it through several financial transactions, such as transferring it into and then out of several bank accounts, or exchanging it for travelers' checks or a cashier's check

3. *Integration*: aggregating the funds with legitimately obtained money or providing a plausible explanation for its ownership

Wire transfers of illicit funds are yet another key vehicle for moving and laundering money through the vast electronic funds transfer systems. More than 465,000 wire transfers, valued at more than two trillion dollars, are moved each day in the United States. Using data mining technologies and techniques for the identification of these illicit transfers could reveal previously unsuspected criminal operations or make investigations and prosecutions more effective by providing evidence of the flow of illegal profits.

There are many ways to launder money. Any system that attempts to identify money laundering will need to evaluate wire transfers against multiple profiles. In addition, money launderers are believed to change their MOs frequently. If one method is discovered and used to arrest and convict a ring of criminals, activity will switch to alternative methods. Law enforcement and intelligence community experts stress that criminal organizations engaged in money laundering are highly adaptable and flexible. For example, they may use nonbank financial institutions, such as exchange houses and check cashing services and instruments like postal money orders, cashier's checks, and certificates of deposit. In this way, money launderers resemble individuals who engage in ordinary fraud: They are adaptive and devise complex strategies to avoid detection. They often assume their transactions are being monitored and design their schemes so that each transaction fits a profile of legitimate activity.

In a study entitled *Information Technologies for the Control of Money Laundering*, completed in September 1995, the Office of Technology Assessment (OTA) was asked by the Permanent Subcommittee on Investigations of the

Senate Committee on Governmental Affairs to assess the proposed use of techniques derived from AI research (data mining) to monitor wire transfer traffic and recognize suspicious transfers. The OTA report rejected the use of data mining due in part to a lack of useful profiles, high false positives, high cost, and privacy issues, but, most importantly, the major challenges in constructing an effective wire transfer analysis system was related to the incomplete, spotty, and poor condition of the data, not the AI technologies. "In several cases, technologies are available that would be appropriate for wire transfer analysis, but data and (government) expertise do not exist to make those technologies effective."

As with other criminal detection applications the major obstacle to using data mining techniques is the absence of data uniformity. Related issues, such as the absence of experts, high costs, and privacy concerns, are being reevaluated in light of the recent terrorist attacks. The post-9/11 environment is changing the priorities of years ago. One of the biggest obstacles to using data mining to detect the use of wire transfers for illegal money laundering was the poor quality of the data; ineffective standards did not ensure that all the data fields in the reporting forms were complete and validated. New legislation is already changing this, ensuring that the quality of data is improved to the level that data mining can be used by government analysts from the U.S. Treasury Department's Financial Crimes Enforcement Network (FinCEN) and other investigative agencies.

9.5 Insurance Crimes

Insurance fraud and health care–related crimes are widespread and very costly to carriers, the government, and the consumer public. Insurance fraud involves intentional deception or misrepresentation intended to result in an unauthorized benefit. An example would be billing for health care services that have not been rendered. Health care crime involves charging for services that are not medically necessary, do not conform to professionally recognized standards, or are unfairly priced. An example would be performing a laboratory test on a large numbers of patients when only a few should have it. Health care crime may be similar to insurance fraud, except that it is not possible to establish that the abusive acts were done with intent to deceive the insurer.

Although no precise dollar amount can be determined, some authorities contend that insurance fraud constitutes a $100-billion-a-year problem. The U.S. General Accounting Office estimates that $1 out of every $7 spent on Medicare is lost to fraud and health care crime. Medicare lost nearly $12 billion last year alone to fraudulent or unnecessary claims. It is important that carriers have the intelligence to process claims with payment, recall them, cancel them, reduce them, or seek clarification from medical staff or patient.

9.5.1   False Claims

False-claim schemes are the most common type of health-insurance fraud. The goal in these schemes is to obtain undeserved payment for a claim or series of claims.

MO: This includes billing for services, procedures, or supplies that were not provided or used, as well as misrepresentation of what was provided, when it was provided, the condition or diagnosis, the charges involved, or the identity of the provider recipient. This may also involve providing unnecessary services or ordering unnecessary tests.

Detection Technique: Depending on the insurance carrier, there are various methods used in an attempt to identify false claims, including red-flag reviews by fraud specialists, both on-line and behind the scenes. A carrier may also use an expert system, which is a rule-based program that codifies the rules of a human reviewer. Link analysis may be used to look for a ring of fraudulent providers, and, of course, data mining tools, such as neural networks, may be used for training and detection if samples of fraud cases exist. The net amount of the claim may be too large compared to the average amount of similar claims.

9.5.2   Illegal Billing

Illegal billing schemes involve charging a carrier for a service that was not performed.

MO: This includes unbundling of claims—that is, billing separately for procedures that normally are covered by a single fee. A variation is double billing, charging more than once for the same service, also known as upcoding, the scam of charging for a more complex service than was performed. This may also involve kickbacks in which a person receives payment or other benefits for making referrals.

Detection Technique: The methods are the same as with false claims. In addition, a carrier may use models and rules developed by insurance specialists, coupled with those from data mining analyses, such as decision trees or rule generators to detect these schemes.

9.5.3 Excessive or Inappropriate Testing

Billing for inappropriate tests—both standard and nonstandard—appears to be much more common among chiropractors and joint chiropractic/medical practices than among other health care providers.

MO: The most commonly abused tests include:

- *Computerized inclinometry*: Inclinometry is a procedure that measures joint flexibility.

- *Nerve conduction studies*: Personal injury mills often use these inappropriately to follow the progress of their patients.

- *Surface electromyography*: this measures the electrical activity of muscles, which can be useful for analyzing certain types of performance in the workplace. However, some chiropractors claim that the test enables them to screen patients for "subluxations." This usage is invalid.

- *Thermography*: Chiropractors who use thermography typically claim that it can detect nerve impingements, or "nerve irritation" and is useful for monitoring the effect of chiropractic adjustments on subluxations. These uses are not medically appropriate.

- *Ultrasound screening*: Ultrasonography is not appropriate for diagnosing muscle spasm or inflammation or for following the progress of patients treated for back pain.

- *Unnecessary X rays*: It is not appropriate for chiropractors to routinely X-ray every patient to measure the progress of patients who undergo spinal manipulation.

- *Spinal videofluoroscopy*: This procedure produces and records X-ray pictures of the spinal joints that show the extent to which joint motion is restricted. For practical purposes, however, a simple physical examination procedure, such as asking the patient to bend, provides enough information to guide the patient's treatment.

Detection Technique: Many insurance administrators are concerned about chiropractic claims for "maintenance care," which is a periodic examination and "spinal adjustment" of symptom-free patients, which is not a covered service. To detect such care, many companies automatically review claims with more than 12 visits. However, this number can be adjusted. In 1999, the U.S. Inspector General recommended automatic review after no more than 12 visits for Medicare recipients. Some chiropractors attempt to avoid review by issuing a new diagnosis after the 12th visit. Link analysis has been used to detect some of these perpetrators, as well as have data mining and expert systems. Data mining analyses should zero in on the percentage of diagnostic test costs to the average net amount of similar claims, as well as a comparison of the cost of one or more diagnostic tests to the average amount of similar claims.

9.5.4 Personal Injury Mills

Many instances have been discovered in which corrupt attorneys and health care providers, usually chiropractors or medical clinics, combine to bill insurance companies for nonexistent or minor injuries. The typical scam includes "cappers" or "runners," who are paid to recruit legitimate or fake auto-accident victims or worker's compensation claimants. Victims are commonly told they need multiple visits.

MO: Mills fabricate diagnoses and reports, providing expensive, but unnecessary, services. The lawyers then initiate negotiations on settlements based upon these fraudulent or exaggerated medical claims.

Detection Technique: Mill activity can be suspected when claims are submitted for many unrelated individuals who receive similar treatment from a small number of providers. These claims are typically manually reviewed by claim specialists; however, link analysis and rule generators can also be used for screening large volumes of claims.

9.5.5 Miscoding

In processing claims, insurance companies rely mainly on diagnostic and procedural codes recorded on the claim forms. Their computers are programmed to detect services that are not covered. Most insurance policies exclude nonstandard or experimental methods. To help boost their income, many nonstandard practitioners misrepresent what they do and may misrepresent their diagnoses.

MO: Brief or intermediate-length visits may be coded as lengthy or comprehensive visits. Patients receiving chelation therapy may be falsely diagnosed as suffering from lead poisoning and may be billed for infusion therapy or simply an office visit. The administration of quack cancer remedies may be billed as chemotherapy. Live-cell analysis may be billed as one or more tests for vitamin deficiency. Nonstandard allergy tests may be coded as standard ones.

Detection Technique: Any code that is not standard must be subject to review and matched against prior claims from similar clinics or practitioners, typically performed by red-flag claim specialists. Clustering of historical data can be used to detect outliers automatically, and to check a disease (illness) against average duration and cost using a historical claims database to generate a histogram.

In the insurance industry, there are various methods by which carriers attempt to review for fraud while processing policy claims. The following are some important data attributes for detecting potential fraud claims:

- Duration of illness

- Net amount cost

- Illness (disease)

- Claimant sex

- Claimant age

- Claim cost

- Hospital

Using these variables, analyses can be performed to identify outliers for each, such as test costs, hospital charges, illness duration, and doctor charges. These are some temporal parameters for analyzing insurance claims. Table 9.1 illustrates the various methods of insurance fraud detection, along with some advantages and disadvantages of each. The chart is not all-inclusive but simply provides an overview of trends in the industry.

Detecting insurance fraud, as in the case of financial crimes, also requires the combined efforts of human experts—investigators, fraud specialists, claim reviewers and forensic auditors—along with the use of data mining tools, such as link analysis, SOMs, neural-network models, decision trees, and rule generators.

Table 9.1   *Methods of Insurance Fraud Detection*

Method	Advantages	Disadvantages
On-line red-flag review by fraud specialist	Provides immediate feedback to claim handler	Is limited to current claim
		Limited number of red flags can be reviewed
		Must still evaluate the significance of the set of red flags detected
Behind-the-scenes red-flag review by fraud specialist	Can scan for a larger number of red flags	Does not provide immediate feedback to claim handler
	Can detect ring activity or repeat fraudulent behavior by the same individuals	Must still evaluate the significance of the set of red flags detected
	Doesn't interfere with the claim handling process	
Interactive expert systems (this is a rule-based system)	Can detect qualitative red flags as well as quantitative	Is time-consuming for claim handler
Data mining or statistical modeling	Weighs the relative importance of claim information in predicting fraud	Requires that data mining skills be developed
	Provides consistent fraud evaluation for all claims	Requires periodic revision of model as the nature of fraud changes
Outlier clustering detection	Is self-adjusting to different types of populations	Need specialized skills to develop
		Needs large amounts of transaction data

→

Table 9.1   *Methods of Insurance Fraud Detection (continued)*

Method	Advantages	Disadvantages
Link analysis	Provides easy-to-understand graph or map of patterns of fraud	Needs specialized software to display results
	Links can detect and uncover fraud rings	Needs some proactive fraud-detection preliminary work to reduce the amount of claim data to represent pictorially
		Has limited effectiveness at determining whether an individual claim is fraudulent

9.6   Death Claims That Did Not Add Up: A Case Study

A major insurance company was concerned with finding patterns in death claims that occur within and shortly after the two-year contestability period. During this time frame, the insurance company has the right to contest benefit payments. Therefore, it is imperative that fraudulent claims be detected in a timely fashion.

This particular insurance company database consisted of over 100,000 policies. A traditional auditing tool was first used as a preprocessor to manipulate the files and sort the data according to date clusters. The contestability date was selected and the period two years before (back to the issuing date) and two years after formed the total four-year period of interest. The data was sorted into six-month clusters or a total of eight clusters over the four years, and the records containing death claims were selected. Each resulting cluster of interest consisted of an average of about 550 records.

Once the preliminary step was taken with a traditional auditing tool, Wiz-Rule from WizSoft was used to analyze the data. This firm also offers Wiz-Why, a data mining rule generator tool. WizRule is a data auditing application that automatically reveals all the rules in a given database and points out deviations and potential errors in the data. WizRule can search and find all the IF/THEN rules in a data set and calculate the level of unlikelihood of each deviation when analyzing a database. In the case of this insurance carrier, WizRule analyzed each cluster of interest for patterns in the data and for deviations.

Since WizRule finds all the rules and relationships in the data without requiring preknowledge of the auditor, interesting and unexpected results can be discovered. Among the unusual patterns detected by WizRule were cases where the death occurred in a state other than either the state of insurance or the state the decedent lived in during the coverage of the policy. In some cases, a pattern of foreign-issued death certificates pointed to a potential ring of fraud. These cases are currently under investigation by the appropriate agencies.

9.7 Telecommunications Crime MOs

Wireless telephony fraud is a worldwide phenomenon. The $1.5 trillion phone industry loses approximately 10% to fraud, that is, $150 billion at current estimates. Nearly 70% of this fraud is "fraud for profit." The remaining fraud is social or expense-saving fraud. More disturbing are estimates that the telephony industry is growing at an average annual rate of 3% to 8%. Wireless crime, however, is growing at a rate of 11% to 25%, or even faster in some parts of the world.

Industry reports indicate that nearly 70% of all phone fraud, wittingly or unwittingly, originates inside the telecommunications company. Unscrupulous or venal company personnel can be knowingly working with outside criminals to defraud the phone company. Alternatively, unwitting company personnel may be used by outside criminals. Antifraud management systems must therefore be secure from internal, as well as external, threats and attacks. Because of the nature of this crime, senior security management needs to monitor the day-to-day activities of subordinates and conduct periodic security audits. Clearly, data mining can assist in detecting crime. However, in situations such as this, it is also a case of monitoring employees closely. Systems must be put in place to monitor personnel closely in search of deviations from standard measurements.

The basic strategy used by telecommunications criminals is very simple and is twofold: (1) they counterfeit their identity, and (2) they mechanically trick the systems and networks. Tactics, however, are another story; there are literally hundreds of tactics, with many changing daily, even hourly. For this reason, it is estimated that most carriers, even those using fraud-detection management systems, will miss 45% to 55% of the fraud that takes place in their networks.

Types of phone fraud can be subdivided in many ways, depending on how they are classified. There are several methods of classifying telecommunications crimes. Briefly, the following are the most two most common:

1. *Technical cloning and network alterations*: This is done by copying or changing the telephone mechanical equipment, switches, PBX, etc., or by spoofing and surfing, involving the capturing of calling-access information electronically or visually.

2. *Counterfeit identity*: This can be as simple as a dishonest application for subscription telecom service or use of a stolen name identify (identity theft).

Because of advances in security management systems, the trend of telecommunications crime is moving away from technical cloning and toward identity theft. However, identity fraud and wireless cloning fraud operations are often very similar. The distinction is in the technique used. Clone brokers counterfeit valid mobile identification number–electronic serial numbers (MIN-ESNs). Identity brokers counterfeit valid identities.

Indeed, identity fraud threatens to be the preferred wireless fraud of the new millennium. A likely scenario is the blending of cloning fraud and identity fraud operations. Due in part to anticloning technology, the migration of cloning fraud will most likely be to identity fraud, and a new type of criminal: the identity broker. An identity broker is a criminal who sells stolen accounts to other individuals. When carriers discover bogus accounts, most often an identity broker is involved, and usually a *behavioral signature* is found—an MO. The MO of the identity broker commonly has the following signatures.

9.7.1 Reuse of Identity Patterns

An identity broker will often reuse the same call-back telephone number with different accounts. They often reuse the same or a very similar billing address. Also their customers tend to use the stolen services within the same geographic areas. More often a local carrier will have checked the credit on the same identity. This inquiry will be present on their credit report for several months. This fact is a clue that can be used when "scoring" applicants because these inquiries will be present in all credit reports (see Chapter 2).

9.7.2 Signature Calling Patterns

There is often a set of commonly dialed numbers originating in a consistent geographic area. Upon activation, there may be a signature test call that fits a pattern. If international calling is important, the broker will often make a trial direct-dial international call, just to see if it works, before delivery to the customer. Another signature call pattern includes calls to obtain the time (767-2676) or information (411) to see if the number is activated. These test calls will be performed to these nondescript numbers because the perpetrators will not want to make a test call to a dialed number that might link the calls back to them.

9.7.3 Delay Patterns

Often there is a delay in usage beyond the test call. This pattern occurs for a few days until the new service is delivered to customers who buy the stolen accounts.

9.7.4 Association Patterns

Often the customers of identity brokers call each other on common pager numbers. Since business is often via word-of-mouth, common links often exist. This pattern of association lends itself to link analysis, as well as analysis via decision trees.

9.7.5 Telecommunications Crime Detection Techniques

An initial task is to develop models designed to identify the MO of operating identity brokers, to search for the patterns discussed above. These indicators of identity fraud can be matched to a specific MO. After all, analysis of known *past* fraud yields hard data that can be used to combat *future* fraud. Quantification of reoccurring indicators and the various patterns discussed here can be used to score and identify accounts with a probability of being obtained by fraud. This includes classic fraud indicators such as the reuse of a Social Security number, call back number or address, suspicious change requests, and unusual calling activity and call destinations.

But, the eventual solution is to authenticate the identity of the person applying for an account. This may entail the use of digital signatures, biometrics, and authentication processes designed to verify the identity of the faceless customer. Data mining, specifically the use of rule generators can be used to extract conditions, such as those covered in the patterns of these MOs to assist investigators in filtering suspected stolen accounts. The analysis can be complex and convoluted, but the rewards may be high. If a single identity broker organization can be identified and stopped, hundreds, or even thousands, of cases can be stopped at their source. Identity fraud has become so lucrative that a cottage industry of newly-minted identity brokers now flourishes in most big cities. According to the FBI, most of these perpetrators specialize in the wireless industry; however, some brokers also specialize in credit-card fraud, especially with regard to e-commerce and on-line auctions.

9.8   **Identity Crimes**

A study of identity theft conducted by the National Fraud Center found the following patterns in these crimes:

1.   Identity theft is no different from any other type of crime when committed by the professional perpetrator.

2.   Identity theft is difficult to track because it is a tool used for committing numerous other types of crimes, such as credit-card, bank, Internet, and telecommunications fraud.

3.   The growth of identity theft appears to be tied to technology, particularly the Internet and the wireless industry.

4.   Identity theft, largely as a result of the Internet, is rapidly developing internationally.

For wireless carriers, an applicant's good credit rating is the equivalent of a "bearer" financial instrument. Potential creditors are willing to hand over thousands of dollars in goods and services based upon a verbal promise to pay. All they require is someone who is the bearer of an acceptable credit history; this is really what an identity broker is stealing. In truth, most wireless service providers are more interested in verifying available credit rather than identity. This is a mistake, but in the highly competitive marketplace, it is a fact of survival and doing business.

Credit-card purchases rarely require identification, but verification of a credit balance is standard. Government regulations require financial institutions to check identification, but in the nonregulated private sector, the rules are generally lax, especially for wireless services. As a rule of thumb, businesses usually align their identification policies with their fraud and bad-debt experience.

Most wireless carriers verify the legitimacy of new customers with a credit check. If the credit history comes back as acceptable, it is *assumed* that the person is who they say. Since 99% of the time the assumption is correct, rarely is additional verification, such as photographic identification requested. However, the increasing use of telephonic "sign-up" for service makes photographic identification impractical.

One of the problems with detecting identity fraud for most wireless carriers is the length of time between activation and the realization that a crime has been committed, which is typically three to four months. Absent suspicious or unusual conditions, the account will not attract attention until a payment is sufficiently overdue. Generally, the initial bill is due about 60 days after activation. An additional 30 to 45 days will pass before the account is treated as seriously overdue. Meanwhile, collection notices of overdue payments will have begun. Telephone contact will be attempted and disconnect notices sent. Typically 120 days elapse before the service is actually deactivated.

For the telecommunication service provider, as with the credit-card issuer, a crime-detection system must be designed and developed by professionals who are very knowledgeable about industry practices. The statistical models developed and deployed must be dynamic and fast. They must be able to flag alerts directly to the fraud analyst within seconds after a suspected call is completed. The detection system must be customizable, because no two carriers' infrastructures are alike. In addition, their customers' demographics will likely be somewhat different; the types of services sold and their equipment will also be different. Reliability and security are essential. The system must be at least 99.9% reliable and secure with little or no maintenance downtime. Most importantly, the crime detection system must be designed to be self-learning, using multidimensional data mining models, as well as responsive to human experts.

Some of the larger telecommunications carriers have developed in-house fraud-detection systems based on each of their customers' signatures of usage, using a stream of transactions about each consumer yielding acceptable false-alarm rates. They create a signature of predicted usage behavior for each customer and update it with each nonsuspicious transaction that the customer makes. They next score transactions for fraud using predicted behavior for the customer as the baseline, and then accumulate translation scores into account fraud scores that are updated with each new transaction that the customer makes.

They create and maintain usage and fraud signatures for each customer, which they update with each transaction that the customer makes. They used periodic timing variables, such as day of week or hour of day, to construct these customer signatures. However, no information is available on what percentage of actual fraud even these high-end systems are able to detect. The AT&T network alone handles over 350 million long-distance calls and over 75 million wireless calls each day. Their InfoLab, which is responsible for mining their toll-usage data, has over 50 individuals working not only on identifying signatures, but also on squashing the data into an approximation format suitable for modeling, a major task in view of the high volume of data involved.

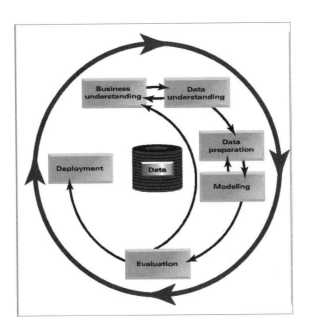

Figure 9.1 *The CRISP-DM process.*

9.9 A Data Mining Methodology for Detecting Crimes

The following methodology is proposed for detecting and deterring these various types of digital and entity crimes, not only for the industries covered in this chapter, but for those in other market sectors. First, in order to be cost-effective and accurate, the methodology should adhere to the CRoss-Industry Standard Process–Data Mining (CRISP-DM). CRISP-DM is a nonproprietary, documented, and freely available data mining model methodology.

CRISP-DM encourages best practices and offers a set structure for obtaining better and faster results from data mining. The CRISP-DM methodology was developed several years ago by a consortium of companies and organizations with the idea of standardizing some of the data mining processes for multiple and diverse data mining objectives, including crime detection.

CRISP-DM divides the life cycle of a data mining project into six major phases. The sequence of the phases is not strict. Moving back and forth between different phases is always required. The outcome of each phase determines what phase will follow or which particular task of a phase needs to be performed next. The arrows in the CRISP-DM diagram in Figure 9.1 indicate the most important and frequent dependencies between phases. The outer circle in the diagram symbolizes the cyclic nature of the data mining process. The concept of CRISP-DM is that data mining is a process, which continues well after a solution has been deployed. The lessons learned during this process could trigger new and often more focused investigative questions and queries, leading to subsequent data mining processes, which will benefit from the experiences of previous ones.

The objective of CRIP-DM is to establish a data mining standard process that is applicable in diverse industries, including criminal detection, with the objective of making data mining projects faster, more efficient, more reliable, more manageable and less costly. The CRISP-DM model defines the following data mining processes.

One: Understand the Investigation's Objective

Understand the insight or outcome sought by the agency, department, or business. During the course of the investigative data mining project, the analysts need to understand the type of crime they are trying to detect, the costs of positive and negative predictions, and the enforcement and preemptive actions that can be taken in each case. This initial phase focuses on understanding the project objectives and requirements from a business or law enforcement perspective, and then converting this knowledge into a data mining problem definition and a preliminary plan designed to achieve these objectives. The overall costs and benefits of the entire data mining project should be estimated and quantified.

Two: Understand the Data

Understand the crime that needs to be detected. This will ensure that the appropriate data will be collected and used to achieve a strong prediction. The data-understanding phase starts with an initial data collection and proceeds with exploratory activities necessary to get familiar with the data, to identify data-quality problems, to gain an initial insight into the data or to detect interesting subsets, and to form hypotheses from the hidden information. During this phase, consideration is given to the quality of the data and how that will impact the results obtained. Consideration is also given to how we will access the data and understand confidentiality and privacy issues. At this juncture, considering appending additional information, such as demographics or data from another governmental agency or commercial database, may be warranted.

Three: Data Preparation

The data-preparation phase covers all related activities needed to construct the final dataset, the data that will be fed into the data mining tool(s) from the initial transactional raw data. Data-preparation tasks are likely to be performed multiple times and not in any prescribed order. Tasks include table, record, and attribute selection, as well as transformation and cleaning of data for modeling tools. At this phase, data-quality issues must be addressed, a determination on how much data will be needed must be made, and in what format. For example, decisions need to be made on how to handle missing values, which in fraud detection takes on an especially important dimension. A process and a plan on how to obtain and prepare the data in the most efficient way possible must be made at this stage, with consideration given to other applications accessing the same data, and to server and network restrictions.

Four: Modeling

In this phase, various modeling techniques are selected and applied, and their parameters are calibrated to optimal values. Typically, there are several techniques for the same data mining problem type. Some techniques have specific requirements, depending on the structure of the data; therefore, stepping back to the data-preparation phase is often needed. For example, some algorithms, like CART, can work only with numeric data. During this phase, the construction of multiple models should take place to compare error rates. For crime detection it is essential that a number of techniques and models be employed and used in cooperation, via an ensemble—this is fundamental to a viable methodology and success in acheiving a cost-effective solution.

Five: Evaluation

At this stage in the project, the models have been constructed and appear to have a high degree of quality from a data-analysis perspective. However, before proceeding to final deployment of the models, it is important to evaluate them thoroughly and review the steps executed to construct them to be certain they properly achieve the detection objectives. A key objective is to determine if there is some important issue that has not been sufficiently considered, such as a high number of false positives, which can impact the total cost of deployment. At the end of this phase, a decision on the use of the data mining results should be reached. The entire process is iterative, and this evaluation phase should ensure and validate the results before final deployment.

Six: Deployment

The deployment of the models is often the neglected stage in most data mining projects. For crime detection, this phase requires continuous learning, automated monitoring and evaluation, and instantaneous refreshing of new models to capture the ever-changing characteristics of criminal avoidance. Creation of the model is generally not the end of the project. Even if the purpose of the model is to increase knowledge of the data, the knowledge gained will need to be organized and presented in a way that it can be used in a production environment. Code or rules may need to be exported into a production system, such as a call site, intranet, network, servers, or Web site. Depending on the requirements, the deployment phase can be as simple as generating a report or as complex as implementing a repeatable data mining process with streams of code generated on a regular basis.

9.10   Ensemble Mechanisms for Crime Detection

The optimal methodology for crime detection is to avoid designing a system that is rigid and based on a set of rules or thresholds that can be easily avoided by knowledgeable perpetrators. In addition, the detection system and models cannot be based on a single algorithm or technique; instead they should be based on the paradigm of a *committee of models*. The methodology should employ an ensemble of techniques and models, with each providing a *vote of confidence* regarding the legitimacy of any transaction, whether it be credit-card purchase, insurance claim, phone call, or any other type of event an investigator or analysts is trying to detect. The following are some essential steps that need to be considered in this process.

Random Sampling

Random samples of criminal evidence should be collected and used in the construction of multiple models. That is, fraudulent transactions need to be used in the analysis and an adequate sample for each crime that needs detection is required. For example, to construct a model to detect theft through credit cards on an e-commerce site, random samples of criminal transactions should be sampled from different product lines and, if possible, different times of days. Models will require samples of legal transactions in order to discriminate them from the criminal ones. This is especially important when using a neural network as one of the components in the ensemble.

Balance the Data

Another important step is having an adequate sampling of all types of criminal transactions along with an even number of legal ones. Again, this is especially important when working with neural networks, as they are essentially software memories that need an adequate number of observations to be able to recognize the phenomena (crime) the models are attempting to detect.

Split the Data

It is a common and standard practice in data mining to split the data into at least two parts, a training data set for constructing predictive models and a testing data set for evaluating the prediction and error rates of the models.

However, due to the nature of criminal detection, where samples tend to be very small, such as that of fraudulent transactions, an extra step should be taken and the data should be split into three segments: training, testing, and validating datasets.

Rotate the Data

As an extra precaution, aside from splitting the data into three segments for training, testing and validating, they should also be rotated; again, this is because of the relatively small samples of criminal transactions. The rotation can be as follows:

Training	Data set 1	Data set 2	Data set 3	Results A
Testing	Data set 2	Data set 3	Data set 1	Results B
Validating	Data set 3	Data set 1	Data set 2	Results C
	Results A	Results B	Results C	Solution Z

In this rotation scheme, the objective is to arrive at an average optimum of Solution Z by averaging the results of A, B, and C.

Evaluate Multiple Models

The optimum method for ensuring the best possible detection system is through the use and comparison of multiple models created with decision trees, rule induction generators, and neural networks. If time permits, multiple neural network architectures should be tried and tested to optimize their performance. In addition, the neural networks should be optimized if possible using a genetic algorithm component, which some data mining tools provide.

Combine Models

After evaluating and comparing individual models, create an ensemble:

Decision tree	Data set 1	Data set 2	Data set 3	Results A
Rule generator	Data set 2	Data set 3	Data set 1	Results B
Neural network	Data set 3	Data set 1	Data set 2	Results C
	Results A	Results B	Results C	Solution Z

The model ensemble combines the results from the best-performing decision tree, rule generator, and neural networks to optimize the detection capability. This scheme is also known as bagging for combining the prediction results from multiple models or from the same type of model for different data. It is used to address the inherent instability of results when applying complex models to relatively small data sets. Another technique, called *boosting*, is to derive weights to combine the predictions from those models in which greater weight goes to those observations that are difficult to classify (fraud transactions) and lower weights to those that are easy to classify (legal transactions).

Measure False Positives

Consideration should be given to the overall performance of the model ensemble, especially in regard to the misclassification costs—that is, the wrong alerts (false positives) and undiscovered cases (false negatives):

	Crime	No crime	
Alert	Correct	False positive	Alert
No alert	False negative	Correct	No alert

Cost considerations are different for both of these misclassification errors. For false positives, for example, there is the manpower consideration for checking on a potential criminal case that turns out to be legal. For false negatives, the cost is in the potential loss of revenue by not identifying a criminal incident. This may turn out to be the most expensive of both errors.

The biggest obstacle in any criminal detection system is the prediction of false positives. This is where a legitimate transaction, conducted by a legitimate credit-card or cell-phone customer or insurance policy holder, is classified as potentially fraudulent. There are two problems with false positives. If this happens too often, the (valuable) legitimate customer is likely to get upset by the intrusion and the delay of his business. Worse yet is the implication that he or she is a criminal. Also, if the numbers of false positives are large, the business or governmental process may be unable to handle the required investigative procedures, which may be manual and expensive, such as assigning suspected cases of fraud to a call center operator to handle or the detainment of individuals at a point of entry at a border or at an airport.

Deploy and Monitor

Once the model ensemble has been built and tested, it must be deployed in a real-time business environment. This can be accomplished by the export of its rules, weights (formulas), and assorted code from the models, which most data mining tools support. The continuously changing environment and skewed distributions, coupled with the cost-sensitive requirements, complicate the evaluation of the performance of a criminal-detection system. However, it must be continuously evaluated and improved, as the methods of criminal behavior change and attempts to go undetected will no doubt continue. Crime does not stop, nor should the mining of its pattern of behavior.

Compounding the challenge of data mining for criminal detection is that often systems rely on a history of fraud examples, which means they are often only capable of detecting fraud activities that match or correspond closely with those training samples, leaving many more fraudulent activities undetected. There is no single technique or model that will solve this. However, the ensemble-of-models technique provides an optimum method for making the best possible decision on the predicted legitimacy of the transaction, along with a measure of confidence to support that decision and course of action through continuous monitoring, evaluation, and improvement. Finally, as a means to identify new, undetected criminal transactions, a clustering analysis should be performed, using a SOM neural network. The objective is to look for transactions that fall out of the pattern of normal transactions, to look for outliers. These are cases that don't adhere to the way the majority of business activities are carried out.

Resources

AI and Fraud Detection

http://www.dinkla.net/fraud

AI Techniques in Fraud Management

http://www.aaai.org/AITopics/html/fraud.html

Association of Certified Fraud Examiners

http://www.cfenet.com

Communications Fraud Control Association

http://www.cfca.org

National Fraud Information Center

http://www.fraud.org

National Healthcare Anti-Fraud Association

http://www.nhcaa.org

9.11 Bibliography

Intelligent Enterprise (May 28, 2002), "The Hidden Truth."

10

Intrusion Detection: Techniques and Systems

10.1 Cybercrimes

Increasingly, crime, as we have said, is digital in nature: burglary, destruction, and thefts are perpetrated via remote system break-ins by computer hackers. Unlike the burglar of a building, cybercriminals will enter through a network port using a variety of utilities and tools for the purpose of obtaining the secret passwords and privileges designed to protect a system, so that they can destroy or steal digital property. In this chapter we will concentrate on the detection of computer system intrusions, which, in our prevailing networked environment, are becoming more common, leading to spiraling costs and massive destruction.

Of 500 organizations that responded to a recent computer crime and security survey conducted by the Computer Security Institute and the FBI, 90% detected an intrusion to their systems. The average loss due to a cybercrime is $6.6 million, up from $954,700 just five years ago. The most damaging attacks are targeted intrusions involving theft and financial fraud. Worms and viruses can also cause worldwide economic damage. Some worms, such as Code Red, enable intrusions, which can run into the billions of dollars in costs for government and corporate networks.

An intrusion is when a hacker attempts to break into or misuse a computer system, Web site, or network. Yet another way to define an intrusion is any set of actions that attempt to compromise the integrity, confidentiality, or availability of a computer resource. First, we will provide a brief overview on some of the techniques, utilities, and tools most commonly used by cybercriminals. Next, we will cover some of the preventive techniques and detection systems that have been developed, including how data mining is increasingly being used to counter these intrusions by forecasting attacks. As with the other types of crimes discussed previously, recognizing criminal patterns is the objective of the investigative data miner.

There are two types of potential intruders, the outside hacker and the inside one. Remarkably, FBI studies have revealed that 80% of intrusions and attacks come from within organizations. So, despite the fact that most security measures are put in place to protect the inside from a malevolent outside world, most intrusion attempts actually occur from within an organization. Whether the intrusion takes place from outside or within, it is important to find out how it happened to prevent any future break-ins. Computer forensics stress the need to preserve the crime scene once a break-in is discovered, which we will discuss at the end of this chapter.

Whether they attack from outside or inside, there are generally several steps taken by most hackers. Not surprising, the most common method of breaking in is via the Internet. The majority of these perpetrators use readily available tools or utilities to target computer systems and gain entry by remotely scanning for ports to achieve access, steal passwords, and eventually take control of networks, Web sites, computers, and their data.

There are several methods by which to prevent these types of cybercrimes. There are firewalls, antivirus software, and, of course there are countermeasures system administrators can take to protect their systems. There are also network-based and host-based intrusion detection systems (IDS), some of which use pattern-recognition techniques to detect and deter these types of system break-ins. However, before we get into a discussion of these data mining and intrusion detection techniques, it is important to describe the sequential steps cybercriminals have taken in the past to gain entry and take control of systems and networks.

An intrusion can occur as innocently as when an unsuspecting person opens an e-mail message or downloads an MP3 file. Free software can also harbor a stealth intruder with destructive applications hitching a ride, compromising privacy and security. Java applets downloaded with free software can transmit private information without the user's knowledge or permission. Spyware—JavaScript in an e-mail or invisible graphics (Web bugs; see Chapter 2)—downloaded or transmitted from a Web site can transmit user names and passwords without a user's knowledge, which at times is all cybercriminals want. Often a single password compromised from a user can destroy an entire system, Web site, or network.

10.2 Intrusion MOs

Before we detail how an intrusion detection systems work, it is important that a scenario be provided describing some of the common techniques, utilities, tools, and schemes used by hackers. There are several stages to an intentional system intrusion. There are half a dozen states, from the start of targeting a system to more daring probes, escalating to an all-out attack, to a system take-over and the setting of backdoors to enable the criminal to return. For those investigators who are not knowledgeable about some of these tools and utilities, it highly recommended that a search engine, such as Google.com, be used to research and even download them.

10.2.1   Intelligence

Any attack, just like a common burglary, starts with an intruder "casing the joint," or assessing the premises where the crime will take place, whether it is a bank or a server. The thief needs to know where the cameras and exits are to make a quick getaway without revealing his or her identity. This is the initial information-gathering process, and it can involve the use of open source search engines, Whois servers, USENet, Edgar, and domain name service lookups to obtain a composite of the target system.

MO

Edgar This is the Security and Exchange Commission (SEC) database at http://www.sec.gov, which provides a comprehensive view of publicly traded companies. Documents like 10Q and 10K provide a quick snapshot of a company's recent activities, especially with respect to new acquisitions, which may be the easiest path to a system penetration. Since the parent company will often scramble to bring new entities into its networks and Web site, with security often lagging behind, a hacker will note the new entities on file and target them first.

UseNet Mail postings by anybody associated with the company seeking technical assistance may signal a possible opening for an intrusion. This is readily available on the Internet to any hacker that knows what to look for.

Whois Whois servers can identify domain names and associated networks related to a particular firm or organization. These domain databases can be queried at http://www.networksolutions.com, http://www.arin.net, http://wwwallwhois.com or http://samspade.org. These databases can provide such intelligence, which a hacker can use prior to an intrusion attack as domain names, registration data, organization, point of contact and network IP address. The administrative contact is an important bit of intelligence, which a hacker can use to send spoofed e-mail, posing as the administrative contact, requesting a change of the password. Here is a sample of the information a Whois server provides:

webminer.com

Request: webminer.com

Registrant:
WebMiner (WEBMINER-DOM)
   2101 Shoreline Drive Suite 290
   Alameda, CA 94501
   US

   Domain Name: WEBMINER.COM

   Administrative Contact, Billing Contact:
      Martines, Earl (ECF327) earl@LUMINAAMERICAS.COM
      Webminer
      760 Broadway 2nd Floor
      New York, NY 10012
      US
      648.437-3331 646.437-3366
   Technical Contact:
      Hostmaster, Intermedia (HO2936-ORG)
      hostmaster@INTERMEDIA.NET
      Intermedia Corporation
      953 Industrial Ave. Ste.121
      Palo Alto, CA 94303
      US
      650-424-9935
      Fax- - 650-424-9936
      Fax- - - 650-424-9936

   Record last updated on 10-May-2001.
   Record expires on 01-May-2003.
   Record created on 30-Apr-1997.
   Database last updated on 18-Apr-2002 02:25:00 EDT.

   Domain servers in listed order:

   NS2.INTERMEDIA.NET   207.5.44.2
   NS3.INTERMEDIA.NET   207.5.1.222

Domain Name Service (DNS) After identifying associated domains, an attacker may begin to query the DNS, which is a distributed database used to map IP addresses to hostnames and vice versa, used mainly for redundancy of primary addresses with secondary ones. This service may be violated. If a DNS is configured insecurely, internal IP addresses may be disclosed to an attacker via the Internet, providing a complete map of a firm's internal network.

10.2.2 Scanning

At this phase an intruder will begin to use a different set of tools for the identification of listening services in search of the primary place for the break-in. This involves performing ping sweeps, port scans via the use of automated discovery tools. The objective of the perpetrator is to determine what ports are in a listening state and accessible via the Internet.

MO

fping Ping is a basic utility used to find out if a system is alive. It sends a packet to a target system; fping will send mass ping requests in parallel, sweeping multiple IP addresses. fping is a ping-like program, which uses the Internet Control Message Protocol (ICMP) echo request to determine if a host is up. fping is different from ping in that the user can specify any number of hosts on the command line or specify a file containing the lists of hosts to ping. Instead of trying one host until it times out or replies, fping will send out a ping packet and move on to the next host in a round-robin fashion. If a host replies, it is noted and removed from the list of hosts to check. If a host does not respond within a certain time or retry limit, it will be considered unreachable. Unlike ping, fping is used with scripts, and its output is easy to parse.

icmpenum This is yet another utility for sending packets to test if a system is alive. This tool allows packets dropped by border routers or firewalls using the ping utility. Host enumeration is the act of determining the IP address of potential targets on a network. Icmpenum uses not only ICMP echo packets to probe networks, but also ICMP timestamp and ICMP information packets as well. Furthermore, it supports spoofing and promiscuous listening for reply packets. Icmpenum is great for enumerating networks that block ICMP echo packets but have failed to block timestamp or information packets, or for upstream sniffing of trusted addresses. This is a proof-of-concept tool to demonstrate possible distributed attacking concepts, such as sending packets from one workstation and sniffing the reply packets on another.

Nmap Nmap is a port scanning tool used to determine the type of operating system a target computer is using, a key bit of intelligence for a preemptive attack. Other tools include NetScan, SuperScan, WinScan, ipEye, and WUPS. Nmap ("Network Mapper") is an open source utility for network exploration or security auditing. It was designed to scan large networks rapidly, although it works fine against single hosts. Nmap uses raw IP packets in novel ways to determine what hosts are available on a network, what services (ports) they are offering, what operating system version they are running, what type of packet filters/firewalls are in use, and dozens of other characteristics. Nmap runs on most types of computers, and both console and graphical versions are available. Nmap is free software, available with full source code. Counter port scanning tools include Snort, a freeware site-based system IDS and network-based IDSs, such as RealSecure.

10.2.3   Probing

At this phase, an attacker will attempt to identify user accounts, network resources, users and groups, file-sharing lists, and applications. These probes will differ depending on the operating system of the target computer: Windows NT/2000, Novell NetWare, Linux, and UNIX.

MO

DumpSEC This is a tool for discovering and listing a system network's user accounts. DumpSec is a security auditing program for Microsoft® Windows NT™. It dumps the permissions (DACLs) and audit settings (SACLs) for the file system, registry, printers, and shares in a concise, readable listbox format, so that holes in system security are readily apparent. DumpSec also dumps user, group, and replication information.

Sid2user This is another utility for revealing user accounts. It works with User2sid.exe, which can retrieve a SID from the Security Accounts Manager (SAM) from a local or a remote machine. Sid2user.exe can then be used to retrieve the names of all the user accounts and more. These utilities do not exploit a bug, but call the functions *LookupAccountName* and *LookupAccountSid*, respectively. What is more, these utilities can be called against a remote machine without providing logon credentials, except those needed for a null session connection.

OnSite Admin This utility can list user accounts for Novell systems. Originally a multi-server analysis, maintenance, and configuration tool for NetWare servers, it allows the user to monitor, analyze, update, and configure multiple servers all from a single workstation.

10.2.4 Attack

This is the phase when an intruder has enough information about ports and users to mount an attempt to access a target system or network. Depending on the operating system, this may take different routes. Windows 95/98 and Millennium are the most susceptible to break-ins. Since they are end-user operating systems lacking the security of NT/2000 and other network OSs, they are the easiest to attack via the Internet or e-mail.

MO

tcpdump This is utility for eavesdropping for passwords. It is the most popular network sniffer and analyzer for UNIX systems.

NAT When invoked, will work for file share privileges via brute force.

pwdump2 This is another password file-grabbing utility. It dumps the password hashes (OWFs) from NT's SAM database.

It should be noted at this juncture that most IDS and data mining analyses concentrate on looking for these probes in the log files of systems for the detection of potential intrusion attempts and attacks.

10.2.5 Control

At this phase the perpetrator will seek full control of a target system. For example, when ports 135 or 139 show up on a scanning probe, the system is identified to be running NT and the following tools will be used to gain administrator privileges.

MO

L0phtrack This is a tool for password cracking. L0phtcrack can brute-force hashes taken from network logs or programs like pwdump and recover the plaintext password; it also breaks the new NT-style password hashes.

getadmin This is a program that adds a user to the Administrators group, thus allowing an intruder to become the Administrator of an NT machine and gain total control of the target system.

sechole This utility also adds a user to the Administrators group. The utility performs a very sophisticated set of steps that allows a nonadministrative user to gain debug-level access on a system process. Using this utility, the non-administrative user is able to run code in the system security context and, thereby, grant local administrative privileges on the NT system.

10.2.6 Stealth

In this final phase, total ownership of the target system is secured, and the attacker will likely begin to cover his or her tracks from the system administrators, setting trapdoors to secure privileged access, and enabling return.

MO

rhosts This utility will evaluate hosts and list hosts and users who are trusted by the local host.

zap This is a tool for clearing logs and removing the evidence of an intrusion.

rootkits This is a utility for hiding tools. Perpetrators will use it to hide and secure their presence in a system, modifying ls and ps programs not to display intruder activities: ls is altered not to display the intruder files, and ps is modified not to display their processes.

cron This is a tool for scheduling batch jobs. Cron is a background-only application which, quietly and efficiently, launches other applications or opens documents at specified dates and times.

netcat This is a utility for planting remote-control services. It reads and writes data across network connections, using TCP or UDP protocol. It is designed to be a reliable backend tool that can be used directly or easily driven by other programs. It is a feature-rich network debugging and exploration tool that can create almost any kind of connection a perpetrator needs.

VNC Is a program for remotely hijacking NT GUIs. VNC stands for virtual network computing. It is, in essence, a remote display system that allows the perpetrator to view a computing desktop environment not only on the machine where it is running, but from anywhere on the Internet and from a wide variety of other machine architectures.

B02K This is Back Orifice 2000, an NT hacker tool for complete takeover of a Microsoft system.

As previously noted, cybercriminals can be classified as either external intruders who are unauthorized users of the machines they attack, or internal intruders who do not have permission to access certain portions of their host system. These internal intruders may also masquerade as another user, such as one with legitimate access to especially sensitive data. The most dangerous type is the clandestine intruder who has the power to turn off audit trails and take control of systems. System intrusions can also be viewed based on the following main categories:

1. Attempted break-ins or masqueraded attacks, which may be detected by atypical behavior profiles or violations of security constraints.

2. Penetration of the security control system, which may be detected by monitoring for specific patterns of activity.

3. Leakage or denial of service, which may be detected by atypical use of system resources.

4. Malicious use, which is detected by atypical behavior profiles, violations of security constraints, and the use of special privileges.

10.3 Intrusion Patterns

Software systems known as IDSs have been constructed to attempt to automatically detect these break-ins. They are based on the analysis of certain behavior patterns. These intrusions come down to two main types of patterns of detection: misuse and anomaly.

Misuse intrusions are well-defined attacks on known weak points of a system and involve some of the hacking techniques described in the preceding section. They can be detected by data mining audit-trail information. For example, an attempt to create a `setuid` or `tcpdump` call file can be caught by examining log messages resulting from these types of system calls; this can be done using a pattern-matching approach.

Anomaly intrusions are based on observations of deviations from normal system usage patterns. They are detected by building up a profile of the system being monitored and detecting significant deviations from normal behavior. These metrics are computed from available system parameters, such as average CPU load, number of network connections per minute, number of processes per user, type of application accessed, etc. An anomaly, or deviation from a system profile, may be an indication of a possible intrusion.

A hybrid system that combines the pattern-matching profiles of an anomaly system with the vigilance of a misuse detection computer program may be the best solution. Such a hybrid program would always be monitoring the system for potential intrusions, but would be able to ignore spurious false alarms if they resulted from legitimate user actions.

10.4 Anomaly Detection

Anomaly detection software systems and services start first by establishing normal usage patterns for users by looking at their CPU and I/O behavior to build a profile. Anomaly detection techniques assume that all intrusive activities are necessarily anomalous. This means that if we could establish a "normal activity profile" for a system, we could, in theory, flag all system states varying from the established profile by categorizing statistically significant amounts as intrusion attempts. This can result in anomalous activities that are not intrusive being flagged as intrusive. Or, worse, intrusive activities that are not anomalous could result in false negatives, that is, events that are not flagged as intrusive, though they actually are. This is a dangerous problem, and is far more serious than the problem of false positives.

10.5 Misuse Detection

The main issues in anomaly detection systems thus become the selection of threshold levels, so that neither of these two problems occurs, and the selection of what system features to monitor. Anomaly detection systems are also computationally expensive because of the overhead of keeping track of, and possibly updating, several system profile metrics. Audit data needs to be collected in order to update profiles and generate them dynamically so as to issue attack alerts on statistically deviant behavior. Anomaly detection has been performed via several mechanisms, including neural networks and machine-learning algorithms.

Misuse detection systems encode and match the sequence of hackers' signature actions, such as the changing ownership of a file in known intrusion scenarios. The main shortcomings of misuse systems are that known intrusion patterns have to be hand-coded; they are unable to detect unknown intrusions, which have no matched (future) patterns. The concept behind misuse detection schemes is that there are ways to represent attacks in the form of a pattern or a signature so that even variations of the same attack can be detected. This means that these systems are not unlike virus-detection systems—they can detect many or all known attack patterns, but they are of little use for as yet unknown attack methods. An interesting point to note is that anomaly detection systems try to detect the complement of "bad" behavior. Misuse detection systems try to recognize known "bad" behavior, with new rules being continuously needed to issue alert attacks.

10.6 Intrusion Detection Systems

As the threats of hacker attacks and other type of break-ins increase in complexity and number, new software tools and services for analyzing networks attacks, known as IDSs, are being developed. These security programs and services are capable of investigating network traffic in order to recognize suspects, irregular patterns, and possible attacks. IDSs are automated applications designed to monitor systems and networks, providing alerts when a suspected unauthorized event occurs.

An IDS will typically work with the audit records of operating system calls, including such data as the following:

- A resource, which draws data from the CPU, memory, I/O, etc.

- A subject, which identifies a user, a session, or a location

- An object, which identifies what the subject acted upon

- An action, which identifies the action attempted

- A timestamp or an error code

The most common way to detect intrusions is using the audit data generated by the operating system. An audit trail is a record of activities on a system that are logged to a file in a chronologically sorted order. Since almost all activities are logged on a system, it is possible that a manual inspection of these logs can allow intrusions to be detected. However, the incredibly large size of audit data generated make manual analysis impossible. IDSs automate the drudgery of wading through these log files. Audit trails are particularly useful because they can be used to establish the guilt of perpetrators for prosecution, and they are often the only way to detect unauthorized, but subversive, user activity. As such, IDSs can increasingly be used as forensic tools for prosecution purposes, documenting the break-in and trail taken by cyberperpetrators.

An IDS attempts to detect both an intruder breaking into a system and a legitimate user misusing system resources. A key advantage of an IDS is that it runs constantly, working away in the background, only notifying the administrator in real-time when it detects something it considers suspicious or illegal. Most IDSs only take preventive measures when an attack is detected and leave it up to the human administrator to determine the course of action after an alert is issued. Some IDSs base their operations on analysis of these operating system audit trails. This data forms a footprint of system usage over time. It is a convenient source of data and is readily available on most systems. From these observations, the IDS will subsequently compute metrics about the system's overall state and decide whether an intrusion is currently occurring or a system has been jeopardized.

The IDS may also perform its own system monitoring and keep aggregate statistics about a system usage profile. These statistics can be derived from a variety of sources, such as CPU usage, disk I/O, memory usage, activities by users, or number of attempted logins. These statistics must be updated continually to reflect the current system state. They may be correlated with an internal model that will allow the IDS to determine if a series of actions constitutes a potential intrusion. This model may describe a set of intrusion scenarios or possibly encode the profile of a clean system. Ideally, an IDS should address the following issues, regardless of what mechanism it is based on:

1. It must cope with changing system behavior and configuration as new applications and users are added; the IDS must be able to adapt.

2. It must impose minimal overhead on the system without slowing the network.

3. It must resist subversion; the system must be able to monitor itself to ensure that it has not been compromised.

4. It must be fault-tolerant, able to survive a system crash without loosing its content at restart.

5. It must be difficult to fool; some inherent intelligence must be designed into the IDS.

6. It must run continually in the background of the system being observed.

7. It must be easily customized to a system and its usage patterns.

8. It must observe deviations from normal behavior.

As with all classification problems, an IDS is subject to system errors. These can be categorized as either false-positive, false-negative, or subversion errors. A false positive occurs when the system classifies an action as anomalous, a possible intrusion, when in fact it is a legitimate action. A false negative occurs when an actual intrusive action has occurred but the system allows it to pass as nonintrusive behavior. A subversion error occurs when an intruder modifies the operation of the intrusion detector to force false negatives to occur.

As with the problem encountered in the previous chapter involving fraud detection, if too many false positives are generated by an IDS, the administrator will come to ignore the output of the system over time, which may lead to an actual intrusion being detected, but ignored. False-negative errors are more serious than false-positive errors because they give a misleading sense of security by allowing all actions to proceed. A suspicious action will not be brought to the attention of the operator. Subversion errors are more complex and tie in with false-negative errors. An intruder could use his or her knowledge about the internals of an IDS to alter its operation, possibly allowing anomalous behavior to proceed. The intruder could then violate the system's operational security constraints, but it would appear that the intrusion detection system was still working correctly.

Another form of subversion error is fooling the system over time. As mentioned previously, an IDS is continually updating its usage patterns profiles. But if an intruder could perform actions over time which were just slightly outside of normal system usage, then it is possible that the actions could be accepted as legitimate, although they really formed part of an intrusion attempt. The detection system would have come to accept each of the individual actions as slightly suspicious, but not a threat to the system. It would not realize that the combination of these actions was a planned to mask an attack of the system.

10.7   Data Mining for Intrusion Detection: A Case Study from the Mitre Corporation

In the Network Operations Center of the future, the security analyst will come to work in the morning, sit down with a cup of coffee, and press the What's New? button on the network monitoring and analysis screen. A list of suspicious incidents and attempted intrusions (more commonly called attacks) on the network will appear. Perhaps there is a file transfer at 2:00AM from a host that usually only has activity during business hours. The analyst will then investigate these incidents to identify them as, for example, attack or false alarm. The analyst will also be presented with distilled descriptions of attacks that he or she had identified the previous day.

An essential technology in this scenario will be data mining. Data mining analysis will determine the bounds for normal network activity, and data mining techniques will enable the software to spend the night determining which characteristics of a previously identified attack activity distinguish it from normal network usage.

To understand the improvement this will represent, it is necessary to understand the current network intrusion detection (ID) environment. Software sensors deployed along the network record activity: the initiation of an Internet connection from host A to host B, for example, or a single outside host trying to connect to every MITRE host. Each sensor records certain important pieces of information about this activity, such as the time of day and the duration of the connection. This information is stored in a database that easily accrues millions of records each day. On a regular basis, security analysts sift through this data looking for the most serious attacks. There can be thousands of suspicious activity alarms, and each requires further analysis to understand its purpose fully. Moreover, as commercial ID software currently favors heightened sensitivity, many of the alerts generated are false alarms and result in wasted time.

One of the most serious limitations in identifying and describing new attacks is that there is simply so much data that security experts are not able to examine thoroughly every single alerted activity. And, as data collection grows with increased network usage, little is being done to help mitigate this situation by performing analysis to determine which data is the most relevant and which data is unnecessary to collect.

This area of data overload is where data mining can make its most significant contribution. A number of MITRE research projects have begun to explore the use of data mining to address data overload in ID by taking one of two basic approaches: profiling or classification. In profiling, the goal is to establish some notion of normal and then look for deviations from that. In classification, we take known attacks and try to determine meaningful features that distinguish that set of traffic from the remainder of the traffic.

Of these two approaches, classification has been used less often in the ID environment. This is because it is crucial for classification analysis that there be adequate collections of data representing both attacks and nonattacks. Because this type of analysis is new to the ID world, rarely is this information collected in the proper form. Without explicit identifiers on identified attack records, it has been nearly impossible for classifiers to learn to discriminate between attacks and nonattacks.

MITRE's current Data Mining in ID project is starting to address this deficiency by enabling security analysts to tag important records in the database and assign them to meaningful classes (e.g., attack, probe, legitimate). By providing the necessary capabilities for labeling attacks and a better way to maintain the history of intrusion behavior, this work represents a significant enhancement to the existing security infrastructure. This labeled data will be used to explore and test various data mining classification techniques. This project has also begun to perform profiling on individual hosts. This profiling analysis can operate on the basic network traffic data that is already collected.

The hope is that by looking at the traffic to and from specific machines, unusual activity can be identified. The initial approach involves doing simple statistical analyses of isolated features. For example, Figure 10.1 shows a 30-day summary of the frequency of File Transfer Protocol (FTP) connections to a particular host for each hour of the day. Notice that the activity from 1AM to 2AM is outside the hours during which the vast majority of connections are

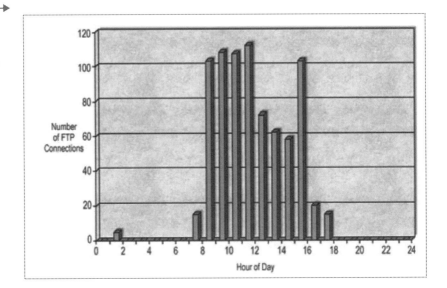

Figure 10.1
Thirty-day summary of File Transfer Protocol connections.

made; analysts should be alerted so they can investigate that activity further. The next stage of this project will use data clustering techniques to identify more sophisticated partitions of common activity for that host. Then, traffic that does not fit into any of the normal groups will be reported to the security analyst for further investigation.

In other emerging work, MITRE is addressing the issue of false alarms produced by current ID sensors. This work uses data mining to look for recurring sequences of alarms to help understand which alarms might be the result of legitimate usage. For example, alarm A may be frequently followed by alarm B as a result of legitimate operations. Once this is recognized, future occurrences of this sequence can be filtered out. MITRE is working on an approach that includes filtering out data that captures "common" connection activity. It makes use of association rule detection to identify frequent host parings. For example, perhaps host X regularly connects to host Y four times a day. Once these common connections have been removed, the remaining data is fed to a classification system to detect attacks. This work has been successfully tested on synthetically generated data, and it will soon be applied to actual network data.

MITRE, like other organizations and agencies, currently makes heavy use of human analysts in identifying real intrusion attacks from the large amount of log data collected. Standard procedure is to review the previous day's sensor events in the morning. The large numbers of raw sensor events, most of which are uninteresting, make detecting real attacks or potential problems difficult. In this context, data mining is not used to replace the human analyst, but to reduce the burden by allowing him to focus his expertise on those alarms most likely to be real intrusion attacks. The following details the overall objective of the project:

The Problem:
Data consists of individual sensor events (sensorlog
database records) that need to be both aggregated
into an incident and classified, but which do we do
first?

The Approach:
Construct features for individuals that capture
relationship to aggregate
* How many other records have the same srcip
  as this record?
* How many other records have the same srcip
  and dstport as this record?

An Intrusion Event:
Base - collected by network sensors
Examples: date, type of sensor, protocol, srcip, dstip,
          srcport, dstport

Incident - relationship to known security incidents
Example: has this srcip/dstip been listed in an
          incident recently?

Record - data lookups specific to a single record
Example: duration, endtime, starttime, highport,
          srczone, hostsrcip

Host - data related to the source or destination host
Example: #alarms with same srcip &dstip,
          #other alarms with same srcip

Time Window - statistics gathered over time
Example: avg. time between connections for a srcip
          or dstip

The Goal: To automatically identify *interesting*
anomalous behavior

The Tasks:
* Use sensor log events *not* identified as incidents
* Filter attributes based on analyst feedback
* Build Web interface for easy viewing of generated anomalies
* Classify anomalies into incident categories

Example of Anomalies:
Anomaly #14. 3 case(s). Signficance level: 0.015
        highdstport = no   (281 cases, 98.6% `yes`)
            synflag = no
RECORD:130330539,we1,log,2000/02/13,2000,02,13,14,
        38,46,sun,bus,?,?,?,?,?,?,3,netbios-ns,
        tcp,23,137,206.184.139.134,192.47.242.29,
        r,2451588,in,no,no,no, ?,no,no,no,no

Interpretation: This is a possible scan attempt to bypass firewall?

Anomaly #32. 4 case(s). Signficance level: 0.004
        srcmitre = no   (1692 cases, 99.65% `yes`)
            dstip = 192.188.104.221

RECORD:143722187,we1,log,2000/03/05,2000,03,05,02,
        53,05,sun,sleep,2000,03,05,02,53,23,18,1min,
        3,ftp,tcp,1098,1,195.145.0.130,
        195.145.0,192.188.104.22,192.188.104,
        s_[sa]_fa_[fa]_[fpa]_fa_[fa]_[fpa]_r,2451609,
        in,no,no,no,no,no,yes,no,no,no,no,no

Interpretation: This is a scan for ftp servers

Results:
Machine-learning decision tree (99% training set accuracy) used here was trained on the same month as the data used for generating anomalies (September)

Classification Model Accuracy:
High predictive accuracy for initial model: 96%

The fields of network intrusion detection and data mining are just beginning to work together. MITRE research is beginning to demonstrate that the network activity data, whose sheer quantity has been one of the primary challenges to current ID efforts, can be amenable to analysis via a variety of data mining techniques. The application of those techniques has already begun to prove useful in filtering out false alarms and characterizing normal connection pairs. In the near future, data mining should be able to help us understand what normal behavior is for individual host machines and better discriminate network attacks from innocuous activity.

10.8   Types of IDSs

There are either host- (and multihost-) based IDSs or networked-based IDSs. The networked-based systems are a specialized type of network sniffers. A sniffer monitors and reports on the movement of data packets in a network. A network IDS sits between a host and a gateway or clients, viewing the traffic moving, looking for evidence of unauthorized activity. A common practice is to have a centralized IDS providing logging and alert functions based on the data provided by multiple remote sensors, each located in different segments of a local area network. Sensors are placed in multiple ports, all reporting to the centralized networked IDS. Host-based IDSs tend to be more expensive because more devices are monitored and, hence, tend to be more accurate with fewer false positives and catch a higher number of intrusions.

IDSs can also be categorized based on the type of intrusions they issue alerts on; some detect specific events (misuse), while others report on changes in patterns (anomaly), the two main intrusion detection types. Event or misuse IDSs monitor for specific sequences of events, or sequences that are characteristic of attempts to gain unauthorized access to a system. An example is issuing an alert when a specific number of failed login attempts take place. This type of IDS detects intrusions by looking for activity that corresponds to known intrusion techniques (signatures) or system vulnerabilities.

10.9   Misuse IDSs

Event or misuse IDSs have been constructed using expert systems, which are encoded with rules and are designed in such a way as to separate the rule matching phase from the action (rule firing) phase. The rule matching is done based on the audit trail events. A new prototype IDS known as the Next Generation Intrusion Detection Expert System (NIDES) was developed by SRI and takes this expert-system approach. However, NIDES combines a hybrid intrusion detection technique consisting of a misuse detection component, as well as an anomaly detection component. This is the best of both types of detection techniques. The anomaly detector is based on the statistical approach and flags events as intrusive if they are largely deviant from the expected behavior. To do this, it builds user profiles based on over 30 different criteria, such as CPU and I/O usage, commands used, local network activity, and system errors, with the profiles updated at periodic intervals.

The expert-system misuse detection component encodes known intrusion scenarios and attack patterns. The rule database can be changed for different systems. One advantage of the NIDES approach is that it combines both data mining and expert system components. This is the bottom-up and top-down solution to the intrusion detection problem. This increases the chances of one system catching intrusions missed by the other component. Another advantage is that the problem's control reasoning is cleanly separated from the formulation of the solution.

The drawback to the expert-system approach is that its rules are only as good as the knowledge of the security professional who programs it. It is for this reason that NIDES has an anomaly, as well as a misuse, detection component. These two components are loosely coupled in the sense that they perform their operations independently for the most part. The NIDES system suffers from the same drawbacks of other expert systems: the high cost of maintaining its rules. Furthermore, additions and deletions of rules from the rulebase must take into account their sequential order, which could be problematic. The SRI system was able to establish a historical behavior profile for each desired entity (e.g., user, group, device, process). It was able to compare current behavior with the profiles. The system could detect departures from established norms, although the profiles had to be continuously updated to learn changes in subject behavior and address unanticipated intrusion types.

10.10 Anomaly IDSs

The anomaly detection model is based on a system detecting intrusions by looking for activity is different from a user's or system's normal behavior. The main approach is to use a statistical model of user behavior—a profile. In this method, initial behavior profiles for subjects are generated. As the system continues running, the anomaly detector constantly generates the variance of the present profile from the original one. There may be several measures that affect the behavior profile (e.g., like activity measures, CPU time used, number of network connections in a time period, applications normally used).

In some systems, the current profile and the previous profile are merged at intervals, but in some other systems, profile generation is a one-time activity. The main advantage of statistical systems is that they are adaptive; they learn the behavior of users and are, thus, more sensitive than security administrators. One potential flaw with anomaly IDSs is that they can gradually be trained by intruders so that eventually, intrusive events are considered normal. False positives and false negatives are generated depending on whether the threshold is set too low or too high, and relationships between events are missed because of the insensitivity of statistical measures to the order of events.

An open issue with all anomaly IDSs is the selection of measures to monitor. It is not known exactly what subset of all possible measures most accurately predicts intrusive atacks. Static methods of determining these measures are sometimes misleading because of the unique features of a particular system. Thus, it seems that a combination of static and dynamic determinations of the set of measures should be done. As with most investigative data mining projects, a hybrid solution mixing machine-learning or statistical models with human insight is usually the best.

Anomaly IDSs have also been developed using a predictive pattern-generation methodology. This method of intrusion detection tries to predict future events based on the events that have already occurred. The rules may be based on data mining analyses. Therefore, we could have a rule like the following:

```
IF       Event 1
AND      Event 2
THEN     Event 3 = 80%
         Event 4 = 15%
         Event 5 = 5%
```

This would mean that given that events 1 and 2 have occurred, with event 2 occurring after event 1, there is an 80% probability that event 3 will follow, a 15% chance that event 4 will follow, and a 5% probability that event 5 will follow. The problem with this is that intrusion scenarios not described by the rules will not be recognized, identified, and flagged.

However, there are several advantages to this approach. First, rule-based sequential patterns can detect anomalous activities that were difficult with traditional methods. Second, systems built using this model are highly adaptive to change. The rules can be based on a combination of machine-learning models and human domain observations. This is because low-quality patterns are continuously eliminated, finally leaving the higher-quality patterns behind. Third, it is easier to detect users who try to train the system during its learning period. And fourth, anomalous activities can be detected and reported within seconds of receiving audit events.

10.11 Multiple-Based IDSs

There are host-based IDSs as well, also known as event log viewers. This kind of IDS monitors event logs from multiple sources for suspicious activity. These host-based IDSs are ideal for detecting computer misuse from inside users or outsiders who have already infiltrated a network. There is an added benefit to these types of IDS in that because they operate in near real time, system faults are often detected quickly.

There are also network-based IDSs that monitor all network traffic, reacting to any packet anomaly or signature-based suspicious activity. Basically, they are specialized packet sniffers, and they come in the guise of plug-and-play, appliance-based products. These network-based IDSs analyze every packet, looking for the signature of intruder attacks; some will block suspicious packets. Because many network IDSs are unreliable at high speeds dropping a high percentage of network packets, new network-node IDSs are becoming popular, as they delegate the network-IDS function down to individual hosts, alleviating the problems of both high-speed failures and packet switching.

A network-based IDSs view is restricted to what passes over a given line. Also, a tremendous amount of data must be examined and logged, a process considerably weakened if encryption is used. Further, these IDSs can only monitor a limited number of machines or entities. Most of the current crop of network IDSs lack the robustness to deal with missing, incomplete, untimely, or otherwise faulty data.

Lastly, there are hybrid IDSs that are combinations of network and host systems in a single package. This solution gives maximum coverage. Many networks and system administrators reserve these hybrid IDSs for critical servers because they tend to be the most expensive products available.

10.12 Data Mining IDSs

Data mining has been around for years; however, its application to intrusion detection is a relatively new concept. Some of the obstacles are encountered in the amount of data to be analyzed and its complexity. It is possible for a company to collect millions of records per day that need to be analyzed for malicious activity. What data needs to be looked at needs to be determined. Data mining can be integrated with anomaly detection and misuse detection to create an IDS that will allow an analyst to accurately and quickly identify an attack or intrusion on a network more quickly.

There has been increased interest in data-mining–based approaches to building detection models for IDSs. These methods can generalize models of both known attacks and normal behavior to detect unknown attacks. Domain experts can also generate them in a faster and more automated method than manually encoded models that require difficult analysis of audit data. Several effective data mining techniques for detecting intrusions have been developed, many of which perform as well as or better than systems engineered by domain experts.

The key ideas are to use data mining techniques to discover consistent and useful patterns of system features that describe program and user behavior and to use the set of relevant system features to compute inductively learned classifiers that can recognize anomalies and known intrusions. Experiments have been performed using the *sendmail* system call data and the network *tcpdump* data to construct concise and accurate models to detect anomalies. Machine-learning algorithms have been used to compute the intra- and inter-audit record patterns, which are essential in describing program or user behavior. The discovered patterns can guide the audit data-gathering process and facilitate feature selection.

IDSs have been developed using neural networks. The idea is to train and construct a model to predict a user's next action or command based on patterns of historical behavior. The network is trained on a set of representative user commands. After the training period, the network tries to match actual commands with the actual user profile already present in the model. Any incorrectly predicted events are considered deviations from the user's established profile. Some advantages of using neural networks are that they cope well with noisy data, their success does not depend on statistical assumptions about the nature of the underlying data, and they are easier to modify for new user profiles.

IDSs have also been constructed using machine-learning algorithms to create a massive decision tree of thousands of statistical "rules" of acceptable user and system behavior. Branches on the decision tree are labeled with conditional probabilities. These machine-learning decision trees can be trained from a few days of data. However, they cannot be updated to learn new rules as usage patterns change. With these machine-learning IDSs activity is considered abnormal if it does not match a branch in the decision tree or if it matches a branch with low conditional probability.

Security of network systems is becoming increasingly important as more and more sensitive information is being stored and manipulated online. IDSs have thus become a critical technology to help protect networks and systems. As we have seen, most IDSs are based on hand-crafted signatures developed by the manual encoding of expert knowledge. These systems match activity on the system being monitored to known signatures of attacks. The major problem with this approach is that the system cannot generalize to detect new attacks.

Data mining can help improve intrusion detection by adding a new level of focus to anomaly detection. Data mining can automate the process of detection by identifying bounds for valid network activity; it can assist security analysts in their ability to distinguish attack activity from common everyday traffic on the network. Data mining can also play a vital role in the area of data reduction. Current data mining techniques have the ability to identify or extract the data that is most relevant and provide analysts with different views of the log files to aid in their analysis.

10.13 Advanced IDSs

Metalearning IDSs have been developed at Columbia University. Metalearning integrates a number of different classifiers. This type of IDS benefits from a multilayered approach in which machine learning and decision procedures detect intrusions locally. The University of California at Santa Barbara has developed model-based IDSs to detect suspicious state transitions. The system uses penetration scenarios as a sequence of actions and keeps track of interesting state changes as it attempts to identify attacks in progress, before damage is done.

The University of California at Davis has developed three types of IDS. One uses graphics to detect intrusions whose activity spans many machines that could be difficult to detect locally. This IDS specifies intrusion scenarios via graphs of actions covering many machines. The graphs provide an intuitive visual display. UC-Davis has also developed a specification-based IDS that detects departures from the security specifications of privileged programs, allowing detection of unanticipated attacks. Lastly, UC-Davis developed a thumbprint-technique IDS that can match and track the path of system users.

In private industry, GTE has developed an IDS that detects anomalous events for telephone service provider networks. This type of IDS is designed for integration into network operation centers; it uses existing systems and tools for data collection, as well as anomaly detection and specific signaling protocols to perform its "sanity checks."

Bellcore has also developed a survivable active networks (SAN) IDS that will allow highly configurable network elements to cooperate with networked hosts to detect, isolate, and recover quickly and automatically from damage due to errors or malicious attacks. This IDS will allow suspect activity to be *"peeled off"* the system, while continuing to operate in a micro environment.

Figure 10.2 *An IDS is only part of the entire deterrence process.*

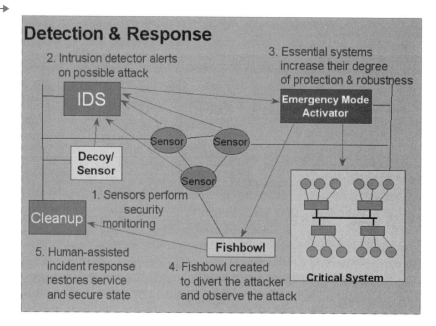

Boeing has developed an IDS with an automated response that integrates firewall, intrusion detection, filtering router, and network-management technologies. This IDS uses local intrusion detectors to determine threat presence, with the firewalls communicating intrusion detection information to each other. In this scheme, firewalls cooperate to locate a foreign intruder. This allows network managers to reconfigure the network automatically to thwart the attack. Firewalls and filtering routers dynamically alter filtering rules to block the intruder, allowing for dynamic reconfiguration of logging, monitoring, and access control in response to detected suspicious activity. This IDS uses different detectors to monitor and adapt a response to an attack.

10.14 Forensic Considerations

As with any other type of crime, even after an attack has occurred, it is important to examine the scene and gather important evidence. In cybercrimes this involves analyzing audit data so that the extent of the system damage can be determined. It also involves tracking down attackers so that preventive steps can be taken to reduce future intrusions. Computer forensics involves preserving and collecting digital evidence, such as usage logs, IP traces, and any other type of audit trails that can be collected about the incident (log files, antivirus reports, router firewall logs and file changes). Basically, anything that can be traced back to the perpetrators, such as where they came in through and how they did it, is collected as evidence. An IDS is only part of the process of detecting, isolating, reconfiguring, and repairing an attack (see Figure 10.2).

To protect a system, it is not only important to thwart attacks; it is also essential to understand how they took place. This may require allowing intruders to continue with their intrusion, leaving the damage, preserving it as evidence, and treating a hack attack as what it is: a crime scene. Often by repairing the damage, administrators destroy the evidence against perpetrators. Instead, an image copy of all hard drives should be made. All investigative activities, including any data mining analyses undertaken with their results, should be documented.

Care should be taken that certain commands that will modify directories or file dates and time stamps are not used. Search activity may also change log files and modify, destroy, or corrupt important forensic evidence. An IDS can also be used to analyze audit data. This makes them valuable not only as real-time deterrence shields, but also as forensic tools for gathering the evidence used in prosecuting internal and external hackers.

10.15 Early Warning Systems

The spiraling cost and damage of intrusions has also led to the creation of some early warning systems, such as those by SecurityFocus and the nonprofit SANS Institute. They represent intrusion detection clearinghouses providing information on vulnerabilities and attack techniques. Both collect and analyze data from monitoring devices around the world, dispersing alerts via the Internet to thousands of customers and subscribers. The SecurityFocus Deep-Sight Threat Management System gathers and correlates data from over 15,000 network intrusion detection, firewall, and router devices from thousands of private, public, and academic networks in 150 countries. The annual subscription for DeepSight is $50,000. Educational institutions that agree to feed their data get a discount.

SANS is a nonprofit educational group for security professionals. SANS accepts logs for analysis. Other security services, such as aris.securityfocus.com, allow victims to also upload IDS logs for purposes of analyzing attacks. McAfee's Visual Trace service can map attacks, offering time and place information like caller ID, and is capable of tracking down attackers by geographic region, IP address, and even street address. Check Point Software Technologies, a firewall maker, allows customers to block traffic from IP addresses SANS lists as attackers.

10.16 Internet Resources

Finally, there are an assortment of Web sites that provide useful information and programs in the area of intrusion detection. The following listings are some of the most popular tools and utilities:

- *DShield.org* is a site that collects data about cracker activity from all over the Internet. The data is cataloged and summarized and can be used to discover intrusion trends. Their Distributed Intrusion Detection System accepts firewall log excerpts for analysis. The site also reports on intrusions worldwide, listing the 10 most wanted IP addresses (http://www.dshield.org).

- *Incidents.org* is a site that provides reports on intrusion attacks. The site provides real-time threat-driven security intelligence through its Internet Storm Center, which performs data correlation collected from thousands of firewalls and intrusion detection systems, monitoring for trends and potential threats (http://www.Incident.org).

- *"DOCSHOW" Security Papers Archive* is a site that has very timely and insightful papers about IDSs, firewalls, and other security tools (http://www.docshow.net).

- *InfoSysSec* is a site that provides a collection of IDS and security resources (http://www.infosyssec.net/infosyssec/intdet1.htm).

- *An Introduction to Intrusion Detection Systems* is a site that provides an introduction to intrusion detection systems illustrated with the Dragon IDS Suite (http://www.intrusion-detection-system-group.co.uk).

Data mining can be used for intrusion detection to automate some of the tasks of data collection and pattern recognition.

10.17 Bibliography

Kruse, W. and Heiser, J. (2002), *Computer Forensics: Incident Response Essentials*, Boston: Addison-Wesley.

McClure, S., Scambray, J., and Kurtz, G. (2001), *Hacking Exposed: Network Security Secrets and Solutions*, New York: Osborne McGraw-Hill.

The Entity Validation System (EVS): A Conceptual Architecture

11.1 The Grid

Identity theft is the nation's fastest-growing crime, and it is not just terrorists who create identities to mask their presence; this crime is also committed by perpetrators who steal credit cards through various schemes on the Web or from trash dispensers. After 9/11, advances have been made to unify state driver's licenses and to regulate Social Security numbers more tightly. While these efforts will lessen the masking of perpetrators, data mining can also be used to validate the identify of individuals. In this chapter, a theoretical architecture for accessing multiple and disparate data sets will be described, the purpose of which is to validate a person's identity via machine-learning algorithms coupled with the experience of seasoned investigators.

The entity validation system (EVS) will develop predictive models that will support a wide range of field personnel and devices in confirming the identity of individuals. The concept is to provide data mining as a Web service for security deterrence purposes. The evolution of the Internet, wireless networks, and a number of information system standards provides the infrastructure for such a system. In the near future, this kind of service will be feasible using a pervasive network, linking systems and agents via a grid, providing real-time intelligence derived from autonomous data mining robots that are self-adjustable, evolutionary, and continuously learning, under the tutelage of experienced analysts.

The envisioned EVS would utilize remote data access via networks and an evolutionary real-time data mining system. The concept advanced here is one of an intelligence-gathering engine with many possible behavioral profiling applications and delivery options. For example, because of the technologies used to assemble this EVS, alerts could be delivered not only to humans but also to machines. At its core, the EVS would use the data mining technologies covered earlier in the book, such as agents and machine learning.

11.2　GRASP

Many years ago, a full decade before the explosion of the Internet, as an analyst for a federal law enforcement agency, I proposed and led a team of programmers in the creation of a system we drolly christened the Gateway Remote Access Service Provider (GRASP). GRASP enabled field agents to access multiple databases in support of their investigations. From that experience, I learned firsthand the problem of connecting and retrieving information from disparate data silos and the endless protocols each required for extracting key intelligence about individuals and business entities. I also learned that simply retrieving the information was not enough; assembling and intelligently analyzing the data was also required, which ironically set me on the path of AI, at first working with expert systems and eventually neural networks and machine learning.

11.3　Access Versus Storage

Rather than bringing the data to a centralized data warehouse, accessing it remotely is just as effective. So, rather than replacing and consolidating isolated data sources, as is the case with many government databases at the federal, state, and local levels, remotely referencing this shared data works as well and is more cost-effective. Sharing data can be difficult in a heterogeneous database environment. There are issues with shared versus replicated data, data consistency, and performance. But there are many applications, such as data mining, that require high flexibility and low maintenance costs, yet impose modest performance requirements for data. Sometimes there are good reasons to leave data in different database systems, whether historical, functional, or cost-related.

When a company or a government agency sets out to build a decision-support system that will make all its data accessible, it does not necessarily mean that a query about a customer or an individual will be restricted to a single database. In fact, the GRASP system allowed users to access multiple databases with a single query. These diverse data silos contained telephone records, vehicle registrations, driver's licenses, public record filings, change of address records, credit bureau data, real estate records, and, of course, internal government databases. No warehouse at that time could have stored the billions of records that the GRASP system accessed: that's because we opted for access rather than storage. We built a network rather than a data warehouse.

11.4   **The Virtual Federation**

Today, leaving the data in place and retrieving it on demand is even easier with the advent of the Web, which facilitates accessing data stored on multiple autonomous computing systems connected by a network presented to users as one integrated database. This virtual database presents data to users by means of user views that, from a user perspective, look exactly like the views of data in a centralized database. User views in this virtual database are mapped to underlying tables or objects that may be stored in any of the various databases in a federation. The federated database system processes queries defined in terms of these views, retrieving data as needed from the other systems in the federation and delivering the results as if all the data were local. Today, almost every Web page on any large site is assembled automatically from multiple sources. Click on a button and data may be retrieved from a federation of remote databases and servers. Users may not be aware of this, but it goes on constantly.

Federated databases operate by means of a similar principle, except that each data resource is defined by means of a database schema or view, providing the user with much more power to access and manipulate the data. Users interact with a front-end system that presents information on what data is available, accepting ad hoc queries. The front-end system decomposes each query into subqueries that can be handled by the various database servers in the federation; the system ships each subquery to the appropriate database server, assembling and delivering the result to the user.

A federated database system will deliver acceptable performance for most applications only if it includes a fully developed cost-based optimizer that is aware of the distribution and heterogeneity of the back-end servers. Some older systems that appear to deliver federated database management such as the GRASP system are really only providing gateways to other databases. GRASP, for example, was able to access all of the major national credit bureaus at that time—Equifax, Trans Union and TRW (now Experian)—and convert their different codes and content into a single easy-to-interpret format, but it wasn't capable of handling real-time queries that accessed these data at multiple locations. It ran batches at night.

Both the servers and the data models in the federation may be heterogeneous. The federation can include different database engines residing on different operating systems and hardware platforms. For example, a federation may include DB2 databases on Sun Microsystems and IBM servers, Informix databases on Hewlett-Packard servers, Microsoft SQL Server on a Unisys ES7000, and a Teradata database on an NCR Worldmark 5250. Database servers can be added to and deleted from the federation over time. It is a fully modular system for accessing diverse data sources.

In terms of data models, the front-end system may present users with a relational view, while retrieving data from database servers that are object-oriented, hierarchical, and so on. Different users or applications may be presented with different views of the data suited to particular uses. Multiple copies of the front end can be distributed throughout the network. Front-end systems may maintain snapshots, materialized views, or summaries of data from various servers. Such snapshots have several advantages, including accelerated query performance. And the snapshot can be available even when the underlying data is not. Snapshots also provide a stable picture of a dynamic phenomenon for data mining analysis and reporting purposes. To access and make available the output of such a federated system, a Web of services would be used

Until recently, the centralized approach represented the more attainable of two limited choices for building intelligent data warehouse support systems: a massive initial investment of time and money to build and load a centralized database or a complicated patching together of existing systems with all the associated integration and maintenance problems. A virtual federated database, however, allows for the data to be left where it is. The users can still access the data they need using an integration layer built on heterogeneous data sources and database views. In order to be linked and have access to an entity validation, a Web service architecture would be used.

11.5   Web Services

Web services comprise sets of standards that allow programs to invoke software services across IP networks through the exchange of XML messages riding on top of HTTP. HTTP is the communication standard for the Internet. This mirrors the everyday Web, except that instead of human beings, the recipients are application programs. The ubiquity of the Internet, intranets, and wireless networks gives Web services the power to reach almost anyone and enables users to access data mining models anytime from anywhere. The term *Web services* is actually an abbreviation for *web of services*, meaning that distributed applications, such as this proposed EVS, will be assembled from a Web of software and databases in the same way that a Web site today is assembled from a disparate number of HTML pages and content from different servers.

Web services are always invoked by means of XML-encoded messages. XML can go anywhere there is an IP network, which nowadays means everywhere, and can be received by any HTTP server. Web services invoke executable programs that are not decided until the XML-encoded message arrives via the IP network. Web services are characterized by late binding just-in-time applications. However, the most distinguishing feature of Web services is that they allow programs, rather than humans, to exchange information and commands in the form of XML messages. This would work for an EVS, in that for example, denial of entry, to board a plane or conduct a transaction at an ATM or other type of terminal, such as an airline ticket dispenser, could be invoked from a centralized data mining server to a machine, rather than to a human inspector.

Tim Berners-Lee, the inventor of the World Wide Web, has embarked on a long-range program called the Semantic Web, which aims to create quasi-intelligent networks through a combination of shared semantics, ontologies, software agents, and service discovery techniques. This EVS would invoke this architecture of distributed intelligence in which a Web service would be used to open up legacy information and data sources from federated databases and process the data through pattern-recognition models populated from IF/THEN rules to authorized users or appliances with access to the Internet, intranet, wireless, or any other proprietary network. Constructing the EVS as a Web service is important because it greatly simplifies the creation and integration of a large-scale system.

11.6   The Software Glue

In the same way that HTML catalyzed a vast web of human-accessible content, several new software standards will enable a web of machine-accessible services, such as this proposed EVS. Web services are defined by three information and communication system standards:

1.   Simple Object Access Protocol (SOAP), which performs the transfer of XML-encoded messages

2.   Web services description language (WSDL), which declares what the Web service can do and is an XML equivalent of a "software resume"

3.   Universal Description, Discovery, and Integration (UDDI), which performs a global lookup at three levels: white pages, yellow pages and green pages, and defines a directory for authorization

SOAP is a lightweight protocol for the exchange of information in a decentralized environment, typically across the Internet or intranet. Based on XML, SOAP has three main parts. First, it provides an envelope that defines a framework for describing what is in a message and how to process it. Secondly, it provides a set of encoding rules for expressing instances of application-defined data types. Thirdly, it contains a convention for representing responses across a network.

WSDL functions like an XML resume; it declares what a Web service can do, where it lives, and how to invoke it. It is a defining interface language, and it is the method by which services in a network can be found and categorized. Coupled with the third standard, UDDI, it allows a Web service to find what Web services exist on the Internet, an intranet, or a proprietary network.

UDDI operates on three separate levels: white pages (address information), yellow pages (business information), and green pages (technical details as to how transactions are to be conducted). As a matter of security and confidentiality, it is obvious that for this EVS, private and restricted UDDI servers would be maintained, accessible only to those individuals and devices with appropriate authorization.

There are currently no security standards specific to Web services, but the existing standards for secure and authenticated HTTP can be used in most cases. HTTPS, which is HTTP running over SSL, uses a digital-certificate scheme that allows the client and server to verify each other's identities and communicate over a secure, encrypted channel. Then, there is HTTP basic authentication, which allows specific URLs to be password protected, so that only client users with the appropriate credentials can gain access. Finally, there are SOAP security extensions, which allow individual pieces of a payload to be electronically signed and encrypted. IBM has already released a prototype called SOAP Security Extensions that is part of its Web services toolkit.

Increasingly, the trend in information systems is toward decentralization. In a few short years we have gone from mainframes to minicomputers, PCs, laptops, and wireless organizers. We have gone from client/server architectures to the Web, to peer-to-peer networks, and soon to Web services. As the world moves toward decentralized information storage, the problem of validating a person's identity in a network arises. Because an entity can be described as a set of information nuggets, it should be possible to store these nuggets in various databases in a network and to reconstruct a profile from these nuggets when needed. This would enable different Web services to store specific aspects of a person's profile and identity. For example, one set of Web services could store credit information, whereas another set of services could store license data, another financial, yet another travel activity data, another pictures of the person with details about data appearance, income, public records, and so forth.

The critical point is that a secured EVS, as a high-level Web service, would be able to reconstruct part or all of a person's profile by orchestrating the information nuggets held by the lower-level Web services. And because of the

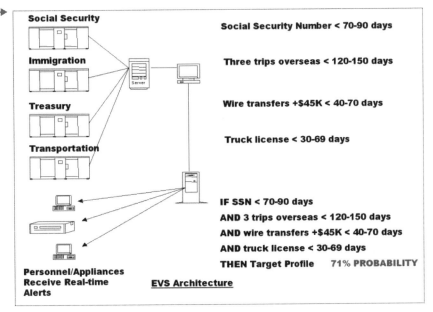

Figure 11.1
Incremental profiles are distributed.

Social Security

Social Security Number < 70-90 days

Immigration

Three trips overseas < 120-150 days

Treasury

Wire transfers +$45K < 40-70 days

Transportation

Truck license < 30-69 days

IF SSN < 70-90 days
AND 3 trips overseas < 120-150 days
AND wire transfers +$45K < 40-70 days
AND truck license < 30-69 days
THEN Target Profile   71% PROBABILITY

Personnel/Appliances
Receive Real-time
Alerts

EVS Architecture

technologies used by such a service, alerts could be sent not only to human personnel, such as a customs inspector, but also to devices, such as an airline kiosk or an ATM. This is the EVS architectural design; however, challenges remain in the development of a truly evolutionary data mining system, which would be the creator and assembler of these profile nuggets. There nuggets must be able to be dynamically updated and created with new data by advanced new algorithms, guided by experienced counter-intelligence human analysts, who would know that if a person is 40 years old and has no public records, something is amiss.

11.7 The Envisioned EVS

The EVS envisioned would dramatically improve the capability of human analysts and Internet and wireless appliances to make inferences in complex, data-intensive domains. The EVS would vastly increase the ability to identify individuals at point-of-entry border crossings, airports, and other locations warranting the validation of their identity. The system would search for key facts hidden in immense quantities of irrelevant information and assemble large numbers of disparate facts to reach valid conclusions in real time (see Figure 11.1).

The system would be capable of learning in the following ways:

- Learn from the data: make effective use of a wide variety of public records from government and commercial databases

- Learn actively: request new data and analyses that optimally improve learning and inference

- Learn cumulatively: incrementally improve existing knowledge and make use of that knowledge in subsequent learning and inference

- From humans and machine algorithms: make use of data mining techniques under the direction of knowledgeable analysts and investigators

11.8 Needles in Moving Haystacks

Whereas conventional data mining is sometimes described as finding a needle in a haystack, the EVS architecture would be designed to help analysts, investigators, inspectors, and other personnel to reassemble needles from pieces that have been deliberately hidden in many haystacks. Hence, the challenges for such an EVS would be as follows:

1. It must be able to deal with patterns involving relations among multiple objects, such as people, places, and events, which are dynamic.

2. It must be able to make inferences concerning organizations and activities and associate of individuals with them.

3. The amount of criminal data is small; terrorist-related activity is even scarcer, making it difficult to induce predictive patterns of such activity and to profile these perpetrators. An ensemble mechanism, such as the one proposed in section 9.10, must be used.

4. Effective learning and inference requires large amounts of general and domain-specific knowledge; because of this, experienced investigators and analysts need to guide the EVS.

5. Much of the available knowledge concerns patterns of events in time and space, often with large gaps introduced intentionally for the purpose of obscuring clandestine activities and perpetrator identities. Again the EVS must be able to deal with these challenges.

6.   Relevant data are drawn from many different sources, such as databases of sightings, financial transactions, phone calls, travel records, and news stories. Those sources contain many different types of items, such as numbers, text, photos, audio, and video feeds and have varying degrees of reliability, overlap, and correlation. A major task of the EVS is unifying this mixed media into a cohesive view of entity profiles.

7.   The available data represent only a fraction of what could be known; part of effective learning is reasoning about what additional data to request. This will require the direction of experienced analysts in guiding and training the EVS.

8.   The organizations and individuals that wish to avoid detection deliberately obscure patterns of behavior; this fact must be taken into consideration in the general scheme and design of the sources referenced by the EVS.

9.   A single missed terrorist event could have catastrophic consequences, as we now know after 9/11. The EVS must have a low false-positive ratio.

10. Changes in individuals, organizations, technologies, and political events all produce changes in underlying behavior. The EVS must be adaptive to its environment.

An EVS with these capabilities could greatly improve the detection of perpetrators involved in criminal and terrorist activities, such as money laundering, cybercrime, fraud, entity theft, and weapons of mass destruction acquisition. Conventional data mining techniques and applications, as we have discussed throughout the book, generally fall into two classes: anomaly detection and pattern recognition or signature discovery. Yet another method of seeing how investigative data mining processes work is via clustering and searching for anomalies or outliers, while the other process involves segmentation and classification of criminal signatures, such as fraud or misuse intrusions.

The first type of data mining, anomaly detection, identifies unusual events in a consistent stream of structured data. Such an event might be a sudden shift in telephone calling behavior or increased purchases with a credit card, both of which are indicative of fraud or identity theft, or altered usage of a computer system or application in the context of an intrusion. In this context, a SOM neural network might be used to search for a hidden cluster in a very large data set.

The second class of data mining techniques is pattern discovery, which constructs models from structured data that can be used to infer unknown variables. For example, a discovered pattern might construct a set of IF/ THEN rules that infers a questionable identification based on known patterns of prior deception. In this case inferences are based on the MO of individual instances of captured or killed perpetrators; for example:

```
IF DOB                      =      07/06/66
AND SSN issue date          =      02/01/01
AND # of Credit Cards       <      0
EVS                       Score  87
```

In this situation a high EVS score of 87 means that the identity of this individual is highly questionable in light of the missing information, lack of credit history, new Social Security number, and high age.

11.9   **Tracking Identities**

The data initially presented to the EVS is assumed to be complete; however, the system should posses the logic to decide whether to seek additional data. Analysts must assemble many individual records into larger patterns before they are meaningful. Taken alone, each source of data may not reveal any strong anomalies or patterns. But taken together, a clear picture may emerge. For example, possessing a truck drivers, license or having a biochemical degree does not identify that individual as a terrorist; however, having a Social Security number that is out of sequence and no public records on file in combination may warrant a high EVS score that calls that identity into question.

The correct interpretation of data requires substantial and diverse domain knowledge. For example, insurance fraud specialists are aided by knowledge about medical scams, crime trends and patterns, criminal organizations, and legitimate business operations. Many of the EVS tasks will require knowledge about these criminal scams, as well as knowledge about diverse cultures, religious beliefs, political events, and chemical, biological, and nuclear weapons, their components, and construction. Rules coded from human experts knowledgeable about criminal and terrorist techniques as well as rules extracted from data mining analyses, would be combined to interpret all the data correctly in order for the EVS to generate its scores.

The important relationships among some records are temporal and spatial. Such relationships often require special data structures, analysis techniques, and domain knowledge for correct interpretation, such as common duration of certain events, minimum travel times, etc. This is particularly true when large temporal and spatial gaps are intentionally introduced to hide illegitimate activities. Analysis requires many different types of records from a variety of local and remote databases. The EVS will require access to multiple data sources with the potential that these sources will have a different type of record structures However, the Web service architecture and the standards used will enable the integration of these diverse data sources.

The data themselves are fragmentary, sparse, and largely unlabeled. The data about any one subject, such as a person's name, address, date of birth, or occupation, are necessarily fragmentary and incomplete. One of the primary goals of the EVS is to determine whether additional data gathering is warranted. Terrorists and other organized criminals intentionally evade detection. Thus, patterns and anomalies will be much more subtle, because perpetrators intentionally attempt to cover their illegal activities within a haystack of legal activities. The EVS must be designed to deal with these attempts to evade detection. Domain experts will play a key role in determining what and where to gather this information and what clues to recognize.

The structure of criminal and terrorist organizations and their methods of operation can shift frequently. Hence, the kinds of patterns and anomalies that must be detected by the EVS data mining mechanism are inherently dynamic. This is true in some commercial applications, such as e-commerce personalization systems, which are dynamically able to customize Web pages to each individual in real time based on past behavior and preferences. This EVS must have the same type of capability to adjust and learn.

11.10 The AI Apprentice

In the true spirit of AI, the EVS should have the capabilities of incremental learning, incorporating genetic algorithms and the ability to gain insight and knowledge using machine-learning algorithms. This visionary goal requires the development of a learning apprentice system that can use a variety of knowledge and data sources and an interactive interface to acquire human expertise. The EVS should be able to integrate and comprehend direct natural language instruction and advice from criminal and counter-intelligence experts; it should also be able to learn solutions from sample cases.

Such a visionary system would combine an ability to mine large amounts of data, as well as to learn from its interaction with experienced intelligence analysts and law enforcement investigators. For example, an analyst could provide an initial description of a profile of a "smuggler entity" using a language that allows him or her to specify an initial set of defining objects and relations. Using this profile and an existing domain-general knowledge base, the EVS would search through a variety of databases to identify individuals that satisfied this profile and retrieve a set of matching smuggler entities.

The analyst would next examine these entities and label some of them as correct or incorrect, possibly providing some distinguishing properties or relations to help explain the errors. Using these matched and mismatched samples and the analyst's comments, the EVS would revise its knowledge base, which could be a set of hundreds of IF/THEN rules. This interactive process would repeat for several cycles, resulting in a significantly improved knowledge base and reduced error rates and could be used for future searches by the EVS in profiling potential smugglers.

In order to construct such an EVS, techniques are required for organizing knowledge, such as abstraction hierarchies that allow the efficient use of prior knowledge during learning. Already such knowledge bases are being developed under DARPA's High Performance Knowledge Bases Program. Domain-specific knowledge bases of concepts and theories for particular applications, such as narcosmugglers, money laundering, or bioterrorist activities, need to be developed and deployed. They would be a key component of the envisioned EVS.

Interactive theory refinement algorithms need to be developed that handle incremental addition of prior knowledge and exploit directed examples and advice from the human experts. Learning algorithms that exploit forms of prior knowledge other than declarative domain theories need to be developed. This includes methods that automatically extract knowledge using data and text mining agents. The algorithms need to utilize procedural prior knowledge and additional relevant unsupervised data to guide the EVS in learning.

11.11 Incremental Composites

To outline the visionary capabilities of this EVS, picture the following scenario: An investigative analyst identifies a group of suspects as possible perpetrators. The EVS searches the multiple government and commercial databases that it has direct access to and develops some working hypotheses about what makes these individuals similar to one another and different from most other people in the general population. Next, the EVS profiles other individuals with very similar patterns of behavior and data attributes and asks the analyst if these persons are possible perpetrators. The analyst examines the records of the individuals and finds that only a few of the selected group are in fact criminals; the analyst communicates this information to the EVS.

The EVS proceeds, moving on to test information in more expensive databases and asking the analyst a few, more refined questions. Finally, EVS generates a diagnostic procedure for identifying possible perpetrators. The analyst looks at the rules and sees that the EVS has discovered a set of signatures in calling patterns and financial transactions that had not previously been associated with this type of crime. The diagnostic procedure is set up to run as a background job, looking through the databases. Whenever the EVS finds someone suspicious, it initiates more active diagnosis, perhaps asking additional questions from investigators or calling for additional data collection. Through this incremental learning process, the EVS refines its profiling process under the tutelage of human experts refining new rules continuously.

For example, in profiling, say, a suspected smuggler, the EVS might first check internal government databases, such as citizenship, type of license, travel data, or passport. If those data had certain values, then the procedure would call for gathering more external and expensive data, such as financial, real estate, and credit information. In this context, a profile can include several data dimensions such as behavior, property, nationality, planes, financial transactions, cartels, cells, bombs, targets, and criminal records. These objects are mapped graphically, as we found out in Chapter 3 on link analysis, as are properties and relations for these profiles:

```
entity_narco-trafficker(Antonio_Diaz),
last_seen (Antonio_Diaz,Juarez_6/12/2001),
ownership(Antonio_Diaz,LadiesBar,
         KentuckyClub,Submarine),
citizen(Antonio_Diaz,Mexico),
         bank-transfer(Antonio_Diaz,
         BofA_account-00801287,MexCom_account-004453,
         $1,500,000,11/10/2002).
```

Such representations are crucial for profiling via an EVS, but they add significantly to the complexity of learning. In a conventional attribute-vector representation, all of the possibly relevant attributes are enumerated and the set of possible hypotheses is large, but clearly circumscribed. In a relational representation, arbitrarily long chains of information and complicated networks of relationships may be relevant for learning and profiling.

The EVS will be required to capture complex, time-varying patterns and features of individuals. Existing data mining technologies can be divided into two general types: local neural networks and machine-learning algorithms. Local search algorithms, such as neural networks, start with an initial random pattern representation and incrementally make adjustments to recognize signatures in the data, while machine-learning algorithms start with a null pattern and gradually refine, elaborate, and segment a data set to improve its predictive power. The EVS will require a mixture of both of these top-down and bottom-up algorithms to discover complex patterns. In the end, the EVS will combine the best features of human knowledge and data mining algorithms and their brute-force ability to crunch data for converging on a profile solution.

11.12 Machine Man

The EVS will be a hybrid of human intuition and data mining technologies working in tandem on an on-going basis to detect individuals involved in terrorism and criminal activity. The capabilities of machines and people clearly complement each other: Computers are able to process very large amounts of data, whereas analysts and investigators are able to bring to bear large amounts of knowledge about human behavior, criminal activity and alliances, and the politics and cultures of terrorist and criminal organizations.

A hybrid human-knowledge and machine-learning EVS has the potential to be an effective system if the data mining process can be made dynamic as it develops its profiles, where the induction process requires that it be ongoing and incremental under the guidance of knowledgeable human investigators and analysts. Data relevant to assessing perpetrators is received continually over long periods of time. The structure of criminal and terrorist organizations and their methods of operation can change over time, so patterns of behavior may change without any real change in the severity of the terrorist threat. After 9/11, it is highly unlikely that a similar attack could be undertaken; however, other groups and methods exist by which other types of attacks could be attempted.

The hybrid combination of human knowledge and machine learning must go through an incremental process to couple the analyst's insight with the data mining power of algorithms and access to a vast network of data sources. For example, an initial profile may be developed by intelligence analysts to formulate a description of a perpetrator. This profile is then used to guide a more focused search to detect additional confirming or disconfirming evidence via machine-learning techniques. This back-and-forth process of human-computer interaction will continue as part of the development and the refinement of the perpetrator profile. The EVS must be capable of integrating data from a variety of disparate, dynamic, and possibly conflicting data sources. When new data or entirely new data sources become available, the system must be able to analyze the impact of the new data and incrementally reevaluate and revise its conclusions as it validates the identity of individuals.

11.13 Bibliography

Glass, G. (2002), *Web Services: Building Blocks for Distributed Systems*, Upper Saddle River: Prentice Hall PTR.

Goldszmidt, M. and Jensen, D. (June 13–14, 1998), *DARPA Workshop on Knowledge Discovery, Data Mining, and Machine Learning (KDD-ML)*, Carnegie Mellon University.

Mapping Crime: Clustering Case Work

There are spatial and temporal features to crimes, and today's data analysis tools allow for the display and examination of this digital data. Increasingly, police departments are beginning to use new mapping applications and geographic information systems (GIS) to measure and analyze the spatial relationships of this criminal data. With these new graphical tools, analysts are able to examine place-based crime and develop contiguity matrices to view relationships between criminals and victims. In addition to these analytical advances, computerized police records management systems and computer-aided dispatch (CAD) systems of citizen calls to police make it possible to systematically quantify varying levels of criminal activity and types at different locations within a city.

There are two methods by which crimes can be mapped. One is human-driven, where an analyst interactively explores the features of crimes by different dimensions, such as type of crime by time of day or day of week. This is a top-down approach to mapping criminal activity. The second method of mapping crime, the machine-driven method, where criminal data is autonomously clustered using a data mining tool, such as a SOM neural network. This type of map is driven by the criminal data itself and may lead to the discovery of new, previously unseen patterns and can provide very important insights that a human-driven analysis might miss. This is a bottom-up approach to mapping criminal activity. In the end both the top-down and bottom-up approaches should be considered for they can compliment each other; the bottom-up approach may discover a trend or pattern, which the top-down approach can be used to validate.

12.1 Crime Maps

A crime map may be viewed as the end product of a process that starts with a 911 call and the first-responding officer's report, which is then processed and entered into a database and eventually transformed into a digital report, then

Figure 12.1
MAPS links to crime maps and statistics to various cities.

Please contact the **WEBMASTER** if you would like to submit a link for consideration.

Agencies with Data/Maps on the Web

Local Law Enforcement	Information Available
Baltimore County, MD	Crime statistics and maps by community
Berkeley, CA	Crime statistics by census tract
Beaverton, OR	Neighborhood maps, neighborhood Part One and Two Crime year to date, 1999 compared to 2000 Calls for Service and Crime year to date
Boulder, CO	Weekly crime maps and crime stats
Cambridge, MA	Total City crimes and Part 1 charts
Charlotte-Mecklenburg, NC	Part 1 monthly citywide
Cheyenne, WY	Limited interactive aggregate calls and crime types
Chicago, IL	Query the Chicago Police Department's database of reported crime
Cincinnati, OH	Crime maps and statistics for selected crimes
Clearwater, FL -Pinellas County	In-progress, county-wide crime maps
Dallas, TX	Part I crime totals by Beat
Detroit (Tri-County), MI	Crime maps and statistics for selected crimes for 3 area counties
Evansville, IN	Weekly maps for selected crimes
Fort Lauderdale, FL	Produces a monthly report which depicts our crime and service statistics
Fremont, CA	Sex offender maps
Hobbs, NM	Crime View Maps produced on website
Illinois State Police	Viewing of crime data, sex offender data, and traffic data
Jefferson Parish, LA	Interactive maps by civic association or zip code
Lenexa, KS	Yearly crime statistics by patrol district boundary

into a graphical map. In one interpretation, a crime map is merely a picture of a database of criminal data. However, by inspecting a map, police analysts may notice a relationship or discover a correlation between environmental factors that otherwise might have gone unnoticed. Crimes occur where an opportunity exists, be it due to a lack of night lights, police patrols, or surveillance cameras; a map may bring these facts to light.

Maps are also integral tools for the exploration and testing of hypotheses about crimes and perpetrators. For example, a crime map may confirm an investigator's hunch about the burglary pattern of a repeat offender who is using a specific bus route and its associated stops to enter a neighborhood, commit his crimes, and escape. If so, the map might be used to view the hypothesis and possibly deter the criminal. At the core of this method is an interactive process involving the development and testing of a hypothesis on the basis of the best available information derived from the investigator's experience, the physical evidence, and the distribution of the criminal data. Maps may reveal a pattern not expected, leading to such questions as did the discovered cluster of burglaries pop up by chance? Do officers in the field have a potential suspect? What is this perpetrator's signature MO? Are there other unsolved burglaries that match this pattern?

Maps of crimes are highly persuasive because people tend to instantly grasp graphs, believing what they can see. In 1997 the National Institute of Justice established the Crime Mapping Research Center, whose goal is the promo-

Figure 12.2 *A view of crimes by types in the central part of the city.*

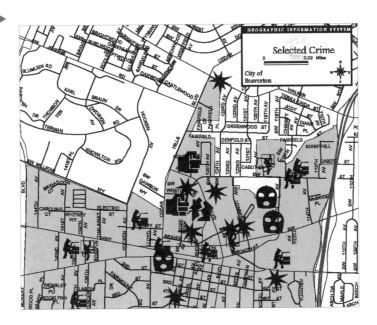

tion, researching, evaluation, development, and dissemination of GIS technology and the spatial analysis of crime. On the CMRC Web site, several links can be found to several police department sites and their GIS maps.

From the CMRC site, shown in Figure 12.1, the user can easily click on any city on the list, such as Beaverton, and view the crimes by each of its 13 neighborhoods (see Figure 12.2).

12.2 Interactive Crime GIS

There are also interactive maps that can map crimes by such parameters as location, time, and type. A GIS is an interactive mapping system that permits information layering to produce detailed descriptions of conditions and analyses of relationships among variables. A GIS is based on drawing different spatial distributions of data and overlaying them on one another to find interrelated points. Conditions, or filters, can be used on a GIS to refine searches at any level an analyst chooses. For example, the most obvious filter would isolate all crimes by specific type. However, filtering can isolate crimes by time of day, neighborhood, and MO. Conditions can be set to specify all the desired criteria, possibly resulting in the isolation of a cluster of incidents that could be linked to the same perpetrator.

Figure 12.3
San Diego interactive crime map.

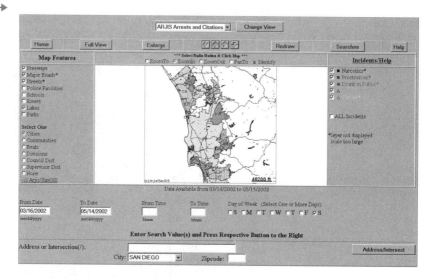

Interactive mapping can also be set by the characteristics of victims, suspects, or both and is easily accomplished with the current generation of GIS software. Maps can be created, for example, to answer such questions as where have females been assaulted? Is there evidence that a cluster of burglaries has occurred at homes occupied by elderly females? Figure 12.3 is an example of a new type of Internet interactive GIS, which is accessible to anyone with a browser; it features an assortment of methods by which to view crimes in San Diego, California.

12.3 Crime Clusters

One of the most notable characteristics of crime is that it tends to organize itself in distinct clusters. Criminal acts do not extend evenly over space, and they are not constant over time; there are variations and patterns in space and time. As far back as the 19th century, statisticians have closely studied the differences in crime across communities. Today, clustering and its implications still play a central role in the study of crime. Clustering occurs in both temporal and cross-sectional data and in both individual and aggregate analyses. Criminologists often perform different type of clustering analyzes, such as individual temporal, aggregate cross-sectional, individual cross-sectional and aggregate temporal.

As stated earlier, yet another method of developing clusters is via the use of data mining to find anomalies, such as discovering unexpected hidden associations between a class of crimes and perpetrators' MO. So far most of the criminal mapping has been human-driven, where hypotheses are performed on the data in search of patterns and clusters. However, data mining, as we have found out, can find unexpected patterns and clusters organized by the data itself, using special types of neural networks. Innovative criminal investigators in the United Kingdom and the United States have begun to use these types of data mining techniques in their quest to solve crimes and gain insight into the crime maps.

As with many other police department, the West Midlands police department in the United Kingdom is faced with shrinking resources, few leads, and aging cases. Investigators find that these challenges can limit the cases they can investigate. High-volume cases without definite leads, such as house burglaries and vehicle theft, that lack clear evidence are often filed away until new evidence is found. However, each West Midlands electronic case file contains physical descriptions of the thieves, as well as their MO. While many cases lacking evidence were previously filed away, the department is now reexamining them with a new type of weapon: data mining.

Inspector Rick Adderley is using two (SOM) Kohonen neural networks to cluster similar physical descriptions and MOs. He then combines clusters to see whether groups of similar physical descriptions coincide with groups of similar MOs. If he finds a good match and perpetrators are known for one or more of the offenses, it is possible that the unsolved cases were committed by the same individuals. Adderley's analytical team further investigates the clusters, using statistical methods to verify the importance of these similarities. If clusters indicate the same criminal might be at work, the department is likely to reopen and investigate the other crimes. Or, if the criminal is unknown but a large cluster indicates the same offender, the leads from these cases can be combined and the case reprioritized.

Adderley is also investigating the behavior of prolific repeat offenders with the goal of identifying crimes that seem to fit their behavioral pattern. He constructs a model using data from cases in which the offender is known, and then applies it to a database of unsolved crimes. Such models can be an invaluable aid in linking known criminals to specific crimes quickly. The following case studies are presented in their original versions in which SOMs are used to construct clusters of criminal data. These analyses signal the advent of a new type of forensic data mining techniques. The following case study is provided in its original version; the author would like to thank Inspector Rick Adderley for his valuable assistance in providing the paper on his innovative work with SOMs.

12.4   Modeling the Behavior of Offenders Who Commit Serious Sexual Assaults: A Case Study

Richard Adderley
West Midlands Police
Queens Road Police Station
Birmingham, B6 7ND, UK
r.adderley@west-midlands.police.uk

Peter B. Musgrove
University of Wolverhampton
35-49 Lichfield St.
Wolverhampton, WV1 1SB, UK
Tel: +44 1902 321851
P.B.Musgrove@wlv.ac.uk

12.4.1   Abstract

This paper looks at the application of data mining techniques, principally the self-organizing map, to the linking of records of crimes of serious sexual attacks. Once linked, a profile of the offender(s) responsible can be derived automatically.

The data was drawn from the major crimes database at the National Crime Faculty of the National Police Staff College, Bramshill, United Kingdom. The data was encoded from text by a small team of specialists working to a well-defined protocol. The encoded data was analyzed using the self-organizing map tools of SPSS/Clementine. Two experiments were conducted. These resulted in the linking of several offenses in to clusters, each of which were sufficiently similar to have possibly been committed by the same offender(s). A number of interesting clusters were used to form profiles of offenders. Some of these profiles were confirmed by independent analysts as either belonging to offenders who had already been detained in connection with a number of the offenses or as appearing sufficiently interesting to warrant further investigation.

The system described in this paper is a prototype developed over a 10-week period. This contrasts with an in-house study using conventional techniques, which took two years, but achieved similar results. As a consequence of this study, the Home Office intends to devote more resources to a follow-up study to investigate the efficacy of routine application of a derivative of the current system to similar serious offenses.

Keywords

Knowledge discovery, data mining, crime pattern analysis, self-organizing map.

12.4.2 Introduction

Data mining is now a proven technology in many areas of commerce and industry. The challenge now is to extend the range of applications to which data mining is used in order to both spread benefits and investigate any domain-specific problems that require enhancements to current data mining practices.

Police forces across the developed world have attempted to apply advanced computing technologies to tackling crime [2]. However, comparatively little use has been made of data mining techniques in analyzing and modeling the behavioral patterns that occur at each stage of the commission of a crime.

In this paper, we look at applying data mining techniques to the task of linking crimes of a serious sexual nature. The challenge is to decide which of the separate offenses can be linked as being possibly committed by the same offender(s). The intent is to link offenses based on coded data (see section 12.4.4) and to subsequently produce a profile of the offender(s) that describes the linked theme.

This work draws on an earlier study applied to linking crimes of burglaries due to the offender(s) passing themselves off as a bogus official in order to gain access to a dwelling with the intention of committing theft [1]. The current study was conducted on a larger scale and provided with more resources, which enabled the system to be provided with cleaner data.

The commercial data mining package, SPSS Clementine, was used in order to speed development and facilitate experimentation within a Cross Industry Platform for Data Mining (CRISP-DM) methodology [6]. This enabled the prototype system described in this paper to be developed in 10 weeks. This contrasts with an in-house study using conventional techniques, which lasted two years and produced similar results.

In this paper two specific data mining techniques, the self-organizing map and visualization techniques, are used to analyze sexual assaults and rape offenses held in a ViCLASS relational database within the National Crime Faculty (NCF) at Bramshill, the National Police Staff College. The stages of data selection, coding, and cleaning are described, together with the interpretation of the results.

12.4.3   Task Understanding

When a specified offense occurs within the United Kingdom the force in which the offense occurred has the remit to forward full details to the NCF for subsequent entry into the Violent Crime Linkage Analysis System (ViCLASS) system. A specified offense includes a sexually motivated murder, rape where the offender is a stranger or only has limited knowledge of the victim, abduction for sexual purposes, and serious indecent assaults. ViCLASS is a relational database developed in 1991 by the Royal Canadian Mounted Police comprising 53 tables, not all of which are used in the United Kingdom. The system not only stores hard factual information relating to the crime, but the offender's behavior is also encoded. Trained analysts examine a 165, question input document and extract behavioral information from narrative text, such as the offender's speech and physical actions immediately prior to and during the commission of the crime.

On receipt of the document, an analyst assistant uses a quality-control document for guidance to ensure a consistent approach to data interpretation. It is the role of the NCF analysts to examine each new case, the index case, with a view to identifying similarities with existing offenses within the system. If such links are made, it can identify that the index case is part of an emerging series of crimes committed by the same offender(s), who may or may not be known. If a specific series cannot be identified, the analysis may still reveal similarities with other crimes that will assist the senior investigating officer (SIO) in the investigation of the index crime. Current police crime recording systems do not transcend individual police force boundaries; therefore those crimes that occur in different force areas are more difficult to detect. It is within the NCF remit to provide additional assistance in these circumstances.

Before the results of the encoded behavior can be utilized it is important to understand the current research relating to criminology and its relevance to the data set in question.

Routine activity theory requires that there are a minimum of three elements for a crime to occur; a likely offender, a suitable target and the absence of a suitable guardian. Offenders do not offend 24 hours a day committing crime, they have recognizable lives and activities, for example, go to work, support a football team, regularly drink in a public house. They have an awareness space in which feel comfortable, which revolves around where they live, work socialize and the travel infrastructure that connects those places.

One offender from the ViCLASS system committed 12 of his 13 offenses on his way to and home from work, his remaining offense occurred along his route to a repair shop where he took his lawnmower. All of the recorded offenders, who commit their assaults in more than one Force area, offend within an average distance of 3.37 miles of their home current address at the time of committing the offense. This is the entire population of such offenders using the shortest road route.

It has been stated that crimes against the person such as rape, homicide and assault occur closer to the offender's home than property crimes such as burglary. However the authors have established that offenders who commit sexual crimes commit their crimes further from home than burglary offenders. Based on 2 years of burglary crimes in a district of the West Midlands Police area the average distance that a burglary offender travels from his/her home address is 1.47 miles. Sampling a random 60% of recorded offenders from the ViCLASS database who only commit offenses within the border of a single Force, the average distance from their home address is 4.11 miles.

The rational choice perspective states that committing a crime is conscious process by the offender to fulfill his/her commonplace needs such as money, sex and excitement. An unknown offender within the system has committed 22 offenses by committing a burglary and indecently assaulting the female occupant. By these actions he is possibly fulfilling two of the stated needs, sex and excitement.

12.4.4   **Data Understanding**

A copy of the database used in this study contained 2,370 recorded sexual offenses that occurred throughout England, Scotland, Wales, and Northern Ireland between March 1998 and June 26, 2000 and were referred to NCF for analysis. Table 12.1 shows the eight specific crime categories and the numbers of offenses associated with each. The categories are not mutually exclusive, an example being an offender who commits a burglary with a view to sexually assaulting the victim.

Table 12.1   *Classification of Sexual Crimes*

Offense Category	Date Rape	Burglary	Sexual Assault	Multiple Offenders	Abduction	Weapon	Aggravated Assault	Other	Total	Offense Total
Total	22	138	1786	223	230	306	339	266	**3310**	2370

There are 1,015 known offenders (convicted, charged, or suspected), 90 of whom are believed to have committed two or more offenses (see Table 12.2). It is possible, however, that some of the undetected crimes in the database may be attributed to these recorded offenders. Also the offenders of the crimes reported in the database may have committed other similar crimes that have not been reported to the NCF for analysis.

Table 12.2   *Number of Crimes Attributed to Known Offenders*

Number of Offenses	Number of Offenders
18	1
13	1
10	1
9	1
7	1
6	1
5	7
4	8
3	9
2	60

Offenses committed by persons unknown to the victim are particularly difficult to detect. However, within a series, the offender's behavior often has consistencies across the crime set [8, 10]. There is a tendency for the levels of violence to escalate across time.

In attempting to model offender behavior by linking crimes, it is necessary to understand certain fundamental limitations:

- The data set is not complete. Although all forces have the remit to forward specified cases to the NCF, it is apparent that this is does not always occur. In some instances, a force will forward a number of crimes that it has already linked with a view to gaining further assistance with the series.

- It is possible that unsolved crimes held within the database may be attributed to one of the known offenders.

- Although the same team of people has input the crimes, there are discrepancies in the encoding process, which are discussed below.

- Additional information that could be used to identify similarities between the crimes is held in free-text memo fields within the database. They are not currently used in the modeling process.

- The crimes in series identified by NCF analysts for which no offender has been charged, suspected, or convicted are assumed to have been committed by the same person(s) for purpose of validation of the models.

- It has to be assumed that the known offenders have actually committed the crimes that have been attributed to them.

12.4.5   Data Preparation

Ambiguous Data

The results of the mining process are directly proportional to the quality of the data. With a small number of persons responsible for encoding and entering the data, it was assumed that the quality would be high. However, there were some discrepancies within the subsequent encoding. Table 12.3 illustrates an example of confusing encoding of free-text information. In this example, the variable being encoded relates to whether the victim was specifically targeted as an individual (not just targeted due to the type of person he or she was). It is clear that both the yes and no contain the same information and all should have been encoded as no.

Table 12.3   *Data Encoding Examples (3 Yes and 3 No)*

Specifically Targeted = Yes	Specifically Targeted = No
The intention of the group involved in this offense was to pick up a prostitute, so to that extent she was targeted.	Required prostitute, but the individual was not targeted.
In that she was a prostitute, however, it need not have been specifically her.	The offender did not target that particular prostitute.
As being a vulnerable female.	Only in as much as she was a single, young, vulnerable female.

Missing Data

It is not uncommon for the encoded data to have fields that contain unknown or missing values. There are a variety of legitimate reasons why this can happen. In this specific task, one such occurrence might be due to the victim's not recalling certain facts due to the trauma associated with the crime. How should they be treated? Are those fields essential to the mining process? There are a number of methods [12] for treating records that contain missing values:

1. Omit the incorrect field(s)

2. Omit the entire record that contains the incorrect field(s)

3. Automatically enter/correct the data with default values (e.g., select the mean from the range)

4. Derive a model to enter/correct the data

5. Replace all values with a global constant

Within this study, both missing and unknown data have been set to zero when used in dichotomous variables.

Data Encoding

Data was encoded as binary dichotomous variables. Categorical data, such as build, was encoded by a set of mutually exclusive binary variables. An example is the offender's build, which could be Unknown, Thin/Skinny/Slim, Medium, Heavy/Stock/Fat being encoded as a 1 and the remainder as 0.

Three of the data fields each contain a large number of options, some of which appear to be close in meaning:

1. The approach, the type of behavior that the offender exhibited at the beginning of the crime

2. The precautions that the offender took during the commission of the crimes

3. The verbal themes, as described above.

There are 29 options for the approach classification, 22 for precautions, and 28 for the verbal-themes options. Encompassing research [4, 7] the 29 approach options have been reduced to three mutually exclusive dichotomous variables. In conjunction with extensive discussions with the analysts, the precautions options have been reduced to four mutually exclusive dichotomous variables, and the verbal themes reduced to seven fuzzy dichotomous variables.

It is during the data preparation stage in the CRISP-DM cycle that a variety of encoding techniques may be utilized to provide additional fields for analysis and to enable fuzzy concepts.

Variable Selection

It is always difficult to ascertain the correct number and combination of variables that are to be used in the modeling process. Within this paper, it is the intention to model offenders' behavior to establish consistency across crimes. Therefore, to test this, two different sets of twin variable combinations representing particular behavioral traits were used.

Exercise 1

The first modeling exercise used only the approach and verbal-themes sets of variables. This combination was selected to examine behavioral traits at the initial offender/victim point of contact and the subsequent dialogue throughout the crime. This resulted in a total of three approach and seven verbal-themes variables being used in training the model.

Exercise 2

Research conducted on male offenders who have committed rape offenses within the south of England [5] established that they committed their offenses close to their home base. Therefore, in conjunction with the findings discussed in Section 12.4.3, the second modeling exercise was restricted to a single police area. The variable set of approach and precautions was used. This combination was selected to examine behavioral traits at the initial offender/victim point of contact and the precautions that the offender took in committing the crime. This resulted in a total of three approach and four precaution variables being used in training the model.

Model Building

A Kohonen [9] self-organizing map was used in the modeling process for both exercises discussed above. A self-organizing map was selected because it has the ability to cluster similar records into the same cell, while producing a two-dimensional topological map showing the relationship of those records to near neighbors. This can be used to form larger clusters by merging neighboring cells [1]. It also aids in determining the relationship between broad categories of crime. In this application, this could be useful as crimes that are broadly similar may have been split into different clusters due to slight variations in

Figure 12.4
*Approach and
verbal-themes
behavior.*

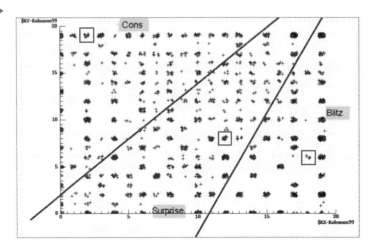

offender behavior due to the specific circumstances in which the crime was committed or even due to missing data.

Figure 12.4 Exercise Mode 1 illustrates the 2D representation of the resulting modeling process for Exercise 1. The map shows the 2,370 crimes on a 20 x 20 grid (400 cells) as points agitated to show density. Lines and a circle have been manually drawn on the graph to show broadly the differing types of approach that the offender used at the point of contact with the victim. These have been broadly categorized as cons, surprise, and blitz. (An alternative automated approach to manually drawing these regions would have been to use a multi-layered perceptron to take the output coordinates from the SOM and label the regions appropriately.) The square shapes contain those crimes from each of the "approach" types that were selected at random from within each broad area for independent verification.

Exercise 2 Model

Figure 12.5 illustrates the 2D representation of the resulting modeling process for Exercise 2 on a 10 x 10 grid (100 cells). Again, individual crimes lying within a cell have been agitated to show density. Lines broadly separate the differing types of approach that the offender used at the point of contact with the victim. The triangle contains those crimes that were independently validated. Again, while the super clusters have been allocated manually, they could have been formed automatically by use of a multilayered perceptron.

Verification

NCF analysts who took no part in the modeling undertook the validation process, but due to their workload they could not examine all crimes within

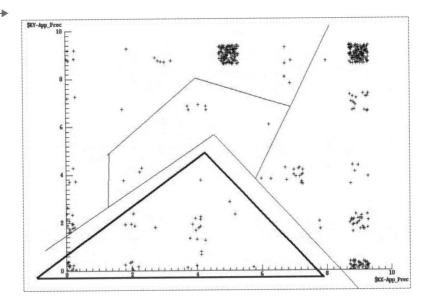

Figure 12.5
Approach and precautions behavior.

all clusters. Each analyst was only presented with a list of crime identification numbers with a remit to ascertain whether there were similarities between the crimes. They had no other information. The narrative was mainly used to ascertain the similarities between the crimes.

Exercise 1

Three clusters represented by the squares in Figure 12.4 were sent for independent verification; the only information provided to the analysts was the unique case reference number and a cluster number. In Exercise 1 the initial clustering process used the approach and verbal-themes variables, and it was established that there were additional similarities between the crimes contained in each cluster.

The similarities in cluster 1 consisted of the following:

- 80% of the victims were under the influence of alcohol.

- The type of sexual assault was 100% consistent.

- Precautions were taken by the offender in 80% of crimes.

- Although the offender immediately overpowered the victim on contact, only minor injuries were caused in 80% of the crimes.

The similarities in cluster 2 consisted of the following:

- 50% of the offenders were of the same nonwhite race.

- 53% of the victims were walking in public places at the time of the offense.

- A further 33% of victims were asleep at the time of the attack.

- There were two partial series contained within this cluster.

- Four crimes were part of a known series.

The similarities in cluster 3 consisted of the following:

- The victim was subjected to a number of sexual acts in 100% of the crimes.

- 100% of the offenders took precautions.

- In 100% of the crimes the offender disrobed himself as well as the victim

Of the three clusters submitted for validation, cluster 2 contained the largest number of offenders and cluster 3 the smallest. It would appear that the number of crimes contained within the clusters indicates the accuracy of the clustering process; the fewer the crimes in the resulting clusters, the more similarities there appear to be.

The three square clusters in Figure 12.4 were examined using the variables identified in Table 12.4 together with a control group formed by averaging attribute values of 100 randomly selected crimes.

The headings in Table 12.4 refer to the attributes in the database tables; for example, Questions refers to whether the offender questioned the victim and the degree of the questioning process.

Both approach and verbal-themes variables, described in the section "Data Encoding" above, comprise a number of subvariables that, individually, are used in this table for comparison purposes. An example is that 91% of offenders in cluster 1 used the same subapproach type on initial contact with the victim as compared with 19% of the control group. This is, therefore, a significant behavioral trait appertaining to that cluster.

It is important to note that such traits that fall below the average are also significant in identifying individual offenders (e.g., only 22% of offenders in cluster 6 try to offer reassurance to their victim's during the commission of the

Table 12.4   *Cluster Comparison*

Cluster	Same Sub Approach	Same Sub Verb Theme	Negotiation	Disrobing	Reassurance	Questions	Victim Build	Victim Marital Status	Victim Drug Use
1	91%	36%	82%	60%	91%	92%	40%	60%	80%
2	53%	80%	67%	20%	80%	55%	46%	65%	52%
3	75%	100%	75%	25%	50%	50%	24%	100%	25%
Cluster Average	58%	82%	68%	22%	67%	49%	48%	73%	34%
S1	20%	60%	70%	40%	70%	50%	40%	90%	40%
S2	10%	20%	70%	20%	40%	60%	30%	50%	40%
S3	20%	60%	70%	50%	70%	50%	10%	30%	30%
S4	20%	60%	70%	50%	70%	50%	40%	50%	40%
S5	10%	30%	70%	10%	80%	60%	50%	70%	30%
	20%	10%	80%	30%	90%	80%	60%	60%	20%
	20%	40%	80%	30%	90%	70%	60%	60%	20%
	10%	30%	70%	40%	60%	70%	50%	60%	20%
	30%	40%	60%	20%	70%	50%	40%	60%	20%
	30%	30%	90%	10%	70%	50%	60%	50%	10%
Control Cluster	19%	38%	73%	30%	71%	59%	44%	58%	27%

offense, as compared with 71% from the control group). This indicates that the majority of offenders reassure their victim in some way, whereas the offenders in cluster 6 do not, thereby identifying the particular behavioral trait of that cluster.

Exercise 2

The crimes belonging to the single-approach type that are captured within the triangle in Figure 12.5 were passed to an analyst for validation purposes. Individual clusters were not identified due to the group of 54 crimes being considered a Super Cluster.

Within the triangle, a complete crime series of four and five partial series were identified and the following similarities were found:

- 92% of offenses were committed by person(s) unknown to the victim.

- 59% of offenders had the same motive.

- Full intercourse took place in 51% of offenses.

- 46% of victims were fondled by the offender.

- 41% of offenders committed burglary to commit the offense.

- 38% of offenders were concerned about their own safety.

- 35% of offenders used the attack for ego satisfaction/pleasure.

- A weapon was visible in 32% of offenses.

None of the above was used in the modeling process.

12.4.6   Discussion

Given the existing limitations identified in Section 12.4.4, the results are encouraging. In both exercises, based on the results of the validation process, the authors have illustrated that the models identify consistency in offender behavior. The analysts established that crimes in individual clusters exhibited strong similarities, with adjacent clusters that are based on a variable theme having similar traits, as illustrated in Figure 12.4.

An analyst currently compares the index case against the remainder of the database by selecting one or more variables from the screen, which is then translated into a SQL query. This process relies on the analyst's skill and intuition, often resulting in a time-consuming process of multiple queries returning different overlapping sets in order to ensure that all variances are returned for examination. In both exercises, the analysts report that all crimes that they would have wished to examine were contained within the clusters.

The results from Exercise 1 demonstrate that crimes within a single cluster have strong similarities and, as in the results from cluster 2, may even contain crimes that have been committed by the same offender. With further refinements, it should be possible to suggest names from the known offender list as being responsible for as yet unsolved crimes.

The results from Exercise 2 indicate that this type of model could be used as an initial match against the index case by restricting the search space to the police force area in which that crime occurred. A second pass through the data would include those crimes from the adjacent force areas and a third pass could include national data.

This prototype system took 10 weeks to develop from being unfamiliar with the data and its structures to gaining domain understanding, encoding and modeling the data, and passing the results through the validation process. Prior to and independent of this study, three persons, a medical psychologist, a statistician, and a researcher, took two years to complete a piece of work that reached broadly similar results. As a result of this study, the NCF plans to commence an in-depth 12-month pilot using the software.

12.4.7 Further Work

Only two sets of two variable types were used in this study. There is scope to increase the number of sets and the number of variables within each set, model each, and ascertain the behavioral consistency across each type. An example would be approach, verbal themes, and precautions within the same model.

Use several combinations of two variable sets and establish whether the same crimes are clustered in more than one of the resulting models. Greater numbers of crimes clustered across the models may indicate that the same offender is responsible.

Cluster on a single two-variable combination, for example, approach and precautions as in training the model.

Exercise 2 and recluster the results from the triangle using a different set of variables.

12.4.8 Acknowledgments

Our thanks to the National Crime Faculty of the National Police College, Bramshill United Kingdom, for providing the data and independent verification of the results.

References

1. Adderley, R., and Musgrove, P.B. (1999), *Data Mining at the West Midlands Police: A Study of Bogus Official Burglaries*. BCS Special Group Expert Systems, ES99, London, Springer-Verlag, pp. 191–203.

2. Adderley, R., and Musgrove, P.B. (2001), "Police Crime Recording and Investigation Systems, a User's View." *Policing an International Journal of Police Strategies and Management*, 24(1), pp. 100–114.

3. Brantingham, P.L., and Brantingham, P.L. (1991), "Notes on the Geometry of Crime," *in Environmental Criminology*, USA: Wavelend Press, Inc.

4. Canter, D., and Heritage, R. (1990), "A Multivariate Model of Sexual Offense Behaviour: Developments in Offender Profiling I." *The Journal of Forensic Psychiatry*, 1(2), pp. 185–212.

5. Canter, D., and Larkin, P. (1993), "Environmental Range of Serial Rapists" *Journal of Environmental Psychology*, 13 pp. 63–69.

6. Chapman, P., Clinton, J., Kerber, R., Khabaza, T., Reinartz, T., Shearer, C., and Wirth, Rudiger. (2000), *CRISP-DM 1.0 Step-by-Step Data Mining Guide*, USA: SPSS Inc. CRISPWP-0800 2000.

7. Davies, A. (1992), "Rapists' Behaviour: A Three Aspect Model As a Basis for Analysis and the Identification of Serial Crime." *Forensic Science International*, 55 pp. 173–194.

8. Hazelwood, R.R., Reboussin, R., and Warren, J.I. (1989), "Series Rape: Correlates of Increased Aggression and the Relationship of Offender Pleasure to Victim Resistance." *Journal of Interpersonal Violence* 4 pp. 65–78.

9. Kohonen, T. (1984), "Self-organisation and associative memory," *Springer Series in Information Sciences*, Vol 8. New York: Springer-Verlag.

10. LeBeau, J.I. (1987), "Patterns of Stranger and Serial Rape Offending: Factors Distinguishing Apprehended and at Large Offenders." *Journal of Criminal Law and Criminology* 78 pp. 309–326.

11. Rhodes, W.M., and Conly, C. (1991), *The Criminal Commute: A Theoretical Perspective in Environmental Criminology*, USA: Wavelend Press, Inc.

12. Weiss, S.M., and Indurkhya, N. (1998), *Predictive Data Mining: A Practical Guide*. San Francisco: Morgan Kaufman Publishers, Inc.

12.5 **Decomposing Signatures Software**

New data mining software has been developed for handwriting identification without the bias that often accompanies human analysis of handwriting. Who wrote the Jon-Benet Ramsey ransom note? A computer program in development at the University at Buffalo may soon be able to assist in answering such a question. It is currently 98% effective in determining the authorship of handwritten documents.

The Center of Excellence in Document Analysis and Recognition (CEDAR) project funded by the National Institute of Justice has produced the first software program designed to develop computer-assisted handwriting-analysis tools for forensic applications. In criminal cases, the question of who penned a ransom note or forged a check is now the domain of human handwriting analysts. Because they are human, even the best graphologists cannot claim complete objectivity. The University of Buffalo's software is the first that can identify who wrote a particular document based on purely scientific criteria.

"A human expert may put in his or her own bias even unconsciously," says Sargur Srihari, Ph.D., principal investigator and SUNY Distinguished Professor in the Department of Computer Science and Engineering in the College of Arts and Sciences and the School of Engineering and Applied Sciences at University of Buffalo. "We have built the foundation for a handwriting analysis system that will quantify performance and increase confidence in determining a writer's identity. This is about validating individuality in handwriting," Srihari notes. "The idea that everyone's handwriting is different is taken for granted. What we have done is to develop purely scientific criteria for that premise."

It is the first time researchers have attempted to do pattern recognition based on a large database of handwriting and using a totally automated means of measuring specific features of human handwriting, according to Srihari, who also is the director of CEDAR. CEDAR is primarily devoted to a new set of pattern-recognition technologies that can recognize and read handwriting. It was CEDAR's expertise in developing systems that can read and interpret handwritten addresses on envelopes for the U.S. Postal Service—now used around the world—that attracted interest from the National Institute of Justice, which funded the work with a $428,000 grant.

Providing a scientific basis for establishing the individuality of handwriting has become essential for admitting handwriting evidence in U.S. courts due to a number of recent rulings concerning expert testimony, Srihari says; "In this project, we are developing a technology whose job it is to authenticate documents." The University of Buffalo researchers developed the software by first collecting a database of more than 1,000 samples of handwriting from a pool of individuals representing a microcosm of the U.S. population in terms of gender, age, and ethnicity.

Multiple samples of handwriting were taken from subjects, each of whom was asked to write the same series of documents in cursive. Instead of analyzing the documents visually, the way a human expert would, Srihari explains, the researchers deconstructed each sample, extracting features from the writing, such as measuring the shapes of individual characters, descenders, and the spaces between lines and words. The researchers then ran the samples through their software program.

"We tested the program by asking it to determine which of two authors wrote a particular sample, based on measurable features," says Srihari. "The program responded correctly 98 percent of the time." Human experts look for arcades and garlands, features that may distinguish one person's penmanship from another's, he explains. The current software should be able to conduct that type of advanced analysis within the year.

The goal of authenticating documents in criminal cases is usually to determine whether or not a particular suspect wrote the document in question. The scientific approach that Srihari and his colleagues are developing, however, also may be useful in establishing individuality, as with DNA, fingerprints, or facial features, in the emerging field of biometrics, which is the automated identification of a person based on precise measurements of physiological or behavioral characteristics. For more information on CEDAR, go to its Web site at http://www.cedar.buffalo.edu/index.html.

The following case study is again provided in its original version. The author would like to thank Lars Kangas for his valuable assistance in providing the materials relating to his work with the CATCH investigative data mining project.

12.6 Computer Aided Tracking and Characterization of Homicides and Sexual Assaults (CATCH)

Lars J. Kangas,[1] Kristine M. Terrones, Robert D. Keppel, and Robert D. La Moria

Battelle Pacific Northwest Division, MS K7-22, Richland, WA 99352

Attorney General of Washington, Criminal Division

1. Correspondence: Email: lars.kangas@pnl.gov; Telephone: (509) 375-3905

12.6.1   Abstract

When a serial offender strikes, it usually means that the investigation is unprecedented for that police agency. The volume of incoming leads and pieces of information in the case(s) can be overwhelming as evidenced by the thousands of leads gathered in the Ted Bundy murders, the Atlanta child murders, and the Green River murders. Serial cases can be long-term investigations in which the suspect remains unknown and continues to perpetrate crimes. With state and local murder investigative systems beginning to crop up, it will become important to manage that information in a timely and efficient way by developing computer programs to assist in that task. One vital function will be to compare violent crime cases from different jurisdictions so investigators can approach the investigation knowing that similar cases exist.

CATCH (Computer Aided Tracking and Characterization of Homicides) is being developed to assist crime investigations by assessing likely characteristics of unknown offenders, by relating a specific crime case to other cases, and by providing a tool for clustering similar cases that may be attributed to the same offenders.

CATCH is a collection of tools that assist the crime analyst in the investigation process by providing advanced data mining and visualization capabilities. These tools include clustering maps, query tools, geographic maps, timelines, etc. Each tool is designed to give the crime analyst a different view of the case data.

The clustering tools in CATCH are based on artificial neural networks (ANNs). The ANNs learn to cluster similar cases from approximately 5,000 murders and 3,000 sexual assaults residing in a database. The clustering algorithm is applied to parameters describing modus operandi (MO), signature characteristics of the offenders, and other parameters describing the victim and offender. The proximity of cases within a two-dimensional representation of the clusters allows the analyst to identify similar or serial murders and sexual assaults.

12.6.2   Introduction

CATCH is being developed to provide crime analysts enhanced means for interpreting large databases of crime data. These databases store a large number of crimes with each case described in a large number of details. Battelle Memorial Institute's Pacific Northwest Division developed CATCH in collaboration with the Attorney General of Washington, Criminal Division. Investigators at the Criminal Division are currently evaluating CATCH.

The development of CATCH was made possible with the HITS (Homicide Investigation Tracking System) database system. Police involved in the infamous Green River and Ted Bundy murder investigations in the State of Washington developed HITS circa 10 years ago to enable the computer-based analysis of murders. The database now contains several thousand violent crimes primarily from the Pacific Northwest, USA.

CATCH provides analysts tools for efficiently viewing crime details and comparing crimes against each other. An initial set of one or more crimes is selected by using point-and-click methods that generate SQL queries to retrieve the set of crimes from the database. This set of crimes is then refined with tools that tell the analyst that specific crimes do not "belong" in the set. The analyst can also add other crimes to the set that should "belong" to the set. The set of crimes may belong together because they appear to be committed by the same offender.

There are two versions of CATCH, one for murders and one for sexual assaults. Although the version of CATCH described here is custom configured specifically for the HITS database of violent crimes, it can be applied against other crime databases through relatively minor changes in the software.

12.6.3 Clustering Algorithm

CATCH uses ANNs for analysis. The benefit of ANNs is often described by means of their information (sensor) fusion capabilities. Information fusion is the process of extracting information from several data sources in parallel. More information can frequently be gained by this approach, compared to processing each data source individually. Another benefit with some ANNs is their ability to extract nonlinear information from data.

The clustering algorithm in CATCH is based on self-organizing maps (SOMs). These networks are also called self-organizing feature maps or Kohonen networks after the inventor, Professor Teuvo Kohonen [11, 6].

The SOMs belong to the unsupervised neural-network class, meaning that the network is not provided any labels that describe the data vectors during a learning phase. Instead, the SOM organizes data vectors into clusters of similar data in regions on a two-dimensional map. Two dimensions provide a convenient visual representation, though it is not a requirement.

The HITS Unit staff at the Attorney General of Washington, Criminal Division use standard forms to record the large number of details describing each crime, which are then entered into the HITS database. CATCH processes these crime details and generates data vectors for numerical analysis. Each data vector includes more than 200 details of each crime.

Figure 12.6
The SOM represents about 5,000 murders in the HITS database.

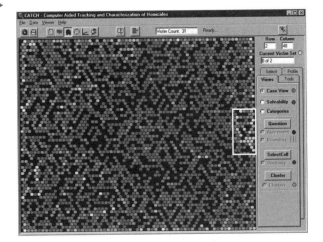

The SOM in CATCH has 4,096 cells organized as a 64 x 64 grid (see Figure 12.6). The learning phase assigns each crime to exactly one of these cells. The specific cell to which each crime is assigned is based on a clustering algorithm applied during a learning phase. Similar crimes are placed in closer proximity to each other. Identical or nearly identical crimes may be placed in the same cell. Some cells may not be assigned any crimes during the learning phase, but these cells may be assigned new crimes as they are entered into the database between retrainings of the SOM. The SOM should periodically be retrained when a sufficient number of new cases are added to the database to take advantage of all the crime data available.

The self-organizing map in Figure 12.6 represents about 5,000 murders in the HITS database. Each of the cells in the 64 x 64 map typically contains eight or fewer crimes. The black cells contain no crimes. The lighter the cell color, the more crimes are in the cell. (The cells are colored in different shades in the application.) The overlaid light rectangle contains light-colored cells that are selected into a current set of crimes being analyzed. (The example set of clustered crimes in the figure is the Green River murders believed to have been commited by one serial offender.)

12.6.4 Database Mining

The tools in CATCH are of two types. First, there are database mining tools to give the crime analyst a better understanding of the content of the database. Second, there are tools that let the analyst retrieve and compare specific crimes.

The self-organizing map is like a window into the database. Each crime in the database has a location on the SOM and the clusters on the SOM link

Figure 12.7
Crimes are mapped by modus operandi descriptions.

together similar crimes in the database. Thus, the database can be mined for related crimes through the SOM. These mining tools, which use the SOM, include a search tool that lets the analyst select a combination of crime details and see where on the SOM there are crimes for which these details hold true (see Figures 12.7 and 12.8). Another tool allows the analyst to select one crime case and see where in the SOM there are other similar crime cases, based on any combination of the details describing the crimes. CATCH allows the analyst to add to, remove from, or crop the current set of crime cases by selecting areas of cells in the SOM, while mining the database.

The SOM is overlaid by boundaries around areas of common crime details. The small window shows which details are selected and the color-coding of the boundaries. The user can select crimes that are in the unions of the bounded areas, shown as light-colored cells in the figure.

In Figure 12.8, the depicted tool emphasizes cells containing crimes for which all selected details correctly describe the crimes. The cells in the SOM are colored lighter according to the correlation of the selected crime details (i.e., lighter cells have higher correlation with the selected crime details).

The "starmap" of crimes in CATCH is shown in Figure 12.9. This representation of all crimes in the database is a three-dimensional cube, where the data vectors describing the crimes have been reduced down to three eigenvalues. The cube is viewed by selecting any two of the dimensions. Although a significant amount of information is lost when high-dimensional data is reduced to a few dimensions, the visualization of the data still conveys significant structure of the data in the database. The user can select volumes in the cube to retrieve, remove, and crop crimes from the current set of crimes being analyzed.

Figure 12.8
*Order and
description of
crimes such as
rape, serial and
rituals can be
queried.*

Figure 12.9 shows all the crime data vectors as points in a three-dimensional eigenspace. The cube of crimes is viewed in any two of the three dimensions. This cube of crimes gives an alternate view of the clusters and structure of the crimes in the database. Similar crimes form denser areas of "stars" in the cube. The highlighted crimes within the overlaid square are selected into the current working set.

The geographic map in CATCH is shown in Figure 12.10, with crimes placed as pins at the locations where they were committed. This map also allows the user to select an area and retrieve all the crimes in that area, or the user can crop or remove crimes from the current working set of crimes.

The geographic map tool in Figure 12.10 places the current set of crimes on the map as pins (see examples in the rectangle). The user can select pins to view additional information about specific crimes.

The tools described above and some additional tools (e.g., a time line tool), allow the crime analyst to retrieve crime data from the database without having to use queries. CATCH automatically generates SQL queries to retrieve requested information from the user's interaction with graphical representations of the data. Thus, although CATCH allows the use of queries in a specific query tool, it has been designed so that a user is removed from having to work with queries when mining the database.

Figure 12.9
The figure shows all the crime data vectors as points in a three-dimensional eigenspace.

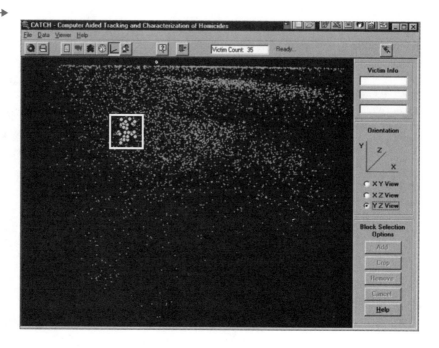

12.6.5   Database Visualization

While the data mining tools are used for rapidly focusing on a set of crimes that may be related, the data visualization tools become the priority for more

Figure 12.10
Crimes can be mapped along highways.

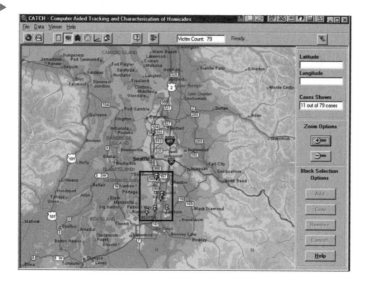

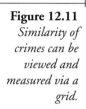

Figure 12.11
Similarity of crimes can be viewed and measured via a grid.

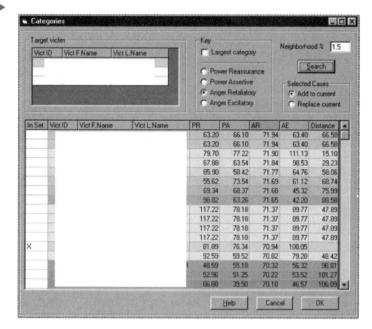

in-depth analysis of crime data. Some graphical data visualization capabilities of CATCH have been partially described above with the data mining tools. This section describes a few of the tools that allow the users to view, analyze, and compare details describing different crimes. (Because CATCH processes sensitive information, it is necessary to restrict the images of these tools in the figures).

Most of the data visualization tools in CATCH show the crime details in grids that are enhanced by color and order of significance. The color enhancement in the grids is used to give the user improved perception of the data without having to focus on numerical values. Typically, grid values representing crime details are lighter in color if the crime detail has a higher numerical value or if the crime detail holds true for a specific crime. The grids can also be sorted to bring more significant details to the top of the grids. The significance of each detail is dynamically computed in the sorting algorithms.

Figures 12.11 and 12.12 show two tools for comparing crime cases based on labels assigned to sexual offenders. These labels—Power Reassurance, Power Assertive, Anger Retaliatory, and Anger Excitation—were conceived by the FBI to describe the behavior of sexual offenders [1-5]. Dr. Robert Keppel [7-10], chief criminal investigator at the Attorney General of Washington, Criminal Division, developed a weighting scheme applied to these labels. Each specific detail describing crimes has associated weights that are based on how much the detail contributes to the different labels and the rarity of that

Figure 12.12
*Comparison of
crime types can
be measured.*

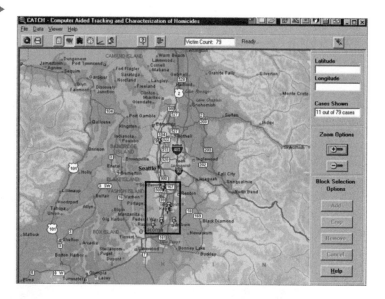

detail occurring in the HITS database of crimes. The weighting scheme incorporates the expertise of the crime investigators, recognizing that some crime details are more important than others for identifying related crimes by serial offenders.

The grid in the Figure 12.11 shows several crimes, one on each row, which have been determined by CATCH to be similar to a crime being analyzed (marked by an X in the first column). The most similar crimes in the database are retrieved and ordered by the overall weight assigned to one of the four sex-

Figure 12.13
*Probability and
distance of
crimes by the
same perpetrator
can be graphed.*

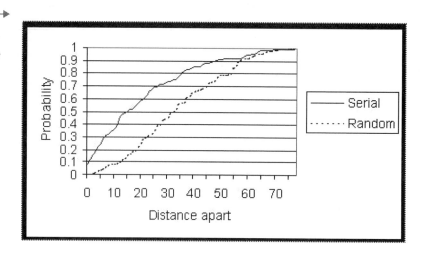

ual offender labels: Power Reassurance, Power Assertive, Anger Retaliatory, and Anger Excitation. The grid can be used for selecting and removing crimes from the current set of crimes.

The tool shown in the Figure 12.12 allows the crime analyst to compare two crimes side by side according to the sexual offender labels: Power Reassurance, Power Assertive, Anger Retaliatory, and Anger Excitation. The figure shows the individual weights assigned to each of the details and the four labels describing each of the two crimes. The details of the two crimes in the figure are sorted to bring the significant details to the top. The two crimes compared in the figure are both described to have "unusual ritual" and "blindfold" in common. These are two crime details that are relatively rare in the database and may suggest that the same offender committed these two crimes.

12.6.6 Evaluation

CATCH was developed to identify serial offenders by recognizing that serial offenders tend to repeat certain aspects of their crimes. Because the neural-network algorithm clusters similar data vectors, we expect the crimes by the same offenders to be clustered close together. The graphs in Figures 12.13 and 12.14 show the summary of distances found between any pair of crimes committed by the same known offenders for murders and sexual assaults, respectively. Distances are measured as the number of cells between two crimes on the self-organizing map. A distance of zero indicates that both crimes are in the same cell, a distance of one indicates that the two crimes are in adjacent cells, etc.

Figure 12.14
The solid line in the graph shows the probability of finding two sexual assaults by one serial rapist n number of cells apart.

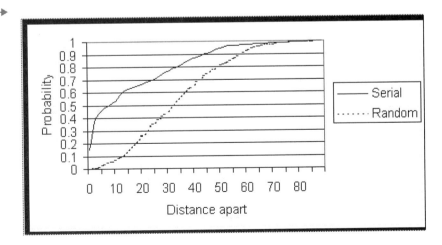

The results shown in Figure 12.13 are based on 189 serial murders committed by 81 known offenders. The graph shows that 50% of serial murders by the same offenders are within 15 cells of each other. The results shown in Figure 12.14 are based on 412 serial sexual assaults committed by 154 known offenders. The graph shows that 50% of serial sexual assaults by the same offenders are within eight cells from each other.

The solid line in Figure 12.13 shows the probability of finding two murders by one serial murderer n number of cells apart. Of the related serial murders 50% are found within 15 cells of each other. The dashed line, in comparison, shows the distance between the same murders as they would appear if randomly placed into cells in the self-organizing map. The confidence is greater than 99% against these two probability distributions having the same mean (two-tailed t-test).

The solid line in Figure 12.14 shows the probability of finding two sexual assaults by one serial rapist n number of cells apart. Of the related serial sexual assaults 50% are found within eight cells of each other. The dashed line, in comparison, shows the distance between the same sexual assaults as they would appear if randomly placed into cells in the self-organizing map. The confidence is greater than 99% against these two probability distributions having the same mean (two-tailed t-test).

12.6.7   Conclusion

Crime analysts at the Attorney General of Washington, Criminal Division, are currently evaluating CATCH. Thus, a statement regarding the utility of CATCH must remain pending until the outcome of this evaluation.

Preliminary evaluations suggest that the clustering algorithms and visualization tools in CATCH have the potential to have considerable value to crime analysts. A new version of CATCH is planned to incorporate additional tools that have been identified from the current research and development. The first set of tools in version one of CATCH was concentrated on researching the value of using artificial neural networks to cluster similar cases. The new version will provide crime analysts a more complete suite of tools; for example, a new tool will provide a more complete method for generating SQL statements from graphical representations.

12.6.8   Acknowledgment

This work was supported by the National Institute of Justice.

12.6.9   References

1.   Copson, G. (1995) "Coals to Newcastle? Part 1: A Study of Offender Profiling: Police Research Group Special Interest Series," Paper 7, Home Office Police Department, London.

2.   Copson, G., R. Badcock, J. Boon, and P. Britton (1997), "Articulating a Systematic Approach to Clinical Crime Profiling," *Criminal Behaviour and Mental Health*, 1997.

3.   Douglas, J.E., A.W. Burgess, A.C. Burgess, and R.K. Ressler (1992) *Crime Classification Manual*, New York: Lexington Books.

4.   Geberth, V.J. and R.N. Turco (1997) "Antisocial Personality Disorder, Sexual Sadism, Malignant Narcissism, and Serial Murder," *Journal of Forensic Sciences* 42 (1): pp. 49–60.

5.   Geberth, V.J. (1996), *Practical Homicide Investigation: Tactics, Procedures, and Forensic Techniques*, Third Edition CRC Publishing, Miami, Florida.

6.   Kaski, S. *Data Exploration Using Self-Organizing Maps*, Acta Polytechnica Scandinavica, Mathematics, Computing and Management in Engineering Series No. 82, Espoo.

7.   Keppel, R.D. and J.P. Weis (1997), "Time and Distance as Solvability Factors in Murder Cases," *Journal of Forensic Sciences*, 39 (2), pp. 386–401.

8.   Keppel, R.D. (1997), *Signature Killers*, New York: Pocket Books.

9.   Keppel, R.D. (1995), "Signature Murders: A Report of Several Related Cases," *Journal of Forensic Sciences*, 40 (4), pp. 658–662.

10. Keppel, R.D. (1995), *The Riverman: Ted Bundy and I Hunt the Green River Killer*, New York: Pocket Books.

11. Kohonen, T. (1997), *Self-Organizing Maps*, Second Edition, Berlin, Springer-Verlag.

12.7   Forensic Data Mining

Neural network have been used to recognize signatures in seized drugs and arson cases; for example, Casale and Watterson produced a paper on "A Computerized Neural Network Method for Pattern Recognition of Cocaine Signatures," which describes a practical procedure for rapidly searching a large database of cocaine signatures to identify database entries that closely resemble a given reference cocaine exhibit. Their procedure takes advantage of the pattern-recognition capability of the multilayer perceptron neural network to identify similar cocaine signatures.

Their pattern-recognition software has been used on a daily basis at the North Carolina State Bureau of Investigation (NCSBI) to aid forensic experts in identifying signatures that originate from the same batch of cocaine. Intelligence reports generated from database searches have been useful to undercover field agents who are striving to build drug-related conspiracy cases. The software was developed as a collaborative effort between the NCSBI and the Center for Systems and Engineering of the Research Triangle Institute.

Another forensic investigator, S.A. Barshick, conducted an analysis of accelerants and fire debris using aroma-detection technology similar to the work done by Matt Vona from the California Department of Justice. Barshick investigated the utility of electronic aroma-detection technologies for the detection and identification of ignitable liquid accelerants and their residues in suspected arson debris.

Through the analysis of known accelerants and residues, a trained neural network was developed for classifying fire-debris samples. Three unknown items taken from actual fire debris that had contained gasoline, kerosene, and diesel fuel were classified using the neural network. One item, taken from the area known to have contained diesel fuel, was correctly identified as diesel fuel residue every time. Barshick also reported success in using neural networks in the classification of kerosene and gasoline residues. His paper, "Analysis of Accelerants and Fire Debris Using Aroma Detection Technology" can be found on the *Journal of Forensic Science* Web site.

12.8 Alien Intelligence

AI software, as we have discovered, can automatically *evolve, breed* solutions, and *learn* criminal behavior on its own when programmed to do so. Sometimes the behavior of this type of AI program is completely unpredictable, or clear, such as that of a neural network. However, when software is designed to learn, it can do so quickly through brute computing force, such as with the CART algorithm. Sometime we can't follow its logic in detail, but we use these AI components because they are very accurate. This is what the renowned computer scientist and writer James Martin calls "alien intelligence," which is a process executed on a computer that is so complex that a human can neither follow the logic step-by-step nor come to the same result by other means. We couldn't write a conventional program, for example, to spot fraud on millions of accounts in real time; we need neural networks to help us.

Alien intelligence refers to the data mining techniques covered in this book that enable computers to recognize patterns too complex or vast for humans to recognize. It also refers to a method by which programs are bred, rather than programmed; software is trained, rather than coded, because humans cannot write their functions—their logical reasoning is too complex. Brain-like mechanisms, such as neural networks, exhibit emergent properties that humans cannot anticipate. These things happen at electronic speed, over vast networks. Only a computer can execute logic millions of times faster than humans can, so we initiate self-evolving computer processes that may become very complex for criminal and terrorist detection and deterrence. The machine-learning algorithms become our defenders and protectors.

Today we have to tell computers blow-by-blow what to do, so coding or writing programs is a very slow process. However, with data mining techniques we don't give the computer blow-by-blow instructions. Instead we train it by giving it a narrowly focused initiative, such as learning the *signature* of a crime, or the task of profiling a perpetrator, which machines with very limited functionality but extreme speed are able to accomplish. This is creating systems and software that breed and evolve and are capable of changing themselves automatically. They are the future of criminal detection and security deterrence. When software breeds or evolves, it does so in order to meet goals that humans specify. The twenty-first century will be an era of emerging alien intelligence. As the century progresses, computers will become immensely more powerful than they are today—eventually billions of times more powerful— and there will be billions of machines interconnected by worldwide networks communicating at the speed of light.

When a system learns it improves its knowledge, as a human does, but this is a mechanistic process. There is no cognizance involved; the computer merely becomes better able to exploit choices of action among an almost infinite number of possibilities. A computer can learn about human behaviors and recognize them for behavioral profiling. Systems and agents coupled with electronic sensors can be relentless in monitoring and collecting information. Some people may feel uncomfortable about this, but because of the threat of terrorism, this will be part of the society we are creating. Machines can observe our behavior and update their knowledge continuously.

With alien-intelligence techniques, computers can be trained to detect patterns that humans couldn't possibly recognize. They can be put to work analyzing, trying to make sense of overwhelming quantities of data, and taking action on the basis of knowledge acquired from the process. They can forage through masses of data, learning about criminals, intrusions, theft, terrorism, fraud, computer viruses, bioterrorism, and other threats to society. Already we have software capable of recognizing faces, emotions, and deception, and with the attacks of 9/11 more are bound to follow, exceeding the abilities of man.

However, in the end, it is the combination of human and machine intelligence and recognizing their fundamental differences as well as each of their strengths that will triumph. Increasingly, alien intelligence can be used to combat crime and terrorism; in this book, you have seen some of the technologies, tools, techniques, and case studies of precrime.

12.9   Bibliography

Martin, J. (2000), *After the Internet: Alien Intelligence*, Washington, DC: Capital Press.

1,000 Online Sources for the Investigative Data Miner

Locator Web Sites

http://locateme.com
Locate Me – Professional locator service.

http://www.who-me.com
Who? Me? – Search registry for those searching for others.

http://www.yellowpages.ca
Canadian Yellow Pages – Online searchable listings for Canada.

http://www.netpartners.com/locator.htm
Company Web Site Locator – A search engine for a companies Web or FTP site.

http://www.corptech.com
Corptech Database – 50,000+ manufacturers and developers of high-tech products.

http://dotcomdirectory.com/nsi/basic.hm
Dot Com Directory – Dot com's business directory.

http://yp.superpages.com/sform.phtml?SRC=lycos&STYPE=S
GTE's Yellow Pages – Searchable by name, category, and state.

http://www.earthcommerce.com/cig-win/upd.exe/activity
Help Findit – Multiple searchs for products and businesses.

http://www.hongkongyellowpages.com
Hong Kong Yellow Pages – Searchable yellow pages.

http://www.jewishbiz.com
Jewish Business Directory – Listings of Jewish businesses.

http://www.newquestcity.com/dir.htm
National Business Directory – Searchable business directory.

http://www.ndiyp.com/usa/yellow_index.html
National Direct – Internet yellow pages.

http://pronet.ca
Pronet Global Business Center – Database of 1.6 million business listings.

http://www.worldpages.com
World Yellow Pages – On-line yellow page listings.

http://www.yellowpages.com
Yellow Pages – Yellow page listings.

Military Personnel Web Sites

http://www.af.mil/search
Air Force Link – Air force link search site.

http://www.aiipowmia.com
Information and search resources for POWs and MIAs.

http://members.aol.com/veterans/warlib13.htm
American Veteran/military Registry – Names of every American who served in uniform since the birth of our nation.

http://www.army.mil
Army Homepage – Latest army news, location resources, links, and large library of army-related information.

http://www.dtic.mil/armylink/faq/index.html
Army Link – FAQ on how to obtain various army records.

http://www.dtic.mil/dpmo
Defense POW/Missing Personnel.

http://members.aol.com/forvets/htomr.htm
Getting Military Records – Offers detailed information on how to go about obtaining military records.

http://www.thefew.com/search.html
Marine Search – Search for U.S. Marines located throughout the United States and abroad.

http://www.familygenealogy.com/military.htm
Military Record Search – Medical, personnel, and pension information.

http://www.militarycity.com
Military Locator Service – Many different databases, which will aid you in searching for active duty personnel, overseas personnel, duty losses, reserves, and military bases.

http://www.nara.gov/regional/mpr.html
Military Personal Records – A repository of millions of military personnel, health, and medical records.

http://www.militaryusa.com/index.html
MilitaryUSA – Searchable database of military records and reunions.

http://www.vets.org
National Veterans Archives – Searchable veteran listings.

http://www.bupers.navy.mil
Navy Locator – Bureau of Naval personnel sailor search.

http://www.peoplesite.com/indexstart.html
People Finder – Veterans – Offers postings from veterans and those looking for them.

http://www.seeklost.com
Seekers of the Lost – The largest search registry online with over 42,000 records.

http://sites.defenselink.mil
US DOD Defense Link – A personal locator.

Directory Web Sites

http://www.1800ussearch.com
1-800 U.S. Search – Offers various search packages for finding anyone in the United States.

http://www.555-1212.com
555-1212 People Finder – Offers multiple database searches from one search engine for locating e-mail addresses and phone numbers.

http://www.infophil.com/World/Alumni
Alumni.net – Search for previous classmates around the globe.

http://kadima.com
A searchable database service that consists of over 200 million names, 170 million with date of birth, compiled from multiple public, private, and proprietary sources.

http://www.anywho.com
Anywho – Provides various online people searches including reverse phone number lookups.

http://www.aol.com/netfind/emailfinder.adp
AOL E-mail Finder – Find an e-mail address using name or address.

http://www.aol.com/netfind/yellowpages.html
Aol Netfind – Look up phone numbers, addresses, maps, and directions for businesses in any U.S. city.

http://www.bigfoot.com
Big Foot – E-mail and white page listings using a person's name.

http://canada411.sympatico.ca
Canada 411 – Searchable address/telephone listings for Canadians.

http://www.nara.gov/regional/cpr.html
Civilian Records – IRS records, civilian personnel and medical records, and government employee records.

http://www.confi-chek.com/pplloc.html
Confi-chek – Find people by name or phone number.

http://www.emailfinder.com
Email Finder – Internet source for updated e-mail and URL addresses.

http://emailchange.com/emailchange/index.htm
Emailchange.com – Change of e-mail address registry and search engine.

http://www.primeris.com/fonefind
Fone Finder – Local and international phone number database.

http://www.whowhere.com/GovtPages
Government Employee Lookup – Search state and federal levels.

http://www.informus.com/adrrpt.html
Informus – Allows you to perform a name search by previous address.

http://www.infospace.com
Info Space Search – Offers white pages, yellow pages, international listings, government listings, and city guides.

http://www.iaf.net
Internet Address Finder – Find an e-mail address.

http://www.mailtown.com
Mailtown.com – Find an e-mail address using a name.

http://www.peoplesite.com/indexstart.html
People Finder – Registry for finding people.

http://www.populus.net
Populus – Address, phone, college, e-mail, and date of birth.

http://www.searchamerica.com
Search America – Search active databases using the name, address, or phone number of anyone in the USA.

http://www.search.com
Search.com – Phone number and e-mail address searches and searchable yellow pages.

http://www.semaphorecorp.com
Semaphore Corporation – Find people who have changed their address, phone, email, name, etc.

http://www.switchboard.com
Switch Board – Find people using surname, address or telephone number.

http://www.semaphorecorp.com/ff/home.html
USPS – Change Of Address Database.

http://www.whitepages.com
White Pages – USA – Search white pages by name.

http://www.whowhere.com
Who Where – E-mail address and company lookups.

http://www.who-me.com
Who? Me? – Search registry for those searching for others.

http://www.worldemail.com/wede4.shtml
World E-mail Directory – Search for e-mail addresses.

http://www.worldpages.com/reshome.html
World Pages – Addresses and phone numbers; e-mail, businesses, and government information.

http://home.wizard.com/wwpr.html
World Wide Profile Registry – Central database for personal profiles of Internet users from all over the globe.

http://people.yahoo.com
Yahoo People Search – Phone number and e-mail search databases.

Criminal Investigative Web Sites

http://www.tarsearch.com
Accident Reconstruction Experts Database – Traffic accident reconstruction (TAR) expert database.

http://www.polygraph.org
American Polygraph Association – Consists of about 2,000 members in the polygraph field.

http://www.actlabs.com/forensics.htm
Arson – Actlabs – Large collection of resources dealing with arson.

http://www.teleport.com/~peterc/2.html
Data Discovery – Experts that will examine computer hard drives, diskettes, and other media for evidence of a crime.

http://police2.ucr.edu/csi.html
Crime Scene Investigation – Online manual of methods and procedures to be performed at a crime scene.

http://www.acsr.com
Crime Scene Association – Access to experts in the use of scientific methods, physical evidence, deductive reasoning.

http://www.mssm.edu/genetics/dna_dbase.html
DNA Databases – Provides links to numerous DNA-related databases on the Web.

http://www3.sympatico.ca/lindblom.doc.exam
Document Examination Consultants – Provide both expert and objective examinations of questioned documents.

http://www.experts.com
Expert Directory – Online database of experts, expert witnesses, consultants, and spokespersons searchable by topic, keyword, or location.

http://www.expertsearch.com/search.html
Expert Witness Search – Provides an expert witness database that can be searched by state venue or name.

http://www.fcafire.com
Fire Cause Analysis – Provides fire investigation, fire protection engineering, and scientific evaluations.

http://www.geocities.com/CapeCanaveral/4329
Forensic Chemistry Network – Links and articles.

http://users.aol.com/murrk/index.htm
Forensic Science Web Pages – A large collection of forensic-science information and other related material.

http://www.handwriting.com
Handwriting Research Center – Computerized handwriting analysis, psychological tests, personality evaluation, and character assessment for security, screening, employment, etc.

http://www.expertwitness.com
Expert Witness Directory – An interactive Web site reference tool for legal and insurance professionals.

http://expertpages.com
Expert Witness Directory – Searchable directory of witness experts in various fields.

http://www.askanexpert.com
Pitsco's Ask An Expert – Free service that allows you to search for an expert and, once found, ask him or her questions.

http://www.qdewill.com
Questioned Document Examination FAQ – Handwriting examination questions answered.

http://www.projectile.com/AJpro.htm
Shooting Incident Reconstruction.

http://www.poisonlab.com
Toxicology Testing Laboratory – Testing of illegal drugs in hair, urine, or blood.

http://www.atf.treas.gov/wanted/index.htm
ATF's Most Wanted – Descriptions and photographs.

http://www.c-s-i.org
Crime Stoppers International – A list of all Crime-Stoppers
sites on the Web.

http://www.fugitive.com
Fugitive Watch – Fugitive listings.

Credit Report Web Sites

http://www.arsdata.com/acc
Accurate Credit Check – Credit reports for mortgage, real
estate, and tenant screening.

http://bankrupt.com/clerks.html
Bankruptcy Clerks' Offices – A directory of the bankruptcy
clerks' offices found throughout the United States.

http://www.equifax.com
Equifax – Collects and provides credit information.

http://www.experian.com
Experian – Collects and provides credit information.

http://www.ftc.gov/os/statutes/fdcpa/fdcpact.htm
Fair Debt Collection Practices Act – Full text.

http://www.eqmi.com/freeonline.htm
Freeonline – Personal credit reports for free online.

http://www.infotel.net
Infotel Corp – Business and personal background information.

http://www.nfcc.org/index.html
N.F.C.C. – National Foundation for Consumer Credit.

http://www.qspace.com/
Q-Space – Offers credit reports with online retrieval.

http://www.transunion.com
Trans Union Credit Information Co.

http://www.census.gov
US Census Bureau – Provides complete census information
that can be searched by state.

http://www.usgenweb.com
USGenweb – Databases, advice, and other resources.

http://www.acc-u-data.com
Acc-U-Data – Missing person searches, telephone searches,
asset identification, employment, and background checks.

http://anybirthday.com
Birthdate Search
ANYBIRTHDAY.COM – Database of well over 135 million
records for the Birthdate of someone.

http://docusearch.com
Docusearch – Provides various dossier searches, including
locate, personal, businessman's, and prospective employee.

http://www.creative-research.com
Creative Research Inc. – Pre-employment, business, and
consumer research.

http://www.ermoian.com
Ermoian Investigations – Complete selection of online record
searches.

http://searchinfo.com
Global Information Network – Locates people, background
checks, dossier reports, business payment analysis, etc.

http://www.informus.com
Informus – Offers reports on employment, motor vehicle
registration, education verification, and more.

http://www.investigate.com
Instant Data Research – Bank account, criminal, driving, asset
searches, S.S. tracing and credential verification.

http://www.knowx.com
Know-X Free Searches – Online searches for public records.

http://www.wdia.com/ncihome.htm
National Credit Information Network – Locate people,
background checks, dossier reports, and business payment.

http://www.ameri.com/sherlock/sherlock.htm
Sherlock – The Online Detective – Enter what you know
about a person and it will return what reports it can provide.

http://edcwww.cr.usgs.gov/napp/napp_examples.html
Arial Photography Database – Searchable database of
photographs that cover the entire lower 48 states.

http://www.ntis.gov/databases/armypub.htm
Army Manuals and Publications Database – Distributes Army
technical manuals, searchable database.

http://zeno.simplenet.com/marks
/gerrit_volckerycks_cars_database.htm
Automobile and Tire Track Database – Information on tires,
track widths, wheelbases and other specifications of about
4,000 cars.

http://208.222.214.185
Internet Autopsy Database – Searchable collection of over
49,000 autopsy facesheets.

http://www.s9.com/biography
Biographical Dictionary – Biographical information on
thousands of notable people.

http://www.lookupusa.com
Sales Leads Database – Information about a business,
including business size, sales volume, key executives, credit
code, and more.

http://www.secure-data.com/info.html
Computer Evidence Recovery – Large collection of articles and other resources.

http://virtuallibrarian.com/legal/ccsearch.html
Computer Crime Database – A searchable index to the online Computer Crime Database (2,900 URLS).

http://www.crimelibrary.com
Crime Library – Library of articles including topics, such as major crimes, notorious criminals, and great crime fighters.

http://www.crime.org/homepage.html
Crime Statistics Site – Crime statistics site with tutorials, search engine, and link guide.

http://www.internets.com/spolice.htm
Criminology Database – Criminology database.
http://www.trancenet.org
Cults – Information on cults, links, and support.

http://www.disinfo.com
Disinformation – Information on current affairs, politics, new science and the "hidden information."

http://uncweb.carl.org
Uncover Document Database – Database of current article information taken from over 17,000 multidisciplinary journals.

http://www.elibrary.com/id/2525
Electronic Library – Search thousands of newspapers, magazines, journals, and books using a keyword.

http://excite.com
Excite's Newstraker – Offers a free Web clipping service; searches over 300 publications.

http://library.uwaterloo.ca/./databases/database.html
Fasnet Databases – Offers links and information on hundreds of databases that you can search over the Internet.

http://www.primeris.com/fonefind
Fone Finder – Public search engine that finds the geographic location of any phone number in the world.

http://www.virtuallibrarian.com/gangs
Gang Info Database – Internet links to gang-related information.

http://www.gebbieinc.com
Gebbie Inc. – Listing of newspapers and other media within the United States arranged by state.

http://hatewatch.org
Hate Watch – Provides information about hate groups and offers links to various related sites and material.

http://www.mayhem.net/Crime/archives.html
Internet Crime Archives – Online crime archives, mostly dealing with serial killers and cults.

http://www.libraries.rutgers.edu/rulib/ref.html
Internet Reference Library – List of general Internet reference resources.

http://www.security.org
Locks, Safes And Security Information Database – Information on locks, safes, and other security information.

http://missing.inthe.net
Missing Persons Database – Online searchable database of missing persons reports.

http://www.gwu.edu/~nsarchiv
Security Archive – An independent nongovernmental research institute and library that collects and publishes declassified documents acquired through the Freedom of Information Act (FOIA).

http://www.sexoffender.com
National Sex Offender Database – Searchable database of sex offenders across the nation.

http://www.ncjrs.org/database.htm
NCJ Reference Database – National Criminal Justice Reference Service Abstracts Database; contains summaries of more than 150,000 criminal justice publications, including federal, state, and local government reports, books, research reports, journal articles, and unpublished research.

http://www.parolewatch.org
Parolewatch – Cases in which violent felons are coming up for parole.

http://www.payphone-directory.org
Pay Phone Directory – Pay phone numbers located throughout the United States and Canada.

http://investigative.on.ca/medical.htm
Professional and Medical License Search – Directory includes the license holder's name and address, license type and number, degree, date of issue, date of expiration, and any disciplinary actions taken.

http://www.rcmp-grc.gc.ca/html/graphics/wanted/list.htm
Royal Canadian Mounted Police Most Wanted – Canada's most wanted criminals.

http://realestate.yahoo.com/realestate/homevalues
Real Estate – Home Values – Searchable by location or price range.

http://www.cs.utk.edu/~bartley/saInfoPage.html
Sexual Assault Information Page – Provides information concerning acquaintance rape, child sexual abuse/assault, incest, rape, ritual abuse, sexual assault, and sexual harassment.

http://www.poliisi.fi/wgm/library.htm
Shoemark/toolmark Examiners Library – A library of articles
containing texts of all the various sub-disciplines of
comparative visual examinations of interest to the shoeprint
toolmark examiners.

http://www.Nashville.Net/speedtrap
Speedtrap Registry – Database of speedtraps located
throughout the United States and internationally.

http://www.terrorism.com
Terrorism Research Center – Site on terrorism; links,
documents, research papers, etc.

http://www.druglibrary.org
The Drug Library – Library of drug policy and related
searchable databases.

http://www4.thomasregister.com/index.cgi?balancing
Thomas Register of American Manufacturers – American
manufacturers and the products they offer.

http://www.watchman.org/indxmenu.htm
Watchman Cult Index – Index to cults, occult organizations,
new age groups and religious movements.

http://www.MostWanted.org
World's Most Wanted Criminals And Unsolved Crimes DB
– International fugitives and unsolved crimes.

http://www.teleport.com/~links/news.shtml
World Newspapers – A list of on-line international
newspapers.

http://www.apbnews.com
APB News – Security- and crime-related news and other
resources of interest to law enforcement.

http://www.apbonline.com
APB Online – Police- and crime-related news, information,
and other related resources.

http://www.defenselink.mil/news
Defenselink News – Defense Public Affairs press releases.

http://www.emergency.com
Emergencynet News Service – 24-hour news, information,
analysis, and coverage of disasters and major emergency events.

http://www.indigo-net.com/intel.html
Intelligence Online – Electronic edition of Intelligence
Newsletter on the Internet.

http://www.icg.org/intelweb/index.html
Online Intelligence – International news, security, commerce,
and references.

http://www.pinkertons.com/pgis
Pinkertons Global Intelligence Services – Weekly intelligence
summaries and other related stories.

http://www.ccnet.com/~suntzu75/pirn.htm
Public Intelligence Review – News and press releases from
Public Intelligence Review and Newsletter.

http://www.dso.com
Sources – Investigative intelligence on issues of concern to
governments, businesses, and global citizens.

http://www.ancestry.com/ssdi/advanced.htm
SSN Death Index – Online searchable database of deaths
within the United States by name or SSN.

http://www.informus.com/ssnlkup.html
Informus – Social Security Lookup – Allows you to look up
information with a Social Security number.

http://www.ssa.gov/employer_info/quick_ref_guide.html
Social Security Administration Homepage – Information on
the administration of social security.

http://www.cas.muohio.edu/~security
Social Security Educational Center – Overview of the Social
Security system.

http://www.socsec.org/index.html
Social Security Network – The social security network.

http://www.wdia.com/yahoo/ssn-tracking.htm
Social Security Online – SSN tracking and verification reports
for name and address identification, previous address
information, and age.

http://users.aol.com/navyspies/ssn.htm
Social Security Number Verifier – Determine if a SSN is valid.

http://www.cpsr.org/cpsr/privacy/ssn/ssn.structure.html
Social Security Number Structure – How SSNs are structured
and what information you can obtain from a given number.

http://www.cloakanddagger.com/dagger
Cloak and Dagger Books – New and out-of-print books on
intelligence and related fields.

http://www.cb-security.com
Chatain-blanchon – Manufacturer of hardware for phone-
interception, jamming, tracking, and GSM-detection.

http://www.force-ten.com
Force Ten – Revenge, spying, police and military equipment;
will ship internationally.

http://www.globalspy.com/shop.htm
Global Spy Shop – Investigative aids.

http://www.pimall.com/nais/e.menu.html
Spy Exchange and Security Center – Spy equipment and
related resources.

http://www.w2.com/docs2/z/spyshop.html
The Spy Shop – Products and related resources.

http://www.spysite.com
Spy Site – Spy equipment and related resources.

http://www.spystuff.com
Spy Stuff – Investigative and spy equipment, including protection-related devices, surveillance systems and bug/bomb detection equipment.

http://www.spysupplies.net
Spy Supplies – Online catalog.

http://www.spyworld.com
Spy World – Surveillance equipment.

http://www.spyzone.com
Spy Zone – Spy equipment and related resources.

http://www.uspystore.com/htmls/uspyhome.htm
U Spy Store – Complete catalog of spy related items.

http://www.jewishgen.org/ajgs/jgs-sacramento/vit-recs.html
Introduction To Vital Records.

http://www.medaccess.com/address/vital_toc.htm
Med Access – Contact addresses for vital records.

http://www.genfindit.com/index.html
Online S&I – Scottish and Irish vital records ordering service.

http://travel.state.gov/vital_records_services.html
U.S. State Department – Vital records services.

http://www.vitalchek.com
Vitalchek Network – Get a certified copy of a birth certificate, death certificate, marriage certificate, and other vital records.

http://vitalrec.com/index.html
Vital Records Links – Provides many links to state vital records.

http://www.cdc.gov/nchswww/howto/w2w/w2welcom.htm
Vital Records – How and Where – Provides information, addresses, and procedures for obtaining vital records from all 50 states.

http://airsafe.com
Air Safety Page – Airline safety information.

http://www.ior.com/~jdmoore
Armed Robbery Page – Armed-robbery information and prevention measures.

http://www.gwu.edu/~nsarchiv/NSAEBB/NSAEBB4/ciaguat2.html
C.I.A – Manual on Assassinations – Informative manual on assassinations, methods, diagrams, etc.

http://www.odci.gov/cia/publications/pubs.html
C.I.A. Publications – Complete online resource to C.I.A. publications.

http://www.ifs.univie.ac.at/~pr2gq1/rev4344.html
Computer-Related Crime Prevention Manual – Online manual dealing with computer-related crimes.

http://www.courttv.com
Court TV – Live broadcast on the Web of selected court cases.

http://www.crimescene.com
Crime Scene Evidence File – A repository of investigative information.

http://www.cyberangels.org
CyberAngels – Internet safety awareness.
http://www.federalprison.com
Federal Prison – A Survival Guide.

http://www-medlib.med.utah.edu/WebPath/TUTORIAL/GUNS/GUNINTRO.html
Firearms Tutorial – Investigative techniques employed by the forensic pathologist.

http://www.eff.org
Freedom of Information Kit – Files for individuals or organizations who wish to make an FOIA application to a federal agency.

http://www.glr.com/fbiform.txt
FBI File – Form and the addresses for your FBI file.

http://www.homefires.org/book.html
Criminal Offender Public Records – Guide to obtaining criminal offenders records and other information.

http://nsi.org/Tips/hotel.html
Hotel Room Security – Article on hotel room security.

http://www.mail2web.com
Mail2Web – Read and write e-mail right from the Web.

http://www.vix.com/pub/men/domestic-index.html
Men and Domestic Violence Index – Large selection of articles and resources dealing with domestic violence and men.

http://www.metaspy.com
MetaSpy – View searches on the search engines in real time.

http://members.tripod.com/steganography/stego.html
Steganography – Complete guide to the process of hiding a message inside another message.

http://www.policescanner.com
Police Scanner – Listen to police in Los Angeles, CA, Dallas, TX, Plano, TX, and New York, NY.

http://www.pihome.com
Private Investigator's Homepage – Resources for the private investigator; licensing information, associations, and education sources.

http://www.pimall.com
Private Investigator's Mall – Many different private
investigators and goods related to the P.I. trade.

http://www.nashville.net/~police/risk
Rate Your Risk – Determine what risk you have of becoming a
victim of various types of crime.

http://www.fjc.gov/EVIDENCE/science/sc_ev_sec.html
Scientific Evidence Manual – Manual on scientific evidence
and related topics.

http://edcwww.cr.usgs.gov/Webglis/glisbin/search.pl?DISP
Satellite Images of United States – Searchable index of satellite
images.

http://www.blackcatsystems.com/numbers/numbers.html
Shortwave Spy Number Stations – How to tune in to the spies.

http://www.thesmokinggun.com
The Smoking Gun – Material obtained from government
sources, via FOIA requests.

http://www.spyzone.com/ccslink.html
Spy Links – Numerous security- and spy-related links.

http://www.pimall.com/nais/n.spouse.html
Tell-tale signs of a wayward spouse.

http://www.queendom.com/tests.html
Tests, Tests, Tests – Personality and intelligence tests.

http://informant.dartmouth.edu
The Informant – A free service that will save your favorite
search engine queries and Web sites, check them periodically,
and send you e-mail whenever there are new or updated Web
pages.

http://www.tscm.com/outsideplant.html
Wiretapping 101 – Provides information on wiretapping and
other related issues; also sells wiretapping equipment.

Government Web Sites

http://www.state.ak.us/dmv
Alaska Motor Vehicles – Regulations, manuals, forms, and
information.

http://www.dmv.ca.gov
California Motor Vehicles – Regulations, manuals, forms, and
information.

http://dmvct.org
Connecticut Motor Vehicles – Records information, manuals,
forms, and information.

http://www.dmvsearch.com
DMVSearch.com – Online (e-mail returned results) DMV
searches.

http://www.hsmv.state.fl.us/html/dlnew.html
Florida Motor Vehicles – Public records and computerized
data.

http://www2.state.ga.us/Departments/DOR/dmv
/dmv_indx.shtml
Georgia Motor Vehicles – Driver's license information,
manuals, regulations, and other related information.

http://www.dps.state.la.us/omvwww.nsf?OpenDatabase
Louisiana Motor Vehicles – Driver's license information,
manuals, regulations, and other related information.

http://www.state.me.us/sos/bmv/bmv.htm
Maine Motor Vehicles – Driver's license information, manuals,
regulations, and other related information.

http://mva.state.md.us
Maryland Motor Vehicles – Driver's license information,
manuals, regulations, and other related information.

http://www.magnet.state.ma.us/rmv
Massachusetts Motor Vehicles – Driver's license information,
manuals, regulations, and other related information.

http://www.sos.state.mi.us/dv/index.html
Michigan Motor Vehicles – Information on all aspects of
motor vehicles, including public records.

http://www.dps.state.mn.us/dvs/index.html
Minnesota Motor Vehicles – Driver's license information,
manuals, regulations, and other related information.

http://www.nol.org/home/DMV/index.htm
Nebraska Motor Vehicles – Driver's license information,
manuals, regulations, and other related information.

http://www.nydmv.state.ny.us
New York Motor Vehicles – Driver's license information,
manuals, regulations, and other related information.

http://www.state.oh.us/odps/division/bmv/ol_info.html
Ohio Motor Vehicles – Driver's license information, manuals,
regulations, and other related information.

http://www.odot.state.or.us/dmv
Oregon Motor Vehicles – Driver's license information,
manuals, regulations, and other related information.

http://idt.net/~tagman71
Pennsylvania Motor Vehicles – Driver's license information,
manuals, regulations, and other related information.

http://www.aot.state.vt.us/dmv/dmvhp.htm
Vermont Motor Vehicles – Driver's license information,
manuals, regulations, and other related information.

http://www.dmv.state.va.us
Virginia Motor Vehicles – Driver's license information,
manuals, regulations, and other related information.

http://www.census.gov
Census Bureau – Timely, relevant, and quality data about the people and economy of the United States.

http://www.access.gpo.gov/su_docs/aces/aaces002.html
United States Congress – Hundreds of publications in both text and PDF formats.

http://www.webslingerz.com/jhoffman/congress-email.html
Congressional E-Mail Directory – A directory of e-mail addresses for U.S. Senators and Congressional Representatives.

http://www.pueblo.gsa.gov
Consumer Information Center – Full-text versions of hundreds of the best federal consumer publications.

http://lcweb.loc.gov/copyright
United States Copyright Office – Offers copyright searches (1978 to present).

http://www.tray.com/fecinfo/zip.htm
FEC Info – Database of political contributors by zip code or name.

http://www.access.gpo.gov/su_docs/aces/aces140.html
Federal Register – Provides a searchable database of the Federal Register.

http://www.well.com/user/fap/foia.htm
Freedom of Information Act – Tells you how you may go about obtaining information under the Freedom of Information act.

http://www.fedworld.gov
Gov Bot Database – Online search of GovBot's 535,000 Web pages from government sites around the country.

http://www.usgs.gov/gils
Government Information Locator – Describes information resources that can be found from the federal government.

http://www.gpo.gov
Government Printing Office – Documents published by various government agencies.

http://www.usia.gov
United States Information Agency – Offers a vast amount of information on U.S. foreign affairs and relations.

http://www.irs.ustreas.gov
Internal Revenue Service – IRS forms and publications.

http://www.nara.gov/genealogy
NARA Genealogical Holdings – Order microfilm for a variety of topics including military, census records, and immigrant records.

http://www.cdc.gov/nchswww
National Health Statistics – Databases and reports dealing with health statistics, including death, birth, AIDS, etc.

http://ltpwww.gsfc.nasa.gov/ndrd
Natural Disaster Reference Database – A historical database of natural disasters that can be searched by subject.

http://sunsite.unc.edu/patents/intropat.html
Patents – Internet Patent Search System – Searchable databases for U.S. patents.

http://www.sec.gov/cgi-bin/srch-edgar
SEC Filing – Offers a large database containing detailed information on corporate information.

http://thomas.loc.gov
Thomas – Contains the Congressional Records of the United States and every pending bill before congress.

http://www.access.gpo.gov/congress/senate/constitution/toc.html
U.S. Constitution – The complete text of the U.S. Constitution, history of proposed changes, and related court decisions.

http://www.stolaf.edu/network/travel-advisories.html
U.S. State Department Travel Warnings – A rundown of the risks, visa requirements, medical facilities, and safety recommendations.

http://www.whitehouse.gov
White House – Homepage of the White House.

http://www.atf.treas.gov
Bureau of Alcohol, Tobacco and Firearms – Website.

http://www.coramnobis.com/CDW/index.html
Capital Defender's Toolbox – Articles, information, and a newsletter for those interested in capital punishment.

http://www.odci.gov
Central Intelligence Agency – Links to CIA publications, press releases, speeches, recently declassified material, etc.

http://www.coplink.com
CopLink – Web site devoted to law enforcement professionals.

http://www.corrections.com/index.html
Corrections Connection Network – Correction's white and yellow pages, news center, library, and correction links.

http://www.familytreemaker.com/00000229.html
Court House Finder – Allows you to find the address of court houses located throughout the United States.

http://www.c-s-i.org
Crime Stoppers International – Website.

http://www.cybercrimes.net
Cybercrimes – An informative site dealing with many aspects of computer-related crime on the Internet; provides online seminars and many related articles.

http://www.essential.org/dpic
Death Penalty Information Center – Information on just about anything in relation to the death penalty.

http://pw2.netcom.com/~jrosgood/page5.htm
Criminal Defense Attorneys Multi-state Listing – Provides an online listing of practicing defense attorneys by state.

http://www.drunkdrivingdefense.com/map.htm
DUI State Defense Attorney Listings – Listing of drunk-driving defense attorneys by state.

http://www.fedcrimlaw.com
Federal Criminal Law – Weekly issues of *Punch and Jurists*, the newsletter that summarizes recent significant Federal criminal cases.

http://www.findlaw.com
Find Law – Searchable database of law-related sites and links on the Internet.

http://www.fbi.gov
Federal Bureau of Investigation – Website.

http://www.bop.gov
Federal Bureau of Prisons – Information on the prison system.

http://vls.law.vill.edu/Locator/fedcourt.html
Federal Court Locator – Information related to the federal judiciary, including slip opinions; information can be viewed online or downloaded.

http://www.fedworld.gov/supcourt/index.htm
Flite – Supreme Court Decisions – Over 7,000 Supreme Court decisions dating from 1937 to 1975. You may search by case name or keyword.

http://ourworld.compuserve.com/homepages/ISCPP
International Society of Crime Prevention – Website.

http://www.ncjrs.org/database.htm
Law Abstracts Database – Contains summaries of more than 150,000 criminal justice publications, including federal, state, and local government reports, books, research reports, journal articles, and unpublished research.

http://www.icpsr.umich.edu/NACJD/home.html
Criminal Justice Data – Downloadable data collections relating to criminal justice.

http://www.ncsc.dni.us
National Center for State Courts – An independent, nonprofit organization dedicated to the improvement of justice.

http://www.nsa.gov
National Security Agency – Site provides information on their activities.

http://www.ncjrs.org/database.htm
NCJ Reference Database – Contains summaries of more than 150,000 criminal justice publications, including federal, state, and local government reports, books, research reports, journal articles, and unpublished research.

http://www.ojp.usdoj.gov/ovc
Office for Victims of Crime – Oversees many various programs that benefit victims of crime.

http://www.islandnet.com/~wwlia/diction.htm
Online Legal Dictionary – Allows you to obtain definitions to legal terms.

http://WWW.RCMP-GRC.GC.CA
Royal Canadian Mounted Police RCMP – Information about the Royal Canadian Mounted Police.

http://www.treas.gov/usss
Secret Service – History, investigation information, protection, and FAQ.

http://www.divorcecentral.com/states/laws/index.html
State Divorce Laws Database – State-by-state listing of current divorce laws.

http://www.epic.org/privacy/consumer/states.html
State Privacy Laws Database – State by state privacy laws.

http://supct.law.cornell.edu/supct
Supreme Court Rulings – Updates its information as quickly as 15 minutes after a decision has been announced; currently, decisions from 1990 to present are available.

http://uscode.house.gov/usc.htm
U.S. Code – Provides a search interface to the full text of the U.S. code; allows for keyword and concept searches.

http://www.ussc.gov
U.S. Sentencing Commission – Guidelines for sentencing in federal courts; collecting data about crime and sentencing.

http://www.lawoffice.com
West's Legal Dictionary – Directory of Canadian and U.S. government offices, law firms and lawyers.

State Web Sites

http://www.state.al.us
Alabama – State government information and services.

http://www.gsiweb.net
Alabama – Felony Fugitives Listing.

http://www.gsiweb.net/abiweb/missing_frame.html
Alabama – Listing of missing children and adults.

http://www.innosoft-solutions.com/states/alabama.html
Alabama – Public Record Links – Public records information and links.

http://www.gsiweb.net/so_doc/so_index_new.html
Alabama – Sex Offenders Database – Listing of sexual
offenders with address information.

http://arc-sos.state.al.us/CGI/SOSCRP01.MBR/INPUT
Alabama Corporations Database – Searchable database of
corporate filings and other information.

http://www.sos.state.al.us/cf/election/borjop1.cfm
Alabama Elections Officials Database – Searchable database of
elections officials.

http://www.alalinc.net
Alabama Legal Information Center – Information on court
decisions, state laws, civil and criminal appeals.

http://arc-sos.state.al.us/CGI/sosnot01.mbr/input
Alabama Notaries Public Database – Searchable by name.

http://www.arec.state.al.us/search/search.asp
Alabama Real Estate License Database – License status by
name.

http://arc-sos.state.al.us/CGI/SOSUCC01.MBR/INPUT
Alabama Uniform Commercial Code Database – Online
searchable database that allows you to query debtors and
secured party names.

http://www.state.ak.us
Alaska state government information and services.

http://www.co.fairbanks.ak.us/database/aurora/default.asp
Alaska – Fairbanks – Property Records – Searchable by name,
address, or account number.

http://www.borough.kenai.ak.us/assessingdept/Parcel
/SEARCH.HTM
Alaska – KPB – Property Records – Searchable by name or
parcel number.

http://www.innosoft-solutions.com/states/alaska.html
Alaska – Public Record Links – Public records information and
links.

http://www.dced.state.ak.us/occ/search1.htm
Alaska Corporations/License Database – Searchable database
of corporate filings and other information.

http://www.dced.state.ak.us/occ/search3.htm
Alaska Occupational License Search – Occupational and
professional licenses issued by the Alaska Division of
Occupational Licensing and its licensing boards.

http://www.dps.state.ak.us/sorcr
Alaska Sex Offender Database – A central registry of sex
offenders found within the state.

http://www.revenue.state.ak.us/tax/divisions
/unclaimproperty.htm

Alaska Unclaimed Property Database – Online database of
unclaimed property listings.

http://www.state.az.us
Arizona state government information and services.

http://www.sosaz.com/scripts/Charity_Search_engine.cgi
Arizona – Charitable Organizations Database – Searchable by
name or DBA.

http://www.rc.state.az.us/database.htm
Arizona – Contractor database.

http://www.apltwo.ct.state.az.us/casendx.html
Arizona – Court Case Database – Listing of all open court
cases; including case proceedings.

http://www.accountancy.state.az.us/roster.htm
Arizona – CP Accountants – Certified Public Accountants
listing.

http://156.42.28.232/newdocket/docketformmain.asp
Arizona – Maricopa – Civil/Criminal Records – Superior court
records searchable by name or case number.

http://recorder.maricopa.gov/recdocdata
Arizona – Maricopa – County Recorder's Database –
Searchable by document number, name, or code.

http://www.sosaz.com/scripts/Notary_Search_engine.cgi
Arizona – Notary Public Database – Searchable by name or zip
code.

http://iissvr.jp.co.pima.az.us/webinfo/findcase.asp
Arizona – Pima – Criminal/Civil Records – Justice court
records, searchable by name, case number or citation number.

http://www.asr.co.pima.az.us/apiq/index.html
Arizona – Pima – Property Records – Searchable by parcel,
taxpayer, or subdivision.

http://www.innosoft-solutions.com/states/arizona.html
Arizona – Public Record Links – Public records information
and links.

http://www.azbar.org/MemberFinder
Arizona – State Bar Member Database – Searchable by
numerous fields.

http://www.azleg.state.az.us/ars/ars.htm
Arizona – Statutes Database – Searchable by keyword or title
number.

http://www.primenet.com/~coyypd/sex3.html
Arizona – Yuma – Sex Offenders – Listing of sex offenders
within the city of Yuma.

http://ecf.azb.uscourts.gov
Arizona Bankruptcy Records – Limited information.

http://www.cc.state.az.us
Arizona Corporation Records – Corporate filings, reports, news, and information.

http://www.azll.com/query.html
Arizona Liquor License Database – Searchable for license information by owner name, license number, address or business name.

http://www.sosaz.com/scripts/lobbyist_engine.cgi
Arizona Lobbyist Database – Online searchable database of active state lobbyists.

http://www.docboard.org/az/df/azsearch.htm
Arizona Medical License Database – Online database that allows you to look up detailed information on a medical professionals' licensing information.

http://www.sosaz.com/ucc.htm
Arizona Uniform Commercial Code Database – Online searchable database that allows you to query debtors and secured party names.

http://www.state.ar.us
Arkansas State government information and services.

http://www.sosweb.state.ar.us/corps/coop
Arkansas – Bank Cooperatives Database – Searchable by name.

http://208.154.254.51
Arkansas – Benton – County Records – Search for property, deeds, court, and other county records.

http://courts.state.ar.us/search/index.html
Arkansas – Court Cases Database – Searchable by case name, date or keyword.

http://www.are.uscourts.gov/default.html
Arkansas – East District Court – Some searchable databases including case information.

http://www.innosoft-solutions.com/states/arkansas.html
Arkansas – Public Record Links – Public records information and links.

http://www.state.ar.us/arec/db
Arkansas – Real Estate License Database – Searchable by last name, city, or firm.

http://www.sosweb.state.ar.us/corps/trademk
Arkansas – Trademark Database – Searchable by name, owner, or filing number.

http://www.arwd.uscourts.gov
Arkansas – West District Court – Case information, forms and other useful information.

http://www.sosweb.state.ar.us/corps/bkin
Arkansas Banks and Insurance Companies Database – Online searchable database of state banks and insurance companies.

http://www.sosweb.state.ar.us/corps/incorp
Arkansas Corporation Database – Online searchable database of state based corporations.

http://www.acic.org
Arkansas Crime Information Center – Provides crime statistics, victim information and sex offender registry information.

http://www.sosweb.state.ar.us/corps/homebldr
Arkansas Homebuilders Database.

http://www.sosweb.state.ar.us/corps/notary
Arkansas Notaries Public Database.

http://www.sosweb.state.ar.us/corps/trademk
Arkansas Trademarks Database – Online searchable database of trademark names and owner information.

http://www.state.ar.us/auditor/unclprop
Arkansas Unclaimed Property Database – Online database of unclaimed property listings.

http://www.state.ca.us
California state government information and services.

http://www.co.alameda.ca.us/aswpinq/index.htm
California – Alameda – Property Records – Searchable by parcel number or address.

http://ecf.casb.uscourts.gov/cgi-bin/PublicCaseFiled-Rpt.pl
California – Bankruptcy Court Case Database – Searchable database of cases filed.

http://204.147.113.12/list.html
California – Business Database – Search corporate, LLC records by name.

http://www.cdc.state.ca.us/issues/capital/capital9.htm
California – Condemned Prisoner List – Listing of death row inmates for California.

http://lacountycourts.co.la.ca.us/Locations/Frame.htm
California – County Court Locate – Locate by name.

http://www.co.kern.ca.us/assessor/search.htm
California – Kern – Property Records – Searchable by owner name, ATN, or file number.

http://regrec.co.la.ca.us/fbn/FBN.cfm
California – Los Angeles – Business Database – Searchable by name.

http://lacountycourts.co.la.ca.us/Probate/ProbateSearch.cfm
California – Los Angeles – Probate – Searchable by case prefix, number, or suffix.

http://www.lamuni.org/trafmainin.htm
California – Los Angeles – Traffic Tickets – Searchable by citation number.

http://www.governlink.com/servlet/
CA_Orange?type=birth_certificate&state_code=CA&county_
id=CA-Orange&textOnly=false
California – Orange – Birth Certificates – Order birth
certificates online; fee for county service.

http://www.governlink.com/servlet/
CA_Orange?type=fbn&state_code=CA&county_id=CA-
Orange&textOnly=false
California – Orange – Business Database – Hourly charge.

http://www.governlink.com/servlet/
CA_Orange?type=death_certificate&state_code=CA&county_
id=CA-Orange&textOnly=false
California – Orange – Death Certificates – Order death
certificates online; fee required.

http://www.governlink.com/servlet/
CA_Orange?type=marriage_certificate&state_code=CA&coun
ty_id=CA-Orange&textOnly=false
California – Orange – Marriage Certificates – Order marriage
certificates online; fee required.

http://www.innosoft-solutions.com/states/california.html
California – Public Record Links – Public records information
and links.

http://www.latimes.com/class/realestate/dataquick
California – Real Estate Sales Database – Searchable database
of recent real estate sales.

http://cor400.ci.redding.ca.us/cgi-bin/db2www
/gow3lkap.mbr/input
California – Redding – Assessor's Parcel Database – Searchable
by parcel number or property address.

http://www.saccourt.com/indexes
California – Sacramento – Civil/criminal Records – County
Courts.

http://www.co.san-diego.ca.us/cnty/cntydepts/safety/sheriff
/bookingname.html
California – San Diego Arrest Database – Current sheriff's
department arrest booking log, searchable by last name.

http://www.co.san-diego.ca.us/cnty/cntydepts/safety/sheriff
/whosinname.html
California – San Diego Inmate Database – Search for current
inmates by last name.

http://www.stonehopper.com/fbnc/lookup.html
California – San Mateo – Business Database – Fictitious
business name lookup.

http://www.sb-democracy.com/opis/logon.htf
California – Santa Barbara – Property Records – Online
property information system.

http://www.co.san-bernardino.ca.us/ACR/recsearch.asp
California – Santa Barbara – Grantor/grantee Database –
Searchable by name or date.

http://cdb.tradeport.org/companies/default.cgi
California Company Database – Online searchable database of
state based companies.

http://caag.state.ca.us/piu/crimhist.htm
California Criminal History Inquiries – How to obtain
criminal history information.

http://www.childsup.cahwnet.gov/MOSTWNTD.HTM
California Deadbeat Parents Database – Database of parents
that are being sought by the California Child Support
Enforcement Program for nonpayment of child support.

http://www.casb.uscourts.gov/html/fileroom.htm
California File Room – Numerous files on current cases before
the law and other related searches.

http://www2.cslb.ca.gov
California License Status Database – Contractor license status
check; search by name, business name, or license number.

http://www.abc.ca.gov/LQS/PM_QUERYSYS.SSI
California Liquor License Database – Searchable for license
information by owner name, license number, business address,
or business name.

http://www.ss.ca.gov/prd/ld/contents.htm
California Lobbyist Database – Searchable directory of
lobbyists, lobbying firms, and lobbyist employers.

http://www.docboard.org/ca/df/casearch.htm
California Medical License Database – Searchable database of
medical licensee information, including malpractice judgments
and disciplinary reports.

http://www.dre.ca.gov/licstats.htm
California Real Estate Licensee Database – Online searchable
database of public license information.

http://www.sexoffenders.net
California Sex Offender Database – Provides a listing of
convicted sex offenders by city.

http://www.calsb.org
California State Bar Database – Online searchable database of
state bar memberships.

http://www.sco.ca.gov
California Unclaimed Property Database – Online database of
unclaimed property listings.

http://www.state.co.us
Colorado state government information and services.

http://www.co.arapahoe.co.us/AS/index.htm
Colorado – Arapahoe – Parcel Search – Search for residential
and commercial records.

http://www.denvergov.org/realproperty.asp
Colorado – Denver – Property Database – Searchable by
address, parcel number, or name.

http://www.co.el-paso.co.us/land/default.htm
Colorado – El Paso – Property Database – Searchable by
location.

http://buffy.co.jefferson.co.us/cgi-bin/mis/ats/assr
Colorado – Jefferson – Property Database – Searchable by
address, parcel number, or schedule number.

http://www.laplatainfo.com/search2.html
Colorado – La Plata – Property Database – Searchable by
name, address, or parcel number.

http://205.169.141.11/Assessor/Database/netsearch.html
Colorado – Mesa – Property Database – Searchable by parcel
number or address.

http://aimwebdomain.aspen.com/db/pca/pcareg1.asp
Colorado – Park – Property Database – Searchable by address
or parcel number.

http://www.innosoft-solutions.com/states/colorado.html
Colorado – Public Record Links – Public records information
and links.

http://www.state.co.us/gov_dir/cdphe_dir/hs/search.html
Colorado Marriage and Divorce Database – Online searchable
database of marriage and divorce records.

http://www.dora.state.co.us/medical/main-verification.htm
Colorado Medical License Database – Searchable database of
medical licensee information, including malpractice judgments
and disciplinary reports.

http://www.treasurer.state.co.us/payback.html
Colorado Unclaimed Property Database – Online database of
unclaimed property listings.

http://www.state.ct.us
Connecticut state government information and services.

http://www.jud2.state.ct.us/Civil_Inquiry/GetParty.asp
Connecticut – Civil Court Records Database – Searchable by
party name or location.

http://www.innosoft-solutions.com/states/connecticut.html
Connecticut – Public Record Links – Public records
information and links.

http://sexoffenders.state.ct.us/sor/plsql
/wsor$offender.startup?Z_CHK=0
Connecticut – Sex Offender Database – Searchable by last
name, town, or zip code.

http://www.dss.state.ct.us/wanted/wanted.htm
Connecticut Deadbeat Parents Listing – Listing of parents that
are being sought by the Department of Social Services for
nonpayment of child support.

http://www.state.ct.us/ott
Connecticut Unclaimed Property Database – Online database
of unclaimed property listings.

http://www.state.de.us
Delaware state government information and services.
http://www.2isystems.com/newcastle/Search2.CFM
Delaware – New Castle – Property Database – Searchable by
name or address.

http://www.innosoft-solutions.com/states/delaware.html
Delaware – Public Record Links – Public records information
and links.

http://www.state.de.us/dsp/sexoff/search.htm
Delaware – Sex Offender Database – Searchable by name or
location.

http://courts.state.de.us/supreme/ordsops/list.htm
Delaware – Supreme Court Cases – Listings.

http://www.state.de.us/revenue
Delaware Unclaimed Property Database – Online database of
unclaimed property listings.

http://www.state.fl.us
Florida state government information and services.

http://www.appraiser.co.brevard.fl.us/asp/disclaimer.asp
Florida – Brevard – Property Database – Searchable by address
or owner name.

http://www.bcpa.net/search_1.htm?WebFormID=4
Florida – Broward – Property Database – Searchable by owner,
parcel number, or address.

http://www.ccappraiser.com/record.asp?
Florida – Charlotte – Property Database – Search real property
or sales records.

http://www.pa.citrus.fl.us/ccpaask.html
Florida – Citrus – Property Records – Searchable by address or
parcel number.

http://pawwv.ci.jax.fl.us/pub/property/lookup.htm
Florida – Duval – Property Records Database – Searchable by
number, address, or name.

http://www.co.escambia.fl.us/ectc/taxiq.html
Florida – Escambia – Property Records Database – Searchable
by owner, reference number, or location.

http://www.appraiser.co.highlands.fl.us
Florida – Highlands – Property Database – Searchable by
parcel, owner or address.

http://www.lakeappraiser.com
Florida – Lake – Property Database – Searchable by street, parcel ID or owner.

http://www.property-appraiser.lee.fl.us/Queries/Query.htm
Florida – Lee – Property Database – Searchable by parcel, owner, or address.

http://www.clerk.leon.fl.us
Florida – Leon – Public Records – Offer many different searchable databases of county public records.

http://www.clerkofcourts.com
Florida – Manatee – Court Records – Searchable.

http://www.propertyappraiser.com
Florida – Manatee – Property Database – Searchable by owner.

http://www.propappr.marion.fl.us/agree.html
Florida – Marion – Property Database – Searchable by owner, parcel, or address.

http://www.martin.fl.us/GOVT/co/pa/taxform.html
Florida – Martin – Property Database – Searchable by parcel, owner, price range, or location.

http://www.comptroller.co.orange.fl.us/records/or.htm
Florida – Orange – County Records – Search records by name.

http://www.ocpafl.org/ocpa/owa/record_search
Florida – Orange – Property Database – Searchable by owner, parcel, or address.

http://www2.co.palm-beach.fl.us/papa
Florida – Palm Beach – Property Database – Searchable by address, owner, or parcel.

http://www.doh.state.fl.us/IRM00PRAES/PRASLIST.ASP
Florida – Physician Discipline – Listed by name.

http://polksheriff.org/missing
Florida – Polk – Missing Persons – Listing with pictures.

http://polksheriff.org/wanted/warrants.html
Florida – Polk – Warrants – Search for wanted persons by name or DOB.

http://www.innosoft-solutions.com/states/florida.html
Florida – Public Record Links – Public records information and links.

http://www.srcpa.org/agree.html
Florida – Santa Rosa – Property Db – Searchable by name, address, or parcel ID.

http://www.sarasotaproperty.net/scpa_recs.htm
Florida – Sarasota – Property Database – Searchable by owner, parcel ID, or address.

http://ntweb.scpafl.org
Florida – Seminole – Property Database – Searchable by owner, address, or parcel ID.

http://search.co.st-johns.fl.us/Prop-App/old_html
Florida – St. John's – Property Database – Searchable by name, address, or parcel ID.

http://www.paslc.org/Agree.htm
Florida – St. Lucie – Property Database – Searchable by owner or parcel ID.

http://www.law.ufl.edu/opinions/supreme/index.shtml
Florida – Supreme Court Rulings – Searchable by year, or month.

http://webserver.vcgov.org
Florida – Volusia – Property Database – Parcel record search.

http://fcn.state.fl.us/oraweb/owa/dbprabt2.Qry_ABT_Menu
Florida ABT Delinquencies Database – Search for delinquent invoices.

http://licgweb.dos.state.fl.us/access/agency.html
Florida Agency License Database – Search for state agency licenses within the investigation field by agency name or license number.

http://www.state.fl.us/oraweb/owa/www_dbpr2.qry_lic_menu
Florida Business License Database – Search for license information by owner name, license number, business address, or business name.

http://election.dos.state.fl.us/campfin/cfindb.shtml
Florida Campaign Finance Database – Contains detailed financial records that campaigns and committees are required by law to disclose; view contribution and expense records from candidates or committees.

http://ccfcorp.dos.state.fl.us/COR_menu.html
Florida Corporations Public Records Database – Searchable databases for trademarks, FEI numbers, agents, officers and other corporate information.

http://www.fdle.state.fl.us/FAQ/index.asp#information
Florida Criminal History Inquiries – How to obtain criminal history information.

http://www.fdle.state.fl.us/index.asp
Florida Criminal Offenders Databases – Searchable for state sex offenders, predators, most wanted and missing children; other law enforcement information available as well.

http://tlhora2.dep.state.fl.us/www_pa/owa/www_pa.pa_search
Florida Environmental Permit Database – Search for environmental permits issued within the state of Florida by applicant name, company, or permit number.

http://www.dc.state.fl.us/escapedinmates/inmatesearch.asp
Florida Escaped Inmate Database – Search for escaped inmates
by name or DC number.

http://ccfcorp.dos.state.fl.us/GEN_menu.html
Florida GEN/LLP Partnerships Database – Searchable
database of general limited liability partnerships; searchable by
name, agent, FEI number, or document number.

http://ccfcorp.dos.state.fl.us/FIC_menu.html
Florida Fictitious Names Database – Searchable by fictitious
name, actual name, document number, FEI number, and
more.

http://www.doh.state.fl.us/irm00PRAES/praslist.asp
Florida Health Licensee Database – Searchable for health
licensee information by name, business name, license number,
county, or DBA name.

http://licgweb.dos.state.fl.us/access/individual.html
Florida Individual Licensee Database – Searchable for licensee
information on private investigators and other predefined
categories by name or license number.

http://www.dc.state.fl.us/activeinmates/inmatesearch.asp
Florida Inmate Database – Searchable for inmates within
Florida by name or DC number.

http://www.fbpe.org/pesearch/Pesearch.htm
Florida Professional Engineers Database – Searchable for
professional engineers by last name or PE number.

http://fcn.state.fl.us/oraweb/owa/dbpr2.qry_lic_menu
Florida Professional License Database – Searchable for
professional license information by license number, licensee
name, or business name.

http://www.dc.state.fl.us/inmatereleases/inmatesearch.asp
Florida Released Inmate Database – Searchable for inmates
released by name or DC number.

http://www.fdle.state.fl.us/Sexual_Predators/index.asp
Florida Sex Offenders Database – Searchable for sex offenders
by last name.

http://ccfcorp.dos.state.fl.us/LIEN_menu.html
Florida UCC/FLR Liens Database – Numerous debtor
searches that provide detailed information.

http://www.dbf.state.fl.us/unclaimed/abanprop.html
Florida Unclaimed Property Database – Online database of
unclaimed property listings.

http://www.wc.les.state.fl.us/Provider/index.asp
Florida Workers' Compensation Providers Database –
Downloadable listings of WC providers, including health care
providers, medical advisors, and approved companies.

http://www.state.ga.us
Georgia state government information and services.

http://atlantapd.org/arrests/drugpage.htm
Georgia – Atlanta Drug Offense Database – A listing of
current drug offense arrests within Atlanta.

http://www.atlantapd.org/arrests/sexpage.htm
Georgia – Atlanta Sex Offense Database – A listing of current
sex offense arrests within Atlanta.

http://www.cherokeega-sheriff.org/offender/offender.htm
Georgia – Cherokee – Sex Offenders – Sex offenders listing.

http://www.negia.net/~sherjmas
/Sex%20Offender%20Main.html
Georgia – Clarke – Sex Offenders – Listing of sex offenders.

http://www.dekalbsheriff.org/regnames3.html
Georgia – Dekalb – Sex Offender Database – Alaphbetical
listing of offenders.

http://www.dougherty.ga.us5061/WSG/QAPP0100?taxshttp:
//www.albany.ga.us
Georgia – Dougherty – Business and property records.

http://www.dougherty.ga.us5061/WSG/QAPP0100?taxshttp:
//www.albany.ga.us
Georgia – Dougherty – Property Database – Property and
Business records.

http://www.admin.co.fayette.ga.us/intro.htm
Georgia – Fayette – Property Records – Searchable by name,
address, or district.

http://www.admin.co.fayette.ga.us/intro.htm
Georgia – Fayette – Tax Records – Searchable by taxpayer
name.

http://www.romegeorgia.com/Sheriff/sexoffenders.html
Georgia – Floyd – Sex Offenders – Listing.

http://www.innosoft-solutions.com/states/georgia.html
Georgia – Public Record Links – Public records information
and links.

http://ecf.ganb.uscourts.gov
Georgia Bankruptcy Database – Bankruptcy claims with
limited data.

http://www.sos.state.ga.us/corporations/corpsearch.htm
Georgia Corporation Database – Online searchable database;
name of the entity, filing date, registered agent, and entity's
status are available.

http://www.sos.state.ga.us/ebd-medical/medsearch.htm
Georgia Medical Board Database – Online searchable database
of medical professionals by name or license number.

http://fugitives.dcor.state.ga.us
Georgia Most Wanted – A listing of the states most wanted
fugitives.

http://www2.state.ga.us/Departments/DHR/CSE/mw.htm
Georgia Deadbeat Parents Database – Listing of parents that
are being sought by the Department of Social Services for
nonpayment of child support.

http://www.sos.state.ga.us/ebd/default.htm
Georgia Professional License Database – Searchable for
professional licensee information.

http://www.ganet.org/gbi/sorsch.cgi
Georgia Sex Offender Database – Search by name, city, or zip
code.

http://www.state.ga.us/dor/ptd/ucp
Georgia Unclaimed Property Database – Search for unclaimed
property by name and city.

http://www.hawaii.gov
Hawaii state government information and services.

http://www.innosoft-solutions.com/states/hawaii.html
Hawaii – Public Record Links – Public records information
and links.

http://www.ehawaiigov.com/breg
Hawaii Business Database – Search for a business by name.

http://www.ehawaiigov.com/breg/cog
Hawaii CGS Database – Certificate of Good Standing.
Searchable by name.

http://www.state.hi.us/ag/hcjdc/crimHist.html
Hawaii Criminal History Information – Information and
request form for criminal records.

http://www.state.id.us
Idaho state government information and services.

http://www.adasheriff.org/jailrost/arresta-g.htm
Idaho – Ada – Inmates Database – Alphabetical listing of
current inmates.

http://www.idsos.state.id.us/corp/corindex.htm
Idaho – Business – Information and upcoming databases.

http://www.corr.state.id.us/escapes.htm
Idaho – Fugitives – Listing of escapees at large within Idaho.

http://www2.state.id.us/dle/idmpch/htmlsrc
/mpcpage.htm#Missing
Idaho – Missing Persons – Listing of missing persons within
Idaho.

http://www2.state.id.us/ipels/index.htm
Idaho – Professional License Databases – Information and
searchable databases.

http://www.innosoft-solutions.com/states/idaho.html
Idaho – Public Record Links – Public records information and
links.

http://www.magicvalley.com/offenders
Idaho – Sex Offenders – Listings by county.

http://www.id.uscourts.gov/wconnect/wc.dll?usbc_racer-main
Idaho Bankruptcy Database – Search bankruptcy records by
name, SSN or case number.

http://www.id.uscourts.gov/wconnect/wc.dll?usdc_racer-main
Idaho Court Case Database – Search court case records by
name, lawyer name, or case number.

http://www.state.id.us/tax/unclaimed_idaho.htm
Idaho Unclaimed Property Database – Online database of
unclaimed property listings.

http://www.state.il.us
Illinois state government information and services.

http://www.ilnb.uscourts.gov/ViewImages.htm
Illinois – Bankruptcy Records – Northern district of Illinois.

http://12.17.79.4
Illinois – Chicago – Sex Offenders Database – Searchable by
name or address.

http://www.court.co.macon.il.us/caseinfo.htm
Illinois – Macon – Civil/criminal Records – Search for specific
case information using either the litigant's name or the case
number.

http://www.innosoft-solutions.com/states/illinois.html
Illinois – Public Record Links – Public records information
and links.

http://www.sos.state.il.us/cgi-bin/corpname
Illinois Corporate Records Search – Allows you to search for
corporations by name.

http://www.state.il.us/isp/ucia0001.html
Illinois Criminal History Information – Information and
request form for criminal records.

http://www.state.il.us/lcc/distrib/modify.htm
Illinois Liquor License Database – Searchable state liquor
license database.

http://www.idoc.state.il.us
Illinois Prison Inmate Locator – Online searchable database
that allows you to locate state prison inmates.

http://www.sos.state.il.us/depts/archives/data_lan.html
Illinois Public Land Sales Database.

http://samnet.isp.state.il.us/ispso2/index.htm
Illinois Sex Offender Database – Online searchable database of
registered sex offenders.

http://www.state.in.us
Indiana state government information and services.

http://www.innosoft-solutions.com/states/indiana.html
Indiana – Public Record Links – Public records information
and links.

http://www.ai.org/premium/index.html
Indiana – Public Records – Numerous public records available
for a small fee.

http://www.assessor.evansville.net
Indiana – Vanderburgh – Property Records – Searchable by
name.

http://www.insb.uscourts.gov/public/casesearch.asp
Indiana Bankruptcy Case Database – Searchable by case
number, name, SSN, or ID.

http://www.state.in.us/psb/forms/forms.htm
Indiana Criminal History Information – Information and
request form for criminal records.

http://www.insd.uscourts.gov/casesearch.htm
Indiana Criminal/Civil Case Database – Searchable database of
current and past court cases.

http://www.state.in.us/cji/html/sexoffender.html
Indiana Sexual Offenders DBs – Numerous searchable
databases of sex offenders and related information.

http://www.ai.org/cgi-bin/icpr/cgi-bin/trademarks.pl
Indiana Trademarks Database – Online searchable database of
trademarks found within the state.

http://www.state.in.us/atty_gen/index.html
Indiana Unclaimed Property Database – Online database of
unclaimed property listings.

http://www.state.ia.us
Iowa state government information and services.

http://www.state.ia.us/government/dps/dci/mpic/list.htm
Iowa – Missing Persons – Listing of persons that are currently
reported as missing.

http://www.sos.state.ia.us/NotaryWeb
Iowa – Notary Public Search – Searchable database by name.

http://www.assess.co.polk.ia.us/web/basic/searchI.html
Iowa – Polk – Property Records – Searchable by owner or legal
description.

http://www.pottco.org
Iowa – Pottawattamie – Property Search – Searchable by
owner's name.

http://www.innosoft-solutions.com/states/iowa.html
Iowa – Public Record Links – Public records information and
links.

http://www.state.ia.us/government/dps/dci/isor/publicnot.htm
Iowa – Sex Offenders – Online sex offenders registry.

http://www.state.ia.us/government/dps/crime/unsolved
Iowa – Unsolved Cases – Listing of unsolved cases within
Iowa.

http://www.state.ia.us/government/dps/wanted
Iowa – Wanted Persons – Wanted persons listing.

http://www.sos.state.ia.us/corpweb
Iowa Corporation Database – Search for corporations by name
or number.

http://www.state.ia.us/government/dps/dci/crimhist.htm
Iowa Criminal History Records – Details about how to obtain
criminal history records within the state.

http://www.state.ia.us/government/ag/wanted.htm
Iowa Deadbeat Parents Listings – Listing of parents sought by
the Department of Social Services for nonpayment of child
support.

http://www.docboard.org/ia/find_ia.htm
Iowa Medical Docfinder – Online searchable database of
medical professionals found within the state.

http://www.treasurer.state.ia.us
Iowa Unclaimed Property Database – Online database of
unclaimed property listings.

http://www.sos.state.ia.us/uccweb
Iowa Uniform Commercial Code Database – Search for UCC
filings by name, business name, or UCC number.

http://www.state.ks.us
Kansas state government information and services.

http://hometown.lawrence.com/valuation
Kansas – Douglas – Property Records – Searchable by name or
address.

http://www.jocoks.com/appraiser/disclaim.html
Kansas – Johnson – Property Records – Searchable by owner,
address or legal description.

http://www.ink.org/public/kbi/kbimissingpage.html
Kansas – Missing Persons – Listing.

http://docnet.dc.state.ks.us/offenders/county%20list.htm
Kansas – Parolees Database – Offenders on parole within
Kansas by county.

http://www.innosoft-solutions.com/states/kansas.html
Kansas – Public Record Links – Public records information
and links.

http://kyeasupt1.state.ky.us/krecweb/search/licenseelookup.asp
Kansas – Real Estate License Database – Searchable by name.

http://205.172.12.20/tax/prop_inquire.html
Kansas – Sedgwick – Property Records – Searchable by
address.

http://www.sedgwick.ks.us/sheriff
Kansas – Sedgwick – Sex Offenders – Sex offenders and most wanted listings.

http://www.ink.org/misc/premium.html
Kansas – State Public Records – Fee based; criminal, civil, and business records.

http://www.ink.org/public/kbi/kbiwantedpage.html
Kansas 10 Most Wanted Listings – Listing of the state's 10 most wanted criminals.

http://www.ink.org/public/corps
Kansas Corporation Database – Searchable for corporations using a variety of different search topics.

http://www.ink.org/public/srs/srswanted.html
Kansas Deadbeat Parents Listings – Listing of parents sought by the Department of Social Services for nonpayment of child support.

http://www.docboard.org/ks/df/kssearch.htm
Kansas Medical Professionals Database – Online searchable database of health professionals located throughout the state.

http://www.ink.org/public/kbi/kbiregoffpage.html
Kansas Sex Offenders Database – Online searchable database of registered sex offenders.

http://www.treasurer.state.ks.us/upsearch.htm
Kansas Unclaimed Property Database – Searchable for unclaimed property by owner's name.

http://www.state.ky.us
Kentucky state government information and services.

http://www.innosoft-solutions.com/states/kentucky.html
Kentucky – Public Record Links – Public records information and links.

http://www.sos.state.ky.us/corporate/entityname.asp
Kentucky Business Database – Search for detailed information on over 340,000 Kentucky businesses.

http://38.244.24.105/webpacer.html
Kentucky Case Database – Court cases searchable by number or party.

http://www.state.ky.us/oag/wanted.htm
Kentucky Deadbeat Parents Listings – Listing of parents sought by the Department of Social Services for nonpayment of child support.

http://www.sos.state.ky.us/intranet/default.htm
Kentucky UCC Filings Database – Search state UCC filings by name or document number.

http://www.kytreasury.com/html/kyt_uprop.html
Kentucky Unclaimed Property Database – Searchable for unclaimed property by owner's name.

http://ukcc.uky.edu/~vitalrec
Kentucky Vital Records DBs – Provides searchable databases for deaths, marriages and divorces.

http://www.state.la.us
Louisiana state government information and services.

http://www.sec.state.la.us/NTRINQ.HTM
Louisiana – Notary Database – Searchable by name or zip code.

http://www.dhh.state.la.us/BOARDSbody.HTM
Louisiana – Professional License DBs – Professional license searches for various professions.

http://www.innosoft-solutions.com/states/louisiana.html
Louisiana – Public Record Links – Public records information and links.

http://www.lasocpr.lsp.org/socpr
Louisiana – Sex Offenders – Searchable by name, zip code, or area.

http://www.sec.state.la.us/crpinq.htm
Louisiana Corporation Database – Online searchable database of corporations found within the state; searchable by corporation's or owner's name.

http://www.rev.state.la.us
Louisiana Unclaimed Property Database – Online searchable database of unclaimed property listings.

http://www.state.me.us
Maine state government information and services.

http://www.bangorme.com/crime/warn.html
Maine – Bangor – Sex Offenders – Listing.

http://thor.ddp.state.me.us/archives/plsql
/archdev.death_archive.search_form
Maine – Death Records – Searchable by name or town.

http://www.docboard.org/me/df/mesearch.htm
Maine – Doctor Lookup – Searchable by name.

http://www.state.me.us/sos/sosonline
Maine – Driver/vehicle Records – Can search title, registration, and driving records; requires a subscription.

http://thor.ddp.state.me.us/archives/plsql
/archdev.Marriage_Archive.search_form
Maine – Marriage Records – Searchable by names.

http://www.state.me.us/sos/cec/rcn/notary/not.htm
Maine – Notaries Public Database – Searchable by name or town.

http://www.winslowmaine.org/Assessor.htm
Maine – Property Records – Alphabetical listing.

http://www.innosoft-solutions.com/states/maine.html
Maine – Public Record Links – Public records information and links.

http://www.state.me.us/sos/cec/corp/ucc.htm
Maine – UCC Debtor Database – Searchable by debtor name.

http://www.state.me.us/sos/arc/archives/genealog/genie4.htm
Maine – Vital Records – Information on how to obtain vital records within the state of Maine.

http://www.raynorshyn.com/yorknet/accsel.cfm
Maine – York – Property Records – Searchable by name, or address.

http://www.state.me.us/sos/corpinfo.htm
Maine Corporation Records Database – Lookup corporations by name.

http://www.docboard.org/me/df/mesearch.htm
Maine Medical License Database – Online searchable database of health professionals located throughout the state.

http://www.state.me.us/treasurer/property.htm
Maine Unclaimed Property Database – Online searchable database of unclaimed property listings.

http://www.state.md.us
Maryland state government information and services.

http://www.innosoft-solutions.com/states/maryland.html
Maryland – Public Record Links – Public records information and links.

http://www.mdbusiness.state.md.us/dirco
Maryland Companies Database – Online searchable database of companies found within the state.

http://www.dhr.state.md.us/csea/index.htm
Maryland Deadbeat Parents – Listing of parents sought by the Department of Social Services for nonpayment of child support.

http://www.docboard.org/md/df/mdsearch.htm
Maryland Medical License Database – Online searchable database of medical professionals by name, license number, or town.

http://www.inform.umd.edu/UMS+State/MD_Resources/MDSP/mmw.html
Maryland Most Wanted Criminals – Provides a listing of the state's most wanted criminals.

http://www.dat.state.md.us/realprop
Maryland Property Database – Searches the MDAT Real Property database for property records.

http://www.sos.state.md.us/sos/admin2/html/trade.html
Maryland Trademarks Database – Searchable database of trademarks within the state.

http://www.dat.state.md.us/bsfd
Maryland UCC Filings Database – Search state UCC filings by name or document number.

http://www.comp.state.md.us/unclaim.asp
Maryland Unclaimed Property Database – Online searchable database of unclaimed property listings.

http://www.state.ma.us
Massachusetts state government information and services.

http://www.town.brookline.ma.us/Assessors/property.asp
Massachusetts – Brookline – Property Records – Searchable by name or address.

http://www.town.falmouth.ma.us/propinq.html
Massachusetts – Falmouth – Property Records – Searchable by name or location.

http://registryofdeeds.co.hampden.ma.us/internet.html
Massachusetts – Hampden – Property Records – Access records by name or address.

http://www.magnet.state.ma.us/legis/ltsform.htm
Massachusetts – Legislative Bill Database – Searchable by bill number.

http://www.townonline.com/marblehead/realestate/values/index.html
Massachusetts – Marblehead – Property Records – Alphabetical listing

http://www.capecod.net/mashpee/assess
Massachusetts – Mashpee – Property Records – Searchable by name or address.

http://regdeeds.co.plymouth.ma.us/tview.html
Massachusetts – Plymouth – Property Records – Must apply for title view access.

http://www.state.ma.us/ocpf
Massachusetts – Political Contributors Database – Searchable by name.

http://www.provincetowngov.org/assessor.html
Massachusetts – Provincetown – Property Records – Assessment and property sales databases.

http://www.innosoft-solutions.com/states/massachusetts.html
Massachusetts – Public Record Links – Public records information and links.

http://www.magnet.state.ma.us/sec/cor/cordirec/direcidx.htm
Massachusetts – Public Records – Government subscription service to various business records and other related databases.

http://207.244.88.10/deedsonline.asp
Massachusetts – South Essex – Property Records – Numerous property record databases.

http://www.walpole.ma.us/thdassesorproperty.htm
Massachusetts – Walpole – Property Assessments –
Alphabetical listings.

http://www.townonline.com/watertown/realestate
/assessments/index.html
Massachusetts – Watertown – Property Records – Alphabetical
listing.

http://www.townonline.com/wellesley/realestate/values
Massachusetts – Wellesley – Property Records – Alphabetical
listing.

http://www.townonline.com/weston/realestate/assessments
/index.html
Massachusetts – Weston – Property Records – Alphabetical
Listing.

http://www.magnet.state.ma.us/chsb/pubs.htm
Massachusetts Criminal History Information – Information
and request form for criminal records.

http://www.state.ma.us/cse
Massachusetts Deadbeat Parents Listing – A listing of parents
wanted for failure of child support payments; also offers a
online employee checking service for employers.

http://www.docboard.org/ma/df/masearch.htm
Massachusetts Medical License Database – Medical
professional's licensing information.

http://www.state.ma.us/msp/missing.htm
Massachusetts Missing/unidentified Persons – Listing of
unidentified bodies and missing persons.

http://www.state.ma.us/msp/wanted/wanted.htm
Massachusetts Most Wanted Criminals – A listing of the state's
most wanted criminals.

http://www.state.ma.us/cgi-bin/treasury/abp-main.cgi
Massachusetts Unclaimed Property Database – Online
searchable database of unclaimed property listings.

http://www.migov.state.mi.us
Michigan state government information and services.

http://alpine.data-web.net
Michigan – Alpine – Property Records – Assessment database.

http://www.co.eaton.mi.us/CNTSRV/ONLINE.HTM
Michigan – Eaton – Public Records – Many searchable
databases.

http://www.state.mi.us/mdoc/asp/otis1.html
Michigan – Inmates Database – Offender Tracking
Information System searchable by name.

http://www.jaye.org/MACPSOR.html
Michigan – Macomb – Sex Offenders – Listing by area.

http://www.innosoft-solutions.com/states/michigan.html
Michigan – Public Record Links – Public records information
and links.

http://www.sagtwp.org/pt_scripts/search.cfm
Michigan – Siginaw – Property Records – Assessment records.

http://www.msp.state.mi.us/wanted/fugitiv.htm
Michigan 10 Most Wanted Criminals – A listing of the state's
10 most wanted fugitives.

http://www.sos.state.mi.us/cfr/cfonl.html?#LINKS
Michigan Campaign Financing Database – Online searchable
database of campaign financing statements and information.

http://www.state.mi.us/msp/crd/chrecord.htm
Michigan Criminal History Information – Information and
request form for criminal records.

http://www.jaye.org/MACPSOR.html
Michigan Sex Offenders Registry – A listing of sex offenders
sorted by zip code.

http://www.treas.state.mi.us/unclprop/unclindx.htm
Michigan Unclaimed Property Database – Online searchable
database of unclaimed property listings.

http://www.state.mn.us
Minnesota state government information and services.

http://www2.co.hennepin.mn.us/pins/main.htm
Minnesota – Hennepin – Property Records – Searchable by ID
or address.

http://info.doc.state.mn.us/PublicViewer
Minnesota – Inmate/parole Database – Searchable by name,
DOB, or OID number.

http://www.innosoft-solutions.com/states/minnesota.html
Minnesota – Public Record Links – Public records information
and links.

http://www.mnb.uscourts.gov/cgi-bin/mnb-500-main.pl
Minnesota Bankruptcy Database – Searchable bankruptcy
records by case, SSN, or last name.

http://www.ag.state.mn.us/cgi-bin/charitysearch.taf
Minnesota Charities Database – Online searchable database of
charities found within the state.

http://www.dps.state.mn.us/bca/CJIS/documents
/Page-3-1.html
Minnesota Criminal History Information – Information and
request form for criminal records.

http://www.dps.state.mn.us/bca/CJIS/documents/Page-3.html
Minnesota Criminal History Information – Information for
obtaining criminal records.

http://www.dps.state.mn.us/alcgamb/alcgamb.html
Minnesota Liquor License Database – Various searchable
liquor license databases.

http://www.docboard.org/mn/df/mndf.htm
Minnesota Medical License Database – Medical professional's
licensing information.

http://www.commerce.state.mn.us
Minnesota Unclaimed Property Database – Online searchable
database of unclaimed property listings.

http://www.state.ms.us
Mississippi state government information and services.

http://www.archbd.state.ms.us/roster_tmp.htm
Mississippi – Architects Database – Searchable by name or ID.

http://www.mslawyer.com/LawFirms/#Search
Mississippi – Attorney Database – Listings and searchable
databases.

http://www.sos.state.ms.us/elections/Lobbyists/index.html
Mississippi – Lobbyist Database – Searchable by name.

http://www.sos.state.ms.us/busserv/notaries/notaries.html
Mississippi – Notaries Public Database – Searchable by city or
county.

http://dsitspe01.its.state.ms.us/pepls/EngSurveyors.nsf
Mississippi – Professional Engineer Database – Searchable by
name.

http://www.innosoft-solutions.com/states/mississippi.html
Mississippi – Public Record Links – Public records information
and links.

http://www.mdhs.state.ms.us/mswant.html
Mississippi Deadbeat Parents – Listing of parents sought by
the Department of Social Services for nonpayment of child
support.

http://www.treasury.state.ms.us
Mississippi Unclaimed Property Database – Online searchable
database of unclaimed property listings.

http://www.ecodev.state.mo.us
Missouri state government information and services.

http://168.166.2.55/missouribusinesses
Missouri – Business Database – Searchable by name or ID.

http://ecf.mowd.uscourts.gov
Missouri – Court Case Database – Case files.

http://www.16thcircuit.org/Court/casenet.nsf
/Public+Access?OpenForm
Missouri – Jackson – Court Records – Make an inquiry based
on estate number, if you know it, or a party name.

http://www.innosoft-solutions.com/states/missouri.html
Missouri – Public Record Links – Public records information
and links.

http://168.166.2.55/corporations
Missouri Corporations Database – Online searchable
corporation records database. Perform searches by name, agent,
or charter number.

http://mosl.sos.state.mo.us/bus-ser/corpdata.html
Missouri Corporations Database – Approximately one million
records providing relevant biographical information on all of
the individual business entities registered in Missouri.

http://www.mshp.state.mo.us/HP32P001.NSF
/FAQ?OpenView
Missouri Criminal History Information – How to obtain
criminal history records.

http://casenet.osca.state.mo.us/casenet
Missouri Criminal/civil Records Database – Civil and criminal
records online.

http://www.dor.state.mo.us/dmv/dlrecords.htm
Missouri Drivers Records – Information on how to request
records from the DMV for Missouri

http://www.kcmo-net.org/cgi-bin/db2www/realform.d2w
/report
Missouri KC – Property Records – Searchable by name or
address.

http://www.lylemariam.com/missing.htm
Missouri Missing Children – Listing.

http://lostchild.net/missouri.htm
Missouri Missing Persons – Listing

http://www.dailywatch.com/stlouis/realper2.asp
Missouri Property Database – Searchable by parcel ID for
property within St. Louis and St. Charles counties.

http://mosl.sos.state.mo.us/bus-ser/sosucc.html
Missouri UCC – Information on how to obtain UCC records
in Missouri.

http://www.sto.state.mo.us
Missouri Unclaimed Property Database – Online searchable
database of unclaimed property listings.

http://www.health.state.mo.us/BirthAndDeathRecords
/BirthAndDeathRecords.html
Missouri Vital Records – Information on how to go about
obtaining vital records.

http://www.state.mt.us
Montana state government information and services.

http://www.innosoft-solutions.com/states/montana.html
Montana – Public Record Links – Public records information
and links.

http://www.doj.state.mt.us/csp/CJN_FAQ.htm
Montana Criminal History Information – How to obtain
criminal history records.

http://www.state.mt.us/cor/Esc_Index.htm
Montana Inmate Escapee – Listing.

http://www.com.state.mt.us/License/POL/index.htm
Montana Professional License Databases – Databases and
information on enquires not listed.

http://www.state.ne.us
Nebraska state government information and services.

http://interlinc.ci.lincoln.ne.us/cnty/assess/property.htm
Nebraska – Lancaster – Property Records – Searchable by ID,
owner, or address.

http://www.ci.lincoln.ne.us/city/police/stats/warrant1.htm
Nebraska – Lincoln/lancaster Warrants – Listing.

http://www.madisoncountysheriff.com/#lawenfor
Nebraska – Madison – Warrants Database – Searchable by
name.

http://www.innosoft-solutions.com/states/nebraska.html
Nebraska – Public Record Links – Public records information
and links.

http://www.sarpy.com/sarpycounty/property1.htm
Nebraska – Sarpy – Property Records – Searchable by name or
address.

http://www.nol.org/subscribe/sub.htm
Nebraska Driver's Records – Subscription.

http://www.nol.org/home/SOS/Privatedetectives/pdlist.htm
Nebraska Private Investigator Directory – Alphabetical listing.

http://www.hhs.state.ne.us/lis/lis.asp
Nebraska Professional License Database – Health professional
license information search.

http://www.nol.org/prm.htm
Nebraska Public Records – Various public records offered by
the state by subscription.

http://court.nol.org/opinions/opinindex.htm
Nebraska Supreme Court Records – Categorized by court and
filing date.

http://www.nebraska.treasurer.org
Nebraska Unclaimed Property Database – Online searchable
database of unclaimed property listings.

http://www.state.nv.us
Nevada state government information and services.

http://courtgate.coca.co.clark.nv.us
8490/DistrictCourt/asp/SearchPartyOptions.asp
Nevada – Clark – Criminal Court Database – Searchable by
district, name, lawyer or ID.

http://www.co.clark.nv.us/assessor/Disclaim.htm
Nevada – Clark – Property Records – Numerous searches
available.

http://www.innosoft-solutions.com/states/nevada.html
Nevada – Public Record Links – Public records information
and links.

http://www.nvb.uscourts.gov
Nevada Bankruptcy Database – Search bankruptcy records by
name, SSN, or case number.

http://sos.state.nv.us/default.asp
Nevada Corporation Database – Search for corporation records
by name, agent, officer, or file number.

http://www.state.nv.us/ag/most_wanted/most_wanted.htm
Nevada Deadbeat Parents – Listing.

http://prisons.state.nv.us/inmate%20information.htm
Nevada Inmate Inquiry – How to obtain information on
inmates.

http://lawyers.nevada.nu/search.htm
Nevada Lawyer Search – Search for a lawyer within the state;
legal advice and articles.

http://www.co.clark.nv.us/clerk/clerkhome.htm
Nevada Las Vegas Marriage Records – Online searchable
database of marriage records for Las Vegas.

http://www.missingkids.com/precreate/NV.html
Nevada Missing Children – Listing.

http://www.state.nv.us/ag/ag_wanted/home.htm
Nevada Most Wanted – Listing with pictures.

http://treasurer.state.nv.us/unclaimed
Nevada Unclaimed Property Database – Online searchable
database of unclaimed property listings.

http://www.state.nh.us
New Hampshire state government information and services.

http://www.state.nh.us/pharmacy/nphcst.htm
New Hampshire – Licensed Pharmacists – Listing by name.

http://www.portsmouthnh.com/realestate/index.htm
New Hampshire – Portsmouth – Property Records –
Searchable by owner or address.

http://www.innosoft-solutions.com/states
/new_hampshire.html
New Hampshire – Public Record Links – Public records
information and links.

http://www.state.nh.us/sos/clerks.htm
New Hampshire City and Town Clerks – Listing by name.

http://www.state.nh.us/nhsp/cr.html
New Hampshire Criminal Records – How to obtain criminal
history records.

http://www.state.nh.us/sos/lobname.html
New Hampshire Lobbyist Roster – Listing by name.

http://www.state.nh.us/nhsp/cprmp.html
New Hampshire Missing Persons – Listing.

http://www.state.nh.us/treasury
New Hampshire Unclaimed Property Database – Online
searchable database of unclaimed property listings.

http://www.state.nh.us/nhdoj/Press%20Release
/pressrelease.html
New Hampshire Wanted Persons – Listing.

http://www.state.nj.us
New Jersey state government information and services.

http://www.innosoft-solutions.com/states/new_jersey.html
New Jersey – Public Record Links – Public records
information and links.

http://www.njleg.state.nj.us/cgi-bin/om_isapi.dll?infobase=
mainbill2000.nfo&softpage=Doc_Frame_Pg42
New Jersey Acts Db – Acts searchable by keyword.

http://njuscourts.org
New Jersey Bankruptcy Records – Searchable databases.

http://www.crp.org/capi
New Jersey Campaign Finance Database – Contains financial
records that campaigns and committees are required by law to
disclose.

http://accessnet.state.nj.us/Browse.asp
New Jersey Corporation Database – Searchable by name or
number.

http://www.njlawnet.com/crimes.html
New Jersey Law Network – Civil and criminal law resources
for the state of New Jersey.

http://www.state.nj.us/lps/njsp/missingperson.htm
New Jersey Missing Persons – Listing.

http://www.state.nj.us/lps/njsp/nj12.html
New Jersey Most Wanted – Listing.

http://www.state.nj.us/parole/elig.htm
New Jersey Parole Eligibility Notices – Complete listing by
county.

http://www.state.nj.us/lps/ca/director.htm
New Jersey Prof. License Database – Databases for many
professional licensees within New Jersey.

http://www.taxrecords.com
New Jersey Property Records – Searchable by name or address.

http://www.philly.com/packages/njshore/lookup.htm
New Jersey Shore Property Database – Searchable by address.

http://www.state.nj.us/treasury/taxation/index.html
New Jersey Unclaimed Property Database – Online searchable
database of unclaimed property listings.

http://www.state.nm.us
New Mexico state government information and services.

http://www.nmcourts.com/cgi-bin/factsweb/wsrc01_0
New Mexico – Civil/criminal Records – Searchable by name,
DL number, or SSN.

http://www.innosoft-solutions.com/states/new_mexico.html
New Mexico – Public Record Links – Public records
information and links.

http://www.nmcourt.fed.us/bkdocs/acedoc.htm
New Mexico Bankruptcy Database – Subscription.

http://legis.state.nm.us/scripts/FirstBillFinderForm.asp
New Mexico Bill Database – Searchable by bill number or
keyword.

http://www.nmprc.state.nm.us/ftq.htm
New Mexico Corporation Database – Searchable database for
corporate entities and related information.

http://www.dps.nm.org/dbaccess_m.htm
New Mexico Missing Persons – Listing by name.

http://www.mostwanted.org/NM
New Mexico Most Wanted – Listing.

http://www.eportnm.com/cgi-bin
/viewagency.cgi?RecordEdit_fn=SearchHome
New Mexico Professional License Database – Search licencee
information for many different professions.

http://www.sos.state.nm.us/UCC/UCCHOME.HTM
New Mexico UCC Filings Database – Allows you to search
state UCC filings by name or document number.

http://www.state.nm.us/hsd/wanted.html
New Mexico Deadbeat Parents List – Listing of parents sought
by the Department of Social Services for nonpayment of child
support.

http://www.state.ny.us
New York state government information and services.

http://www.health.state.ny.us/nysdoh/opmc/search/index.htm
New York Physician Discipline Search – Searchable by name.

http://www.pennynet.org/erwin/ertxsrch.htm
New York – Erwin – Property Records – Searchable by name.

http://www.innosoft-solutions.com/states/new_york.html
New York – Public Record Links – Public records information
and links.

http://www.scpl.org/assessments/index.html
New York – Schenectady – Property Records – Assessment
records.

http://www.nysb.uscourts.gov
New York Bankruptcy Database – Run reports on bankruptcy
filings.

http://www.dos.state.ny.us
8099/corp_public/corp_wdb.corp_search_names.show_parms
New York Corporation Database – Searchable by business
name.

http://ecf.nyed.uscourts.gov
New York Court Case Database – Searchable by ID or name.

http://www.parolewatch.org/ndcilinkframe.htm
New York Inmate Database – Search for inmates by crime,
inmate, county, or earliest parole date.

http://www.troopers.state.ny.us/BCI/BCIINDEX.html
New York Missing Persons – Listing.

http://www.troopers.state.ny.us/index.html
New York Most Wanted – Listing.

http://www.op.nysed.gov/opsearches.htm#nme
New York Professional License Database – Searchable by
profession and name.

http://land.netacc.net
New York Property Records – Fee-based.

http://www.osc.state.ny.us
New York Unclaimed Property Database – Online searchable
database of unclaimed property listings.

http://www.sips.state.nc.us
North Carolina state government information and services.

http://web1-sun.aoc.state.nc.us/data/dwi/index.html
North Carolina – Active DUI Cases – Searchable by name,
county, or zip code.

http://www.andassoc.com/gismaps/Aplus/Aplus.htm
North Carolina – Ashe – Property Records – Searchable by
name, parcel number or address.

http://www.aoc.state.nc.us/data/officer/citation_form.html
North Carolina – Citation Lookup – Searchable by number.

http://www.aoc.state.nc.us/www/public/calindx.html
North Carolina – Criminal Trial Calendar – Searchable by
name.

http://www.co.dare.nc.us/interactive/setup.htm
North Carolina – DARE – Property Records – Searchable by
name or address.

http://www.co.davidson.nc.us/asp/taxsearch.asp
North Carolina – Davidson – Property Records – Searchable
by name or address.

http://www.doc.state.nc.us/release
North Carolina – Parolees Database – Searchable by name.

http://www.innosoft-solutions.com/states/north_carolina.html
North Carolina – Public Record Links – Public records
information and links.

http://ndsips01.sips.state.nc.us/NCREC/search.asp
North Carolina – Real Estate License Database – Searchable by
name, firm, or license number.

http://www.wilson-co.com/wctax.html
North Carolina – Wilson – Property Records – Tax records.

http://www.ncwb.uscourts.gov
North Carolina Bankruptcy Database – Search bankruptcy
records by case number or last name.

http://www.ncga.state.nc.us/html1999/billInfo/billInfo.html
North Carolina Bill Database – Searchable by bill number.

http://www.secretary.state.nc.us/corporations
North Carolina Corporation Database – Online searchable
database of corporation names found within the state.

http://www.doc.state.nc.us/escape
North Carolina Inmate Escapes – Listing.

http://www.doc.state.nc.us/prisoner/SEARCH1.HTM
North Carolina Inmate Search – Searchable.

http://www.docboard.org/nc/df/ncsearch.htm
North Carolina Medical License Database – Medical
professional's licensing information.

http://sbi.jus.state.nc.us/missing/missmain.htm
North Carolina Missing Persons – Listing with pictures.

http://ucc.secstate.state.nc.us/debtor.html
North Carolina UCC Database – Searchable by name.

http://www.treasurer.state.nc.us
North Carolina Unclaimed Property Database – Online
searchable database of unclaimed property listings.

http://www.state.nd.us
North Dakota state government information and services.

http://www.innosoft-solutions.com/states/north_dakota.html
North Dakota – Public Record Links – Public records
information and links.

http://www.state.nd.us/sec/senatebills.htm
North Dakota Bills – Listing.

http://www.state.nd.us/sec/contractorsearch.htm
North Dakota Contractor License Database – Searchable by
license number, type, owner name or business name.

http://www.mandanpd.com/wanted/wanted.html
North Dakota Most Wanted – Listing.

http://www.land.state.nd.us
North Dakota Unclaimed Property Database – Online
searchable database of unclaimed property listings.

http://www.state.oh.us
Ohio state government information and services.

http://www.municipalcourt.org/main_dui.asp
Ohio – Delaware – DUI Database – Listing.

http://205.133.113.109/realestate/homepage.htm
Ohio – Hamilton – Property Database – Searchable by owner
name or address.

http://www.innosoft-solutions.com/states/ohio.html
Ohio – Public Record Links – Public records information and
links.

http://www.sheriff.co.stark.oh.us/pr01.htm
Ohio – Stark – Sex Offenders – Listing.

http://www.legislature.state.oh.us
Ohio Acts Database – Searchable by bill number or keyword.

http://www.ohnb.uscourts.gov
Ohio Bankruptcy Database – Run reports on bankruptcy
filings.

http://www.fcmcclerk.com
Ohio Court Records – Franklin County Court case records;
includes speeding tickets and civil cases.

http://www.ohiohistory.org/dindex
Ohio Death Certificate Database – Searchable by name.

http://www.docboard.org/oh/df
Ohio Doctor Database – Searchable by name or license
number.

http://www.drc.state.oh.us/CFDOCS/inmate/search.htm
Ohio Inmate Database – Searchable database of current and
released inmates. Includes photos.

http://www.state.oh.us/scripts/acc/query.asp
Ohio License Database – Accountancy board; search by name
or license number.

http://www.state.oh.us/com/liquor/liquor5.htm
Ohio Medical Board Database – Search for permit holders or
applications being processed.

http://www.state.oh.us/med
Ohio Medical Board Database – Medical professional's
licensing information.

http://www.ag.state.oh.us/juvenile/mcc/posters/index.htm
Ohio Missing Children – Listing.

http://www.drc.ohio.gov/search2.htm
Ohio Parole Violators List – List of parole violators wanted by
the state.

http://www.com.state.oh.us
Ohio Unclaimed Property Database – Online searchable
database of unclaimed property listings.

http://www.oklaosf.state.ok.us
Oklahoma state government information and services.

http://www.oscn.net/pinpoint3/applications/dockets/start.asp
Oklahoma – Civil/criminal Records – Criminal records for
many counties.

http://www.enid.org/police/enidwanted.htm
Oklahoma – Enid – Most Wanted – Listing.

http://www.innosoft-solutions.com/states/oklahoma.html
Oklahoma – Public Record Links – Public records information
and links.

http://www3.lsb.state.ok.us/default.htm
Oklahoma Bill Tracking – Searchable by many categories.

http://www.state.ok.us/~sos/functions
/business%20information.htm
Oklahoma Business Search – Information on how to access
records online; small fee.

http://www.occa.state.ok.us
Oklahoma Criminal Court Records – Searchable court
records.

http://www.osbi.state.ok.us/crimhist/crimhist.html#open
Oklahoma Criminal History Information – Information on
how to obtain criminal records.

http://www.osbi.state.ok.us/crimhist/crimhist.html
Oklahoma Criminal Records – How to obtain criminal history
records.

http://www.okdhs.org/childsupport/TenMostWanted.htm
Oklahoma Deadbeat Parents Listings – Listing of parents
sought by the Department of Social Services for nonpayment
of child support.

http://medbd.netplus.net/physrch.html
Oklahoma Medical License Database – Medical professional's
licensing information.

http://www.geocities.com/CapitolHill/Senate/2198
/index.html
Oklahoma Missing Children – Listing.

http://www.ppb.state.ok.us/Docket/Default.htm
Oklahoma Parole Database – Searchable by name.

http://www.oklahomacounty.org/assessor/disclaim.htm
Oklahoma Property Records – Searchable by name or address.

http://www.kwtv.com/crime/sex_offenders
/sex-offenders-map.htm
Oklahoma Sex Offenders – Searchable by county.

http://www.kocotv.com/5oys/fortune.html
Oklahoma Unclaimed Property Database – Online searchable
database of unclaimed property listings.

http://www.docboard.org/ok/df/oksearch.htm
Oklahoma Doc Finder – Searchable by name.

http://www.state.or.us
Oregon state government information and services.

http://www.co.benton.or.us/sheriff/corrections/bccc/sonote
Oregon – Benton – Sex Offenders – Listing.

http://www.portlandcrusader.com/beaverton_wanted.htm
Oregon – Beverton – Felony Fugitives – Listing.

http://www.open.org/~msheriff/jail.htm
Oregon – Marion – Criminal Database – Various offender
rosters.

http://www.innosoft-solutions.com/states/oregon.html
Oregon – Public Record Links – Public records information
and links.

http://www.barysoftware.com
Oregon Adoption Registry – Searchable.

http://www.oedd.state.or.us/cgi/fm/animal_health
/Search.html
Oregon Animal Health License Database – Searchable by
name.

http://www.sos.state.or.us/corporation/bizreg/bizreg.htm
Oregon Business License – Information on how to obtain
information on business registrations

http://www.cbs.state.or.us/external/imd/database/bcd
/licensing/index.html
Oregon Contractor License Database – Searchable by number,
name, or city.

http://www.osp.state.or.us/orec/index.html
Oregon Criminal History Information – Information on how
to obtain criminal records.

http://www.oedd.state.or.us/cgi/fm/feed_fert/Search.html
Oregon Feed-fertilizer Licenses – Searchable by name, license
number, or address.

http://www.oedd.state.or.us/cgi/fm/food_safety/Search.html
Oregon Food Safety License Database – Searchable by name or
license.

http://www.docboard.org/or/df/search.htm
Oregon Medical License Database – Medical professional's
licensing information.

http://www.columbia-center.org/missing/Default.htm
Oregon Missing Persons – Listing with pictures.

http://www.co.linn.or.us/assessor/PropSearch.asp
Oregon Property Records – Searchable by owner name or
address.

http://www.oda.state.or.us/aclb/search.html
Oregon Real Estate License Database – Searchable by name,
address, or license type.

http://www.sos.state.or.us/cgi-bin/uccsrch.htm
Oregon Ucc Filings Database – Search state UCC filings by
name or document number.

http://www.state.pa.us
Pennsylvania state government information and services.

http://www.berksregofwills.com/search
Pennsylvania – Berks – Vital Records – Marriage, death, birth,
and estate records.

http://www.innosoft-solutions.com/states/pennsylvania.html
Pennsylvania – Public Record Links – Public records
information and links.

http://www.dos.state.pa.us/campaign.htm
Pennsylvania Campaign Finance Database – Listing

http://www.pacode.com/cgi-bin/pacode/secure/titles.pl
Pennsylvania Code Search – By keyword.

http://patch.state.pa.us
Pennsylvania Criminal History Information – How to obtain
criminal history records.

http://www.cor.state.pa.us/cgi-bin/locator.pl
Pennsylvania Inmate Locator – Searchable by name or number.

http://www.state.pa.us/PA_Exec/State_Police/pspfiles
/missing.htm
Pennsylvania Missing Persons – Listing.

http://www.state.pa.us/PA_Exec/State_Police/mwanted
/ten.htm
Pennsylvania Most Wanted – Listing.

http://www.treasury.state.pa.us/Unclaimed.html
Pennsylvania Unclaimed Property Database – Online
searchable database of unclaimed property listings.

http://www.state.ri.us
Rhode Island state government information and services.

http://www.innosoft-solutions.com/states/rhode_island.html
Rhode Island – Public Record Link – Public records
information and links.

http://www.rib.uscourts.gov
Rhode Island Bankruptcy Database – Search for bankruptcy
records by SSN, party, or case number.

http://www.state.ri.us/submenus/leglink.htm
Rhode Island Bill Search – Searchable by keyword.

http://155.212.254.78
Rhode Island Corporate Names Database – Allows you to
lookup corporation names found within the state.

http://www.docboard.org/ri/df/search.htm
Rhode Island Medical License Database – Medical
professional's licensing information.

http://www.risp.state.ri.us/MISSING%20CHILDREN.htm
Rhode Island Missing Children – Listing.

http://www.risp.state.ri.us/MOSTwanted.htm
Rhode Island Most Wanted – Listing.

http://www.ci.woonsocket.ri.us/police.htm#Megan's
Rhode Island Sex Offenders – Listing.

http://www.state.ri.us/treas/moneylst.htm
Rhode Island Unclaimed Property Database – Online
searchable database of unclaimed property listings.

http://www.state.sc.us
South Carolina state government information and services.

http://maps.co.beaufort.sc.us/isa/parcels
South Carolina – Beaufort – Property Records – Searchable by
owner or address.

http://www3.charlestoncounty.org/docs/CoC/index.html
South Carolina – Charleston – Criminal Records – Online
records.

http://www3.charlestoncounty.org/docs/CoC/index.html
South Carolina – Charleston – Public Records – Searchable
databases.

http://greenwood.akanda.com
South Carolina – Greenwood – Property Records – Searchable
by owner.

http://www.innosoft-solutions.com/states/south_carolina.html
South Carolina – Public Record Links – Public records
information and links.

http://www.spt.lib.sc.us/obits/index.html
South Carolina – Spartanburg – Death Records – Listing.

http://www.scsos.com/direct.htm
South Carolina Business Records – Information on how to
obtain business records online.

http://www.sled.state.sc.us/SLED
/default.asp?Category=SLEDCRC&Service=CRC
South Carolina Criminal Records – Fee-based.

http://www.state.sc.us/scdc/fugitive.htm
South Carolina Fugitives – Listing.

http://www.scsos.com/direct.htm
South Carolina Lawyer Database – Searchable by name or
county.

http://www.llr.state.sc.us/dss/dss_menu.htm
South Carolina Licensee Database – Search for professional
licensee information.

http://www.missingkids.com/precreate/SC.html
South Carolina Missing Children – Listing.

http://www.scattorneygeneral.com/public/registry.html
South Carolina Sex Registry – Searchable.

http://www.law.sc.edu/opinions/opinions.htm
South Carolina Supreme Court Decisions – Searchable by
month.

http://www.state.sd.us
South Dakota state government information and services.

http://www.innosoft-solutions.com/states/south_dakota.html
South Dakota – Public Record Links – Public records
information and links.

http://207.222.24.8/wconnect/wc.dll?usdc_racer-main
South Dakota Court Case Database – Search for court cases by
party, case number, or lawyer.

http://www.state.sd.us/corrections/search.htm
South Dakota Inmate Search – Search for inmates within
South Dakota.

http://www.state.sd.us/treasurer/prop.htm
South Dakota Unclaimed Property – Searchable by name.

http://www.state.sd.us/fusebox/shoppingcart
/index.cfm?Fusebox_ID=1
South Dakota Vital Records – Order records online.

http://www.state.tn.us
Tennessee state government information and services.

http://www.hamiltontn.gov/courts/CircuitClerk/dockets
/motion.htm
Tennessee – Hamilton – Court Records – Online records
searchable by various fields.

http://www.innosoft-solutions.com/states/tennessee.html
Tennessee – Public Record Links – Public records information
and links.

http://www.state.tn.us/humanserv/w2.htm
Tennessee Deadbeat Parents List – Listing of parents sought by
the Department of Social Services for nonpayment of child
support.

http://www.tbi.state.tn.us/Fugitives/TBI_MWD4.HTM
Tennessee Felony Fugitives – Listing with pictures.

http://www.ticic.state.tn.us/Missing_Children
/miss_child_new.htm
Tennessee Missing Children – Listing with pictures.

http://www.ticic.state.tn.us/Database/ISC_search_oct.htm
Tennessee Parole/probation Registry – Searchable by name.

http://www.memphisdailynews.com/memphis98
/parcelfree.asp
Tennessee Property Records – Searchable by name or address.

http://www.ticic.state.tn.us/SEX_ofndr/search_short.asp
Tennessee Sex Offender Registry – Searchable by name or zip
code.

http://www.tsc.state.tn.us/OPINIONS/opmaster.htm
Tennessee Supreme Court Search – Various keyword searches.

http://www.treasury.state.tn.us/unclaim/unclaim-s.htm
Tennessee Unclaimed Property – Searchable by name.

http://www.state.tx.us
Texas state government information and services.

http://records.txdps.state.tx.us/dps/default.cfm
Texas – Convictions And Sex Offender Database – Searchable
databases provided by the department of public safety.

http://www.tgcl.co.tom-green.tx.us/datty/Crimhistory.html
Texas Criminal Records – How to obtain records.

http://www.capitol.state.tx.us/fyi/fyi.htm
Texas – Incumbent Database – Searchable incumbent database
for the state of Texas; offers many different search options.

http://www.innosoft-solutions.com/states/texas.html
Texas – Public Record Links – Public records information and
links.

http://ble.state.tx.us/Results/current.htm
Texas Bar Exam Results Database – Lists those that have passed
their bar exams.

http://www.capitol.state.tx.us/tlo/billsrch/search.htm
Texas Bills Database – Search for bills by author/sponsor,
coauthor/cosponsor, committee status, actions taken, and
related subjects.

http://open.cpa.state.tx.us
Texas Corporate Records Database – Search corporation
records by company, tax ID number, or charter number.

http://www.oag.state.tx.us/child/cs_evaders.html
Texas Deadbeat Parents LIST – Listing of parents sought by
the Department of Social Services for nonpayment of child
support.

http://www.tabc.state.tx.us/pubinfo/rosters/default.htm
Texas Liquor License Database – Various information about
permit holders in many different formats.

http://www.docboard.org/tx/df/txsearch.htm
Texas Medical License Database – Medical professional's
licensing information.

http://www.dallascad.org
Texas Property Records – Listing.

http://www.tdi.state.tx.us/general/forms.html
Texas Registered Insurance Agents Lists – Numerous
downloadable listings of registered insurance agents and other
related information.

http://www.sll.courts.state.tx.us
Texas State Law Library – Extensive resource for those needing
legal information within the state of Texas.

http://capitol.tlc.state.tx.us/statutes/statutes.html
Texas Statues Database – Searchable listings of all Texas
statutes.

http://www.window.state.tx.us/comptrol/unclprop
/unclprop.html
Texas Unclaimed Property Database – Online searchable
database of unclaimed property listings.

http://www.state.ut.us
Utah state government information and services.

http://www.innosoft-solutions.com/states/utah.html
Utah – Public Record Links – Public records information and links.

http://www.state.ut.us/serv/bes
Utah Corporation Database – Searchable by company name.

http://www.bci.state.ut.us/FAQ.html
Utah Criminal Records – Information on how to obtain a criminal record.

http://www.cr.ex.state.ut.us/offenders/escapees
Utah Escapees Listing – Listing by name.

http://www.alcbev.state.ut.us/hotmaput.htm
Utah Liquor License Database – Provides information on all the liquor stores in the state, including owner, phone and address.

http://www.bci.state.ut.us/clearinghouse/default.html
Utah Missing Persons – Listing.

http://www.cr.ex.state.ut.us/offenders/mostwanted
Utah Most Wanted – Listing.

http://www.commerce.state.ut.us/dopl/current.htm
Utah Professional License Database – Listing of all licensed professionals within the state.

http://www.cr.ex.state.ut.us/offenders/sexoffenders
Utah Sex Offenders – Listing.

http://ucc.its.state.ut.us/NetDynamics/NetDynamics40/ndNSAPI.nd/UccCode/pgUccSearch
Utah UCC Filings Database – Searchable by file number or name.

http://www.state.vt.us
Vermont state government information and services.

http://www.innosoft-solutions.com/states/vermont.html
Vermont – Public Record Links – Public records information and links.

http://www.sec.state.vt.us/seek/keyword.htm
Vermont Business Records Database – Online searchable database of all registered businesses within the state; also includes trademarks and other related business searches.

http://www.dps.state.vt.us/cjs/questions.htm
Vermont Criminal Records – Information on how to obtain criminal records.

http://www.dps.state.vt.us/vsp/major_cases.html
Vermont Felony Fugitives – Listing.

http://www.sec.state.vt.us/seek/lbylseek.htm
Vermont Lobbyist Database – Searchable directory of lobbyists, lobbying firms, and lobbyist employers.

http://www.docboard.org/vt/df/vtsearch.htm
Vermont Medical License Database – Medical professional's licensing information.

http://www.sec.state.vt.us/seek/lrspseek.htm
Vermont Professional License Database – Online searchable database of all licensed professionals within the state.

http://170.222.200.66/seek/markseek.htm
Vermont Trademark Database – Searchable by name.

http://www.sec.state.vt.us/seek/ucc_seek.htm
Vermont UCC Filings Database – Allows you to search state UCC filings by name or document number.

http://www.state.vt.us/treasurer/abanprop.htm
Vermont Unclaimed Property Database – Online searchable database of unclaimed property listings.

http://www.state.va.us
Virginia state government information and services.

http://www.ci.bedford.va.us/proptax/lookup.html
Virginia – Bedford – Property Records – Searchable by name or address.

http://www.co.fairfax.va.us/dta/re/propadd.asp
Virginia – Fairfax – Property Records – Searchable by address.

http://206.246.204.34/jcc/public/index.htm
Virginia – James City – Property Records – Searchable by name or address.

http://206.246.226.47/RealEstate/search.html
Virginia – Norfolk – Property Records – Searchable by address.

http://www.pwcgov.org/realestate/LandRover.asp
Virginia – Prince William – Property Records – Searchable by name or address.

http://www.innosoft-solutions.com/states/virginia.html
Virginia – Public Record Links – Public records information and links.

http://www.vaeb.uscourts.gov/home/SearchNM.html
Virginia Bankruptcy Database – Searchable by name.

http://sex-offender.vsp.state.va.us/Static/Search.htm
Virginia – Sex Offender Registry – Sex offenders database offered by the Virginia State Police.

http://www.state.va.us/scc/division/clk/diracc.htm
Virginia Corporation DBs (Direct Access) – Offers various databases that can be searched online for corporate and other related information.

http://www.vsp.state.va.us/basrchek.html
Virginia Criminal Records – How to obtain records.

http://www.dss.state.va.us/family/wanted.html
Virginia Deadbeat Parents List – Listing of parents sought by
the Department of Social Services for nonpayment of child
support.

http://www.vipnet.org/premium.html
Virginia Driver's Records – Fee-based.

http://image.vtls.com8000/bibdatabases/henleyabout.html
Virginia Marriage and Death Records – Records from
newspapers.

http://www.vsp.state.va.us/basrmc.html
Virginia Missing Children – Listing.

http://www.vsp.state.va.us/wanted.html
Virginia Most Wanted – Listing.

http://access.wa.gov
Washington state government information and services.

http://www.co.clark.wa.us/sheriff/inter/comminfo
/sexoffender/sex.htm
Washington – Clark – Sex Offenders – Listing

http://www.cowlitzcounty.org/sheriff/rso/default.htm
Washington – Cowlitz – Sex Offenders – Listing.

http://www.metrokc.gov/sheriff/sosch.htm
Washington – King – Sex Offenders – Searchable databases.

http://www.tri-cityherald.com/sexoffenders
Washington – Mid-columbia – Sex Offenders – Listing.

http://okanogancounty.org/Sheriff/soffend.htm
Washington – Okanogan – Sex Offenders – Listing.

http://www.innosoft-solutions.com/states/washington.html
Washington – Public Record Links – Public records
information and links.

http://www.pan.co.yakima.wa.us/sheriff/sexual.htm
Washington – Yakima – Sex Offenders – Listing.

http://204.227.177.194/wconnect/wc.dll?usbcn_racer-main
Washington Bankruptcy Database – Search for bankruptcy
records by SSN, party, or case number.

http://search.leg.wa.gov/pub/textsearch/default.asp
Washington Bill Lookup – Searchable by keyword.

http://www.wa.gov/dor/prd
Washington Business Records Database – Online searchable
database of state business records; searchable by many different
field types.

http://www.lni.wa.gov/contractors/contractor.asp
Washington Contractor License Database – Searchable by
license number, name, or registration number.

http://www.wa.gov/wsp/crime/crimhist.htm
Washington Criminal Records – Information on how to obtain
criminal records.

http://www.wsba.org/adm/search/index.html
Washington Lawyer Database – Searchable by name or city.

http://www.liq.wa.gov/services/storesearch.asp
Washington Liquor Permit Database – Searchable by city,
county, or store number.

http://www.wa.gov/dor/unclaim
Washington Unclaimed Property Database – Online
searchable database of unclaimed property listings.

http://www.state.wv.us
West Virginia state government information and services.

http://www.innosoft-solutions.com/states/west_virginia.html
West Virginia – Public Record Links – Public records
information and links.

http://129.71.161.247/BillT/billsrch.html
West Virginia Bill Lookup – Searchable by bill number.

http://www.wvstatetroopers.com/children
West Virginia Missing Children – Listing.

http://www.wvstatetroopers.com/wanted
West Virginia Most Wanted – Listing

http://www.wvstatetroopers.com/sexoff
West Virginia Sex Offenders – Searchable by name, address, or
zip code.

http://www.wvtreasury.com/unclaimed_property.htm
West Virginia Unclaimed Property Database – Online
searchable database of unclaimed property listings.

http://www.state.wi.us
Wisconsin state government information and services.

http://www.doj.state.wi.us/dles/cib
Wisconsin Criminal Records – Information on how to obtain
criminal records.

http://kenoshapolice.com/offender.htm
Wisconsin – Kenosha – Sex Offenders – Listing.

http://www.ci.madison.wi.us/police/sexoffend.html
Wisconsin – Madison – Sex Offenders – Listing

http://www.tznet.com/comn/mpd/sex.html
Wisconsin – Marshfield – Sex Offenders – Listing.

http://www.mkesheriff.org
Wisconsin – Milwaukee – Most Wanted – Listing.

http://www.milw-police.org/RegSexOffenders.html
Wisconsin – Milwaukee – Sex Offenders – Listing.

http://www.innosoft-solutions.com/states/wisconsin.html
Wisconsin – Public Record Links – Public records information
and links.

http://www.crp.org/wdc/index.html-ssi
Wisconsin Campaign Finance Database – Online searchable
database of contributions made to political parties.

http://ccap.courts.state.wi.us/servlet
/us.wi.state.courts.internet.access.GetJSP
Wisconsin Criminal/civil Records – Criminal/Civil court
records.

http://www.dwd.state.wi.us/bcs/wanted
Wisconsin Deadbeat Parents List – Listing of parents sought
by the Department of Social Services for nonpayment of child
support.

http://www.doj.state.wi.us/missingkids
Wisconsin Missing Children – Listing.

http://165.189.238.43
Wisconsin Professional License Database – Business and health
professionals license information.

http://www.ci.mil.wi.us/citygov/assessor/assessments.htm
Wisconsin Property Assessment Database (Milwaukee) –
Online searchable database of property assessments within
Milwaukee.

http://www.legis.state.wi.us/rsb/stats.html
Wisconsin Statues Database – Searchable by keyword.

http://www.state.wy.us/~sot/unc_prop.html
Wisconsin Unclaimed Property Database – Online searchable
database of unclaimed property listings.

http://www.state.wy.us
Wyoming state government information and services.

http://www.state.wy.us/~ag/dci/so/counties/so_converse.html
Wyoming – Converse – Sex Offenders – Listing

http://www.state.wy.us/~ag/dci/so/counties/so_fremont.html
Wyoming – Fremont – Sex Offenders – Listing.

http://www.state.wy.us/~ag/dci/so/counties/so_laramie.html
Wyoming – Laramie – Sex Offenders – Listing.

http://www.state.wy.us/~ag/dci/so/counties/so_natrona.html
Wyoming – Natrona – Sex Offenders – Listing.

http://www.innosoft-solutions.com/states/wyoming.html
Wyoming – Public Record Links – Public records information
and links.

http://www.wyb.uscourts.gov
Wyoming Bankruptcy Database – Search for bankruptcy
records by SSN, party, or case number.

http://soswy.state.wy.us/corps1.htm
Wyoming Corporation Database – Check the status of any
entity registered in the state of Wyoming.

http://www.state.wy.us/~ag/dci/chc.html
Wyoming Criminal Records – Faq.

http://www.mostwanted.org/WY
Wyoming Felony Fugitives – Listing.

http://www.state.wy.us/~ag/dci/missing.html
Wyoming Missing Persons – Listing

http://www.state.wy.us/~sot/text_unc_prop.html
Wyoming Unclaimed Property List – A searchable listing of
funds held by the Wyoming Unclaimed Property Division.

Forensic Resources and Information Web Sites

http://www.users.interport.net/~tmz/links/avoid
Avoid Frauds and Scams – Large selection of related links.

http://www.bbbonline.org
Better Business Bureau Website.

http://www.bebi.com
Business Ethics Bureau – Online.

http://www.ckfraud.org
National Check Fraud Center.

http://www.consumersgroup.com/crimewatch
/homebusiness.htm
Crime Watch – Consumer fraud watch network.

http://www.cybercops.org
Cybercop – Report consumer scams, rip-offs, and abuses
found on the Internet.

http://www.FlimFlam.com/news.htm
Flim Flam Dot Com – Scam alerts.

http://icp.intnet.mu
ICP – Institute for Consumer Protection online.

http://www.netcheck.com
Net Check – Acts like an Internet better business bureau
whereby you can check on businesses or lodge complaints.

http://www.nettrace.com.au/resource/reference/fraud.htm
Net-trace – Fraud and scam warnings.

http://www.scambusters.com
Scam Busters – Online publication; internet scambusters.

http://www.webguardian.com
Webguardian – Solve your Internet transaction problems.

http://www.cannabisculture.com/index.html
Cannabis Culture – The magazine of marijuana lifestyle and
hemp happenings from around the globe.

http://www.ca.org
Cocaine Anonymous – World services.

http://www.drugfreeamerica.org
Drug Free America – Resource net.

http://www.stealthlinks.com
Drug Screening – Drug screening kits; order online.

http://www.druguse.com
Drug Use – Information about the risks of illegal drug abuse.

http://nepenthes.lycaeum.org/War
Drug War Survival Guide – Information on how to fight
against the drug war.

http://www.urbanext.uiuc.edu/familyworks/drugs-02.html
Family Works – Warning signs and symptoms of common
illegal drugs.

http://www.fsbookco.com
FS Book Company – Specializing in hard to find drug-
education books.

http://www.discover.nl
Highlife – Site with information for cannabis growers and
users.

http://www.hightimes.com
Hightimes magazine site.

http://www.erowid.org
Hyperreal's Drugs Archive – One of the largest illegal drug
archives to be found on the Internet.

http://www.marijuana-anonymous.org
Marijuana Anonymous – World services.

http://www.420.com
Pot Recreation Site – A pro marijuana view of the world.

http://www.cyberfiber.com/news
Cyberfiber – Search for newsgroups of interest.

http://www.DejaNews.com
Deja News – Track any newsgroup messages that someone has
posted within the past few years, or search for specific
messages.

http://www.cuenet.com/ml.html
Email Mailing Lists – List server lists.

http://www.liszt.com
Liszt Newsgroup Locator – Locate newsgroups.

http://www.magmacom.com/~leisen/mlnh/index.html
Master Lists – Master list of newsgroup hierarchies.

http://www.newscene.com/find_news_grp.html
Newscene – Search newsgroups.

http://tile.net/news
Newsgroup Locator – Find newsgroups on subjects of interest.

http://www.nova.edu/Inter-Links/cgi-bin/lists
Nova Mailing Lists – Search for e-mail discussion groups
(mailing lists) using a keyword or sentence.

http://www.reference.com
Stanford Usenet Filter – Search mailing lists and newsgroup
archives.

http://wren.supernews.com
Supernews – Search newsgroup postings.

http://tile.net
Tile Mailing Lists – Search for Internet e-mail lists.

http://www.topica.com
Topica – Find, manage, and participate in electronic lists.

http://www.computerprivacy.org
Americans for Computer Privacy – Website.

http://www.andrebacard.com/privacy.html
Andre Bacard's Privacy Page – Many links to various resources
on Internet privacy and other related issues.

http://www.stack.nl/~galactus/remailers/index.html
Anonymity and privacy on the Internet – Information on how
to be anonymous and how to secure your communications and
files from third parties.

http://www.anonymizer.com/3.0/affiliate
/door.cgi?CMid=14859
Anonymous Surfing on the WWW – Surf the Web
anonymously; keep your activities while surfing private.

http://www.anonymizer.com/3.0/services/email.cgi
Anonymous E-mailer 2 – Send anonymous e-mail over the
Internet.

http://www.cdt.org
Center for Democracy and Technology – Website.

http://www.thelimitsoft.com/cookie.html
Cookie Crusher – Providess software that will enable you to
handle cookies intelligently.

http://www.cyberpass.net
Cyberpass – Provide anonymous Internet accounts.

http://www.cryptosoft.com/html/privacy.htm
Cryptosoft – Huge selection of resources on security and
cryptography.

http://www.catalaw.com/doom
Digital Doomsday – A digital indicator of the threat to
cyberrights everywhere.

http://www.epic.org/crypto/ban
Efforts To Ban Encryption – Website.

http://www.epic.org
Electronic Privacy Information Center – Latest news, articles,
resources and other information on electronic privacy issues.

http://www.fortify.net
Fortify – Free 128-bit encryption for Netscape users.

http://ace.ulyssis.org/~summer/LittlePanda/mail
/compose_no_login.html
Little Panda's Free Anonymous Mailer – Send private e-mail.

http://cryptography.org
North American Cryptography Archives – Libraries, software,
and information.

http://www.vortex.com/privacy.htm
Privacy Forum – Telecommunications, information/database
collection and sharing, and related issues, as they pertain to the
privacy concerns.

http://www.gilc.org/speech/anonymous/remailer.html
Global Internet – WWW anonymous remailer.

http://grc.com/x/ne.dll?bh0bkyd2
Shields Up – Security Utility – Checks the security of your
computer's connection to the Internet.

http://www.commodon.com/threat/frame.htm
Threats to Your Security on the Net – Discusses Trojan horse
applications.

http://www.webroot.com/washop.htm
Webroot – Internet security and privacy tools.

http://www.ziplip.com
Ziplip – Snoop-proof e-mail for free.

http://www.tazzone.com
-=Live 0-Minute SiteZ=-
An underground site dealing with illegal software piracy.

http://www.2600.com
Alt 2600 – The hacker quarterly magazine homesite.

http://www.blackout.org
Black Out – An underground site dealing with illegal software
piracy.

http://www.chaostic.com
Chaostic Hackers Site – Numerous hacking utilities,
information, and other related material.

http://www.eff.org/pub/Publications/CuD
Computer Underground Digest Archives – Collection of
underground digests and articles.

http://www.soci.niu.edu/~cudigest
CU Digest – Weekly digest/newsletter/journal of debates,
news, research, and discussion of legal, social, and other issues
related to computer culture.

http://www.defcon.org
DEF Con – Files, underground information, and various
related material.

http://www.silkroad.com/papers/html/bomb
E-mail Bombs And Countermeasures – Article; discusses mailbombing techniques, automated attack tools, and
countermeasures.

http://easywarez.com
Easy Warez – Files, underground information, and various
related material.

http://www.techline.com/~sheldon/hack/hack.html
Exordium – Underground files, manuals, and related
information.

http://tazzone500.dynip.com/ftc/verified/ftc_whatsnew.htm
FTC File Trading Center – Live online trading of pirated
software.

http://www.flashback.se/arkiv
Flashback – A large collection of underground information
files.

http://www.jya.com/paperF1.htm
Flaws In Security Systems – Article; identifies several secure
operating system features which are lacking in mainstream
operating systems.

http://www.fullversion.com
Full Version Warez – Pirated software, files, underground
information, and various related material.

http://go2warez.com
Go2warez – Software piracy and other related material.

http://www.2600.com/hacked_pages
Hacked Sites – Web pages that have been hacked.

http://www.hackerscatalog.com
Hackers Catalog – Software and hardware tools, files, books,
and videos for cable, satellite, cellular, computing, hacking,
and phreaking.

http://hackers.com
Hackers.com – Information concerning system security holes,
hacking, and related links.

http://www.hackerz.org/index.html
Hackers Defense Foundation – Website.

http://www.hackersclub.com/km/frontpage/index.html
Hackerz Hideout – Website.

http://www.flinthills.com/~hevnsnt/wares.htm
Heaven Sent – Hacking software. War-dialers, decoders, phreaking tools.

http://www.dnaco.net/~kragen/security-holes.html
How To Find Security Holes – The Linux Security Audit project.

http://members.tripod.com/~djwhiz/#projects
How To Hacker's Defense Site – Tools and information on how to defend yourself from hackers.

http://www.illegalnetwork.com
Illegal Network – Software, cracks, FTP sites, and other related material.

http://www.infosecnews.com
Info Security Magazine – Information security issues; many related articles, current news, and other material.

http://www.kopykatz.com
Kopy Katz – An underground site dealing with illegal software piracy and other related issues.

http://www.liquidwarez.com
Liquidwarez – Extensive collection of hacker related resources and pirated programs.

http://l0pht.com
L0PHD – Hard-to-find files from the computer underground and beyond, as well as, other hard to find information.

http://magiklair.com
Magiklair – Illegal software piracy and other related material.

http://www.matarese.com/list.html
Matarese Com – How-to's, hacking, and tracking.

http://members.tripod.com/mp3zone69
Mp3 Zone – Large selection of MP3 files and other related material.

http://www.angelfire.com/on/neosgotya/hacking.html
Neos Hacking World – Large selection of hacking utilities and other related information.

http://www.netice.com
Network Ice – Detect, identify, and stop hackers.

http://www.frame.net/nowarez/index2.html
No Warez – An underground site dealing with illegal software piracy.

http://www.astroquest.com/warez/dark/warez/index.htm
Oh no! More Warez! - An underground site dealing with illegal software piracy.

http://www.pemmy.demon.co.uk/WAREZ.HTM
Pennywise's Warez Page – An underground site dealing with illegal software piracy.

http://www.phrack.com
Phrack Magazine Web Page – Large archive of underground-related text files.

http://catless.ncl.ac.uk/Risks
Risks Digest – Forum on risks to the public in computers and related systems.

http://www.linkhouse.net/top77/topsites.html
ROM Land – ROMS and Emulators for the SNES and n64.

http://www.rozmans.com
Rozman's Empire – Underground site with information on hacking and piracy.

http://www.timecities.com/members/killingyou/index.html
Serial Killer Hack Site – Serial numbers and cracks for commercial software.

http://earthspace.net/jargon/jargon_toc.html
New Hacker's Dictionary – HTML document.

http://www.t50.com
Top Fifty – Lists the top 50 current warez sites (piracy).

http://www.undergroundnews.com
Underground News – Daily news section, files, and articles of interest to hackers.

http://www.focus-asia.com/home/jhanson/index.htm
Vandelay – An underground site dealing with illegal software piracy and software cracks.

http://www.warezcrawler.net
Warez Crawler – Underground search engine.

http://www.warezhangout.com
Warez Hangout – Database of illegal software piracy sites and other related material.

http://warez.com
Warez.com – An underground site dealing with illegal software piracy.

http://warezdimension.com
Warez Dimension – An underground site dealing with illegal software piracy.

http://www.warezfiles.com
Warezfiles.com – A large underground site that deals with all types of software piracy.

http://members.tripod.com/~wuzzworld
Warez Now – An underground site dealing with illegal
software piracy.

http://www.angelfire.com/tn/WarezSafez/index.html
Warez Safez – An underground site dealing with illegal
software piracy.

http://www.warezlist.com/c/in.cgi/nn240rb1v
Warezlist – Software, hacking, password database, cracks, serial
numbers, and other related material.

http://www.abczone.com/common
/newsdet_wut.asp?br=m4&res=2&lan=en&ps=000&qry=2
ABC Zone Virus Alerts – Quick list of latest virus alerts with
detailed information.

http://www.beyond.com/support/antivirus.htm?
Antivirus Center – Virus news and antivirus software.

http://www.antivirus-online.de/english
Antivirus Online – A virus information library, a virus
database, and mailing list.

http://www.metro.ch/avpve
Avp Virus Encyclopedia – An online encyclopedia that can be
searched for information or downloaded; also offers a virus lab
and antivirus software.

http://www.tulane.edu/~dmsander/Big_Virology
/BVFamilyIndex.html
Big Picture Book Of Viruses – Listing of virus types,
descriptions, and other information.

http://www.chaostic.com/virii.html
Chaostic Virus Page – Downloadable virus files.

http://kumite.com/myths/home.htm
Computer Virus Myths – Interesting articles and related
information.

http://www.fmew.com/archive/virus
Computer Viruses – Website.

http://www.datafellows.fi/v-descs/_new.htm
F-Secure – Top 50 Viruses – Listing of current viruses with
descriptions.

http://mft.ucs.ed.ac.uk/pcvirus/pcvirus.htm
PC Virus Library – Collection of virus-related articles and
documents.

http://www.sarc.com
Samantec – AntiVirus Research center.

http://sourceofkaos.com/homes/virus
Virii On The Web – Extensive collection of virus files and
information.

http://www.rahul.net/hacktw/virii.htm
Virii Stuff – Virus makers and macro information.

http://www.virusbtn.com
Virus Bulletin – A technical journal on developments in the
field of computer viruses and anti-virus products.

http://www.datafellows.com/vir-info
Data Fellows Virus Database – A large virus related database
that can be searched by keyword or concept.

http://www.avpve.com
Virus Encyclopedia – Encyclopedia of virus-related
information.

http://www.nai.com/vinfo
Virus Info Library – Look up different viruses by name.

http://www.icsa.net/html/communities/antivirus/index.shtml
Virus Lab – Collection of recent virus news and articles.

http://home.pon.net/waters/virii.htm
The Virus Page – Over 2,250 virii in .zip format for download.

B

Intrusion Detection Systems (IDS) Products, Services, Freeware, and Projects

IDS Commercial Products and Services

Blue Lance LT Auditor+
http://www.bluelance.com
LT Auditor+ enables administrators to track network activity and alerts users to intrusions through e-mail or paging.

Cisco Systems IDS
http://www.cisco.com/warp/public/cc/pd/sqsw/sqidsz/index.shtml
The Cisco Secure Intrusion Detection System is an enterprise-scale, real-time system designed to detect, report, and terminate unauthorized activity throughout a network.

CyberCop
http://www.cybercop.co.uk
Intrusion detection and protection systems, including CyberCop Scanner, CyberCop Monitor, CyberCop Sting, and CyberCop CASL.

CyberSafe
http://www.cybersafe.com
CyberSafe is a software publisher specializing in the development and implementation of network security solutions, such as Centrax IDS.

CyberTrace
http://www.cybertrace.com/ctids.html
A network security management system.

Demrac PureSecure — Total Intrusion Detection System
http://www.demarc.com
Demarc Security offers PureSecure, an all-inclusive network monitoring service that allows users to monitor an entire network of servers from a Web interface; combines NIDS, HIDS and Host/Service monitoring functionality.

eCom Corporation
http://www.e-com.ca/eSCAN
A source for firewall security, intrusion detection systems, network security, network security management, computer network security, network security monitoring, computer security, Web security, e-security, and NT security.

eTrust
http://www.cai.com/solutions/enterprise/etrust/intrusion_detection
Computer Associates' IDS solution.

Internet Security Systems
http://www.iss.net

A host-based tool, S2 identifies and reports exploitable system weaknesses.

Intruder Alert
http://enterprisesecurity.symantec.com/products/products.cfm?ProductID=48&PID=1318145
Allows enterprise security monitoring with detection and response to attacks in real-time.

Intrusion, Inc.
http://www.intrusion.com
Maker of SecureNet Pro, a commercial network intrusion detection (NIDS) product suite.

LANguard
http://www.gfi.com/lanselm/index.html
Intrusion detection, content filtering, security scanner, Internet access control, network security, Internet monitoring.

MacAnalysis
http://www.securemac.com/macanalysis.php
Macintosh security auditing suite.

Neogenesys
http://www.neogenesys.com.mx
Multi-platform security, detect, and audit of AS/400, UNIX, Linux, and Windows NT/2000 operating systems.

NetBrowser Communications, Inc.
http://www.netbrowser.com
Provides Web-based monitoring solutions for mission-critical applications.

Next Generation Security Technologies
http://www.ngsec.com
Home of NGSecureWeb.

Network Flight Recorder
http://www.nfr.net
Clue-gathering tools for network and security managers from
which an IDS can be built; source code is free.

Network Security Associates
http://network-security-associates.com
Service provider specializing in network security using
products from Microsoft and Cisco.

NIKSUN Inc.
http://www.niksun.com
Network performance monitoring, security surveillance, and
forensic analysis tools serving a wide range of protocols and
interfaces, ranging from Ethernet and Gigabit Ethernet to OC-
3; their network appliances continuously capture and analyze
LAN, MAN, and WAN traffic at gigabit rates in a single
platform.

NitroGuard
http://www.nitrodata.com
Suppliers of NitroGuard, the intrusion-prevention device
based on their open-source HogWash software; emphasis is on
prevention rather than detection.

Nokia Intrusion Detection
http://www.nokia.com/securitysolutions/network/iss.html
Nokia's network security appliance featuring the RealSecure
intrusion-detection engine.

nPatrol
http://www.nsecure.net
An adaptive IDS from nSecure.

PENS Dragon IDS
http://www.securityware.co.uk/intrusion-detection/
The PENS Dragon IDS.

Recourse Technologies
http://www.recourse.com
A provider of threat management services designed to contain,
control, and respond to network intrusions and denial-of-
service attacks.

ShadowSecurityScanner
http://www.rsh.kiev.ua
Network security tools and product

Silicon Defense — Intrusion Detection
http://www.silicondefense.com
They offer Snort and technical support services.

SPECTER Intrusion Detection System
http://www.specter.com
Official site of the SPECTER IDS.

TriGeo Network Security, Inc.
http://www.trigeo.com
A software development and network security services firm.

Tripwire, Inc.
http://www.tripwire.com
Data integrity system that detects unauthorized changes to
data on servers and routers and sends notifications; immediate
remediation of altered data is possible.

UAC Intrusion Alert
http://www.uac.com/Products/Intrusion_Detection
/intrusion_detection.html
A Linux-based IDS with an easy-to-use graphical interface.

Veracity
http://www.veracity.com/
A portable data integrity security tool that detects
unauthorized changes in file systems by monitoring the
cryptographic checksums of files.

Who's Spying on you
http://www.spydetect.com
Anti-snoopware, spyware site.

IDS Freeware

Abacus Project
http://www.psionic.com/abacus
A security initiative to produce a suite of tools to provide host-
based security and intrusion detection.

Advanced Intrusion Detection Environment
http://www.cs.tut.fi/~rammer/aide.html
AIDE is a file integrity checker that supports regular
expressions. Licensed with GPL.

IDSA
http://jade.cs.uct.ac.za/idsa
An experimental IDS and reference monitor designed to run at
application level.

LIDS Project — Secure Linux System
http://www.lids.org
LIDS is an enhancement for the Linux kernel; it implements
several security features that are not in the Linux kernel
natively. Some of these include mandatory access controls
(MAC), a port scan detector, file protection, and process
protection.

myNetWatchman.com
http://www.mynetwatchman.com
Intrusion reporting and response services; users forward
firewall logs that are aggregated and analyzed to identify
incidents that are reported to the responsible party.

Pakemon IDS
http://www.sfc.keio.ac.jp/~keiji/ids/pakemon/index.html
A free network intrusion detection system for UNIX systems.

Panoptis
http://panoptis.sourceforge.net
Panoptis is a network IDS that detects and stops DoS/DDoS
attacks.

Snort
http://www.snort.org
A free and very popular lightweight network intrusion detection system for UNIX and Windows.

The Osiris Scripts
http://www.shmoo.com/osiris
A tripwire-like utility that uses MD5 to check files for modifications.

IDS Research Projects

AT&T Information Security Center
http://www.att.com/isc
The AT&T Information Security Center provides government and corporate customers with design and implementation services in intrusion detection, public-key infrastructure, and security consulting.

CERIAS/Purdue University
http://www.cerias.purdue.edu
CERIAS, the world's foremost university center for multidisciplinary research and education in areas of information security (computer security, network security, and communications security) and information assurance.

CIDER Project
http://www.nswc.navy.mil/ISSEC/CID
The Cooperative Intrusion Detection Evaluation and Response project is an effort of NSWC Dahlgren, NFR, NSA, the SANS community, and other interested parties to locate, document, and improve security software.

COAST Intrusion Detection Pages
http://www.cerias.purdue.edu/coast/intrusion-detection
Information about intrusion detection, and intrusion detection research.

Computer immune systems (University of New Mexico)
http://www.cs.unm.edu/~immsec
Four examples of how we are applying ideas from immunology to today's computer security problems are a host-based intrusion-detection method, a network based IDS, a distributable change-detection algorithm, and a method for intentionally introducing diversity to reduce vulnerability.

Cost-sensitive intrusion detection(Georgia Institute of Technology)
http://www.cc.gatech.edu/~wenke/project/id.html
A data mining approach for building cost-sensitive and light intrusion detection models.

EMERALD
http://www.sdl.sri.com/emerald/index.html
EMERALD Event Monitoring Enabling Response To Anomalous Live Disturbances. EMERALD represents the state-of-the art in research and development of systems and components for anomaly and misuse detection in computer systems and networks:

- Scalable Network Surveillance

- High-Volume Event Analysis
- Light-Weight Distributed Sensors
- Generic Infrastructure and Pluggable Components
- Easy Customization to New Targets and Specific Policies

INBOUNDS: Integrated network-based Ohio university network detective service
http://zen.ece.ohiou.edu/inbounds
INBOUNDS is a network-based, real-time, hierarchical IDS being developed at Ohio University. INBOUNDS detects suspicious behavior by scrutinizing network information generated by Tcprace and host data gathered by the monitors of DeSiDeRaTa. INBOUNDS functions in a heterogeneous environment with fault tolerance, very low overhead, and a high degree of scalability.

Intrusion detection projects at UC Davis
http://seclab.cs.ucdavis.edu
Anomaly Detection in Database Systems, Common Intrusion Detection Framework, Intrusion Detection and Isolation Protocol (IDIP), Intrusion Detection for Large Networks, Misuse Detection, and Workshop for Intrusion Detection and Response Data Sharing.

Intrusion detection at the MIT Lincoln Lab, Information Systems Technology Group
http://www.ll.mit.edu/IST
Information assurance focusing on techniques for detecting and reacting to intrusions into networked information systems. We have coordinated several evaluations of computer network IDS.

Intrusion Detection in Columbia University
http://www.cs.columbia.edu/ids
This project approaches the intrusion detection problem from a data mining perspective. Large quantities of data are collected from the system and analyzed to build models of normal behavior and intrusion behavior. These models are evaluated on data collected in real time to detect intruders. There are 12 subprojects, which together compose the Intrusion Detection System Project at the Columbia Project IDS:

- HOBIDS — Host-Based Intrusion Detection System
- HAUNT — Network Based Intrusion Detection System
- DIDS — Distributed Intrusion Detection System
- DW-AMG — Data Warehousing and Adaptive Model Generation
- MEF — Malicious E-mail Filter
- FWRAP — File System Wrappers
- ASIDS — Advanced Sensors for IDS
- TAG — The Attack Group

- IDSMODELS — Intrusion Detection Models Generation
- IDSWATCH — Intrusion Detection Visualization
- DuDE — Denial-of-Service Detection and Response System
- Response — Automated Intrusion Detection and Response Rule-Based System

Intrusion Detection Exchange Format (IDWG)
http://www.ietf.org/html.charters/idwg-charter.html
The purpose of the Intrusion Detection Working Group is to define data formats and exchange procedures for sharing information of interest to intrusion detection and response systems and to management systems, that may need to interact with them. The Intrusion Detection Working Group will coordinate its efforts with other IETF Working Groups.

Institute for security technology studies (Dartmouth Colledge)
http://www.ists.dartmouth.edu
The Institute, with its core program on cybersecurity and information infrastructure protection research, serves as a principal national center for counter-terrorism technology research, development, and assessment.

MAIDS: Mobile Agent Intrusion Detection System (Iowa State University)
http://latte.cs.iastate.edu/Research/Intrusion/index.html
MAIDS design and implementation

RAID: Recent Advances in Intrusion Detection
http://www.raid-symposium.org
The RAID workshop series is an annual event dedicated to the sharing of information related to intrusion detection.

Reliable Software Laboratory of UCSB
http://www.cs.ucsb.edu/~rsg/STAT
The Reliable Software Group (RSG) works on languages and tools for designing, building, and validating software systems. Specific areas that the group has targeted include concurrent and real-time systems. RSG is also investigating techniques for increasing the security of computer systems, with particular emphasis on analyzing encryption protocols using machine-aided formal verification techniques, modeling and analyzing covert channels, modeling and detecting computer intrusions, analyzing mobile code and Web browsers for security violations, and approaches to secure Internet computing with unsecure applications.

ResearchIndex, IDS Section
http://citeseer.nj.nec.com/Security/IntrusionDetection
ResearchIndex is a scientific literature digital library that aims to improve the dissemination and feedback of scientific literature, and to provide improvements in functionality, usability, availability, cost, comprehensiveness, efficiency, and timeliness.

Secure and Reliable Systems Lab at SUNY Stony Brook
http://seclab.cs.sunysb.edu
This group's research is aimed broadly at developing new approaches, technologies, and tools for improving the security and reliability of networks and distributed software systems.

SHANG: Secure and Highly Available Networking Group(NCSU)
http://shang.csc.ncsu.edu/index.html
SHANG's main objective is to build a high-confidence networking infrastructure system, which involves a wide range of research issues in the areas of network security, network management, and networking software development.

The Center for Secure and Dependable Software(University of Idaho)
http://www.csds.uidaho.edu/
Hummer is a distributed component for any IDS; Magpie is a hierarchical network of lightweight, mobile, and adaptive tools designed both to investigate and to guard against intrusions.

Intrusion Detection Glossary

[A]

Active Attack
An attack that results in an unauthorized state change, such as the manipulation of files or the adding of unauthorized files.

Administrative Security
The management constraints and supplemental controls established to provide an acceptable level of protection for data.

AIS
Automated Information System—any equipment of an interconnected system or subsystem that is used in the automatic acquisition, storage, manipulation, control, display, transmission, or reception of data; includes software, firmware, and hardware.

Alert
A formatted message describing a circumstance relevant to network security. Alerts are often derived from critical audit events.

Ankle-Biter
A person who aspires to be a hacker/cracker, but has very limited knowledge or skills related to AISs; usually associated with young teens who collect and use simple malicious programs obtained from the Internet.

Anomaly Detection Model
A model where intrusions are detected by looking for activity that is different from the user's or system's normal behavior.

Application Level Gateway
A firewall system in which service is provided by processes that maintain complete TCP connection state and sequencing. Application level firewalls often re-address traffic so that outgoing traffic appears to have originated from the firewall, rather than the internal host.

ASIM
Automated Security Incident Measurement—Monitors network traffic and collects information on targeted unit networks by detecting unauthorized network activity.

Assessment
Surveys and inspections; an analysis of the vulnerabilities of an AIS. An information acquisition and review process designed to assist a customer in determining how best to use resources to protect information in systems.

Assurance
A measure of confidence that the security features and architecture of an AIS accurately mediate and enforce the security policy.

Attack
An attempt to bypass security controls on a computer. The attack may alter, release, or deny data. Whether an attack will succeed depends on the vulnerability of the computer system and the effectiveness of existing countermeasures.

Audit
The independent examination of records and activities to ensure compliance with established controls, policies, and operational procedures, and to recommend any indicated changes in controls, policy, or procedures.

Audit Trail
In computer security systems, a chronological record of system-resource usage. This includes user login, file access, various other activities, and whether any actual or attempted security violations occurred, both legitimate and unauthorized.

Authenticate
To establish the validity of a claimed user or object.

Authentication
To positively verify the identity of a user, device, or other entity in a computer system, often as a prerequisite to allowing access to resources in a system.

Authentication Header (AH)
A field that immediately follows the IP header in an IP datagram and provides authentication and integrity checking for the datagram.

Automated Security Monitoring
All security features needed to provide an acceptable level of protection for hardware, software, and classified, sensitive, unclassified, or critical data, material, or processes in the system.

Availability
Assuring information and communications services will be ready for use when expected.

[B]

Back Door
A hole in the security of a computer system deliberately left in place by designers or maintainers. Synonymous with trap door. A hidden software or hardware mechanism used to circumvent security controls.

Bell-La Padula Security Model
Formal-state transition model of computer security policy that describes a formal set of access controls based on information sensitivity and subject authorizations.

Biba Integrity Model
A formal security model for the integrity of subjects and objects in a system.

Bomb
A general synonym for crash, normally of software or operating system failures.

Breach
The successful defeat of security controls, which could result in a penetration of the system. A violation of controls of a particular information system such that information assets or system components are unduly exposed.

Buffer Overflow
This happens when more data is put into a buffer or holding area than the buffer can handle. This is due to a mismatch in processing rates between the producing and consuming processes. This can result in system crashes or the creation of a back door leading to system access.

Bug
An unwanted and unintended property of a program or piece of hardware, especially one that causes it to malfunction.

[C]

C2
Command and control.

C2-attack
Effective prevention of C2 of adversary forces by denying information to, influencing, degrading, or destroying the adversary C2 system.

C2-protect
Maintaining effective command and control of own forces by turning to friendly advantage or negating adversary effort to deny information to, influence, degrade, or destroy the friendly C2 system (pending approval in JP 1-02).

CGI
Common Gateway Interface—the method that Web servers use to allow interaction between servers and programs.

CGI Scripts
Allow for the creation of dynamic and interactive Web pages. They also tend to be the most vulnerable part of a Web server (besides the underlying host security).

Check_Password
A hacking program used for cracking VMS passwords.

Chernobyl Packet
Also called Kamikaze Packet. A network packet that induces a broadcast storm and network meltdown. Typically an IP Ethernet datagram that passes through a gateway with both source and destination Ethernet and IP address set as the respective broadcast addresses for the subnetworks being gated between.

Circuit-Level Gateway
One form of a firewall. Validates TCP and UDP sessions before opening a connection. Creates a handshake, and once that takes place, passes everything through until the session is ended.

Clipper Chip
A tamper-resistant VLSI chip designed by NSA for encrypting voice communications. It conforms to the Escrow Encryption Standard (EES) and implements the Skipjack encryption algorithm.

COAST
Computer Operations, Audit, and Security Technology—A multiple project, multiple investigator laboratory in computer security research in the Computer Sciences Department at Purdue University. It functions with close ties to researchers and engineers in major companies and government agencies. Its research focuses on real-world needs and limitations, with a special focus on security for legacy computing systems.

Command and Control Warfare (C2W)
The integrated use of operations security, military deception, psychological operations, electronic warfare, and physical destruction mutually supported by intelligence to deny information to, influence, degrade, or destroy adversary C2 capabilities, while protecting friendly C2 against such actions. C2W is an application of information operations in military

operations and is a subset of information warfare. C2W is both offensive and defensive.

Compromise
An intrusion into a computer system where unauthorized disclosure, modification, or destruction of sensitive information may have occurred.

Computer Abuse
Willful or negligent unauthorized activity that affects the availability, confidentiality, or integrity of computer resources. Computer abuse includes fraud, embezzlement, theft, malicious damage, unauthorized use, denial of service, and misappropriation.

Computer Fraud
Computer-related crimes involving deliberate misrepresentation or alteration of data in order to obtain something of value.

Computer Network Attack (CNA)
Operations to disrupt, deny, degrade, or destroy information resident on computers and computer networks or the computers and networks themselves (DODD S-3600.1 of 9 Dec. 96).

Computer Security
Technological and managerial procedures applied to computer systems to ensure the availability, integrity, and confidentiality of information managed by the computer system.

Computer Security Incident
Any intrusion or attempted intrusion into an AIS. Incidents can include probes of multiple computer systems.

Computer Security Intrusion
Any event of unauthorized access to or penetration of an AIS.

Confidentiality
Assuring information will be kept secret with access limited to appropriate persons.

COPS
Computer Oracle and Password System—A computer network monitoring system for UNIX machines. Software tool for checking security on shell scripts and C programs. Checks for security weaknesses and provides warnings.

COTS Software
Commercial off-the-shelf—Software acquired by government contract through a commercial vendor. This software is a standard product not developed by a vendor for a particular government project.

Countermeasure
An action, device, procedure, technique, or other measure that reduces the vulnerability of an AIS. Countermeasures aimed at specific threats and vulnerabilities involve more sophisticated techniques, as well as activities traditionally perceived as security.

Crack
A popular hacking tool used to decode encrypted passwords. System administrators also use Crack to assess weak passwords by novice users in order to enhance the security of the AIS.

Cracker
One who breaks security on an AIS.

Cracking
The act of breaking into a computer system.

Crash
A sudden, usually drastic, failure of a computer system.

Cryptanalysis
(1) The analysis of a cryptographic system or its inputs and outputs to derive confidential variables or sensitive data, including cleartext.

(2) Operations performed in converting encrypted messages to plain text without initial knowledge of the cryptoalgorithm or key employed in the encryption.

Cryptographic Hash Function
A process that computes a value (referred to as a *hashword*) from a particular data unit in a manner that, when a hashword is protected, manipulation of the data is detectable.

Cryptography
The art or science concerning the principles, means, and methods for rendering plain text unintelligible and for converting encrypted messages into intelligible form.

Cryptology
The science which deals with hidden, disguised, or encrypted communications.

Cyberspace
The world of connected computers and the society that gathers around them; commonly known as the Internet.

[D]

Dark-Side Hacker
A criminal or malicious hacker.

DARPA
Defense Advanced Research Projects Agency.

Data-Driven Attack
A form of attack that is encoded in innocuous-seeming data and is executed by a user or a process to implement an attack. A data-driven attack is a concern for firewalls, because it may get through the firewall in data form and launch an attack against a system behind the firewall.

Data Encryption Standard (DES)
(1) An unclassified crypto-algorithm adopted by the National Bureau of Standards for public use.

(2) A cryptographic algorithm for the protection of unclassified data, published in Federal Information Processing Standard (FIPS) 46. The DES, which was approved by the National Institute of Standards and Technology (NIST), is intended for public and government use.

Defense Information Infrastructure (DII)

The shared or interconnected system of computers, communications, data applications, security, people, training, and other support structures serving the DoDs local, national, and worldwide information needs. DII connects DoD mission support, C2, and intelligence computers through voice, telecommunications, imagery, video, and multimedia services. It provides information processing and services to subscribers over the Defense Information Systems Network and includes C2, tactical, intelligence, and commercial communications systems used to transmit DoD information (pending approval in JP 1-02).

Defensive Information Operations

A process that integrates and coordinates policies and procedures, operations, personnel, and technology to protect information and defend information systems. Defensive information operations are conducted through information assurance, physical security, operations security, counter-deception, counter-psychological operations, counter-intelligence, electronic protect, and special information operations. Defensive information operations ensure timely, accurate, and relevant information access while denying adversaries the opportunity to exploit friendly information and information systems for their own purposes (pending approval in JP 1-02).

Demon Dialer

A program that repeatedly calls the same telephone number. This is benign and legitimate for access to a BBS but malicious when used as a denial of service attack.

Denial of Service (DoS)

Action(s) that prevent any part of an AIS from functioning in accordance with its intended purpose.

Derf

The act of exploiting a terminal that someone has absent-mindedly left logged on.

DES

See Data Encryption Standard.

DNS Spoofing

Assuming the DNS name of another system by either corrupting the name service cache of a victim system or by compromising a domain name server for a valid domain.

[E]

Electronic Attack (EA)

The division of EW involving the use of electromagnetic, directed energy, or antiradiation weapons to attack personnel, facilities, or equipment with the intent of degrading,

neutralizing, or destroying enemy combat capability. EA includes: actions taken to prevent or reduce an enemy's effective use of the electromagnetic spectrum, such as jamming and electromagnetic deception, and employment of weapons that use either electromagnetic or directed energy as their primary destructive mechanism (lasers, radio frequencies, particle beams).

Electronic Protection (EP)

That division of EW involving actions taken to protect personnel, facilities, and equipment from any effects of friendly or enemy employment of EW that degrade, neutralize, or destroy friendly combat capability.

Electronic Warfare (EW)

Any military action involving the use of electromagnetic and directed energy to control the electromagnetic spectrum or to attack the enemy. The three major subdivisions within electronic warfare are electronic attack, electronic protection, and electronic warfare support.

Electronic Warfare Support (ES)

The division of EW involving actions tasked by, or under direct control of, an operational commander to search for, intercept, identify, and locate sources of intentional and unintentional radiated electromagnetic energy for the purpose of immediate threat recognition. Thus, ES provides information required for immediate decisions involving EW operations and other tactical actions, such as threat avoidance, targeting, and homing. ES data can be used to produce signals intelligence (JP 1-02).

Encapsulating Security Payload (ESA)

A mechanism to provide confidentiality and integrity protection to IP datagrams.

Ethernet Sniffing

Listening with software to the Ethernet interface for packets that interest the user. When the software sees a packet that fits certain criteria, it logs it to a file. The most common criteria for an interesting packet is one that contains words like login or password.

[F]

False Negative

Occurs when an actual intrusive action has occurred but the system allows it to pass as nonintrusive behavior.

False Positive

Occurs when the system classifies an action as anomalous (a possible intrusion) when it is a legitimate action.

Fault Tolerance

The ability of a system or component to continue normal operation despite the presence of hardware or software faults.

Firewall

A system or combination of systems that enforces a boundary between two or more networks. Gateway that limits access between networks in accordance with local security policy. The typical firewall is an inexpensive micro-based UNIX box kept clean of critical data, with many modems and public network ports on it, but just one carefully watched connection back to the rest of the cluster.

Fishbowl
To contain, isolate, and monitor an unauthorized user within a system in order to gain information about the user.

Fork Bomb
Also known as Logic Bomb. Code that can be written in one line on any UNIX system; used to recursively spawn copies of itself, eventually "explodes," eating all the process table entries and effectively locking up the system.

[H]

Hacker
A person who enjoys learning the details of programming systems and how to stretch their capabilities, as opposed to most users who prefer to learn on the minimum necessary. A malicious or inquisitive meddler who tries to discover information by poking around.

Hacking
Unauthorized use of, or attempts to circumvent or bypass the security mechanisms of an information system or network.

Hacking Run
A hack session extended long outside normal working times, especially one longer than 12 hours.

Host
A single computer or workstation; it can be connected to a network.

Host-Based
Information, such as audit data, from a single host that may be used to detect intrusions.

[I]

IDEA
International Data Encryption Algorithm—A private key encryption-decryption algorithm that uses a key that is twice the length of a DES key.

IDIOT
Intrusion Detection in our time—A system that detects intrusions using pattern matching.

Information Assurance (IA)
Information operations that protect and defend information and information systems by ensuring their availability, integrity, authentication, confidentiality, and non-repudiation. This includes providing for restoration of information systems by incorporating protection, detection, and reaction capabilities (DODD S-3600.1 of 9 Dec. 96).

Information Operations (IO)
Actions taken to affect adversary information and information systems while defending one's own information and information systems (DODD S-3600.1 of 9 Dec. 96).

Information Security
The result of any system of policies or procedures for identifying, controlling, and protecting from unauthorized disclosure information whose protection is authorized by executive order or statute.

Information Superiority
The capability to collect, process, and disseminate an uninterrupted flow of information while exploiting or denying an adversary's ability to do the same (DODD S-3600.1 of 9 Dec. 96).

Information Warfare (IW)
(1) Actions taken to achieve information superiority by affecting adversary information, information-based processes, and information systems, while defending one's own information, information-based processes, and information systems. Any action to deny, exploit, corrupt, or destroy the enemy's information and its functions, while protecting one's self against those actions; exploiting one's own military information functions.

(2) Information Operations conducted during time of crisis or conflict to achieve or promote specific objectives over a specific adversary or adversaries (DODD S-3600.1 of 9 Dec. 96).

Integrity
Assuring information will not be accidentally or maliciously altered or destroyed.

Internet Worm
A worm program that was unleashed on the Internet in 1988. Written by Robert T. Morris, it was an experiment that got out of hand. *See* Worm.

Intrusion
Any set of actions that attempt to compromise the integrity, confidentiality, or availability of a resource.

Intrusion Detection
Pertaining to techniques that attempt to detect intrusion into a computer or network by observation of actions, security logs, or audit data. Detection of break-ins or attempts either manually or via software expert systems that operate on logs or other information available on the network.

IP Splicing/Hijacking
An action whereby an active, established session is intercepted and coopted by the unauthorized user. IP-splicing attacks may occur after an authentication has been made, permitting the attacker to assume the role of an already authorized user. Primary protections against IP splicing rely on encryption at the session or network layer.

IP Spoofing
An attack whereby a system attempts illicitly to impersonate another system by using its IP network address.

[K]

Key
A symbol or sequence of symbols (or electrical or mechanical correlates of symbols) applied to text in order to encrypt or decrypt.

Key Escrow
The system of giving a piece of a key to each of a certain number of trustees such that the key can be recovered with the collaboration of all the trustees.

Keystroke Monitoring
A specialized form of audit-trail software, or a specially designed device, that records every key struck by a user and every character of the response that the AIS returns to the user.

[L]

LAN
Local-area network—a computer communications system limited to no more than a few miles and using high-speed connections (2 to 100 mbps). A short-haul communications system that connects ADP devices in a building or group of buildings within a few square kilometers, including workstations, front-end processors, controllers, switches, and gateways.

Leapfrog Attack
Use of userid and password information obtained illicitly from one host to compromise another host. The act of Telneting through one or more hosts in order to preclude a trace (a standard cracker procedure).

Letterbomb
A piece of e-mail containing live data intended to do malicious things to the recipient's machine or terminal. Under UNIX, a letterbomb can also try to get part of its contents interpreted as a shell command to the mailer. The results of this could range from silliness to denial of service.

Logic Bomb
Also known as a fork bomb—a resident computer program which, when executed, checks for a particular condition or particular state of the system that, when satisfied, triggers the perpetration of an unauthorized act

[M]

Mailbomb
Mail sent to urge others to send massive amounts of e-mail to a single system or person, with the intent of crashing the recipient's system. Mailbombing is widely regarded as a serious offense.

Malicious Code
Hardware, software, or firmware that is intentionally included in a system for an unauthorized purpose (e.g., a Trojan horse).

Metric
A random variable x representing a quantitative measure accumulated over a period.

Mimicking
Synonymous with impersonation, masquerading, or spoofing.

Misuse Detection Model
Detection of intrusions by looking for activity that corresponds to known intrusion techniques or system vulnerabilities. Also known as rules-based detection.

Mockingbird
A computer program or process that mimics the legitimate behavior of a normal system feature (or other apparently useful function) but performs malicious activities once invoked by the user.

Multihost-based Auditing
Audit data from multiple hosts may be used to detect intrusions.

[N]

Nak Attack
Negative acknowledgment attack—a penetration technique, that capitalizes on a potential weakness in an operating system that does not handle asynchronous interrupts properly and, thus, leaves the system in an unprotected state during such interrupts.

National Computer Security Center (NCSC)
Originally named the DoD Computer Security Center, the NCSC became responsible with the signing of NSDD-145 for encouraging the widespread availability of trusted computer systems throughout the federal government. (AF9K_JBC.TXT) (NCSC-WA-001-85) (NCSC).

National Information Infrastructure (NII)
The nationwide interconnection of communications networks, computers, databases, and consumer electronics that make vast amounts of information available to users. The NII encompasses a wide range of equipment, including cameras, scanners, keyboards, fax machines, computers, switches, compact disks, video and audio tape, cable, wire, satellites, fiber-optic transmission lines, networks of all types, monitors, printers, and much more. The friendly and adversary personnel who make decisions and handle the transmitted information constitute a critical component of the NII (pending approval in JP 1-02).

NCSC
See National Computer Security Center

Network
Two or more machines interconnected for communications.

Network-Based
Network traffic data along with audit data from hosts; used to detect intrusions.

Network-Level Firewall
A firewall in which traffic is examined at the network protocol (IP) packet level.

Network Security
Protection of networks and their services from unauthorized modification, destruction, or disclosure, and provision of assurance that the network performs its critical functions correctly and there are no harmful sideeffects. Network security includes providing for data integrity.

Network Security Officer
Individual formally appointed by a designated approving authority to ensure that the provisions of all applicable directives are implemented throughout the life cycle of an AIS network.

Network Weaving
Another name for Leapfrogging.

Nondiscretionary Security
The aspect of DOD security policy that restricts access on the basis of security levels. A security level is composed of a read level and a category set restriction. For read access to an item of information, a user must have a clearance level greater then or equal to the classification of the information and also have a category clearance, which includes all of the access categories specified for the information.

Non-Repudiation
Method by which the sender of data is provided with proof of delivery and the recipient is assured of the sender's identity, so that neither can later deny having processed the data.

[O]

Open Security
Environment that does not provide sufficient assurance that applications and equipment are protected against the introduction of malicious logic prior to or during the operation of a system.

Open Systems Security
Provision of tools for the secure internetworking of open systems.

Operational Data Security
The protection of data from either accidental or unauthorized, but intentional modification, destruction, or disclosure during input, processing, or output operations.

Operations Security (OPSEC)
(1) The process of denying adversaries information about friendly capabilities and intentions by identifying, controlling, and protecting indicators associated with planning and conducting military operations and other activities.

(2) An analytical process by which the U.S. Government and its supporting contractors can deny potential adversaries information about capabilities and intentions by identifying, controlling, and protecting evidence of the planning and execution of sensitive activities and operations.

(3) A process of identifying critical information and subsequently analyzing friendly actions attendant to military operations and other activities to: (a) Identify those actions that can be observed by adversary intelligence systems. (b) Determine indicators hostile intelligence systems might obtain that could be interpreted or pieced together to derive critical information in time to be useful to adversaries. (c) Select and execute measures that eliminate or reduce to an acceptable level the vulnerabilities of friendly actions to adversary exploitation (JP 1-02).

Orange Book
See Trusted Computer Security Evaluation Criteria.

OSI
Open Systems Interconnection—a set of internationally accepted and openly developed standards that meet the needs of network resource administration and integrated network utility.

[P]

Packet
A block of data sent over the network transmitting the identities of the sending and receiving stations, error-control information, and messages.

Packet Filter
Inspects each packet for user-defined content, such as an IP address, but does not track the state of sessions. This is one of the least secure types of firewall.

Packet Filtering
A feature incorporated into routers and bridges to limit the flow of information based on predetermined communications, such as source, destination, or type of service being provided by the network. Packet filters let the administrator limit protocol-specific traffic to one network segment, isolate e-mail domains, and perform many other traffic-control functions.

Packet Sniffer
A device or program that monitors the data traveling between computers on a network.

Passive Attack
An attack that does not result in an unauthorized state change, such as an attack that only monitors or records data.

Passive Threat
The threat of unauthorized disclosure of information without changing the state of the system. A type of threat that involves the interception, not the alteration, of information.

PEM
Privacy Enhanced Mail—An IETF standard for secure mail exchange.

Penetration
The successful unauthorized access to an automated system.

Penetration Signature
The description of a situation or set of conditions in which a penetration could occur or of system events that in conjunction can indicate the occurrence of a penetration in progress.

Penetration Testing
The portion of security testing in which the evaluators attempt to circumvent the security features of a system. The evaluators may be assumed to use all system design and implementation documentation, which may include listings of system source code, manuals, and circuit diagrams. The evaluators work under the same constraints applied to ordinary users.

Perimeter-Based Security
The technique of securing a network by controlling access to all entry and exit points of the network; usually associated with firewalls or filters.

Perpetrator
The entity from the external environment that is taken to be the cause of a risk. An entity in the external environment that performs an attack (i.e., a hacker).

Personnel Security
The procedures established to ensure that all personnel who have access to any classified information have the required authorizations, as well as the appropriate clearances.

PGP
Pretty Good Privacy—A freeware program primarily for secure e-mail.

Phage
A program that modifies other programs or databases in unauthorized ways, especially one that propagates a virus or Trojan horse.

PHF
Phone book file demonstration program that hackers use to gain access to a computer system and potentially read and capture password files.

PHF Hack
A well-known and vulnerable CGI script that does not filter out special characters (such as a new line) input by a user.

Phracker
An individual who combines phone phreaking with computer hacking.

Phreak(er)
An individual fascinated by the telephone system. Commonly, an individual who uses his knowledge of the telephone system to make calls at the expense of another.

Phreaking
The art and science of cracking the phone network.

Physical Security
The measures used to provide physical protection of resources against deliberate and accidental threats.

Piggy-Back
The gaining of unauthorized access to a system via another user's legitimate connection.

Ping of Death
The use of ping with a packet size higher than 65,507. This will cause a denial of service.

Plain Text
Unencrypted data.

Private Key Cryptography
An encryption methodology in which the encryptor and decryptor use the same key, which must be kept secret. This methodology is usually used only by a small group.

Probe
Any effort to gather information about a machine or its users for the apparent purpose of gaining unauthorized access to the system at a later date.

Procedural Security
See Administrative Security.

Profile
Patterns of a user's activity that can detect changes in normal routines.

Promiscuous Mode
Normally an Ethernet interface reads all address information and accepts follow-on packets only destined for itself, but when the interface is in promiscuous mode, it reads all information (sniffer), regardless of its destination.

Protocol
Agreed-upon methods of communications used by computers. A specification that describes the rules and procedures that products should follow to perform activities on a network, such as transmitting data. If they use the same protocols,

products from different vendors should be able to communicate on the same network.

Prowler
A daemon that is run periodically to seek out and erase core files, truncate administrative logfiles, nuke lost+found directories, and otherwise clean up.

Proxy
A firewall mechanism that replaces the IP address of a host on the internal (protected) network with its own IP address for all traffic passing through it. A software agent that acts on behalf of a user. Typical proxies accept a connection from a user, make a decision as to whether or not the user or client IP address is permitted to use the proxy, perhaps does additional authentication, and then completes a connection on behalf of the user to a remote destination.

Psychological Operations (PSYOP)
Planned operations to convey selected information and indicators to foreign audiences to influence their emotions, motives, objective reasoning, and ultimately the behavior of foreign governments, organizations, groups, and individuals. The purpose of psychological operations is to induce or reinforce foreign attitudes and behavior favorable to the originator's objectives (JP 1-02).

Public Key Cryptography
A type of cryptography in which the encryption process is publicly available and unprotected, but in which a part of the decryption key is protected so that only a party with knowledge of both parts of the decryption process can decrypt the cipher text.

[R]

Red Book
See Trusted Network Interpretation.

Reference Monitor
A security control concept in which an abstract machine mediates accesses to objects by subjects. In principle, a reference monitor should be complete (in that it mediates every access), isolated from modification by system entities, and verifiable. A security kernel is an implementation of a reference monitor for a given hardware base.

Replicator
Any program that acts to produce copies of itself; examples include a program, a worm, a fork bomb, or a virus. It is even claimed by some that UNIX and C are the symbiotic halves of an extremely successful replicator.

Retrovirus
A retrovirus is a virus that waits until all possible backup media are infected too, so that it is not possible to restore the system to an uninfected state.

Rexd
This UNIX command is the Sun RPC server for remote program execution. This daemon is started by inetd whenever a remote execution request is made.

Risk Assessment
A study of vulnerabilities, threats, likelihood, loss or impact, and theoretical effectiveness of security measures. The process of evaluating threats and vulnerabilities, known and postulated, to determine expected loss and establish the degree of acceptability to system operations.

Risk Management
The total process in place to identify, control, and minimize the impact of uncertain events. The objective of the risk management program is to reduce risk and obtain and maintain Designated Approving Authority (DAA) approval.

Rootkit
A hacker security tool that captures passwords and message traffic to and from a computer. A collection of tools that allows a hacker to provide a backdoor into a system, collect information on other systems on the network, mask the fact that the system is compromised, and much more. Rootkit is a classic example of Trojan Horse software. Rootkit is available for a wide range of operating systems.

Router
An interconnection device that is similar to a bridge, but serves packets or frames containing certain protocols. Routers link LANs at the network layer.

Routing Control
The application of rules during the process of routing so as to choose or avoid specific networks, links, or relays.

RSA Algorithm
Rivest-Shamir-Aldeman algorithm—a public-key cryptographic algorithm that hinges on the assumption that the factoring of the product of two large primes is difficult.

Rules-Based Detection
The intrusion detection system detects intrusions by looking for activity that corresponds to known intrusion techniques (signatures) or system vulnerabilities. Also known as misuse detection.

[S]

Samurai
A hacker who hires out for legal cracking jobs, snooping for factions in corporate political fights, lawyers pursuing privacy-rights and First Amendment cases, and other parties with legitimate reasons to need an electronic locksmith.

SATAN
Security Administrator Tool for Analyzing Networks—a tool for remotely probing and identifying the vulnerabilities of systems on IP networks. A powerful, freeware program that helps to identify system security weaknesses.

Secure Network Server
A device that acts as a gateway between a protected enclave and the outside world.

Secure Shell
A completely encrypted shell connection between two machines protected by a super long pass phrase.

Security
A condition that results from the establishment and maintenance of protective measures that ensure a state of inviolability from hostile acts or influences.

Security Architecture
A detailed description of all aspects of the system that relate to security, along with a set of principles to guide the design. A security architecture describes how the system is put together to satisfy the security requirements.

Security Audit
A search through a computer system for security problems and vulnerabilities.

Security Countermeasures
Countermeasures that are aimed at specific threats and vulnerabilities or involve more active techniques, as well as activities traditionally perceived as security

Security Domains
The sets of objects that a subject has the ability to access.

Security Features
The security-relevant functions, mechanisms, and characteristics of AIS hardware and software.

Security Incident
Any act or circumstance that involves classified information that deviates from the requirements of governing security publications. For example, compromise, possible compromise, inadvertent disclosure, and deviation.

Security Kernel
The hardware, firmware, and software elements of a Trusted Computing Base that implement the reference monitor concept. It must mediate all accesses, be protected from modification, and be verifiable as correct.

Security Label
Piece of information that represents the sensitivity of a subject or object, such as its hierarchical classification (e.g., CONFIDENTIAL, SECRET, TOP SECRET), together with any applicable nonhierarchical security categories (e.g., sensitive compartmented information, critical nuclear weapon design information).

Security Level
The combination of a hierarchical classification and a set of nonhierarchical categories that represents the sensitivity of information.

Security Officer
The ADP official having the designated responsibility for the security of an ADP system.

Security Perimeter
The boundary where security controls are in effect to protect assets.

Security Policies
The set of laws, rules, and practices that regulate how an organization manages, protects, and distributes sensitive information.

Security Policy Model
A formal presentation of the security policy enforced by the system. It must identify the set of rules and practices that regulate how a system manages, protects, and distributes sensitive information.

Security Requirements
Types and levels of protection necessary for equipment, data, information, applications, and facilities.

Security Service
A service provided by a layer of communicating open systems that ensures adequate security of the systems or of data transfers.

Security Violation
An instance in which a user or other person circumvents or defeats the controls of a system to obtain unauthorized access to information contained therein or to system resources.

Server
A system that provides network service, such as disk storage and file transfer, or a program that provides such a service. A kind of daemon that performs a service for the requester, which often runs on a computer other than the one which the server runs.

Signaling System 7 (SS7)
A protocol used by phone companies. That has three basic functions: supervising, alerting, and addressing. Supervising monitors the status of a line or circuit to see if it is busy, idle, or requesting service. Alerting indicates the arrival of an incoming call. Addressing is the transmission of routing and destination signals over the network in the form of dial tone or data pulses.

Simple Network Management Protocol (SNMP)
Software used to control network communications devices using TCP/IP.

Skipjack
An NSA-developed encryption algorithm for the clipper chip. The details of the algorithm are unpublished.

Smurfing
A DoS attack in which an attacker spoofs the source address of an echo-request ICMP (ping) packet to the broadcast address

for a network, causing the machines in the network to respond en masse to the victim, thereby clogging its network.

Snarf
To grab a large document or file for the purpose of using it with or without the author's permission.

Sneaker
An individual hired to break into places in order to test their security; analogous to a tiger team.

Sniffer
A program to capture data across a computer network. Used by hackers to capture userid names and passwords. A software tool that audits and identifies network traffic packets. It is also used legitimately by network operations and maintenance personnel to troubleshoot network problems.

Spam
To crash a program by overrunning a fixed-site buffer with excessively large input data. Also, to cause a person or newsgroup to be flooded with irrelevant or inappropriate messages.

Special Information Operations (SIO)
Information operations that by their sensitive nature, due to their potential effect or impact, security requirements, or risk to the national security of the United States, require a special review and approval process (DODD S-3600.1 of 9 Dec. 96).

SPI
Secure Profile Inspector—a network monitoring tool for UNIX, developed by the Department of Energy.

Spoofing
Pretending to be someone else. The deliberate inducement of a user or a resource to take an incorrect action. Attempt to gain access to an AIS by pretending to be an authorized user. Impersonating, masquerading, and mimicking are forms of spoofing.

SSL
Secure Sockets Layer—A session layer protocol that provides authentication and confidentiality to applications.

Subversion
Occurs when an intruder modifies the operation of the intrusion detector to force false negatives to occur.

SYN Flood
The SYN queue is flooded and no new connection can be opened.

[T]

TCP/IP
Transmission Control Protocol/Internet Protocol—the suite of protocols the Internet is based on.

tcpwrapper
A software tool for security that provides additional network logging and restricts service access to authorized hosts by service.

Term Rule-Based Security Policy
A security policy based on global rules imposed for all users. These rules usually rely on a comparison of the sensitivity of the resources being accessed and the possession of corresponding attributes of users, groups of users, or entities acting on behalf of users.

Terminal Hijacking
Allows an attacker on a certain machine to control any terminal session that is in progress. An attack hacker can send and receive terminal I/O while a user is on the terminal.

Threat
The means through which the ability or intent of a threat agent to adversely affect an automated system, facility, or operation can be manifested. A potential violation of security.

Threat Agent
Methods and things used to exploit a vulnerability in an information system, operation, or facility; fire, natural disaster, and so forth.

Threat Assessment
Process of formally evaluating the degree of threat to an information system and describing the nature of the threat.

Tiger
A software tool, that scans for system weaknesses.

Tiger Team
Government- and industry-sponsored teams of computer experts who attempt to break down the defenses of computer systems in an effort to uncover and eventually patch security holes.

Tinkerbell Program
A monitoring program used to scan incoming network connections and generate alerts when calls are received from particular sites, or when logins are attempted using certain IDs.

Topology
The map or plan of the network. The physical topology describes how the wires or cables are laid out and the logical or electrical topology describes how the information flows.

Trace Packet
In a packet-switching network, a unique packet that causes a report of each stage of its progress to be sent to the network control center from each visited system element.

Traceroute
An operation of sending trace packets for determining information; traces the route of UDP packets for the local host

to a remote host. Normally traceroute displays the time and location of the route taken to reach its destination computer.

Tranquillity

A security model rule stating that the security level of an active object cannot change during the period of activity.

Tripwire

A software tool for security. Basically, it works with a database that maintains information about the byte count of files. If the byte count has changed, it will identify it to the system security manager.

Trojan Horse

An apparently useful and innocent program containing additional hidden code that allows the unauthorized collection, exploitation, falsification, or destruction of data.

Trusted Computer System Evaluation Criteria (TCSEC)

A system that employs sufficient hardware and software assurance measures to allow its use for simultaneous processing of a range of sensitive or classified information.

Trusted Computing Base (TCB)

The totality of protection mechanisms within a computer system, including hardware, firmware, and software, the combination of which are responsible for enforcing a security policy. A TCB consists of one or more components that together enforce a unified sewcurity policy over a product or system.

Trusted Network Interpretation

The specific security features, the assurance requirements, and the rating structure of the Orange Book as extended to networks of computers ranging from isolated LANs to WANs.

TTY Watcher

A hacker tool that allows hackers with even a small amount of skill to hijack terminals. It has a GUI interface.

[V]

Vaccine

A program that injects itself into an executable program to perform a signature check and warns if there have been any changes.

Virus

A program that can infect other programs by modifying them to include a possibly evolved copy of itself.

Vulnerability

Hardware, firmware, or software flow that leaves an AIS open for potential exploitation. A weakness in automated system security procedures, administrative controls, physical layout, internal controls, and so forth, that could be exploited by a threat to gain unauthorized access to information or disrupt critical processing.

Vulnerability Analysis

Systematic examination of an AIS or product to determine the adequacy of security measures, identify security deficiencies, provide data from which to predict the effectiveness of proposed security measures, and confirm the adequacy of such measures after implementation.

[W]

WAIS

Wide Area Information Service—an Internet service that allows you to search a large number of specially indexed databases.

WAN

Wide-area network—a physical or logical network that provides capabilities for a number of independent devices to communicate with each other over a common transmission-interconnected topology in geographic areas larger than those served by local area networks.

War Dialer

A program that dials a given list or range of numbers and records those which answer with handshake tones, which might be entry points to computer or telecommunications systems.

Worm

Independent program that replicates from machine to machine across network connections often clogging networks and information systems as it spreads.

The author would like to thank Greg Stocksdale of the National Security Agency Information Systems Security Organization for contributing this glossary.

Investigative Data Mining Products and Services

Acxiom (Data and Demographics) http://www.acxiom.com

AMS (System Integrator) http://www.ams.com

ANGOSS (Data Mining Systems) http://www.angoss.com

ATAC (Link Analysis Visualization Software) http://www.bairsoftware.com

Attar (Data Mining Systems) http://www.attar.com

Attrasoft (Data Mining Systems) http://www.attrasoft.com

Autonomy (Text Mining Software) http://www.autonomy.com

BAE (System Integrator) http:/wwwbaesystems.com

BioComp (Data Mining Systems) http://www.bio-comp.com

BlueLance (Intrusion Detection Software and Services) http://www.bluelance.com

Boeing (System Integrator) http://www.boeing.com

BrainMaker (Data Mining Systems) http://www.calsci.com

Business Objects (Data Mining Systems) http://www.businessobjects.com

CA (System Integrator) http:/www.cai.com

CACI (Data and Demographics) http://www.caci.com

CheckPoint Software (System Integrator) http://www.checkpoint.com

ChoicePoint (Data and Demographics) http://www.choicepoint.com

Cisco (Intrusion Detection Software and Services) http://www.cisco.com

Clairvoyance (Text Mining Software) http://www.clairvoyancecorp.com

ClearForest (Text Mining Software) http://www.clearforest.com

Cognos (Data Mining Systems) http://www.cognos.com

Copernic (Text Mining Software) http://www.copernic.com

Crime Workbench (Link Analysis Visualization Software) http://www.memex.com

CrimeLink (Link Analysis Visualization Software) http://www.crimelink.com

CSC (System Integrator) http://www.csc.com

CyberSafe (Intrusion Detection Software and Services) http://www.cybersafe.com

Daisy (Link Analysis Visualization Software) http://www.daisy.co.uk

DataQuick (Data and Demographics) http://www.dataquick.com

Demrac (Intrusion Detection Software and Services) http://www.demarc.com

DolphinSearch (Text Mining Software) http://www.dolphinsearch.com

DtSearch (Text Mining Software) http:/www.dtsearch.com

EDS (System Integrator) http://www.eds.com

Equifax (Data and Demographics) http://www.equifax.com

eTrust (Intrusion Detection Software and Services) http://www.cai.com

Experian (Data and Demographics) http://www.experian.com

GFI (Intrusion Detection Software and Services) http://www.gfi.com

GTE (System Integrator) http://www22.verison.com

HNC (Text Mining Software) http://www.hnc.com

i2 (Link Analysis Visualization Software) http://www.i2.co.uk

IBM (Text Mining Software) http://www-3.ibm.com

ICrossReader (Text Mining Software) http://www.insight.com.ru

Intruder Alert (Intrusion Detection Software and Services) http://enterprisesecurity.symantec.com

Intrusion, Inc. (Intrusion Detection Software and Services) http://www.intrusion.com

Isoft (Data Mining Systems) http://www.alice-soft.com

ISS (Intrusion Detection Software and Services) http://www.iss.net

Klarity (Text Mining Software) http://www.klarity.com.au

KPMG (System Integrator) http://www.kpmg.com

Kwalitan (Text Mining Software) http://www.kwalitan.net

Leximancer (Text Mining Software) http://www.leximancer.com

Lextek (Text Mining Software) http://www.lextek.com

Lockheed (System Integrator) http://www.lockheedmartin.com

MacAnalysis (Intrusion Detection Software and Services) http://www.securemac.com

Matlab (Data Mining Systems) http://www.mathworks.com

Megaputer (Data Mining Systems) http://www.megaputer.com

MITRE (System Integrator) http://www.mitre.org

NCR (System Integrator) http://www.ncr.com

Neogenesys (Intrusion Detection Software and Services) http://www.neogenesys.com

NetBrowser (Intrusion Detection Software and Services) http://www.netbrowser.com

NetMap (Link Analysis Visualization Software) http://www.altaanalytics.com

NetScreen (Intrusion Detection Software and Services) http://www.netscreen.com

NeuralWare (Data Mining Systems) http://www.neuralware.com

Neurosolutions (Data Mining Systems) http:/www.nd.com

NFR Security (Intrusion Detection Software and Services) http://www.nfr.net

NGST (Intrusion Detection Software and Services) http://www.ngsec.com

NIKSUN (Intrusion Detection Software and Services) http://www.niksun.com

Nokia (Intrusion Detection Software and Services) http://www.nokia.com

Northrop (System Integrator) http://www.northgrum.com

NSA (Intrusion Detection Software and Services) http://network-security-associates.com

Oracle (System Integrator) http://www.oracle.com

PeopleSoft (System Integrator) http://www.peoplesoft.com

Polk (Data and Demographics) http://www.polk.com

ProForma (Text Mining Software) http://www.proformacorp.com

Prudsys (Data Mining Systems) http://prudsys.com

Quadstone (Data Mining Systems) http://www.quadstone.com

Quenza (Text Mining Software) http://www.xanalys.com

Raytheon (System Integrator) http://www.raytheon.com

Readware (Text Mining Software) http://www.readware.com

SAIC (System Integrator) http://www.saic.com

Salford (Data Mining Systems) http://www.salford-systems.com

SAS (Data Mining Systems) http://www.sas.com

Security Focus (System Integrator) http://www.securityfocus.com

Semio (Text Mining Software) http://www.semio.com

Specter (Intrusion Detection Software and Services) http://www.specter.com

SPSS (Data Mining Systems) http://www.spss.com

SRA (System Integrator) http://www.sra.com

Statistica (Data Mining Systems) http://www.statsoftinc.com

SUN (System Integrator) http://www.sun.com

Sybase (System Integrator) http://www.sybase.com

Temis (Text Mining Software) http://www.temis-group.com

TextAnalyst (Text Mining Software) http://www.megaputer.com

ThinkAnalytics (Data Mining Systems) http://www.thinkanalytics.com

Titan (System Integrator) http://www.titan.com

Trans Union (Data and Demographics) http://www.transunion.com

TriGeo (Intrusion Detection Software and Services) http://www.trigeo.com

Tripwire (Intrusion Detection Software and Services) http://www.tripwire.com

VantagePoint (Text Mining Software) http://www.thevantagepoint.com

Veracity (Intrusion Detection Software and Services) http://www.veracity.com

VisualText (Text Mining Software) http://www.textanalysis.com

WizSoft (Data Mining Systems) http://www.wizsoft.com

Wordstat (Text Mining Software) http://www.simstat.com

Index